Lecture Notes in Computer

Commenced Publication in 1973
Founding and Former Series Editors:
Gerhard Goos, Juris Hartmanis, and Jan van L

Stefano Ceri Marco Brambilla (Eds.)

Search Computing

Broadening Web Search

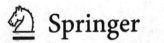 Springer

Volume Editors

Stefano Ceri
Marco Brambilla
Politecnico di Milano
Dipartimento di Elettronica e Informazione
Via Ponzio, 34/5, 20133 Milan, Italy
E-mail: {ceri, mbrambil}@elet.polimi.it

ISSN 0302-9743   e-ISSN 1611-3349
ISBN 978-3-642-34212-7   e-ISBN 978-3-642-34213-4
DOI 10.1007/978-3-642-34213-4
Springer Heidelberg Dordrecht London New York

Library of Congress Control Number: 2012951180

CR Subject Classification (1998): H.3, H.4, H.5, C.2.4, F.2.2, D.1.3, J.1

LNCS Sublibrary: SL 3 – Information Systems and Application, incl. Internet/Web
and HCI

Typesetting: Camera-ready by author, data conversion by Scientific Publishing Services, Chennai, India

Printed on acid-free paper

Springer is part of Springer Science+Business Media (www.springer.com)

Preface

The Search Computing project (SeCo), funded by the European Research Council as an advanced IDEAS grant, aims at building concepts, algorithms, tools, and technologies to support complex Web queries—whose answers cannot be gathered through conventional "page-based" search. Indeed, while the Web search arena is dominated by a few players offering gigantic systems capable of worldwide crawling and indexing Web pages, challenging research problems stem from the need of integrating data sources forming the so-called "deep Web"; this information is available through data collections which are often hardly accessible, requiring data extraction and integration both for understanding their semantics and for mastering their interplay. By studying issues and challenges involved with structured integration of Web data sources, the SeCo project has the ambitious goal of lowering the technological barrier required for building complex search applications, thereby enabling the development of many new applications, covering relevant search needs.

The project is now in the fourth of a five-year lifespan (Nov. 2008-Nov. 2013); during its third year, the project has broadened the spectrum of considered sources, by including structured tables and by including humans and social networks as a new, unconventional, but increasingly relevant source of information. We have also focused on new interaction paradigms, by adding natural language queries to exploratory queries, and by developing techniques for clustering and diversification of results, so as to broaden the spectrum of user experiences. Owing to the high cost of accessing data sources (and to other difficulties in managing them, such as access limitations and lack of stability), we have also considered the need of integrating search with a data materialization system that can produce local copies of most frequently used data.

This is the third book in the Search Computing Series; while the first two books reported the results of SeCo Workshops held in Como in 2009 and 2010, in this book we collect 16 articles which in most cases were contributed to several workshops during 2011, organized by members of the Search Computing project in the context of major international conferences: ExploreWeb at ICWE 2011 (co-chaired by Alessandro Bozzon and Marco Brambilla), Very Large Data Search at VLDB 2011 (co-chaired by Marco Brambilla and Stefano Ceri), DBRank also at VLDB 2011 (co-chaired by Davide Martinenghi), DATAVIEW at ECOWS 2011 (co-chaired by Alessandro Bozzon and Maristella Matera), and OrdRing at ISWC 2011 (co-chaired by Emanuele Della Valle and Alessandro Bozzon).

Articles were selected, extended, and revised in the first semester of 2012, so as to build a rather cohesive set of contributions; they are clustered in four parts according to their thematic similarity.

- Part 1: Extraction and Integration
- Part 2: Query and Visualization Paradigms

– Part 3: Exploring Linked Data
– Part 4: Games, Social Search, and Economics

The first part collects articles dealing with the problem of extracting and integrating data from heterogeneous sources. The first paper, by Blanco et al., addresses the issue of extracting the best estimate of data values which have several replicas on the Web based on extracting all the existing values and then applying a Bayesian model to them, thereby overcoming the uncertainty of accessing a given copy. The second paper, by Mulwad et al., describes the problem of extracting semantics from structured sources in very general terms, by contributing a classification of current tools for data extraction and then describing a specific tool for data extractions which turns relational data into the RDF format. The next two papers are focused on the extraction of semantic information from tables whose content is potentially very useful but whose schema and documentation are missing; in the third paper, by Unbehauen et al., the objective is to connect content to linked data; in the fourth paper, by Brambilla et al., the objective is to extract those tables which are similar both for their schema and for their content, so as to integrate them either through union or through joins. Finally, the last paper, by Bozzon et al., describes the features of a data materialization system – part of the SeCo framework that produces a local copy of content from a frequently queried remote source, thereby providing an active cash; specifically, the paper focuses on seeding the materialization system with data which can be progressively retrieved from the sources.

The second part of the book addresses new paradigms for expressing search queries or for managing query results, in a way that can be most expressive for final users. The first paper, by Guerrisi et al., describes a natural language interface – also part of the SeCo framework—which is capable of understanding complex queries upon multiple domains of interests, by employing rule-based and machine learning methods. The second paper, by Aral et al., discusses the use of mobile interfaces for exploratory Web searches. The third paper, by Brambilla et al., deals with how multi-dimensional data should be clustered together and labeled semantically so as to improve the user's capability of "reading" useful information from results. The fourth paper, by Morales-Chaparro et al., deals with visualization of search results under very different requirements and challenges offered by displays of different format and technology, by presenting a high-level model-driven approach to the development of visualization interfaces.

The third part of the book deals with exploration of semantic data sources presented as linked data. Linked data are clearly the most powerful solution that has been produced by the Semantic Web community for solving data integration and interoperability, hence the exploration of linked data is emerging as a new topic of research. The paper by Bozzon et al. presents how the Sparql query language for accessing RDF sources can be empowered by making ranking a first-class construct, thereby offering a query search paradigm for enabling the use of RDF sources. The paper by Castano et al. offers a method for the thematic exploration of linked data which aims at clustering them, thereby turning messy data into organized collections that expose strong internal cohesion. The paper of Cohen et al. provides an example of a tool for exploring linked data helping users to explore linked data and also to reuse queries that were previously issued, thereby building a personalized collection of queries over linked data repositories.

Finally, the fourth part of the book deals with emerging paradigms for search which deal with social aspects. The first paper, by Cohen et al., studies proximity measures in social networks, which are at the basis for solving problems such as user-centric person search. The second paper, by Bozzon et al., dwells on social search, by describing an architecture that can span a search query of known format to people who are reachable through their social platform; the resulting Crowdsearcher system is an extension of the SeCo framework for alternating exploratory and crowd-based search. The third paper, by Hees et al., proposes a game-based method for associating linked data with popularity, as a measure of its relevance and strength that could then be used for directing exploratory search over linked data. Finally, the paper by Brambilla et al. addresses the problem of economic sustainability of complex search by studying how an ecosystem of application and data source providers could share a revenue system that satisfies the heterogeneity of players and revenue redistribution among them.

The book is the result of collective efforts of many participants of the SeCo project and of a variety of contributors we have met in the context of five workshops. All of them have provided very useful insights on search computing problems and issues. The chapters have been reviewed by several experts. We would like to thank them all for their efforts.

August 2012

Stefano Ceri
Marco Brambilla

Reviewers

Table of Contents

Part 4: Games, Social Search and Economics

Web Data Reconciliation:
Models and Experiences

Lorenzo Blanco[1], Valter Crescenzi[1], Paolo Merialdo[1], and Paolo Papotti[2]

[1] Università degli Studi Roma Tre, Italy
[2] Qatar Computing Research Institute, Qatar

Abstract. An increasing number of web sites offer structured information about recognizable concepts, relevant to many application domains,
such as finance, sport, commercial products. However, web data is inherently imprecise and uncertain, and conflicting values can be provided by
different web sources. Characterizing the uncertainty of web data represents an important issue and several models have been recently proposed
in the literature. This chapter illustrates state-of-the-art Bayesan models
to evaluate the quality of data extracted from the Web and reports the
results of an extensive application of the models on real life web data.
Experimental results show that for some applications even simple approaches can provide effective results, while sophisticated solutions are
needed to obtain a more precise characterization of the uncertainty.

1 Introduction

The Web is offering increasing amounts of data, which are becoming more and
more important in several human activities. Consumers consult online catalogs
to choose products they are willing to buy; individuals and institutions rely on
the financial data available on the Web to take decisions about their trading
activities; many people collect information from specialized web sites for leisure
interests and hobbies. Several tools and techniques are now available to extract
data from the Web, and many applications and services are built by integrating
data provided by multiple sources. However, web data are inherently imprecise
and uncertain, and different sites often provide conflicting data.

To give a concrete example, let us consider the financial domain. On a fixed
date, we looked at the Open value of the Apple Inc. stock quote on 34 web sites
that provide information about NASDAQ stocks: 24 sites reported 204.61, 7
sites reported 204.51, 3 sites reported 204.57. Figure 1 illustrates the number of
distinct values published by the 34 web sites for some information on a random
sample of 819 NASDAQ stock quotes. In particular, for the Open value the 34
sources agreed on a unique value only for 81 stock quotes; for 579 stock quotes
2 values were reported, and for a significant number (about 20%) more than
2 values were provided (with a peak of 6 distinct values for 3 stocks). Similar
results can be observed for the Price and the Volume values.

S. Ceri and M. Brambilla (Eds.): Search Computing III, LNCS 7538, pp. 1–15, 2012.

number of distinct values	Open value	Volume	Price
1	81 (10%)	0 (0%)	261 (32%)
2	579 (71%)	1 (0%)	477 (58%)
3	126 (15%)	44 (5%)	57 (7%)
4	20 (2%)	139 (17%)	15 (2%)
5	10 (1%)	100 (12%)	5 (1%)
6	3 (0.5%)	389 (48%)	4 (0.5%)
> 6	0 (0%)	146 (18%)	0 (0%)

Fig. 1. Number of distinct values reported by 34 web sites on a random sample of 819 NASDAQ stocks quotes. For the *Open value* the 34 sources agree on the same Open value only for 81 (about 10%) objects and there is no stock for which they all propose the same Volume value.

We compared the open values published by each source with the official ones,[1] obtaining that the accuracy (i.e. the error rate) of the 34 source ranges from 0.18 to 0.98 (0.73 on average). Surprisingly, among the sources with the lowest accuracies, we found several popular web sites. Indeed, traditional and popular ranking methods (such as Google's *PageRank*, or Alexa's *Traffic Rank*) provide an indication about the overall popularity of the source, but they rely on properties that do not refer to quality of the published data. Even when sources are authoritative, the quality of data delivered in their pages can be compromised by editorial choices (e.g. numeric values might be deliberately approximated) and by the complexity of the publishing process, which can introduce errors and imprecisions. The problem is even exacerbated because many sources harness and publish data integrating information from other sources, introducing further complications in the process and propagating possible errors.

To evaluate the accuracy of a web source there is the need of an authority that provides the true values for the data of interest. In the above example, we were able to compute the accuracies of the sources with respect to the open values of the NASDAQ stock quotes because the NASDAQ web site publishes the official values. However, in general this is not the case: an authority could be missing, or data consumers could not be aware of its presence. It is worth observing that even in the financial domain, where there exists an obvious authority, the arena of content providers is very crowded and, as our example emphasizes, even the most popular ones may publish erroneous data.

Another important issue that emerges from the example is that the uncertainty of data coming from conflicting web sources should be characterized by a probability distribution function that associates every value found in the sources with a truth probability. In our example, the probability distribution would express the probabilities that `204.61`, `204.51`, or `204.57` is the true open value for the `Apple Inc.` stock quote.

The database research community recently addressed these issues and developed several approaches to characterize the uncertainty of data coming from multiple sources. However, the proposed methods have been tested on real-life

---

[1] The open value of a stock quote is an official information provided by NASDAQ.

web data only to a limited extent, while systematic studies have been done mostly on synthetic data sets. The goal of this chapter is twofold: first, we illustrate the principles of state-of-the-art approaches for evaluating the accuracy of web data and computing a probability distribution for the values they provide. Then, we present the results of the application of an implementation of these approaches on real-life web data from several domains. Our results show that in real life scenarios, even the simplest approach produces reliable results, especially in estimating the accuracy of the sources. More involved solutions outperform simple solution in general and are certainly needed when there is the need to compute precise probability distribution functions. Also, the experiments show that the accuracy of web data source is only marginally related to some popular web ranking indices.

The chapter is organized as follows. Section 2 illustrates the principles and the intuitions of methods for computing the accuracy of data sources by observing the data they provide.[2] Section 3 presents the results of a experimental activity that we have conducted on web data. Section 4 discusses related works. Section 5 concludes the chapter.

2   Probabilistic Models for Uncertain Web Data

Web sources usually provide values for some properties of a large number of objects. For example, financial web sites publish the values for several stocks properties, such as volume, open, max and min values, etc.. Different sources can report inconsistent values of the properties for the same object making data published on the Web inherently uncertain.

The uncertainty of data can be characterized by probability distribution functions: data are associated with functions reporting the probabilities that a property assumes certain values for a given object. These possible values are collected from a set of sources publishing information about that object. Therefore, there is one probability distribution function for each property of each object.

The models to characterize the uncertainty of web data have a twofold goal. They aim at computing (*i*) the probability distributions for data provided by the sources, and (*ii*) the accuracy of the sources with respect to the data of interest, that is, the probability that a source provides the correct values for a set of objects.

State of the art models to characterize the uncertainty of Web data can be classified according to which of the following three main factors they take into account:

consensus given an object, the larger is the number of sources that agree for the same value, the higher is the probability that the value is correct;
accuracy the agreement of the sources' observations contributes in raising the probability that a value is correct in a measure that also depends on the accuracy of the involved sources;

---

[2] The interested reader can find the formal developments of the methods in [11,5,10].

Object	A: authority	I: independent	IC: ind. copied	C1: copier 1	C2: copier 2	NAIVE	ACCU	DEP
			Sources				Model	
obj1	a	c	b	b	b	b	a—b	a
obj2	b	b	c	c	c	c	b	b
obj3	c	b	c	c	c	c	c	c
accuracy	1	$\frac{1}{3}$	$\frac{1}{3}$	$\frac{1}{3}$	$\frac{1}{3}$			

Fig. 2. Running Example: *authority* always reports the correct value; *independent* and *independent copied* provide, independently from the other sources, one correct value out of three; *copier 1* and *copier 2* copy their values from *independent copied*

copiers the presence of copiers, that is, sources that publish data copied by other sources, can generate misleading consensus on the values proposed by the most copied sources.

As an example, consider 5 sources publishing the values of a property for the same 3 objects, as shown in Figure 2. The first source A is an *authority* and provides the true value for each object (a, b, and c respectively), while all the other sources (I, IC , C1, C2) provide a correct value only for one object out of three. The sources I and IC (*independent* and *independent copied*) provide their values independently from the other sources, while the remaining sources C1 and C2 merely copy the values proposed by IC. Notice that in normal settings, the role of the sources is not available as input to the models (i.e., they are not aware that A is an authority, I is independent, and so on).

The simplest model, called NAIVE,[3] for estimating the accuracy of sources and computing data distribution probabilities considers only the consensus: the most probable value is the one published by the largest number of sources, and the probability of a value is estimated by its frequency over the given set of sources. According to NAIVE, in our running example there are 2 possible values for obj2 provided by the 5 sources considered: b is provided by sources A and I, while b is provided by 3 sources (IC and its copiers C1, C2). Similarly for obj1 the most likely value would erroneously be the value b. The example shows how in presence of many sources with different accuracy, a naive voting strategy could lead to incorrect conclusions. The probability distribution of the NAIVE model corresponds to the frequencies of the values. In the running example, the probability for obj1 is a→ 1/5, b→ 3/5, c→ 1/5.

A more involved model, ACCU, considers at the same time the first two factors, consensus and accuracies, and produces as output an estimation of the source accuracies together with the probabilities of the values [15,17,18]. Indeed, consensus among sources and sources' accuracy are mutually dependent: the greater is the accuracy of the sources, the more they agree for a large number of

---

[3] The names of the models presented in this chapter are inspired to those used in [11].

objects and the more they will affect the general consensus. Similarly, the more the sources agree on a large number of objects, the greater is their accuracy.

The role of the accuracies consist in weighting the consensus of the sources. A voting strategy similar to that used with the NAIVE model can be used to estimate the probabilities by means of the consensus: the only difference is that the votes are weighted according to the accuracies of the sources. The accuracy of a source can be estimated by comparing its observations with those of other sources for a set of objects. A source that frequently agrees with other sources is likely to be accurate, and similarly, the most accurate sources will be given the higher weights during the computation of the probabilities of the true values. In our running example, consider the accuracies given at the bottom of the table in Figure 2: 3 sources (IC, C1, and C2) provide the wrong value c for obj2, and they will be given an overall weight of 1, while 2 sources (A,I) provide the correct value b with an overall weight of $\frac{4}{3}$. However, even if the accuracies are known, the model still cannot decide which value, between a and b, is the most likely value for obj1.

A more complex model also considers the presence of copiers, that is, sources that publish values copied by one or more other sources. The presence of copiers makes harder the problem of computing the true values and the accuracies of the sources since they can create "artificial" consensus on values. A copier, even in good faith, can propagate a wrong value originated in one of the sources from which it copies. Provided that there is enough evidence about which are the correct values, it is possible to detect which sources are copying observing that copiers publish the same false values of the sources from which they copy. For instance, if b is considered the most likely value for obj2, the fact the IC, C1 and C2 publish the same false value attests that there are two copiers. The same argument cannot be used for obj3, for which the three sources publish the same value c: since this is a true value, it is not necessarily an evidence of coping.

DEP is a model that considers all the three factors above: consensus, accuracy and copiers [11]. It tries to detect possible copiers by analyzing the dependencies among the sources. Once the copiers has been detected, the consensus created by their presence will be ignored during the computation of the probabilities. The dependence analysis has to consider the mutual feedbacks amongst consensus, accuracy and dependencies: the accuracy of a source depends on the consensus over the values it provides; the dependencies between sources depends on sources accuracy and the consensus over the values they provide; finally, the consensus should take into account both the accuracy of sources and the dependencies between sources. For instance, once that it has been detected that IC, C1 and C2, copy one each other, the voting expressed by two sources will be ignored, and then it can be established that the most likely true value of obj1 is a.

In general, identifying the copiers is a challenging task for two main reasons. First, if in the considered sources there is a lack of evidence, copiers can be missed. Second, if the available evidence is misleading, false copiers can be detected. In Figure 3 we make use of an example to illustrate these issues: four distinct web sources report data about the same three video games. For each

Web Source 1

	genre	publisher	release date
The Sims 3	Simulation	EA	June 5 2009
Doom 3	**FPS**	Activision	August 3 2004
StarCraft 2	RTS	Blizzard	July 27 2010

Web Source 2

	genre	publisher	release date
The Sims 3	Simulation	EA	June 5 2009
Doom 3	**FPS**	Activision	August 3 2004
StarCraft 2	RTS	Blizzard	July 27 2010

Web Source 3

	genre	publisher	release date
The Sims 3	Simulation	EA	June 5 2009
Doom 3	Shooter	**Steam**	**August 2004**
StarCraft 2	Strategy	Blizzard	**July 2010**

Web Source 4

	genre	publisher	release date
The Sims 3	Simulation	**Sims Studio**	June 5 2009
Doom 3	Shooter	**Steam**	**August 2004**
StarCraft 2	Strategy	Blizzard	**July 2010**

True values

	genre	publisher	release date
The Sims 3	*Simulation*	*EA*	*June 5 2009*
Doom 3	*Shooter*	*Activision*	*August 3 2004*
StarCraft 2	*Strategy*	*Blizzard*	*July 27 2010*

Fig. 3. Four web Sources reporting data for three video games. The last table represents the true values for the scenario.

video game three attributes are reported: *genre, publisher*, and *release date*. The fifth table shows the true values for the considered scenario. We remark that such information is not provided in general, in this example we consider it as given to facilitate the discussion.

Consider now the first attribute, the genre of the game. It is possible to argue that web Source 1 and web Source 2 are reporting the same false value for the genre of Doom 3 (errors are in bold). Following the intuition from [11], according to which copiers can be detected as the sources share false values, they should be considered as copiers. Conversely, observe that web Source 3 and web Source 4 report only true values for the genre and therefore there is not any significant evidence of dependence. The scenario radically changes if we look to the other attributes. Web Source 3 and web Source 4 are reporting the same incorrect values for the release date attribute, and they also make a common error for the publisher attribute. Web Source 4 also reports independently an incorrect value for the publisher of The Sims 3. In this scenario our approach concludes that web Source 3 and web Source 4 are very likely to be dependent, while the dependency between web Source 1 and web Source 2 would be very low.

Using the DEP model, therefore by looking only at a single attribute at the time, web Source 1 and web Source 2 would been reported as copiers for the genre attribute because they share the same formatting rule for such data (i.e., false copiers detected), while web Source 3 and web Source 4 would been considered independent sources (i.e., real copiers missed).

Starting from the above observations, the dependence analysis has been further investigated and a more complex model M-DEP has been introduced to consider not only single attributes at a time, but whole tuples [5,10].

M-DEP leverages the evidence accumulated from several attributes to compute the probability that two sources are dependent. The underlying intuition, formalized in the bayesan framework developed in [5], is that the evidence of copying could greatly improve by considering several attributes, since it is much less likely that multiple values provided by two sources for the same object coincide by chance.

3   Experiencing the Models on Web Data

We have developed a Java prototype that implements the models described in the above section in order to experience the models on the data provided by real life web data sources. We used collections of data extracted from web sites from three distinct domains: soccer players, video games, and stock quotes. Data were collected by means of Flint, a system to extract and integrate web data [3,4]. The experiments were executed on a FreeBSD machine with Intel Core i7 2.66GHz CPU and 4GB memory. For all the considered models (except NAIVE) we set the probability of making an error on an independently provided value ϵ=0.5; moreover for DEP and M-DEP we set the a-priori probability of dependence between two data sources α=0.2 and the percentage of copied values over all values provided by a copier c=0.1.

3.1   Experimental Settings

For each domain, we downloaded pages from the Web and extracted the data by means of automatically generated wrappers manually refined to assure the correctness of the extraction rules. The attributes extracted were Height, Weight, and BirthDate for soccer players; Publisher and ESRB for video games; Price, Open Value, and Volume for stock quotes. Overall we collected 50,900 pages: statistics for the extracted data are reported in Figure 4. For each domain we produced

	Soccer Players (20 sources)				Video Games (30 sources)				Stock Quotes (30 sources)			
	Birth	Height	Weight	Avg	ESRB	Publisher	Avg		Price	Open	Volume	Avg
# objects	976	980	972	976	288	166	227		819	819	819	819
# symbols	1435	47	50	510	5	75	40		1892	2011	4812	2902

Fig. 4. Statistics about the data extracted from the Web

the correct (true) values for a set of 861 stock quotes, 200 video games and 100 soccer players. Object were selected randomly, making sure that both popular and rare objects were part of the set. We believe that this is an important requirement, as famous objects are more likely to be curated and updated by the web sites maintainers. For the video game and stocks quote domains, the true values were collected by means of their authoritative sources, www.nasdaq.com and www.esrb.com, respectively, which are the sites of the official organizations always providing correct information. The authoritative source is part of the set of sources for the stock quote domain experiment, but we keep it out of the set for the video games scenario. We will discuss later how the presence of the authority in the input set can impact the performance of the models. For soccer players, since an authoritative source does not exist, the true values of the considered attributes (Height, Weight, and BirthDate) were manually collected by inspecting the official web site of every soccer player whenever available, and the official web site of his current team club, otherwise. In any case, in the soccer domain the sources providing the true value of the players are not part of the set of sources considered for the experiments.

3.2   Evaluation Metrics

Given the truth vector $T = [t_1, \ldots, t_n]$ of correct values, for our experimental evaluation of the quality of web data, we define the *sampled accuracy* as the fraction of true values correctly reported by the site over the number of objects in the truth vector for which it publishes a value. For example, suppose we want to compute the sampled accuracy of a soccer web site w reporting Height values for 1000 objects. We match this set of objects with the true values for Height in T and identify 80 soccer players in the intersection of the two sets. We can now compute the sampled accuracy $\overline{a_i}$ for the source i: if, for example, the values reported by the source coincide with values in T for 40 objects, than we estimate that the source reports true values for 50% of the cases and therefore $\overline{a_i}=0.5$.

We compute in a similar way the sampled accuracy a_i^m for every evaluated model m, the only difference is that the set of values matched with T is the one made by the most probable values computed by m. In other words, even if a model returns a probability distribution for a value, we only consider the most probable one. We then obtain that a model can be treated as a single source and we can compute its sampled accuracy.

We rely also on two metrics, called *Probability Concentration* (PC) and *Accuracy Distance* (AD), to measure the performances of the models in computing the probability distributions and the accuracy of the sources, respectively.

Probability Concentration (PC). The *Probability Concentration* measures the performance of the models in computing the probability distributions for n observed objects. Given the truth vector T, the probability concentration for the model m is the average probability associated to the correct value:

$$PC(m) = \frac{1}{n} \sum_{j=1}^{n} P_j^m \Big(X = t_j \Big).$$

Note that if all the probability distributions associate a probability value of 1 to the correct value, PC equals 1. Conversely, the lower is PC the more the probability distributions are scattered over incorrect values, i.e, they associate probability to incorrect values.

Accuracy Distance (AD). In order to measure the average quality of the accuracies computed for the sources, for each attribute we compare the sampled accuracy a^m computed by every probabilistic model m against the sampled accuracy $\bar{a}$ of the k sources considered:

$$AD(m) = \frac{1}{k} \sum_{i=1}^{k} |a_i^m - \bar{a}_i|.$$

Note that if the estimated values for the accuracy of the sources are identical to the actual ones, then AD equals to 0.

3.3   Accuracy of Web Data Sources

Figure 5 shows sampled accuracies for each source exposing values for it, fixed an attribute for every domain. The results show how attributes from distinct domains may assume quite different behaviours. Conversely, the sampled accuracies of the other attributes in the same domain behave quite similarly, and therefore we do not depict them here.

Overall, the average source accuracy is 70.21% for the soccer domain, 85.78% for stock quotes, and 89.22% for video games. It is important to observe that the sampled source accuracy seems to be better for domains where at least an authority exists. For example, the video game's Publisher exhibits high source accuracy (more than 78%) for every source, while in the case of the soccer players' Height and Weight the source accuracies are sensibly lower in all the sources. It

Fig. 5. The sampled accuracies of the input sources: Height for soccer players, Publisher for video games, and Open Value for stock quotes

is also worth noting that the better accuracy is expected for information that does not change over time (as Publisher for games).

In the finance domain, it can be observed that the source accuracies reflect the presence of clusters of sources that take their data from the same data providers. The source accuracy for the Open Value seems to be affected by two main factors: different sites publish the same value with a different number of digits, and the semantics of this attribute is sometimes confused with a very closely related attribute, that is, the price of the first trade.

In the soccer domain there is a peculiar case, a site whose sampled source accuracy is around zero: by manually inspecting that site, we observed that the site publishes randomly generated data about soccer players and that the published data change every time a page is reloaded.[4]

	Alexa-links	Alexa-traffic	Pagerank
Truth (Open Value)	0,15	-0,22	0,5
Truth (Publisher)	-0,04	0,05	0,11
Truth (Height)	0,13	-0,31	0,21

Fig. 6. The correlation between of Alexa-Incoming-Links, Alexa-Traffic, and Google-PageRank with the sampled source accuracies is negligible. A value of 1 indicates a perfect positive relationship, while a value of -1 represents a perfect negative relationship.

To evaluate how popular ranking models for the Web, namely Google-PageRank [6], Alexa-Incoming-Links, Alexa-Traffic[5], relate to the accuracy of the sources, we computed the Pearson correlation coefficient[6] between these ranking indices and a ranking based on the web sites' data accuracy we computed. As shown in Figure 6, the correlation coefficients of these ranking models with the data accuracy of the sources are negligible. These results suggest that the quality of the data exposed by web sites is not reflected by these popular indices.

3.4 Experiments with Probabilistic Models

The table in Figure 7 reports how the probabilistic models NAIVE, ACCU, DEP, and M-DEP perform by using the three metrics introduced above.

To compute the *Sampled Accuracy* for each model, a vector of candidate true values proposed by the model is needed. Such a vector is obtained by considering as candidate true values the ones that have the highest probabilities according to the computed probability distribution functions.[7] Its results show that on

---

[4] e.g., http://soccer.azplayers.com/players/R/Ronaldo

[5] http://www.alexa.com

[6] A coefficient that represents the relationship between two variables that are measured on the same interval. It is defined as the covariance of the two variables divided by the product of their standard deviations.

[7] If multiple values have the same maximum probability, a random value among them is chosen.

	Sampled Accuracy				Probability Concentration				Accuracy Distance			
	NAIVE	ACCU	DEP	M-DEP	NAIVE	ACCU	DEP	M-DEP	NAIVE	ACCU	DEP	M-DEP
Birthdate	0.98	0.97	0.98	0.98	0.82	0.97	1.00	1.00	8.58	2.28	2.28	2.72
Height	0.66	0.67	0.67	0.67	0.51	0.66	0.67	0.67	4.6	13.86	13.93	16.49
Weight	0.59	0.66	0.66	0.66	0.49	0.67	0.67	0.67	6.37	10.53	10.76	12.11
ESRB	0.89	0.88	0.89	1.00	0.88	0.88	0.89	0.98	5.52	9.21	9.02	0.99
Publisher	0.97	0.97	0.98	1.00	0.92	0.97	0.98	1.00	2.62	1.50.	1.33	0.07
Price	0.96	0.95	0.96	0.96	0.95	0.95	0.95	1	2.1	2.3	3.18	1.58
Open Value	0.97	0.95	0.97	0.97	0.73	0.95	0.96	0.96	11.01	9.56	9.74	8.39
Volume	1	1	1	1	0.83	1	1	1	13.12	0	0	0
AVG	0.88	0.88	0.89	0.91	0.77	0.88	0.89	0.91	6.74	6.16	6.28	5.29

Fig. 7. The Sampled Accuracy (higher is better), the Probability Concentration (higher is better), and the Accuracy Distance (lower is better) for the three domains

average all models are able to identify the correct values with a quite high precision in most cases. As expected, more complex models present better results for all domains, but surprisingly they all perform with similar results, with the best model, M-DEP, outperforming the simplest model, NAIVE, only by a 3.5% on average. It is also worth noting that scores are high for all models for the domains where an authoritative source exists, but this is not directly related to the presence of such authority in the input set of sources. In fact, in the reported results the authority was part of the input only for the stock quote scenario. Moreover, all models performed only slightly better in the video games scenario with an alternative input set containing also the authoritative source.

The *Probability Concentration* measures how much probability a model has concentrated on the known true value. In this case we assume that the NAIVE model proposes probability distribution functions that merely reflect the frequencies of the observed values. This metrics shows that on average the most complex models ACCU, DEP, and M-DEP constantly outperform NAIVE by 14.2%, 15.5%, and 18.2%, respectively, as tools for estimating probability distribution functions. Again, we notice that the most sensible differences are in the domain where an authoritative source does not exists.

Finally, the *Accuracy Distance* metrics measures the distance between the sources quality estimation made by a model and their real sampled accuracy. The result shows that on average NAIVE is only marginally outperformed by the other models in estimating the correct accuracies of the input sources. Surprisingly, NAIVE shows comparable or even better results for half of the attributes (e.g., Height, Weight, Price). The most sensible improvements we observe with more complex models are in the stock quote attributes plus Birthdate. This behavior is due to the very different characteristic of the observed data as reported in Figure 4. In the stock quotes scenario, there is a very large number of distinct symbols in the alphabet and a larger number of instances. Also Birthdate has a much larger alphabet than Height or Weight. We discuss the role of the alphabet in more detail in the following.

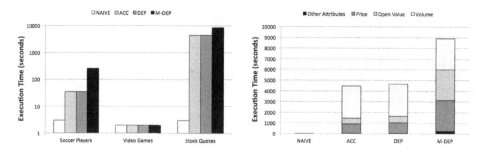

Fig. 8. On the left: execution times for the models over the three domains (logarithmic scale). On the right: detailed analysis of the execution times for different attributes of the stock quote domain.

To conclude our analysis, we examine the execution times for the models considered in the evaluation. Unsurprisingly, Figure 8 shows that NAIVE is always the faster, requiring only a few seconds for all the scenarios. Complex models perform equally well for video games attributes, but are slower in the soccer players scenario, and significantly slower in the stock quotes domain. It is easy to notice that this behavior reflects again the complexity of the data in terms of symbols in the alphabet and number of instances.

3.5 Discussion of the Results

In general, achieving a good accuracy in the estimation of the most probable values is the easy part in characterizing the uncertainty of web data and is generally performed well by all approaches. We then conclude that for applications requiring only a good estimate of the true values, even a simple approach such as the NAIVE model can be considered. However, whenever a more precise characterization of the uncertainty is required, for example to populate a probabilistic database, complex models exhibit significant advantages. In particular, over the three domains complex models show an improvements up to 36.7% for the *Probability Concentration* w.r.t. NAIVE; similar and better results can be observed for the *Accuracy Distance* estimation.

When deciding on what technique to use, we can distinguish three dimensions that can guide the choice: the characteristics of the domain that is used, the requirements on the result, the execution times.

1. If an authoritative source exists for the domain of interest, all models obtain very good results, even if the authority is not part of the input data. However, if the data of interest have large alphabets, complex models are likely to obtain better results. The intuition behind this behavior is quite simple: if the domain of possible values is very large and two sources present the same value it is very unlikely that they agree by chance. Either the value is correct or the fact that they agree on a wrong value is a very strong evidence that they are copiers. As in general identifying copies improves the quality of the results, we can conclude that large alphabets lead to better results.

2. On average, more complex models guaranteed results with better quality. This is particularly evident for the estimation of probability concentration and accuracy of the quality of the sources. But, if the desired output is only the most probable value, then the simple model in many cases returns satisfying results.

3. Execution times depend on the number of instances and the size of the alphabet for the attribute of interest. Experimental activity seems to suggest that only with very large alphabets the execution times of complex models become very expensive (up to hours). In settings with strict efficiency requirements it is crucial to examine carefully the characteristics of the data.

4 Related Work

In this chapter we discussed the application of probabilistic techniques to assign truth probabilities to values gathered from conflicting sources of information. Such information is then used to evaluate the quality of the web sources in terms of their data accuracy. The problem is related to the broader context of data quality [2] and to the issue of combining probability distributions expressed by a group of experts, which has been studied in the statistics community (e.g., [8]).

Many projects have recently been active in the study of imprecise databases and have achieved a solid understanding of how to represent and process uncertain data (see [9] for a survey on the topic).

The development of effective data integration solutions making use of probabilistic approaches has also been addressed by several projects in the last years. In [13] the redundancy between sources is exploited to gain knowledge, but with a different goal: given a set of text documents they assess the quality of the extraction process. Other works propose probabilistic techniques to integrate data from overlapping sources [14].

On the contrary, only recently there has been some focus on how to populate such databases with sound probabilistic data. Even if this problem is strongly application-specific, there is a lack of solutions also in the popular fields of data extraction and integration. Cafarella et al. have described a system to populate a probabilistic database with data extracted from the Web [7], but they do not consider the problems of combining different probability distributions and evaluating the reliability of the sources.

TruthFinder [18] was the first project to address the problem of truth discovery in the presence of multiple web sources providing conflicting information. TruthFinder considers both the consensus on values and the accuracy of sources, and it can be considered as the first work that realizes and exploits their mutual dependency. Based on some heuristics, an iterative algorithm computes the trustiness of values and the accuracy of the sources. A similar direction has been also explored by [17] and [15] which present fix-point algorithms to estimate the true value of data reported by a set of sources, together with the accuracy of the sources.

Some of the intuitions behind TruthFinder were formalized in a probabilistic Bayesan framework by Dong *et al.* [11], who also considered how the presence of copiers (i.e. sources that copy from other sources) affects the evaluation of the source accuracy. While in TruthFinder the effects of possible copying dependencies between sources are handled by means of a simple heuristic, the authors of [11] develop a more principled approach to detect source dependencies. To achieve these results, their model (which corresponds to the DEP model illustrated in Section 2) computes the probability that a pair of sources are dependent by analyzing the co-occurrences of errors. A further variant by the same authors also consider the variations of truth values over time [12]. This latter investigation can lead to identify outdated sources and its first application in a real world scenario shows promising results. Inconsistencies due to temporal aspects such as publication delay and missed updates have been recently studied also by Pal et al., who propose a formal approach to model the history of updates of a real-world entity [16].

The model behind DEP has been extended to improve the quality of the source dependencies detection. In fact, in [11] sources are seen as providers that supply data about a collection of objects, i.e. instances of a real world entity, such as a collection of video games. However, it is assumed that objects are described by just one attribute, e.g. the publisher of a video game. On the contrary, data sources usually provide complex data, i.e. collections of tuples with many attributes, and it has been shown that by considering this information the quality of the results can be improved [5,10].

Notice that in our evaluation we tested for the first time all the models on three common datasets.[8] In fact, evaluations of the above proposals were mainly conducted on synthetic data sets because, as noticed in [15], real-world data sets are hard to find, since they should be annotated with the real truth value in order to carry out the evaluation. Both TruthFinder and the models described in [11] were experimented just on one real data set composed by a collection of data about computer science books taken from www.abebooks.com (by the authors of TruthFinder), with the goal of discovering the books' authors. TruthFinder was also evaluated on a data set composed by a collection of data (the runtime) about movies. The algorithms described in [15] were experimented on a data constructed from the data published by a web-based prediction market: the data set was composed by users' answers on a given topic. Also in [5] the authors tested their solution with only one finance scenario, while in [10] authors used both the www.abebooks.com dataset and another dataset containing weather data.

An experimental comparison of authority and quality results for web sites has been done in [1]. Our work differs from this study in two important points. First, in our comparison against common popularity metrics we exploit the accuracy of the data offered by the web sources, while they compare quality in term of human judgement provided by experts. Second, we study the effectiveness of statistical models for the automatic evaluation of the sources, without requiring any user interaction.

---

[8] Our real-world data sets, as well as our implementation of the models are available on request.

5   Conclusions

In this chapter we have presented an experimental evaluation of state-of-the-art techniques for assessing the quality and accuracy of web data sources. We then used evaluation metrics to compare the considered models on three real-life datasets taken from the Web and manually cured to guarantee precision in the results.

Our evaluations suggest that sophisticated models always compute better results than simple voting strategies, but the decision on which model to use in an application should be done only after an analysis of the desired requirements and of the characteristics of the domain of interest.

References

1. Amento, B., Terveen, L.G., Hill, W.C.: Does "authority" mean quality? predicting expert quality ratings of web documents. In: SIGIR, pp. 296–303 (2000)
2. Batini, C., Scannapieco, M.: Data Quality: Concepts, Methodologies, and Techniques. Springer (2008)
3. Blanco, L., Bronzi, M., Crescenzi, V., Merialdo, P., Papotti, P.: Exploiting information redundancy to wring out structured data from the web. In: Proceedings of the 19th International Conference on World Wide Web, WWW 2010. ACM, New York (2010)
4. Blanco, L., Bronzi, M., Crescenzi, V., Merialdo, P., Papotti, P.: Redundancy-driven web data extraction and integration. In: WebDB (2010)
5. Blanco, L., Crescenzi, V., Merialdo, P., Papotti, P.: Probabilistic Models to Reconcile Complex Data from Inaccurate Data Sources. In: Pernici, B. (ed.) CAiSE 2010. LNCS, vol. 6051, pp. 83–97. Springer, Heidelberg (2010)
6. Brin, S., Page, L.: The anatomy of a large-scale hypertextual web search engine. Computer Networks 30(1-7), 107–117 (1998)
7. Cafarella, M.J., Etzioni, O., Suciu, D.: Structured queries over web text. IEEE Data Eng. Bull. 29(4), 45–51 (2006)
8. Clemen, R.T., Winkler, R.L.: Combining probability distributions from experts in risk analysis. Risk Analysis 19(2), 187–203 (1999)
9. Dalvi, N.N., Suciu, D.: Management of probabilistic data: foundations and challenges. In: PODS, pp. 1–12 (2007)
10. Dong, X., Berti-Equille, L., Hu, Y., Srivastava, D.: Global detection of complex copying relationships between sources. PVLDB 3(1), 1358–1369 (2010)
11. Dong, X.L., Berti-Equille, L., Srivastava, D.: Integrating conflicting data: The role of source dependence. PVLDB 2(1), 550–561 (2009)
12. Dong, X.L., Berti-Equille, L., Srivastava, D.: Truth discovery and copying detection in a dynamic world. PVLDB 2(1), 562–573 (2009)
13. Downey, D., Etzioni, O., Soderland, S.: A probabilistic model of redundancy in information extraction. In: IJCAI, pp. 1034–1041 (2005)
14. Florescu, D., Koller, D., Levy, A.Y.: Using probabilistic information in data integration. In: VLDB, pp. 216–225 (1997)
15. Galland, A., Abiteboul, S., Marian, A., Senellart, P.: Corroborating information from disagreeing views. In: Proc. WSDM, New York, USA (2010)
16. Pal, A., Rastogi, V., Machanavajjhala, A., Bohannon, P.: Information integration over time in unreliable and uncertain environments. In: WWW, pp. 789–798 (2012)
17. Wu, M., Marian, A.: Corroborating answers from multiple web sources. In: WebDB (2007)
18. Yin, X., Han, J., Yu, P.S.: Truth discovery with multiple conflicting information providers on the web. IEEE Trans. Knowl. Data Eng. 20(6), 796–808 (2008)

A Domain Independent Framework
for Extracting Linked Semantic Data
from Tables

Varish Mulwad, Tim Finin, and Anupam Joshi

Computer Science and Electrical Engineering
University of Maryland, Baltimore County
Baltimore, MD 21250 USA
{varish1,finin,joshi}@cs.umbc.edu

Abstract. Vast amounts of information is encoded in tables found in
documents, on the Web, and in spreadsheets or databases. Integrating or
searching over this information benefits from understanding its intended
meaning and making it explicit in a semantic representation language
like RDF. Most current approaches to generating Semantic Web representations from tables requires human input to create schemas and
often results in graphs that do not follow best practices for linked data.
Evidence for a table's meaning can be found in its column headers, cell
values, implicit relations between columns, caption and surrounding text
but also requires general and domain-specific background knowledge. Approaches that work well for one domain, may not necessarily work well
for others. We describe a domain independent framework for interpreting
the intended meaning of tables and representing it as Linked Data. At the
core of the framework are techniques grounded in graphical models and
probabilistic reasoning to infer meaning associated with a table. Using
background knowledge from resources in the Linked Open Data cloud,
we jointly infer the semantics of column headers, table cell values (e.g.,
strings and numbers) and relations between columns and represent the
inferred meaning as graph of RDF triples. A table's meaning is thus cap-
tured by mapping columns to classes in an appropriate ontology, linking
cell values to literal constants, implied measurements, or entities in the
linked data cloud (existing or new) and discovering or and identifying
relations between columns.

Keywords: linked data, RDF, Semantic Web, tables, entity linking,
machine learning, graphical models.

1 Introduction

The Web has become a primary source of knowledge and information, largely
replacing encyclopedias and reference books. Most Web text is written in a narrative form as news stories, blogs, reports, letters, etc., but significant amounts
of information is also encoded in structured forms as stand-alone spreadsheets
or tables and as tables embedded in Web pages and documents. Cafarella et al.
[5] estimated that the Web contains over 150 million high quality relational html
tables.

S. Ceri and M. Brambilla (Eds.): Search Computing III, LNCS 7538, pp. 16–33, 2012.
© Springer-Verlag Berlin Heidelberg 2012

Tables are also used to present and summarize key data and results in documents in many subject areas, including science, medicine, healthcare, finance, and public policy. As a part of a coordinated open data and transparency initiative, nearly 30 nations are publishing government data on sites in structured formats. The US data.gov site shares more than 390,000 datasets drawn from many federal agencies and is complemented by similar sites from state and local government organizations. Tables are used to represent significant amount of information and knowledge, yet, we are not able to fully exploit it. Both integrating or searching over this information will benefit from a better understanding of the intended meaning of the data and its mapping to other reference dataset.

The goal of our research is to unlock knowledge encoded in tables. In this paper, we present a domain independent framework for automatically inferring the intended meaning and semantics associated with tables. Using the Linked Open Data [2] (or an provided ontology, knowledge base [KB]) as background knowledge, our techniques grounded in graphical models and probabilistic reasoning, map every column header to a class from an ontology, links table cell values to entities from the KB and discovers relations between table columns. The inferred information is represented as a graph of RDF triples allowing other applications to utilize the recovered knowledge.

2   Impact

Many real world problems and applications can benefit from exploiting information stored in tables including evidence based medical research [22]. Its goal is to judge the efficacy of drug dosages and treatments by performing meta-analyses (i.e systematic reviews) over published literature and clinical trials. The process involves finding appropriate studies, extracting useful data from them and performing statistical analysis over the data to produce a evidence report.

Key information required to produce evidence reports include data such as patient demographics, drug dosage information, different types of drugs used, brands of the drugs used, number of patients cured with a particular dosage etc. Most of this information is encoded in tables, which are currently beyond the scope of regular text processing systems and search engines. This makes the process manual and cumbersome for medical researchers.

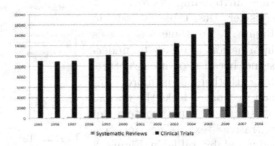

Fig. 1. The number of papers reporting on systematic reviews and meta-analyses is small compared to those reporting on individual clinical trials, as shown in this data from MEDLINE

Presently medical researchers perform keyword based search on systems such as PubMed's MEDLINE which end up producing many irrelevant studies, requiring researchers to manually evaluate all of the studies to select the relevant ones. Figure 1 obtained from [6] clearly shows the huge difference in number of meta-analysis and number of clinical trials published every year. By adding semantics to tables like Figure 2, we can develop systems that can easily correlate, integrate and search over different tables from different studies to be combined for a single meta-analysis.

Web search is another area that can benefit from understanding information stores in tables. Search engines work well at searching over text in web pages, but poorly when searching over tables. If recovered semantics are available, search engines can answer queries like *dog breeds life span, wheat production in Africa* or *temperature change in the Arctic,*with tables or web pages containing them as results. We also see our work helping to generate high quality semantic linked data, which in turn will aid the growth of the Semantic Web.

3   Inferring the Semantics of Tables

Analyzing tables provide unique challenges. One might be tempted to think that regular text processing might work with tables as well. After all tables also store text. However that is not the case. To differentiate between text processing and table processing consider the text "Barack Hussein Obama II (born August 4, 1961) is the 44th and current President of the United States. He is the first African American to hold the office."

The over-all meaning can be understood from the meaning of words in the sentence. The meaning of each word can be can be recovered from the word itself or by using context of the surrounding words. Now consider the table shown in Figure 2. In some ways, this information is easier to understand because of its structure, but in others it is more difficult because it lacks the normal organization and context of narrative text. The message conveyed by table in Figure 2 is different eradication rates for different drug dosages and treatment regimes for the disease *H pylori*. Similarly consider the table shown in Figure 3. The table

Table 2 *H pylori* eradication rates for each treatment regimen

	ITT		PP	
	n	% (95% CI)	n	% (95% CI)
OAC1W	240/301	79.7 (74.8 to 83.9)	183/219	83.6 (78.1 to 87.9)
OAC2W	246/301	81.7 (77 to 85.7)	185/218	84.9 (79.5 to 89.0)
OA	136/305	44.6 (39.1 to 50.2)	96/224	42.9 (36.5 to 49.4)

ITT, intention-to-treat; PP, per protocol; OA, omeprazole 20 mg twice daily and amoxicillin 1 g twice daily and placebo for 2 weeks; OAC1W, omeprazole 20 mg twice daily and amoxicillin 1 g twice daily and clarithromycin 500 mg twice daily for 1 week, followed by omeprazole 20 mg twice daily and placebo for 1 week; OAC2W, omeprazole 20 mg twice daily and amoxicillin 1 g twice daily and clarithromycin 500 g twice daily for 2 weeks.

Fig. 2. Tables in clinical trials literature have characteristics that differ from typical, generic Web tables. They often have row headers well as column headers, most of the cell values are numeric, cell values are often structured and captions can contain detailed metadata (From [32]).

represents information about cities in the United States of America. A closer look at the table tells us that the cities in column one are the largest cities of the respective states in column three.

City	State	Mayor	Population
Baltimore	MD	S.C.Rawlings-Blake	640,000
Philadelphia	PA	M.Nutter	1,500,000
New York	NY	M.Bloomberg	8,400,000
Boston	MA	T.Menino	610,000

Fig. 3. A simple table representing information about cities in United States of America

To extract such information from tables, it will be important to interpret the meaning of column (and row) headers, correlation between columns, and entities and literals mentioned in tables. Additional context and information can be also be obtained from caption of the table as well text surrounding the table.

The intended meaning of column headers can be extracted by analyzing the values in the columns. For example, the strings in column one in Figure 3 can be recognized as entity mentions that are instances of the *dbpedia-owl:Place class*. Additional analysis can automatically generate a narrower description such as major U.S. cities. The string in the third column match the names of people and also the narrower class of politicians. The column header provides additional evidence and better interpretation that the strings in column three are the mayors of the cities in column one. Linking the table cell values to known entities enriches the table further. Linking S.C.Rawlings-Blake to *dbpedia:Stephanie_C._Rawlings-Blake*, T.Menino to *dbpedia:Thomas_Menino* , M.Nutter to *dbpedia:Michael_Nutter* we can automatically infer the additional information that all three belong to the Democratic party. Discovering correlations between table columns also add key information. For example, in this case, correlation between columns one and two help us infer that cities in column one are *largestCities* of the respective states in column three.

The techniques above will work well when the table cell values are strings; but not necessarily when cell values are literals, for e.g. numerical values such as the ones from the table in Figure 2 or values from column four of the table in Figure 3. We discuss the challenges posed by such literals and how to tackle them later in the paper.

Producing an overall interpretation of a table is a complex task that requires developing an understanding of the intended meaning of the table as well as attention to the details of choosing the right URIs to represent both the schema as well as instances. We break down the process into following major tasks: (i) assign every column (or row header) a class label from an appropriate ontology; (ii) link table cell values to appropriate LOD entities, if possible; (iii) discover relationships between the table columns and link them to linked data properties; and (iv) generate a linked data representation of the inferred data.

4   DIF-LDT: A Domain Independent Framework

We present DIF-LDT - our domain independent framework for inferring the semantics associated with tables in Figure 4. With little or no domain dependence, the framework should work equally well with tables found on web pages,

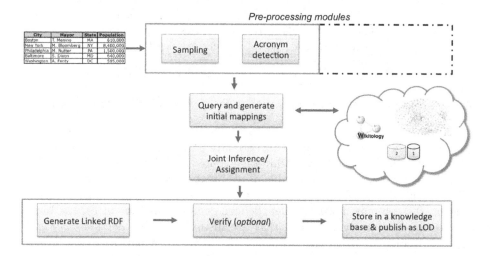

Fig. 4. We are developing a robust domain independent framework for table interpretation that will result in a representation of the information extracted as RDF Linked Open Data

in medical literature or tabular datasets from sites like data.gov. The goal of this framework is also to address a number of practical challenges, including handling with large tables containing many rows, tables with acronyms and encoded values, and literal data in the form of numbers and measurements.

At the core of the framework are two modules - a) module that queries and generates initial set of mappings for column headers, cell values and relation between columns in a table and b) a module grounded in probabilistic graphical model, which performs joint inference. Once the table passes through initial preprocessing, the query phase generates a set of candidate classes, entities and relations between columns, for every column header and cell values in a table. The module for joint inference will jointly assign values to column headers, cell values and relations between columns in a table. The table interpretation will be useful only when we are able to generate an appropriate representation of it which can be reasoned and queried over by other systems. Thus, the next step would be generating an appropriate representation of the inferred information. Certain applications may require that the user review and if necessary change the generated interpretation. To incorporate this requirement, an additional module provides a interactive framework to allow a human to work with the system to produce the interpretation. In the following sections we describe each module in detail.

4.1   Pre-processing

The goal of the preprocessing modules at the start of the process is for dealing with special cases. For example, certain tables or datasets can be too large to be dealt by the module for joint inference. In such cases, it would better to sample the table, generate a smaller version and let that pass through the rest of workflow. While applying joint inference/joint assignment techniques to large tables is not feasible, we believe that it is also not necessary. We note that people can usually understand a large table's meaning by looking only at its initial portion. Our approach will be similar – given a large table, we will sample the rows to select a smaller number to which we will apply the graphical model. The other pre-processing module we present is for acronyms. Many tables tend to use acronyms. Replacing them with their expanded forms, will provide a more accurate context and thus help in generating a better interpretation. While, we present only two such modules, given the independent nature of the modules, more modules can be easily added without breaking the rest of the workflow.

4.2   Generate and Rank Candidates

The goal of the querying phase is to access knowledge sources and generate a initial set of mappings of classes, entities and relations for each mention in the table. The knowledge sources used in the query process will include datasets such as DBpedia [3], Yago [25] from the LOD cloud. For other specialized domains such as the medical domain or open government data, additional ontologies and knowledge resources may be needed. For general tables, like the ones found on the web, DBpedia, Yago and Wikitology [26] provide very good coverage.

Presently, we use Wikitology, a hybrid kb based on Wikipedia's structured and unstructured information augmented with information from structured sources like DBpedia, Freebase [4], WordNet [17] and Yago, to generate our initial mappings. The query module generates a set of candidate entities for each cell value in a table by querying Wikitology, using query techniques described in [19].

Each returned entity has a set of associated classes (or types). For example, a subset of classes associated with the entity *dbpedia:Baltimore* are *yago:IndependentCitiesInTheUnitedStates, dbpedia-owl:PopulatedPlace, dbpedia-owl:City, yago:CitiesInMaryland*. The set of candidate classes for a given column in a table can be obtained by taking a union of the set of classes associated with the candidate entities in that column. Our current focus is restricted to column headers and entities in a table.

Once the candidate sets are generated, the next step is to rank the candidates. We developed two functions ψ_1 and ψ_2 for this purpose. ψ_1 ranks the candidate classes in a given set, whereas ψ_2 ranks the candidate entities. ψ_1 will compute the 'affinity' between a column header string (e.g., *City*) and a class from the candidate set (say *dbpedia-owl:City*). We define ψ_1 as the exponential of the product of a weight vector and a feature vector computed for column header. ψ_1 will assign a score to each candidate class which can be used to rank the candidate classes. Thus,

$$\psi_1 = exp(w_1^T . f_1(C_i, L_{C_i}))$$

where w_1 is the weight vector, L_{C_i} is the candidate class label and C_i is the string in column header i. The feature vector f_1 is composed of the following features:

$$f_1 = [LevenshteinDistance(C_i, L_{C_i}), DiceScore(C_i, L_{C_i}),$$
$$SemanticSimilarity(C_i, L_{C_i}), InformationContent(L_{C_i})]$$

f_1 includes a set of string similarity metrics (Levenshtein distance [15], Dice score [24]) to capture string similarity between the class and column header string. To overcome cases where there is no string or content match (e.g. *dbpedia-owl:AdministrativeRegion* and *State*), we also include a metric to capture Semantic Similarity [10] between the candidate class and column header string.

Selecting 'specific' classes is more useful than selecting 'general' classes. For example it is better to infer that a column header is of type of *dbpedia-owl:City* as compared to inferring it as *dbpedia-owl:Place* or *owl:Thing*. Thus, to promote classes of the likes of *dbpedia-owl:City*, f_1 incorporates an Information content measure. Based on semantic similarity defined in [21], we define Information Content as, $I.C(L_C) = -log_2[p(L_C)]$, where $p(L_C)$ is the probability of the class L_C. We computed $I.C.$ for classes from the DBpedia ontology and noticed that specific classes will have a higher value for $I.C.$ as compared to more general classes.

We also develop a function ψ_2 to rank and compute the affinity between the string in the table row cell (say *Baltimore*) and the candidate entity (say *dbpedia:Baltimore*). We define ψ_2 as the exponential of the product of a weight vector and a feature vector computed for a cell value. Once again ψ_2 will assign a score to each entity which can be used to rank the entities. Thus,

$$\psi_2 = exp(w_2^T.f_2(R_{i,j}, E_{i,j}))$$

where w_2 is the weight vector, $E_{i,j}$ is the candidate entity and $R_{i,j}$ is string value in column i and row j. The feature vector f_2 is composed as follows:

$$f_2 = [LevenshteinDistance(R_{i,j}, E_{i,j}), DiceScore(R_{i,j}, E_{i,j}),$$
$$PageRank(E_{i,j}), KBScore(E_{i,j}), PageLength(E_{i,j})]$$

f_2 is consists a set of string similarity metrics (Levenshtein distance, Dice score) and also a set of popularity metrics(Predicted Page Rank [27], Page Length and Wikitology KB score for the entity). When it is difficult to disambiguate between entities, the more popular entity is likely to be the correct answer; hence the inclusion of popularity metrics. The weight vectors w_1, w_2 can be tweaked via experiments or can be learned using standard machine learning procedures. As we continue to make progress in our work, in the future, we will develop a similar function for ranking candidate relations.

4.3   Joint Inference

Given candidate sets for column headers, cell values and relation between table columns, the joint inference module is responsible for joint assignment to mentions in the table and infer the meaning of a table as a whole. Probabilistic graphical models [13] provide a powerful and convenient framework for expressing a joint probability over a set of variables and performing inference or joint assignment of values to the variables. Probabilistic graphical models use graph based representations to encode probability distribution over a set of variables for a given system. The nodes in such a graph represent the variables of the system and the edges represent the probabilistic interaction between the variables.

Based on the graphical representation used to model the system, the graph needs to be parametrized and then an appropriate inference algorithm needs to be selected to perform inferencing over the graph. Thus constructing a graphical model involves the following steps: (i) identifying variables in the system; (ii) specifying interactions between variables and representing it as a graph; (iii) parameterizing the graphical structure; and (iv) selecting an appropriate algorithm for inferencing. Following this plan, we describe how a graphical model for inferring the semantics of tables is constructed.

Variables in the System. The column headers, cells values (strings and literals) and relation between columns in a table represent the set of variables in an interpretation framework. Each variable has a set of candidates associated, which are generated as described in section 4.2. The initial assignment to each variable will be its top ranked candidate.

Graphical Representation. There are three major representation techniques for encoding the distribution over set of variables: directed models (e.g., Bayesian networks), undirected models (e.g., Markov networks), and partially directed models. In the context of graphical models, Markov networks are undirected graphs in which nodes represent the set of variables in a system and the undirected edges represent the probabilistic interactions between the them. The edges in the graph are undirected because the interaction between the variables are symmetrical. In the case of tables, interaction between the column headers, table cell values and relation between table columns are symmetrical. Thus we choose a Markov network based graphical model for the inferring the semantics of tables.

Figure 5(a) shows the interaction between the variables in a table. In a typical well formed table, each column contains data of a single syntactic type (e.g., strings) that represent entities or values of a common semantic type (e.g., people). For example, in a column of cities, the column header *City* represents the semantic type of values in the column and *Baltimore*, *Boston* and *Philadelphia* are instances of that type. Thus knowing the type (or class) of the column header, influences the decision of the assignment to the table cells in that column and vice-versa.

To capture this influence, we insert an edge between the column header and each of the table cells in the column. Edges between the table cell themselves in the same column are not needed since they become independent of each other once the column header is known. To keep the figure simple, we show interaction between column header and row values for one column only. The same interactions apply, of course, to the rest of the columns.

Table cells across a given row are also related. Consider a table cell with a value *Beetle*. It might be referring to an insect or a car. The next table cell

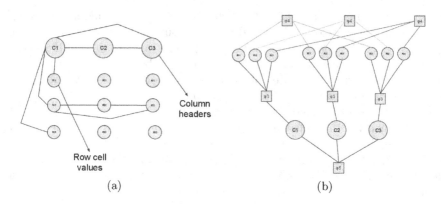

Fig. 5. (a) This graph represents the interactions between the variables in a simple table. Only some of the connections are shown to keep the figure simple. (b) This factor graph is a parameterized Markov network with nodes for variables and factors.

has a value *red* which is a color. The value in the last table cell is *Gasoline*, a type of fuel source. All the values considered together, indicate that the row is representing values of a car rather than an insect. This can be further confirmed by the evidence from type of the column header. Thus to disambiguate a table cell correctly, the context from the rest of table cells in the row should be used. To capture this context, we insert edges between all the table cells in a given row. Again for simplicity, we show interaction between the table cells of only one row.

Similar interaction also exist between the column headers. The column header *City* might suggest that the strings in the columns are cities. However if *City* appears in the table with other columns which are Basketball players, Coach and Division, we can infer that the column of cities is referring to a team itself – an example of metonymy in which the team is referenced by one of its significant properties, the location of it's base. Thus to correctly disambiguate what the column header means, we should use evidence from rest of the column headers as well. To capture this interaction, we insert edges between all the column headers as well.

The model we have presented captures interactions between the column headers and table cell values. Our initial plan is to experiment with the current model and then further extend it to incorporate the variable to capture relations between table columns in the graph as well.

Parametrizing the Network. To represent the distribution associated with the graph structure, we need to parameterize the structure. Since Markov networks are undirected, the goal of parameterization is to capture the *affinity* between the interacting variables. That is if variable A is assigned a value a_1 and variable B is assigned b_1, the question we ask is whether A and B are likely to agree or not. The function that computes this *affinity* is known as a *factor*.

One way to parameterize a Markov network is to represent it as a *factor graph*. A factor graph is an undirected graph containing two types of nodes: variables and factors. The graph has edges only between the factor nodes and variable nodes. The factor nodes are responsible for computing the *affinity* between the variable nodes to which it is connected. Figure 5(b) presents the parametrized network. The column headers (all C_i) and cell values (all R_{ij}) are the variable nodes and ψ_3, ψ_4 and ψ_5 are factor nodes in the graph.

ψ_3 is a factor node that captures the affinity between the class label assigned to a column header and the entities linked to the cell values in the same column; i.e., its goal is to check whether *dbpedia-owl:City, dbpedia:Baltimore, dbpedia:-Philadelphia* and *dbpedia:Boston* are 'compatible' or not. ψ_3 has two goals - to detect if any of cell values have been linked to incorrect entities or if the class label assigned to the column header is incorrect.

Each entity is associated with a set of classes (or types). For example the classes associated with *dbpedia:Baltimore* include *dbpedia:City, yago:IndependentCitiesInTheUnitedStates,* and *yago:CitiesInMaryland.* ψ_3 will assign a score to the class mapped to the column header as follows. Each entity in the column will contribute a score between zero and one to the class. The score contributed will be 0.0 if the class assigned to the column header is not in the set of classes associated with the entity and 1.0 if its the best match. An entity will contribute a lower score if the class assigned to the column header has a more "descriptive" or specific class in its set. For example, the class *dbpedia:City* is more descriptive and informative as compared to *dbpedia:Place.* The score assigned to the class label will be the average of the sum of scores assigned by each of the individual entities in the column.

What inferences can be drawn from the score? A score of 0.0 indicates either that the class label assigned is incorrect or all the entities linked to the cell values are incorrect. A score of 1.0 strongly suggests that class and entity assignments are correct. Scores tending towards 1.0 will indicate higher level of agreement whereas scores closer to 0.0 indicate less agreement. We will discuss how this information is used in the section on inferencing over the graph.

ψ_4 is a factor node that captures the affinity between the entities linked to the values in the table cells in a given row in the table, i.e., the affinity between *dbpedia:Baltimore, dbpedia:Maryland,* and *dbpedia:Stephanie_Rawlings-Blake.* Entities across a given row are likely to be related to each other. We use Pointwise mutual information (PMI) as a measure to capture the relatedness between entities. The PMI between totally unrelated entities will be zero, whereas the value will be non zero for related entities. For example, the PMI between *dbpedia:Baltimore* and *dbpedia:Seattle_Seahawks* will be 0.0, since they are unrelated. We have computed PMI values for Wikitology entities based on statistics derived from Wikipedia and DBpedia.

The factor node ψ_4 will compute pairwise PMI for a entity with the rest of entities in the row. Thus, in this case, for *dbpedia:Baltimore*, ψ_4 will compute PMI between *dbpedia:Baltimore, dbpedia:Maryland* and *dbpedia:Baltimore, dbpedia:Stephanie_Rawlings-Blake.* If a cell value in the row is mapped to a incorrect entity, the entity will have zero PMI with every other entity present in the row. This can be used as a indicator to detect incorrect mapping for a given cell value.

Similarly, ψ_5 is a factor node that captures the affinity between classes that have been assigned to all the column headers in the table, i.e., the affinity between *dbpedia-owl:City*, *dbpedia-owl:AdministrativeRegion*, and *dbpedia-owl:Mayor*. We again rely on the PMI data to capture the association between the class labels assigned to column headers. For every class label, ψ_5 will compute PMI between the class label and each of the other class labels across the column header. A unrelated class label will have zero PMI with every other class label, which can be used as indicator of incorrect mapping.

The factor nodes are dependent on measures such as *PMI* and the *score* assigned by entities to a class. These measures can be computed from the domain knowledge source. We see these functions as first iteration and expect them to evolve as continue to experiment. Similarly as the graph is extended to incorporate relations between table columns, more factor nodes are likely to be added.

Inference. The objective of the inference process is to determine the best possible assignments to the column headers and table cell values and eventually relations between table columns. We will use a variation of message-passing/belief propagation [13] for this process. Our inference algorithm will work as follows. The process will start with the variable nodes sending a message to all its connected factor nodes. The message will be composed of the current value assigned to the variable node.

Once a factor node receives messages from all the connected variable nodes, it will compute if the values assigned are in agreement or not. If the values are not in agreement, it will identify the variable node(s) that may have a wrong assignment. For all the nodes with possible wrong assignments, the factor node will send a message requesting the node to change its assignment to a different value. It will also send a confidence measure; i.e., how confident is the factor node about the assertion that the variable node has a wrong assignment. For the variable nodes with correct assignment, the factor node will send a message of 'no change'.

The factor nodes will use the functions defined above to determine agreement. For example, the factor node ψ_4 can conclude that all the values are in agreement, if every entity assigned in a row is connected (i.e., has non-zero PMI) with at least one other entity in the same row. ψ_4 will send a message of change assignment to a variable, if the entity assigned has zero PMI will all other entities in the row. Similarly if the score assigned to a class mapped to the column header is one, ψ_3 will conclude that the class and the entities in the column are in agreement.

Once a variable node receives messages from all the factor nodes to which it is connected, the variable nodes determines whether it needs to change its assigned value or not. For example, if a node receives a 'no change' message from all factor nodes, the variable node will not change its value. If the node receives a change message from all the factor nodes, the node will change its value and select a new assignment. In the long run, our goal will be to develop a generic function that nodes will use to decide whether to change values or not. The function will take into account factors such as the 'change' and 'no change' messages received, confidence associated with each message and overall 'global temperature'. This last measure will capture whether most (or all) variable nodes are satisfied with their assignment or not. If there is high level of agreement/satisfaction across all nodes, the variable told to change its assignment with low confidence, may not change. We expect that this mechanism will ensure or at least promote convergence to a solution, much like the temperature concept of simulated annealing.

All variable nodes which change their assigned value to a new one send a message to all their connected factor nodes, announcing the update as well the updated value. Every factor node which receives such a message, will redo the computation with the new value and the above process is repeated. This continues until all the variables do not change their values. To ensure that this process converges, variations like penalizing a change in assignment as the number of iterations increase, will be included.

4.4   Generate Linked Data

The table interpretation will be useful only when we are able to generate an appropriate representation of it which can be reasoned and queried over by other systems. Figure 6 presents our preliminary template for representing the inferred information as Semantic Linked Data.

In the future, we will extend our preliminary template and develop an richer ontology for annotating and representing tabular data as linked data. The ontology will provide terms for expressing the provenance of the interpretation and annotating some mappings certainty information.

```
@prefix rdfs: <http://www.w3.org/2000/01/rdf-schema#>.
@prefix dbpedia: <http://dbpedia.org/resource/>.
@prefix dbpedia-owl: <http://dbpedia.org/ontology/>.
@prefix dbpprop: <http://dbpedia.org/property/>.

"City"@en is rdfs:label of dbpedia-owl:City.
"State"@en is rdfs:label of dbpedia-owl:AdminstrativeRegion.
"Baltimore"@en is rdfs:label of dbpedia:Baltimore.
dbpedia:Baltimore a dbpedia-owl:City.
"MD"@en is rdfs:label of dbpedia:Maryland.
dbpedia:Maryland a dbpedia-owl:AdministrativeRegion.
```

Fig. 6. A preliminary represented of inferred knowledge from a table

With the use of a probabilistic graphical model, it is possible to generate certainty information. Since we are dealing with tables on the web, different tables are likely to generate contradictory information. Thus provenance and source of tables will be important to applications reasoning over our data. Our representation will also capture table meta data such as number of columns and rows as well as the table in its raw form. We wish to allow applications to be able to reconstruct the original table from the linked data representation.

4.5   Human in the Loop

Since achieving perfect accuracy in automatically translating a table into linked data is infeasible, we will develop a interactive framework to allow a human to work with the system to produce the interpretation. Our approach will have two phases: interpretation exploration and providing feedback. The first phase will allow a person to inspect and explore the interpretation, determining the entities, concepts and relations to which table components are mapped. The human user will also be able to see the ranked list of alternatives for each mapping along with any associated scores or confidence measures. The second phase will permit the user to identify one of the mappings an incorrect and optionally select and "lock down" one of the alternate interpretations. The system will then rerun the graphical model, producing a new overall interpretation. This sequence of inspection and correction can be repeated until an acceptable interpretation is produced.

4.6   Challenges – Literals

Literals pose unique challenges. Unlike strings in table cells, literals are not entities that can be linked to existing entities from a knowledge base; but rather they represent values of properties. The properties themselves can be associated with other entities in the table. Thus techniques that will work with string based values will not necessarily work for literals.

So how do we treat literals such as numerical data ? We can take the intuition that humans use to understand columns of numerical data as a starting point. To begin with, the range of numbers in a given column can start providing evidence about what the column is about. If a person looks at a column (without a column header) that contains numbers in the range of 0–100, the person is likely to infer that the column could be percentages or ages. The row (or column) header may have additional clues. For example, in the case of percentages, the % sign maybe associated with the numbers in the table cell or it may be present in the row (or column) header in the table.

Successfully understanding numerical data, will require understanding what properties do values from a column map to and extracting unit associated with numbers or unit symbols (like %).

5   Related Work

Our work is closely related to two threads of research. The first focuses on generating RDF and linked data from sources such as databases, spreadsheets and CSV files. The second, and more recent one, addresses understanding and inferring the implicit semantics of tables.

Several systems have been implemented to generate semantic web data from databases [23,28,20], spreadsheets [11,14] and CSV files [8]. All are manual or at best partially automated and none have focused on automatically generating *linked* RDF data for the entire table. These systems have mainly focused on relational databases where the schema is available or on simple spreadsheets. In the domain of open government data, [8] presents techniques to convert raw data (CSV, spreadsheets) to RDF. However the generated RDF data does not use existing classes or properties for column headers, nor does it link cell values to entities from the LOD cloud. To generate a richer, enhanced mappings, users will need to manually specify a configuration file. Their focus has been on generating massive quantity linked government data rather quality linked government data.

The key shortcoming in such systems is that they rely heavily on users and their knowledge of the Semantic Web. Most systems do not automatically link classes and entities generated from their mapping to existing Semantic Web resources – their output turns out to be just *raw string data* represented as RDF, instead of fully linked RDF. Figure 7 shows a part of RDF representation of

```
<rdf:Description rdf:about="#entry1">
<value>6444</value>
<label>Number of Farms</label>
<group>Farms with women principal operators</group>
<county_fips>000</county_fips>
<state_fips>01</state_fips>
<state>Alabama</state>
<rdf:type rdf:resource="http://data-gov.tw.rpi.edu/2009
/data-gov-twc.rdf#DataEntry"/>
</rdf:Description>
```

Fig. 7. A portion of the RDF representation from dataset 1425 - Census of Agriculture Race, Ethnicity and Gender Profile Data from data.gov.

dataset 1425 from *data.gov* [7]. The property names in the representation are column headers from the raw dataset and the values of the properties represent row values for the respective columns.

The representation fails to use existing vocabulary terms to annotate the raw data and most of the column headers are mapped to properties local to the RDF file. Mapping column headers to classes and properties from the LOD cloud, provides richer description as compared to the local properties. Such a representation often uses string identifiers for table cell values instead of linking them to existing entities in the LOD cloud. Linking the string cell values can further enrich the semantic representation of the data. Our framework will link and reuse existing classes, properties and entities with dereferenceable URIs from the LOD cloud. Our goal is to generate linked data in a form which is identified as "five star" by Tim Berners-Lee [1].

Early work in table understanding focused on extracting tables from documents and web pages [12,9] with more recent research attempting to understand their semantics. Wang et al. [30] began by identifying a single 'entity column' in a table and, based on its values and rest of the column headers, associates a concept from the Probase [31] knowledge base with the table. Their work does not attempt to link the table cell values or identify relations between columns. Ventis et al. [29] associate multiple class labels (or concepts) with columns in a table and identify relations between the 'subject' column and the rest of the columns in the table. Both the concept identification for columns and relation identification is based on maximum likelihood hypothesis, i.e., the best class label (or relation) is one that maximizes the probability of the values given the class label (or relation) for the column. Their work also does not attempt to link the table cell values. Limaye et al. [16] use a graphical model which maps every column header to a class from a known ontology, links table cell values to entities from a knowledge-base and identifies relations between columns. They rely on Yago for background knowledge.

The core of our framework is a probabilistic graphical model that captures a much richer semantics, including relation between column headers as well relation between entities across a given row. Our model has a single 'factor' node to capture relation between column header and strings in the column, which makes it possible to deal with missing values (e.g., absent column header).

Current systems for interpreting tables rely on semantically poor and possibly noisy knowledge-bases and do not attempt to produce a complete interpretation of a table. None of the current systems propose or generate any form of linked data from the inferred meaning. The work mentioned above will work well with string based tables but we know of no systems that interpret columns with numeric values and use the results as evidence in the table interpretation. Doing so is essential for many domains, including medical research.

6   Discussion and Conclusion

We built a baseline system [19] to evaluate the feasibility in tacking the problem. The baseline system was a sequential system that did three things : i) predict class labels for column headers ii) link table cell values to entities and iii) discover correlation between column headers. We evaluated our baseline system using a dataset of 15 tables obtained from the web, Google Squared and tables from Wikipedia articles. Excluding the columns with numbers, the 15 tables have 52 columns and 611 entities for evaluation of our algorithms. We used a subset of 23 columns for evaluation of relation identification between columns.

In the first evaluation of the algorithm for assigning class labels to columns, we compared the ranked list of possible class labels generated by the system against the list of possible class labels ranked by the evaluators. For 80.76% of the columns the average precision between the system and evaluators list was greater than 0 which indicates that there was at least one relevant label in the top three of the system ranked list. The mean average precision for 52 columns was 0.411.For 75% of the columns, the recall of the algorithm was greater than or equal to 0.6. We also assessed whether our predicted class labels were reasonable based on the judgement of human subjects. 76.92% of the class labels predicted were considered correct by the evaluators. 66.12% of the table cell strings were correctly linked by our algorithm for linking table cells. Our dataset had 24 new entities and our algorithm was able to correctly predict for all the 24 entities as new entities not present in the KB. We did not get encouraging results for relationship identification with an accuracy of 25%.

Analysis of our evaluation provided useful lessons. First, we noticed, with a sequential system, the error percolated from stage one to stage three, thus leading to an overall poor interpretation of the semantics of tables. This lead us to developing a framework based around probabilistic graphical model for joint inference over a table. Secondly, our baseline system was giving preference to 'general classes' over 'specific classes', which we address by introducing measures like Information Content of a class. Our framework also goes beyond web-tables and aims to deal with tables across multiple domains – from medical literature to open government data. We are in the process of implementing the graphical model. Once the model is implemented, we will evaluate it against a dataset of tables shared by Limaye et al. [16].

Generating an explicit representation of the meaning implicit in tabular data will support automatic integration and more accurate search. We described general techniques grounded in graphical models and probabilistic reasoning to infer a tables meaning relative to a knowledge base of general and domain-specific knowledge expressed in the Semantic Web language OWL. We represent a table's meaning as a graph of OWL triples where the columns have been mapped to classes, cell values to literals, measurements, or knowledge-base entities and relations to triples. We believe that knowledge recovered from tables can enable and assist various application and lead us towards a web of semantics, concepts and entities.

Acknowledgements. This research was supported in part by NSF awards 0326460 and 0910838, MURI award FA9550-08-1-0265 from AFOSR, and a gift from Microsoft Research.

References

1. Berners-Lee, T.: Linked data (July 2006), http://www.w3.org/DesignIssues/LinkedData.html
2. Bizer, C.: The emerging web of linked data. IEEE Intelligent Systems 24(5), 87–92 (2009)
3. Bizer, C., Lehmann, J., Kobilarov, G., Auer, S., Becker, C., Cyganiak, R., Hellmann, S.: Dbpedia - a crystallization point for the web of data. Journal of Web Semantics 7(3), 154–165 (2009)
4. Bollacker, K., Evans, C., Paritosh, P., Sturge, T., Taylor, J.: Freebase: a collaboratively created graph database for structuring human knowledge. In: Proc. ACM Int. Conf. on Management of Data, pp. 1247–1250. ACM (2008)
5. Cafarella, M.J., Halevy, A.Y., Wang, Z.D., Wu, E., Zhang, Y.: Webtables: exploring the power of tables on the web. PVLDB 1(1), 538–549 (2008)
6. Cohen, A., Adams, C., Davis, J., Yu, C., Yu, P., Meng, W., Duggan, L., McDonagh, M., Smalheiser, N.: Evidence-based medicine, the essential role of systematic reviews, and the need for automated text mining tools. In: Proc. 1st ACM Int. Health Informatics Symposium, pp. 376–380. ACM (2010)
7. Dataset 1425 - Census of Agriculture Race, Ethnicity and Gender Profile Data (2009), http://explore.data.gov/Agriculture/Census-of-Agriculture-Race-Ethnicity-and-Gender-Pr/yd4n-fk45
8. Ding, L., DiFranzo, D., Graves, A., Michaelis, J.R., Li, X., McGuinness, D.L., Hendler, J.A.: Twc data-gov corpus: incrementally generating linked government data from data.gov. In: Proc 19th Int. Conf. on the World Wide Web, pp. 1383–1386. ACM, New York (2010)
9. Embley, D.W., Lopresti, D.P., Nagy, G.: Notes on Contemporary Table Recognition. In: Bunke, H., Spitz, A.L. (eds.) DAS 2006. LNCS, vol. 3872, pp. 164–175. Springer, Heidelberg (2006)

10. Han, L., Finin, T., McNamee, P., Joshi, A., Yesha, Y.: Improving word similarity by augmenting pmi with estimates of word polysemy. IEEE Transactions on Knowledge and Data Engineering (2012)
11. Han, L., Finin, T., Parr, C., Sachs, J., Joshi, A.: RDF123: From Spreadsheets to RDF. In: Sheth, A.P., Staab, S., Dean, M., Paolucci, M., Maynard, D., Finin, T., Thirunarayan, K. (eds.) ISWC 2008. LNCS, vol. 5318, pp. 451–466. Springer, Heidelberg (2008)
12. Hurst, M.: Towards a theory of tables. IJDAR 8(2-3), 123–131 (2006)
13. Koller, D., Friedman, N.: Probabilistic Graphical Models: Principles and Techniques. MIT Press (2009)
14. Langegger, A., Wöß, W.: XLWrap – Querying and Integrating Arbitrary Spreadsheets with SPARQL. In: Bernstein, A., Karger, D.R., Heath, T., Feigenbaum, L., Maynard, D., Motta, E., Thirunarayan, K. (eds.) ISWC 2009. LNCS, vol. 5823, pp. 359–374. Springer, Heidelberg (2009)
15. Levenshtein, V.I.: Binary codes capable of correcting deletions, insertions, and reversals. Tech. Rep. 8, Soviet Physics Doklady (1966)
16. Limaye, G., Sarawagi, S., Chakrabarti, S.: Annotating and searching web tables using entities, types and relationships. In: Proc. 36th Int. Conf. on Very Large Databases (2010)
17. Miller, G.A.: Wordnet: a lexical database for english. CACM 38, 39–41 (1995)
18. Mulwad, V.: T2LD - An automatic framework for extracting, interpreting and representing tables as Linked Data. Master's thesis, U. of Maryalnd, Baltimore County (August 2010)
19. Mulwad, V., Finin, T., Syed, Z., Joshi, A.: Using linked data to interpret tables. In: Proc. 1st Int. Workshop on Consuming Linked Data, Shanghai (2010)
20. Polfliet, S., Ichise, R.: Automated mapping generation for converting databases into linked data. In: Proc. 9th Int. Semantic Web Conf. (November 2010)
21. Resnik, P.: Semantic similarity in a taxonomy: An information-based measure and its application to problems of ambiguity in natural language. Journal of Artificial Intelligence Research 11(1), 95–130 (1999)
22. Sackett, D., Rosenberg, W., Gray, J., Haynes, R., Richardson, W.: Evidence based medicine: what it is and what it isn't. BMJ 312(7023), 71 (1996)
23. Sahoo, S.S., Halb, W., Hellmann, S., Idehen, K., Thibodeau Jr., T., Auer, S., Sequeda, J., Ezzat, A.: A survey of current approaches for mapping of relational databases to rdf. Tech. rep., W3C (2009)
24. Salton, G., Mcgill, M.J.: Introduction to Modern Information Retrieval. McGraw-Hill, Inc., New York (1986)
25. Suchanek, F.M., Kasneci, G., Weikum, G.: Yago: A Core of Semantic Knowledge. In: 16th Int. World Wide Web Conf. ACM Press, New York (2007)
26. Syed, Z., Finin, T.: Creating and Exploiting a Hybrid Knowledge Base for Linked Data. In: Filipe, J., Fred, A., Sharp, B. (eds.) ICAART 2010. CCIS, vol. 129, pp. 3–21. Springer, Heidelberg (2011)
27. Syed, Z., Finin, T., Mulwad, V., Joshi, A.: Exploiting a Web of Semantic Data for Interpreting Tables. In: Proc. 2nd Web Science Conf. (April 2010)
28. Vavliakis, K.N., Grollios, T.K., Mitkas, P.A.: Rdote - transforming relational databases into semantic web data. In: Proc. 9th Int. Semantic Web Conf. (November 2010)
29. Venetis, P., Halevy, A., Madhavan, J., Pasca, M., Shen, W., Wu, F., Miao, G., Wu, C.: Recovering semantics of tables on the web. In: Proc. 37th Int. Conf. on Very Large Databases (2011)

30. Wang, J., Shao, B., Wang, H., Zhu, K.Q.: Understanding tables on the web. Tech. rep., Microsoft Research Asia (2011)
31. Wu, W., Li, H., Wang, H., Zhu, K.: Towards a probabilistic taxonomy of many concepts. Tech. rep., Microsoft Research Asia (2011)
32. Zagari, R., Bianchi-Porro, G., Fiocca, R., Gasbarrini, G., Roda, E., Bazzoli, F.: Comparison of 1 and 2 weeks of omeprazole, amoxicillin and clarithromycin treatment for helicobacter pylori eradication: the hyper study. Gut 56(4), 475 (2007)

Knowledge Extraction from Structured Sources

Jörg Unbehauen, Sebastian Hellmann, Sören Auer, and Claus Stadler

Universität Leipzig, Postfach 100920, 04009 Leipzig, Germany
{unbehauen,hellmann,cstadler,auer}@informatik.uni-leipzig.de
http://aksw.org

Abstract. This chapter surveys knowledge extraction approaches from structured sources such as relational databases, XML and CSV. A general definition of knowledge extraction is devised that covers structured as well as unstructured sources. We summarize current progress on conversion of structured data to RDF and OWL. As an example, we provide a formalization and description of SparqlMap, which implements the relational database to RDF mapping language R2RML currently being standardized by the W3C.

Keywords: Triplification, Knowledge Extraction, RDF.

1 Introduction

In recent years, the availability of data in Semantic Web formats such as RDF and OWL has drastically increased. Nevertheless, the data that is currently available constitutes just a fraction of existing data that could be exposed and distributed as RDF and OWL. As the Web of Data, envisioned by Tim Berners-Lee[1], gains momentum, the demand to extract knowledge and to "triplify" data is steadily increasing, especially in the areas of commerce, science and government. This "triplification" process, however, is due to the heterogeneity of information and data models challenging. Although tools exist to support the generation of RDF from legacy sources, several obstacles remain for automated approaches. Such obstacles and cost factors include in particular:

Identification of Private and Public Data. Legacy sources always contain information which should not be made public on the Web such as passwords, email addresses or technical parameters and configurations. Automatically distinguishing between strictly confidential, important and less relevant information is very hard, if not impossible.

Proper Reuse of Existing Vocabularies. Even the most elaborated approaches to ontology mapping fail in generating certain mappings between the legacy data (e.g. database entities such as table and column names) and existing RDF vocabularies, due to lacking machine-readable descriptions of the domain semantics in the database schema.

---

[1] http://www.w3.org/DesignIssues/Semantic.html

S. Ceri and M. Brambilla (Eds.): Search Computing III, LNCS 7538, pp. 34–52, 2012.

Missing Schema Descriptions. Many legacy sources do neither provide proper documentation nor extensive schema definition (e.g. MySQL does not contain definitions for foreign keys or constraints, XML data type definition only provides information about the validity of the data, but not about the semantics). Syntactic approaches for detecting schema descriptions are likely to fail, since schemas were often grown evolutionary and naming conventions are not enforced. In most cases, the structure of the data needs to be manually reverse engineered by a domain expert, who has an understanding of the content and the domain.

URI Generation. The quality of legacy data sources do often not match the requirements for RDF datatypes and URIs. Strings and terms have to be normalized and cleaned to admit a transition to URIs. The choice which entities to use for identifiers (e.g. convert primary keys to URIs) is not always obvious. It often depends on the particular use case whether a database entry should be transformed to a URI or an RDF literal.

The aim of this article is to present an overview on approaches to tackle these obstacles. In Section 2 we discuss some prerequisites and then define "Knowledge Extraction" as a general concept. The presented definition was used to bootstrap the Wikipedia article on the topic[2]. Our definition also explains the relation between extracted "knowledge" and "triplification" into RDF/OWL. Subsequently, we compare popular existing structured data models with RDF/OWL in Section 3 to shed light on the impedance mismatch. In Section 4 we introduce the *Knowledge Extraction Tools Survey Ontology* (KETSO) to classify existing tools. The ontology differs greatly from previous survey methodologies as it introduces a flat property based classification approach in comparison to previous hierarchical ones [8,6,10,12]. The main rationales for employing an ontology based approach (using OWL datatype and object properties) to classify the tools are:

1. Not all tools use the full set of properties as they vary greater than tools from one source (e.g. XML).
2. Hierarchical classification are shown to be inconsistent in the first place and also become obsolete once we generalize the classification to other sources.
3. The scheme and the data are made freely available. By providing an OWL class for classification, future work can be incorporated as an extension or related with `owl:equivalentClass` and `owl:disjointWith` axioms. The data can be used to visualize approaches and match them to given use cases.

We provide an in-depth look at one particular knowledge extraction approach with the formalization and description of SparqlMap, which implements the relational database to RDF mapping language R2RML currently being standardized by the W3C. Finally, we conclude and give an outlook on potential future work in Section 6.

---

[2] http://en.wikipedia.org/wiki/Knowledge_extraction

2   Definition of Knowledge Extraction

Although the term *knowledge extraction* is widely used in the literature, no surveys exist that have succeeded in creating a framework to cover unstructured as well as structured sources or provide a clear definition of the underlying "triplification" process and the required prerequisites. Other frameworks and surveys as well as individual approaches especially lack the following aspects:

1. Clear boundaries to existing research areas such as *Information Extraction* (Text Mining), *Extract-Transform-Load* (Data Warehouse) and *Ontology Learning* have not yet been established. Such boundaries are defined by stating distinctive criteria and also by specifying the meaning of knowledge w.r.t. the main data model of our concern, RDF and OWL (see next item).
2. The idea that "knowledge" is extracted has not been well-defined. Although, RDF and OWL can serve as knowledge representation formalisms, the mere usage of RDF/OWL as a format can not sufficiently define the notion of "knowledge". The main questions are: "What is the result of a *triplification* process?" "Structured data or represented knowledge?", "When does structured data become knowledge?"
3. Although, the area of extraction of RDF from relational databases has been been researched extensively, approaches were hardly comparable to extraction methods employed on other sources, thus preventing generalisation.
4. Most individual approaches were driven by very specific use cases that came with a specific data source and required the transformation into RDF and, thus, are lacking a more general view on the problem. The main questions were: "What are the properties of such a transformation?" and "How do they differ from previous efforts?"

Knowledge Extraction is the creation of knowledge from structured (relational databases, XML) and unstructured (text, documents, images) sources. The resulting knowledge needs to be in a machine-readable and machine-interpretable format and must represent knowledge in a manner that unambiguously defines its meaning and facilitates inferencing. Although, it is methodically similar to Information Extraction (NLP) and ETL (Data Warehouse), the main distinguishing criteria is that the extraction result goes beyond the creation of structured information or the transformation into a relational schema. It requires either the reuse of existing formal knowledge (reusing identifiers or ontologies) or the generation of a schema based on the source data. Because of the last part, Ontology Learning can be considered a sub-discipline of Knowledge Extraction.

For the RDF and the OWL data model, we can identify two different criteria for identifying Knowledge Extraction processes: *Reusing identifiers.* (1) generated RDF properties are globally unique and have a well-defined meaning. If de-facto standard vocabularies, for example FOAF[3], are reused, then the extracted RDF can be unambiguously related to other data in the Web of Data. (2) `owl:sameAs` or `owl:equivalentClass` linking of extracted entities to existing entities in the Web of Data.

---

[3] `http://www.foaf-project.org/`

Schema generation. Schema (or Ontology) generation from legacy sources is a weaker form of knowledge extraction when compared to reusing identifiers. Although hierarchies [4] or OWL/DL axioms of varying expressivity are generated (see [3] for generation of subclass relations from databases and [13] for generating expressive axioms from text) no disambiguation is created by linking the newly created classes to existing ontologies. The relation of the generated taxonomy of terms remains unclear and requires methods from the field of ontology matching to become part of the global network of knowledge.

3   Comparison of the RDF/OWL Data Model to Relational Databases and XML

In this section we describe the characteristics of different structured data models and compare them to RDF/OWL. We selected Relational Databases (RDBs) and the Extensible Markup Language (XML) as these structured data sources cover a wide array of usage scenarios and real world applications. RDBs residing in Relational Database Management Systems (RDBMSs) are the dominant data storage solution for enterprise data, web sites and community created content. XML is widely adopted for data exchange, both for importing/exporting data and data access through web services. In order to juxtapose and compare these data models we determined the following characteristics:

Data Structure & Model. Describes whether the data structures and the data model are based on a certain abstraction. Also the fundamentally used data structures are identified.
Entity Identification. The mechanisms provided for identifying entities.
Schema. Describes the capabilities of the data model, i.e. which properties and features are inherent of the data model (e.g. inference or constraints).
Schema Data Separation. Can the schema be accessed in the same way as the instance data? A strictly separated schema on the contrary requires different access and manipulation methods.
Schema Reuse. An external schema definition allows the (partial) inclusion and reuse of previously defined schemata.
Conceptual and Physical Model Separation. Is the model of the data affected by its physical representation or is the data following a purely conceptual or logical model?
Expressivity. Describes the focus of expressiveness of the data model.
Data Access. The means by which the data is typically made available.
Data Integration. Describes the prevalent data integration paradigm followed.
Serialization. What serialization options are available for transmitting data.
World Model. Closed or Open World. Describes whether the truth-value of a statement is independent of whether or not it is known by a particular observer or agent to be true.

Table 1 summarizes the comparison of RDF with the relational and XML data models.

Table 1. Comparison of structured data models

	RDF/OWL	Relational Data	XML/XML Schema
Data structure & model	Statements represented as subject-predicate-object triples, using IRIs, blank-nodes and literals as components.	Entities described with a fixed number of attributes using tables, columns, rows.	Tree with nodes of different types (element, attribute, text etc.).
Entity identification	IRIs for globally unique identification of entities and relationships.	Only locally unique identifiers.	Use of IRIs is possible, but not enforced.
Schema	RDF-Schema and OWL allow definition of vocabularies and formal ontologies, including inference and consistency checks.	Schema defines and labels the relations, enforces data types and constraints.	Multiple schema definition languages allow to define data types, structures and constraints.
Schema/data separation	The same representation is used for schema and data, schema reuse is strongly encouraged.	Schema is stored as external meta data. Local schema only.	Schema can be expressed as XML. External schemata possible.
Conceptual and physical model separation	Conceptual model only.	Mixed physical and conceptual model (includes indexes, denormalizations).	Conceptual model only.
Expressivity	Focus: entities and relationships forming a graph; Problematic: lists, n-ary relations, constraints, graphs.	Focus: n-ary relations, schema adherence; Problematic: trees and graphs.	Focus: Flexible model allows representation of arbitrary data structures; Problematic: requires external knowledge for interpretation.
Data access	Linked data dereferencing (HTTP), SPARQL queries.	ODBC/JDBC, ORM.	DOM, XQuery/XPath, Web services, files.
Data Integration	Entity matching, schema matching, similarity measures.	ETL & data warehousing, middleware & mediation.	Structural analysis of trees, similarity measures.
Serialization	RDF/XML, turtle, N-Triples.	SQL-DDL	XML
World Model	Open world.	Closed world.	Closed world.

4   The Knowledge Extraction Tool Survey

In this section, we summarize the results of the Knowledge Extraction Tool Survey [7], which is also available online[4]. The Knowledge Extraction Tool Survey Ontology (KETSO) is used for the classification of knowledge extraction tools. In the following we summarize the main properties defined in KETSO for the characterization of tools. Note that some of the properties (e.g. Data Exposition and Data synchronization) are not completely orthogonal (e.g. values "dump" and "static"), but on the other hand not dependent as well (e.g. "SPARQL" can be "dynamic" or "bi-directional"). The flat modelling as single independent features does not produce any bias or encode assumptions into the data and it is much easier to add new values.

Vocabulary Reuse. The tool is able to reuse existing vocabularies in the mapping. For example the table column 'firstName' can be mapped to `foaf:firstName`. Some automatic approaches are not capable of reusing/mapping vocabularies. Boolean.

Data Exposition. Is SPARQL or another query language possible? Values can be either ETL (Dump), SPARQL (or another Query Language) or Linked Data. Note that the access paradigm also determines whether the resulting RDF model updates automatically. ETL means a one time conversion, while Linked Data and SPARQL always process queries versus the original database.

Data Source. The type of the data source the tool can be applied on. RDB, XML, CSV, etc.

Data Synchronization. Is a dump created once or is the data queried live from the legacy source? Static or Dynamic. If the tool writes the changes made to the RDF back to the legacy source it is bi-directional.

Has GUI. Does the tool have a visual user interface?

Mapping Automation. The degree to which the mapping creation is assisted / automatized. Manual, GUI, semi-automatic, automatic.

Mapping Language. The mapping language used by the approach (e.g. SQL, R2O, D2RQ, R2RML). The used mapping language is an important factor for reusability and initial learning cost as well as flexibility and expressiveness. Most of the users are for example familiar with SQL and no additional training is necessary. But, although SQL has extensive capabilities for selecting data in the WHERE clause, an additional mechanism for conversion and mapping is needed.

Requires a Domain Ontology. A pre-existing ontology is needed to map to it. Boolean.

We surveyed existing tools for knowledge extraction according to these characteristics. Table 2 summarizes the results of the survey.

---

[4] http://tinyurl.com/KETSurvey

Table 2. Survey of Knowledge Extraction Tools, references and more detailed information can be found in `http://tinyurl.com/KETSurvey` or [7]

Application	Data Source	Data Exposition	Data Synchronisation	Mapping Language	Vocabulary Reuse	Mapping Automatisation	Requires Domain Ontology	Uses GUI
CSV2RDF4LOD	CSV	ETL	static	none	✓	manual	-	-
Convert2RDF	Delimited text file	ETL	static	RDF DAML	✓	manual	-	✓
D2R Server	RDB	SPARQL	bi-direct.	D2R Map	✓	manual	-	-
DartGrid	RDB	own query language	dyn.	Visual Tool	✓	manual	-	✓
DataMaster	RDB	ETL	static	prop.	✓	manual	-	✓
Google Refine's RDF Extension	CSV, XML	ETL	static	none		semi-automatic	-	✓
Krextor	XML	ETL	static	xslt	✓	manual	✓	-
MAPONTO	RDB	ETL	static	prop.	✓	manual	✓	-
METAmorphoses	RDB	ETL	static	prop. xml	✓	manual	-	✓
MappingMaster	CSV	ETL	static	prop.	✓	GUI	-	✓
ODEMapster	RDB	ETL	static	prop.	✓	manual	-	✓
OntoWiki CSV Importer	CSV	ETL	static	prop.	✓	semi-automatic	-	✓
Poolparty Extraktor (PPX)	XML, Text	LD	dyn.	RDF (SKOS)	✓	semi-automatic	✓	
RDBToOnto	RDB	ETL	static	none	-	automatic, fine tunable	-	✓
RDF 123	CSV	ETL	static	-	-	manual	-	✓
RDOTE	RDB	ETL	static	SQL	✓	manual	✓	✓
Relational.OWL	RDB	ETL	static	none	-	automatic	-	-
T2LD	CSV	ETL	static	-	-	automatic	-	-
TopBraid Composer	CSV	ETL	static	SKOS	-	semi-automatic	-	✓
Triplify	RDB	LD	dyn.	SQL	✓	manual	✓	-
Virtuoso RDF Views	RDB	SPARQL	dyn.	Meta Schema Laguage	✓	semi-automatic	-	✓
Virtuoso Sponger	structured and semi-structured	SPARQL	dyn.	Virtuoso PL & XSLT	✓	semi-automatic	-	-
VisAVis	RDB	RDQL	dyn.	SQL	✓	manual	✓	✓
XLWrap: Spreadsheet to RDF	CSV	ETL	static	TriG Syntax	✓	manual	-	-
XML to RDF	XML	ETL	static	-	-	manual	-	-

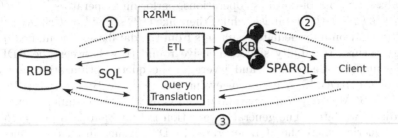

Fig. 1. Query rewriting and knowledge extraction

The results indicate, that most tools focus on extraction from relational data sources (i.e. RDB or CSV). Only few tools for the extraction from XML are available. Also, the dynamic extraction (i.e. translation of SPARQL queries into queries on the underlying data model) is relatively rare and ETL approaches are prevalent. Surprisingly, none of the tools offers mapping axiomatization, vocabulary reuse and a GUI.

5   RDB2RDF Extraction and Mapping with SparqlMap

The mapping of relational data to the RDF data model is a crucial knowledge extraction technique. Since data management according to the relational data model is still an order of magnitude faster than RDF data management and we do not expect this gap to close, relational data management will be prevalent in the next years. Still, for facilitating data exchange and integration it is of paramount importance to provide RDF and SPARQL interfaces to RDBMS. In this section we present *SparqlMap*[5], a SPARQL-to-SQL rewriter based on the specifications of the W3C R2RML working group[6]. The rationale is to enable SPARQL queries on (possibly existing) relational databases by rewriting them to corresponding SQL queries based on mapping definitions. The general approach is depicted in Figure 1. In essence, the R2RML standard describes how a relational database can be transformed into RDF by means of term maps and triple maps (1). The resulting RDF knowledge base can be materialized in a triple store and subsequently queried using SPARQL (2). In order to avoid the materialization step, R2RML implementations can dynamically map an input SPAQRL query into a corresponding SQL query (3), which renders exactly the same results as the SPARQL query being executed against the materialized RDF dump.

SparqlMap is in terms of functionality similar to D2R [1], a state-of-the-art standalone SPARQL-to-SQL translations tool. SparqlMap is likewise designed as a standalone application for facilitating light-weight integration into existing enterprise data landscapes. Compared to D2R we focus on performing all query operators in the relational database in a single unified query. D2R mixes

---

[5] http://aksw.org/Projects/SparqlMap
[6] http://www.w3.org/TR/r2rml/

in-database and out-of-database operations, performing operators like *AND* or (some) *FILTER* in the database, while others like *OPTIONAL* or *UNION* are executed in D2R on intermediate result sets from the database. The unified query strategy ensures scalability since expensive round trips between the RDBMS and the mapper are reduced and leverages the query optimization and execution of the RDBMS. We run an evaluation with the Berlin Sparql Benchmark [2] (BSBM) comparing SparqlMap and D2R with the results presented on the projects website[7]. The general observation is that SparqlMap outperforms D2R for queries where the SQL generated by D2R results in huge intermediate result sets. To the best of our knowledge no detailed or formalized description of a mapping based SPARQL-to-SQL translator exists. In this section we, therefore, present an overview over SparqlMap which is structured as follows. In Section 5.1 we formalize the mapping and query syntax. The process of rewriting a query on a mapping is outlined in the following three steps:

Mapping Candidate Selection. As the initial step of the process, we describe in Section 5.2 how candidate mappings are identified. These are mappings that potentially contribute to the query's result set. Informally, this is the set of mappings that yield triples that could match the triple patterns of the query, as shown in Figure 4. The relation between the candidate mappings and the triple patterns is called a binding.

Query Translation. The identified candidate mappings and the obtained bindings enable us to rewrite a SPARQL query to an SQL query. This process is described in Section 5.3.

Query Execution. Finally, in Section 5.4 we show how from the SQL result set of the executed SQL query the corresponding SPARQL result set is constructed.

5.1 Definitions

In this section we define the syntax of RDF, SPARQL and the mapping. The RDF and SPARQL formalization is closely following [9].

Definition 1 (RDF definition). *Assume there are pairwise disjoint infinite sets I, B, and L (IRIs, blank nodes, and RDF literals, respectively). A triple $(v_s, v_p, v_o) \in (I \cup B) \times I \times (I \cup B \cup L)$ is called an RDF triple. In this tuple, v_s is the subject, v_p the predicate and v_p the object. We denote the union $I \cup B \cup L$ as by T called RDF terms.*

Using the notion $t.i$ for $i \in \{s, p, o\}$ we refer to the RDF term in the respective position. In the following, the same notion is applied to *triple patterns* and *triple maps*. An RDF *graph* is a set of RDF triples (also called RDF dataset, or simply a dataset). Additionally, we assume the existence of an infinite set V of variables which is disjoint from the above sets. The W3C recommendation SPARQL[8] is a query language for RDF. By using *graph patterns*, information can be retrieved

---

[7] http://aksw.org/Projects/SparqlMap/benchmark
[8] http://www.w3.org/TR/rdf-sparql-query/

from SPARQL-enabled RDF stores. This retrieved information can be further modified by a query's solution modifiers, such as sorting or ordering of the query result. Finally the presentation of the query result is determined by the *query type*, return either a set of triples, a table or a boolean value. The graph pattern of a query is the base concept of SPARQL and as it defines the part of the RDF graph used for generating the query result, therefore *graph patterns* are the focus of this discussion. We use the same graph pattern syntax definition as [9].

Definition 2 (SPARQL graph pattern syntax). *The syntax of a SPARQL graph pattern expression is defined recursively as follows:*
1. *A tuple from $(I \cup L \cup V) \times (I \cup V) \times (I \cup L \cup V)$ is a graph pattern (a triple pattern).*
2. *The expressions $(P_1 \ AND \ P_2)$, $(P_1 \ OPT \ P_2)$ and $(P_1 \ UNION \ P_2)$ are graph patterns, if P_1 and P_2 are graph patterns.*
3. *The expression $(P \ FILTER \ R)$ is a graph pattern, if P is a graph pattern and R is a SPARQL constraint.*

Further the function $var(P)$ returns the set of variables used in the graph pattern P. SPARQL constraints are composed of functions and logical expressions, and are supposed to evaluate to boolean values. Additionally, we assume that the query pattern is well-defined according to [9].

We now define the terms and concepts used to describe the SPARQL-to-SQL rewriting process. The basic concepts are the relational database schema denoted s and a mapping for this schema m. The schema s has a set of relations R and each relation is composed of attributes, denoted as $A_r = (r.a_0, r.a_1, ..., r.a_l)$. A mapping m defines how the data contained in tables or views in the relational database schema s is mapped into an RDF graph g. Our mapping definitions are loosely based on R2RML. An example of such a mapping is depicted in Figure 2 and used further in this section to illustrate the translation process.

Definition 3 (Term map). *A term map is a tuple $tm = (A, ve)$ consisting of a set of relational attributes A from a single relation r and a value expression ve that describes the translation of A into RDF terms (e.g. R2RML templates for generating IRIs). We denote by the range $range(tm)$ the set of all possible RDF terms that can be generated using this term map.*

Term maps are the base element of a mapping. In Figure 2 an example for such a *term map* is (1). With ve being the template `http://comp.com/emp{id}` and $A = \{Employee.id\}$ it is possible to produce resource IRIs for employees. The RDF term (2) in Figure 2 creates a constant value, in this case a property. Consequently, for this RDF term $A = \emptyset$ holds.

Definition 4 (Triple map). *A triple map trm is the triple (tm_S, tm_P, tm_O) of three term maps for generating the subject (position s), predicate (position p) and object (position o) of a triple. All attributes of the three term maps must originate from the same relation r.*

A triple map defines how triples are actually generated from the attributes of a relation (i.e. rows of a table). This definition differs slightly from the R2RML

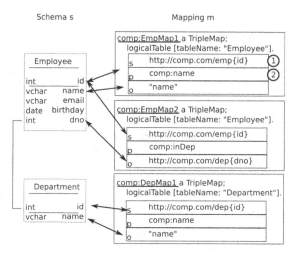

Fig. 2. Exemplary mapping of parts of two relations using three triple maps. R2RML's construct `logicalTable` specifies the source relation of a triple map.

specification, as R2RML allows multiple predicate-object pairs for a subject. These two notions, however, are convertible into each other without loss of generality. In Figure 2 the triple map `comp:EmpMap1` defines how triples describing the name of an employee resource can be created for the relation `Employee`.

A mapping definition $m = (R, TRM)$ is a tuple consisting of a set of relations R and a set of triple maps TRM. It holds all information necessary for the translation of a SPARQL query into a corresponding SQL query. We assume in this context that all data is stored according to the schema s is mapped into a single RDF graph and likewise that all queries and operations are performed on this graph [9].

5.2 Mapping Candidate Selection

Mapping selection is the process of identifying the parts of a mapped graph that can contribute to the solution of a query q. This selection process is executed for every query and forms the basis for the following step – the translation into SQL. The parts of a query that are used for matching the parts of a graph examined are the graph patterns. The graph of a mapped database is the set of triples defined by the *triple maps*. Consequently, we propose the selection of candidate *triple maps* to match the *graph pattern*. The general approach described here aims at first binding each *triple pattern* of q to a set of candidate triple maps, and then to reduce the amount of bindings by determining the unsatisfiability of constraints (e.g join conditions) based on the structure of the SPARQL query.

Before we formally introduce the operators used, we give a brief overview of the process in Figure 3. The simple query q depicted here represents a tree-

---

[9] Note, that support for named graphs can be easily added by slightly extending the notion of triple map with an additional term map denoting the named graph.

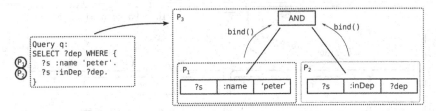

Fig. 3. Mapping candidate selection overview. The patterns of a query parsed into a tree. The bind function recurses over that tree.

like structure according to Definition 2. In a bottom-up traversal we first search for mapping candidates for the triple patterns P_1 and P_2. In the next step, indicated by the $bind()$ function, these mapping candidates are examined on the next higher level of the tree. Based on the semantics of P_3 the $bind()$ function reduces the mapping candidates for P_1 and P_2. Before we formally describe this process we define the notion of a binding.

Definition 5 (Triple Pattern Binding). *Let q be a query, with TP_q being its set of triple patterns. Let m be the mapping of a database, with TRM_m being its set of all triple maps. A triple pattern binding tpb is the tuple (tp, TRM), where $tp \in TP_q$ and $TRM \subseteq TRM_m$. We further denote by the set QPB_q for a query q the set of triple pattern bindings TPB, such that there exists for every $tp \in TP_q$ exactly one tpb.*

In this context we assume that in case q contains a triple pattern more than once, for each occurrence there exists in QPB_q a separate *tpb*. The set *TRM* for a triple pattern *tp* is also called the set of mapping candidates for *tp*. We now define successively the basic terms and functions on the triple pattern bindings and illustrate them using the sample query introduced in Figure 3. In Figure 4 the result of the process is depicted. The dotted squares indicate the triple pattern bindings *tpb* with their patterns and triple maps.

Definition 6 (Term map compatibility). *We consider two term maps tm_1 and tm_2 to be compatible, if $range(tm_1) \cap range(tm_2) \neq \emptyset$. We further consider a term map tm compatible with an RDF term t, if the term $t \in range(tm)$. A variable v is always considered compatible with a term map.*

With the boolean function $compatible(t_1, t_2)$ we denote the check for compatibility. This function allows us to check, if two term maps can potentially produce the same RDF term and to pre-check constraints of the SPARQL query. Mapping candidates that cannot fulfill these constraints are removed from the binding. Further it allows to check, if a triple map is compatible with a triple pattern of a query. In the example given in Figure 4 term map compatibility is used to bind *triple maps* to *term maps*. At position (1) in Figure 4 the triple pattern P_2 is bound to the term map :`EmpMap2` because the resource IRI at the predicate position of P_2 is compatible with the constant value term map of :`EmpMap2` in the same position. The notion of term compatibility can be extended towards checking bindings for compatibility by the functions *join* and *reduce*.

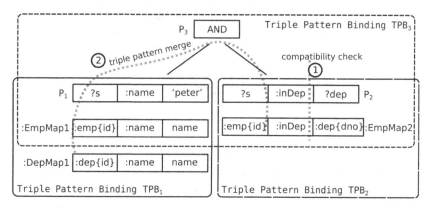

Fig. 4. Binding operations on a sample query. In (1) a simple check for compatibility at the predicate position is performed, in (2) the triples maps are merged between two triple pattern bindings, checking compatibility at the subject position.

Definition 7 (Join of triple pattern bindings). *Let $tpb_1 = (tp_1, TRM_1)$ and $tpb_2 = (tp_2, TRM_2)$ be triple pattern bindings. Further, let $V = var(tp1) \cap var(tp2)$ be the set of shared variables.*

We define $join(tpb_1, tpb_2) : \{(trm_a, trm_b) \in TRM_1 \times TRM_2 |$ for each variable $v \in V$ the union of the corresponding sets of term maps of trm_a and trm_b is either empty or its elements are pairwise compatible.[10] }

Definition 8 (Reduction of triple pattern bindings). *The function $reduce(tpb_1, tpb_2)$ is defined as $proj(join(tpb_1, tpb_2), 1)$, i.e. the projection of the first component of the tuples obtained by the join operation.*

Reduction is the base operation for minimizing the set of *triple maps* associated with every *triple pattern*. It rules out all candidate tuples that would eventually yield unsatisfiable SQL join conditions. In Figure 4 the reduction process follows the dotted line indicated by (2). The triple patterns P_1 and P_2 share the variable ?s which is in both cases in the subject position of the triple pattern. Consequently, each triple map in TPB_1 is compared at the subject position with all subject term maps of TPB_2 for compatibility. If no compatible triple map is found, the triple map is removed from the candidate set. The term map :DepMap1 in Figure 4 is therefore not included in TPB_3, as the subject of :DepMap1 is not compatible with the subject of :EmpMap2. The reduction function now allows the definition of two operators that perform a reduction of mapping candidates along the syntax of a SPARQL query.

For the two sets of *triple pattern bindings* TPB_1 and TPB_2 we define two merge operations for the triple pattern bindings as follows:

Binding Merge $merge(TPB_1, TPB_2)$ reduces all triple pattern bindings with each other, as illustrated in Figure 5a.

---

[10] Note, that the same variable may occur multiple times in a triple pattern and therefore map to multiple term maps.

(a) $merge(TPB_1, TPB_2)$

$TPB \leftarrow TPB_1 \cup TPB_2$
$TPB' \leftarrow \emptyset$
for $tpb_1 in\ TPB$ **do**
  for $tpb_2 in\ TPB$ **do**
    $tpb_1 \leftarrow reduce(tpb_1, tpb_2)$
  end for
  $TPB' \leftarrow TPB' \cup \{tpb_1\}$
end for
return TPB'

(b) $optmerge(TPB_1, TPB_2)$

$TPB' \leftarrow TPB_1$
for $tpb_1 in\ TPB_1$ **do**
  for $tpb_2 in\ TPB_2$ **do**
    $tpb_2 \leftarrow reduce(tpb_2, tpb_1)$
  end for
  $TPB' \leftarrow TPB' \cup \{tpb_2\}$
end for
return TPB'

Fig. 5. The merge and optmerge algorithms

Binding Opt Merge $optmerge(TPB_1, TPB_2)$ reduces all triple pattern bindings of TPB_2 with the all triple pattern bindings of TPB_1, as illustrated in Figure 5b.

Both merge operations preevaluate the join conditions of the later SQL execution. The compatibility check for the shared variables of two triple patterns rule out unfulfillable join or respectively left join conditions.

We can use these operators to define the recursive function $bind_m(P)$, which computes for a mapping m and the graph pattern P the set of triple pattern bindings TPB_p, similar to the recursive evaluation function defined in [9].

Definition 9. *Let TRM_m be the set of all triple maps in m, P_1 and P_2 be graph patterns and tp be a triple pattern of a query. The function $bind_m(P)$ is the recursive binding of the TRM_m to the triple patterns of a query for the following cases:*

1. *If P is a triple pattern tp, $bind(P) = \{(tp, TRM_{tp})| TRM_{tp} = \{trm|trm \in TRM_m \wedge compatible(trm.s, tp.s) \wedge compatible(trm.p, tp.p) \wedge compatible(trm.o, tp.o)\}\}$*
2. *If P is $(P_1\ AND\ P_2)$, $bind(P) = merge(bind_m(P_1), bind_m(P_2))$*
3. *If P is $(P_1\ OPT\ P_2)$, $bind(P) = optmerge(bind_m(P_1), bind_m(P_2))$*
4. *If P is $(P_1\ UNION\ P_2)$, $bind(P) = (bind_m(P_1) \cup bind_m(P_2)$*
5. *If P is $(P_1\ FILTER\ R)$, $bind(P) = \{tpb|tpb \in bind_m(P_1) \wedge$ if tpb is sharing variables with R, the constraint is pre-evaluated. If the filter is always false, the term map is not included.\}*

The complete binding process can now be illustrated using the example in Figure 4. Starting from the bottom, $bind(P_1)$ evaluates to $TPB_1 = \{(P_1, \{$:empMap1,:depMap1\})\} and $bind(P_2)$ to $TPB_2 = \{(P2, \{$:empMap2\})\}. For P_1 the triple map :empMap2 is not bound, because $compatible(P1.p,$:empMap2.p$)$ = *false*. In the next step of the recursion, the pattern binding merge is evaluated between the two sets, creating TPB_3. The sets of triple maps of TPB_1 and of TPB_2 are reduced on the shared variable s. The term map at the subject position of :depMap1 is not compatible with the subject from another triple map of TPB_1 and is not included in TPB_3. Here the recursion halts, the set obtained in the last step represents the full mapping of the query $QPB = TPB_3$. QBP is

```
Select cast(1 as numeric) s_type,        ⎫ Type columns
       cast(1 as numeric) s_datatype,    ⎬
       cast(null as text) s_text,        ⎫
       cast(null as numeric) s_num,      ⎬
       cast(null as bool) s_bool,        ⎬ Literal columns
       cast(null as time) s_time,        ⎭
       cast(2 as numeric) s_reslength,   ⎫
       cast('http://comp.com/emp' as text) s_res_1,  ⎬ Resource
       cast("Employee"."id"  as text) s_res_2        ⎭ columns
```

Fig. 6. Column group for variable ?s of graph pattern P_1

a set of two triple pattern bindings, each with one triple map, and is ready to be used for creating the SQL query in the next step of the process.

The approach described in Definition 9 has some limitations. Variables used in both sub-patterns of UNIONs are not exploited for reducing the candidate triple maps. This for example could be overcome by using algebraic equivalence transformations which are described in [11]. Another limitation is that not all candidate reductions are applied to triple patterns that are not directly connected by shared variables. The modifications to the query binding strategy dealing with this limitation are part of the future work on SparqlMap.

5.3   Query Translation

Query translation is the process of generating a SQL query out of the SPARQL query using the bindings determined in the previous step. We devise here a recursive approach of query generation, similar to the one presented for mapping selection. The result of this translation is a nested SQL query reflecting the structure of the SPARQL query. Each translation we devise here creates a SQL select query which nests the recursions in subselects. We first describe the function $toCG(tm) = CG$ that maps a term map tm into a set of column expressions CG, called a *column group*. The utilization of multiple columns is necessary for efficient filter and join processing and data type compatibility of the columns in a SQL union. In a CG the columns can be classified as:

Type Columns. The RDF term type, i.e. resource, literal or blank node is encoded into these columns using constant value expressions. The column expression `cast(1 as numeric) s_type` Figure 6 declares the RDF terms produced in this column group to be resources.

Resource Columns. The IRI value expression VE is embedded into multiple columns. This allows the execution of relational operators directly on the columns and indexes.

Literal Columns. Literals are cast into compatible types to allow SQL UNION over these columns.

In Figure 6 the column group created for the variable ?s of triple pattern P_1 is depicted.

The following aspects of query translation require the definition of additional functions.

Align. The alignment of of two select statements is a prerequisite for performing a SQL union as the column count equality and data type compatibility of the columns are mandatory. The function $align(s_1, s_2) = s_1'$ for two SQL select statements s_1 and s_2 modifies s_1 by adding adding columns to s_1 such that s_1' contains all columns defined in s_2. The columns added do not produce any RDF terms.

Join. Filter conditions are performed on column groups, not directly on columns. As already outlined in [5] this requires embedding the filter statements into a conditional check using `case` statements. This check allows the database to check for data types and consequently to select the correct columns of a column group for comparison. For two SQL queries s_1, s_2 the function $joinCond(s_1, s_2)$ calculates the join condition as an expression using `case` statements, checking the column groups bound to of shared variables.

Filter. For R being a filter expression according to Definition 2, the function $filter_f(R)$ translates a filter expression into an equivalent SQL expression on column groups.

Triple Pattern. The RDF literals and resources used in a triple pattern tp are implicit predicates and need to be made explicit. The function $filter_p(tp)$ maps these triple patterns into a set SQL predicates, similar to the definition of $filter_f(R)$.

Alias. The renaming of a *column group CG* is performed by the function $alias(CG, a) = CG_a$ that aliases all column expressions of CG, by adding the prefix a. For the scope of this paper, we assume that proper alias handling is performed and is not further explicitly mentioned.

Using the previously defined function $toCG(tm)$ and the usage of the SQL operators *JOIN, LEFT JOIN and UNION* we can now devise a simple recursive translation function.

Definition 10 (Query translation). *Let QPB be a query pattern binding, P_1 and P_2 be graph patterns and tp be a triple pattern and $tpb = (tp, TRM)$ be triple pattern binding for tp with the set of term maps TRM. The relation for each $trm \in TRM$ is denoted r. The translation of a graph pattern P into a SQL query $Q_{sql} = t_{QPB}(P)$ is performed as follows.*

1. *If P is a triple pattern:* $t_{QPB}(P) =$ UNION ALL $\{\forall trm \in TRM :$ SELECT $toCG(trm.s), toCG(trm.p), toCG(trm.o)$ FROM r WHERE $filter_p(P)\}$
2. *If P is $(P_1$ AND $P_2)$:* $t_{QPB}(P) =$ SELECT $*$ FROM ($t_{QPB}(P_1)$) p1 JOIN ($t_{QPB}(P_2)$) p2 ON($joinCond(p1, p2)$)
3. *If P is $(P_1$ OPT $P_2)$:* $t_{QPB}(P) =$ SELECT $*$ FROM ($t_{QPB}(P_1)$) p1 LEFT JOIN ($t_{QPB}(P_2)$) p2 ON($joinCond(p1, p2)$)
4. *If P is $(P_1$ UNION $P_2)$:* $t_{QPB}(P) =$ ($align(t_{QPB}(P_1), t_{QPB}(P_2))$) UNION ($align(t_{QPB}(P_2), t_{QPB}(P_1))$)
5. *If P is $(P_1$ FILTER $R)$:* $t_{QPB}(P) =$ SELECT $*$ FROM $t_{QPB}(P)$ WHERE $filter_f(R)$

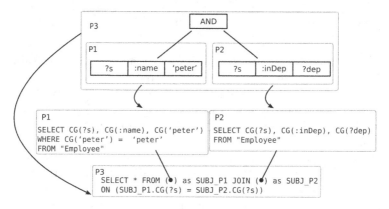

Fig. 7. Query nesting for a sample query

The translation of the example of Figure 4 is depicted in Figure 7. The column groups are indicated here by the notion (CG(t)), where t is the RDF term or variable the column group was created for.

5.4   Query Execution

The SQL query created in the previous chapter can now be executed over the mapped database. The result set of this SQL query is then mapped into a SPARQL result set. Depending on the query type of the SPARQL query, the SQL result set is transformed. Each row of a SQL result set produces for every column group an RDF term which then can be used to create the SPARQL result set. In the case of an SPARQL select query, for each projected variable the corresponding column group is used to generate the RDF term. We use the result set for the query initially described in Figure 3 to illustrate the result set translation process. In the following listing the result set snippet for the column group of variable ?dep is presented. As this column group represents a resource, no columns for literal values are given in this example.

```
dep_type|dep_datatype|dep_reslength|     dep_res_1      |dep_res_2
|--------|------------|-------------|--------------------|---------|
|       1|           1|            2|http://comp.com/dep|        1|
|--------|------------|-------------|--------------------|---------|
```

The RDF term is according to dep_type a resource. The IRI of the resource is generated from 2 columns, indicated by dep_reslength. The IRI is constructed by concatenating the prefix from s_res_1 with the percent-encoded[11] value from dep_res_2.

The SPARQL result set corresponding to the sample query is consequently:

---

[11] As defined in http://tools.ietf.org/html/rfc3986

```
<?xml version="1.0"?>
<sparql xmlns="http://www.w3.org/2005/sparql-results#">
  <head><variable name="dep"/></head>
  <results>
    <result>
      <binding name="dep"> <uri>http://comp.com/dep1</uri></binding>
    </result>
  </results>
</sparql>
```

6   Conclusion and Outlook

Knowledge-extraction approaches are crucial for the bootstrapping and further development of the Data Web. In this article, we devised a definition of the concept knowledge extraction and we compared the popular data models relational data and XML with RDF. We derived a number of characteristics of knowledge extraction approaches and surveyed the state-of-the-art with regard to tools being available in that area. Our results revealed that most tools focus on extraction from relational data sources. The dynamic extraction (i.e. translation of SPARQL queries into queries on the underlying data model), however, is still challenging and ETL approaches are prevalent. With SparqlMap we presented an implementation of the relational database to RDF mapping language R2RML currently being standardized by the W3C. SparqlMap allows the dynamic translation of a SPARQL query based on a mapping into a single SQL query on the underlying relational database. This will ensure that we can capitalize on existing work in relational database query optimization.

In future work, we aim to add further optimizations to SparqlMap, such as support for the SPARQL REDUCED construct, which can boost the execution of certain queries. The query generation overhead in SparqlMap can be substantially reduced by enabling prepared SPARQL queries, where a SPARQL query template is already precompiled into the corresponding SQL query template and subsequently reoccurring queries using the template do not have to be translated anymore. A first evaluation of SparqlMap with the Berlin SPARQL Benchmark (BSBM) showed a significant performance improvement compared to the state-of-the-art. However, certain features that are particularly challenging for an RDB2RDF tool (such as queries over the schema) are not part of BSBM. We plan to perform comprehensive benchmarks and also to evaluate SparqlMap with large-scale real-world data.

Acknowledgments. We would like to thank our colleagues from AKSW research group for their helpful comments and inspiring discussions during the development of SparqlMap. This work was partially supported by a grant from the European Union's 7th Framework Programme provided for the project LOD2 (GA no. 257943).

References

1. Bizer, C., Cyganiak, R.: D2r server publishing relational databases on the semantic web. Poster at the 5th International Semantic Web Conference, ISWC 2006 (2006)
2. Bizer, C., Schultz, A.: The berlin SPARQL benchmark. Int. J. Semantic Web Inf. Syst. 5(2), 1–24 (2009)
3. Cerbah, F.: Learning Highly Structured Semantic Repositories from Relational Databases: In: Bechhofer, S., Hauswirth, M., Hoffmann, J., Koubarakis, M. (eds.) ESWC 2008. LNCS, vol. 5021, pp. 777–781. Springer, Heidelberg (2008)
4. Cimiano, P., Hotho, A., Staab, S.: Learning concept hierarchies from text corpora using formal concept analysis. Journal of Artificial Intelligence Research 24, 305–339 (2005)
5. Cyganiak, R.: A relational algebra for SPARQL. Technical report, Digital Media Systems Laboratory, HP Laboratories Bristol (2005)
6. Ghawi, R., Cullot, N.: Database-to-Ontology Mapping Generation for Semantic Interoperability. In: Third International Workshop on Database Interoperability, InterDB 2007 (2007)
7. Hellmann, S., Unbehauen, J., Zaveri, A., Lehmann, J., Auer, S., Tramp, S., Williams, H., Erling, O., Thibodeau Jr., T., Idehen, K., Blumauer, A., Nagy, H.: Report on knowledge extraction from structured sources. Technical Report LOD2 D3.1.1 (2011), http://lod2.eu/Deliverable/D3.1.1.html
8. Konstantinou, N., Spanos, D.-E., Mitrou, N.: Ontology and database mapping: A survey of current implementations and future directions. J. Web Eng. 7(1), 1–24 (2008)
9. Pérez, J., Arenas, M., Gutierrez, C.: Semantics and complexity of sparql. ACM Trans. Database Syst. 34(3):16:1–16:45 (2009)
10. Sahoo, S.S., Halb, W., Hellmann, S., Idehen, K., Thibodeau Jr., T., Auer, S., Sequeda, J., Ezzat, A.: A survey of current approaches for mapping of relational databases to rdf, 01 (2009)
11. Schmidt, M., Meier, M., Lausen, G.: Foundations of sparql query optimization. In: Proceedings of the 13th International Conference on Database Theory, ICDT 2010, pp. 4–33. ACM, New York (2010)
12. Spanos, D.-E., Stavrou, P., Mitrou, N.: Bringing relational databases into the semantic web: A survey. Semantic Web 3(2), 169–209 (2012)
13. Völker, J., Hitzler, P., Cimiano, P.: Acquisition of OWL DL Axioms from Lexical Resources. In: Franconi, E., Kifer, M., May, W. (eds.) ESWC 2007. LNCS, vol. 4519, pp. 670–685. Springer, Heidelberg (2007)

Extracting Information from Google Fusion Tables

Marco Brambilla[1], Stefano Ceri[1], Nicola Cinefra[1], Anish Das Sarma[2],
Fabio Forghieri[1], and Silvia Quarteroni[1]

[1] Politecnico di Milano, Dipartimento di Elettronica e Informazione,
Piazza L. Da Vinci, 32. 20133 Milano, Italy
{mbrambil,ceri,quarteroni}@elet.polimi.it
[2] Google Inc.,
anish@google.com

Abstract. With Fusion Tables, Google has made available a huge repository that
allows users to share, visualize and manage structured data. Since 2009, thousands
of tables have been shared online, encompassing data from virtually any domain
and entered by all kinds of users, from professional to non-experts. While Fusion
Tables are a potentially precious source of freely available structured information
for all sorts of applications, complex querying and composing them is not supported natively, as it requires understanding both the structure and content of
tables' data, which are heterogeneous and produced "bottom-up". In this paper,
we discuss ongoing and future work concerning the integration of Fusion Tables
in the aim of efficiently integrating, visualizing, and querying them.

Keywords: semantic annotation, service description, search services.

1 Introduction

With Fusion Tables [10], Google has given to the general public a powerful set of
tools for managing, querying and visualizing structured content; as a result, since
2009, several thousands of Google Fusion Tables (henceforth GFTs) have been published, encompassing data from virtually any domain entered by all kinds of users,
from professional to non-experts. Thus, GFTs are a potential source of freely available structured information that could in principle form a knowledge base usable in all
sorts of applications. However, GFTs have a number of characteristics making their
direct exploitation difficult. First, the data they contain is not "curated" by their authors, as GFTs are generally meant for "private" consumption (e.g. as address books
of association members or lists of properties of a real estate agency). More importantly, in the vast majority of cases, GFTs are not designed by knowledge representation
or database experts, but rather by end-users themselves. This often results in unclear
descriptions, as illustrated in Figure 1, where the column containing coffee shop
names is denominated "Text"; but even good-quality column names can be quite different, e.g. "coffee shop" vs "coffee store" vs "café", requiring some kind of integration. Automatic approaches to understand the structure and content of GFTs are chal-
lenged by their heterogeneity and poor data quality.

S. Ceri and M. Brambilla (Eds.): Search Computing III, LNCS 7538, pp. 53–67, 2012.

Thus, GFTs bring about an interesting challenge: how to "make sense" of heterogeneous, messy data for understanding and composing them. Our ultimate aim is to support a high-quality search process over this type of data that not only leverages their content in a meaningful way, but is also capable of integrating data deriving from different tables, thanks to a deep understanding of their content. This is particularly meaningful to us as it is an excellent showcase for the Search Computing (SeCo) project, where we design models to integrate data services in a coherent fashion with the purpose of efficient querying and result ranking, and in line with the efforts in the Fusion Tables group [7].

NYC Coffee Shops

Text ▼	Number ▼	Location ▼
Ground Support	3	399 West Broadway, New York, NY
Mud	4	307 East 9th Street, New York, NY
Bluebird Coffee Shop	6	72 East 1st St. New York, NY
Iris Cafe	13	20 Columbia Pl., Brooklyn NY
Bouchon Bakery	16	10 Columbus Circle, New York, NY
Cafe Pedlar	20	210 Court Street, Brooklyn, NY
Gorilla Coffee	21	97 Fifth Ave., Brooklyn, NY

Fig. 1. A public Google Fusion table describing coffee shops in New York

In this paper, we pursue the objective of interpreting GFT semantics from two complementary perspectives: we infer information both at the schema level, by understanding the meaning of tables and of their columns, and at the instance level, by finding matching content within the tables. Understanding GFT semantics enables us to find relationships across GFTs, which can drive several applications such as combining multiple GFTs to obtain higher quality tables, and enhancing table search by augmenting search results with inter-table relationships. We also believe that understanding the semantics of GFTs developed by Google users worldwide is a complex task, due to the intrinsic ambiguity of terms used in GFTs and to their nonprofessional design. Following such considerations, we propose Games With A Purpose (GWAP) methods as means of inviting humans into the understanding loop.

In Section 2 we introduce the issues of dealing with GFTs interpretation. Section 3 shows our first experiments of GFT registration using SeCo supervised methods. Section 4 shows our methods for automatic clustering of GFTs, the main contribution of this paper. Section 5 hints to methods for improving the content of GFTs by means of GWAP.

2   Related Work

Search Computing focuses on integrating [7], querying [6], visualizing [2] and exploring [4] structured Web data sources, made available by third party providers in different formats and through various kinds of Web interfaces (e.g., APIs implemented as REST or WSDL services). In this paper we consider a particular kind of data sources, namely the Google Fusion Tables [10,11], which can be managed using an API made available by Google for defining, managing, querying and visualizing structured content. GFTs represent a potential source of freely available structured information that could in principle form a basis of knowledge usable in all sorts of applications. However, their content is quite heterogeneous, because each user loads and manipulates limited datasets, typically not consistent with others and not cleansed and curated in terms of coherence and completeness.

There is a very rich research on schema matching problems, well represented by seminal papers of Ullman [26] and Lenzerini [27]. However, schema matching is only one part of the problem, as we search for tables that are related not just by their structure, but also by their content. Indeed, we aim at extracting sensible meaning out of thousands of tables with a scalable approach, capable of identifying sets of tables that are internally coherent, both in terms of topics (schemas) and of data instances. The GFT research group has independently taken a similar approach to ours [13], by defining metrics of table similarity which take into account both schema and value similarity; their method is based on computing relatedness scores among all pairs of tables; they also propose to use filters to optimize computing times.

Our approach uses a clustering method, which partitions a set of objects into clusters such that objects in the same cluster are more similar to each other than objects in different clusters according to some defined criteria. Clustering methods are generally divided in two categories: hard clustering, where each element can belong to only one cluster, and soft or fuzzy clustering, where items can have different "degrees of belonging" to different clusters. In this paper, we apply hard clustering with partitional methods, which divide the set of tables into non-overlapping groups; in particular, our choice fell on then well-known *k-means* algorithm [14]. The similarity metrics we adopt as clustering criteria account for both schema- and instance- level information. At the schema level, we adopt known metrics such as the *Levenshtein* [25], *Wu-Palmer* [24] and *Jiang-Conrath* [23] distances. At the instance level, similarity is based on geographical coherence, i.e., on the possibility of associating different GFTs to the same geographical entity. This enables interesting information exploration scenarios as the ones described in [5] and is in line with the most typical usage of GFTs, where information integration is strongly based on geographical maps.

In addition to automated algorithms for clustering, another line of research uses human involvement in the problem. Crowdsourcing is a valuable paradigm to make this technique scale to large amounts of questions and answers [19, 20, 21]. Our preliminary work on social search and question answering [3] shows that the approach is feasible also for the search domain. Games with a purpose (GWAP) can be used to engage people to participate in problem-solving tasks, by involving them in information collection tasks that appear in the form of games [16, 17, 18].

3   Semi-supervised GFT Registration

Our first approach for managing GFTs consists in registering them by means of a semi-automatic registration process, which aims at capturing the meaning of the schema names of GFTs (table and column names). A semi-automatic registration algorithm, adapted from the service registration framework of SeCo [7], maps such names into the terminology of a reference open-domain knowledge base; we have used YAGO2 [22], which in turns integrates WordNet [15] and WikiPedia[1].

The method tries to match a YAGO2 entity to each table and column name; it then decides, based upon the quality of the mapping that is automatically established, whether such a mapping requires confirmation. In few cases, when no mapping is determined, a human supervisor is involved to introduce a new name. Table names are mapped to entity names; whenever two tables share columns with identical names or are mapped to the same type/property in the knowledge base, they may be connected by relationships. In this way, GFTs are mapped to an Entity-Relationship diagram, which can then be navigated by using exploration techniques available in SeCo [4] or queried in natural language. The registration process is semi-automatic: a human supervisor may be involved to help in the process.

Deploying the SeCo registration algorithm on GFTs allowed us to observe that the registration method has good potential for inferring their semantics. We considered 100 GFTs with 350 columns, and we mapped them to an entity-relationship diagram consisting of 46 entities and 50 relationships. This provides evidence that the registration algorithm is able to unify the semantics of GFTs to the point of reducing the number of entities required to represent them to about 50% (46/100). Figure 2 illustrates the domain diagram with 28 entities, obtained after registering 50 tables.

It must be noted however that the contribution of a human expert to suggest/disambiguate mappings with modeled items was very intense, with e.g. 298 confirmation queries for the 450 parameters. While the effort of supervising with yes/no answers to the system's hypotheses requires far less effort and expertise than to draw an ER schema from scratch, without the help of a disambiguation environment, human intervention appears to be too heavy to dominate a situation with potentially millions of tables; henceforth, in the following we move to methods requiring no human intervention.

We also point out that most GFTs share location information (see Fig. 2, where the LOCATION entity appears to be connected to most other entities). From a deep inspection of a random selection of GFTs, we observed that 70-80% of them include location and spatial information; we therefore we decided to use the location-dependent nature of GFTs for suggesting location-based instance clustering, as discussed in the next Section.

---

[1] http://en.wikipedia.org

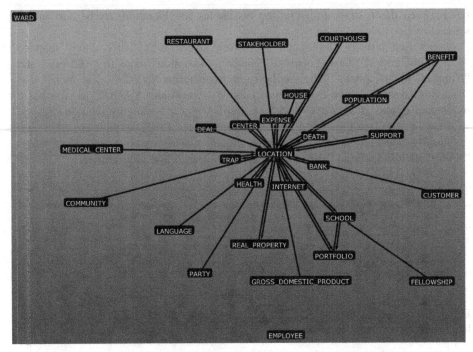

Fig. 2. Domain diagram resulting from the registration of 50 Google Fusion Tables

Tap Restaurants

Number ▼	Name ▼	Type ▼	Address ▼	Phone ▼
5	Gobo Upper East Side	Vegetarian	1426 Third Avenue,New York, NY 10028	212.288.5099
55	Gobo Greenwich Village	Vegetarian	401 Avenue of the Americas,New York, NY 10014	212.255.3242
3	Kellari Taverna	Seafood	1700 K Street, N.W.,Washington, DC 20006	202.535.5274
16	SUSHI TARO	Seafood	1503 17TH ST NW,Washington, DC 20036	202.462.8999
18	Hank's Oyster Bar- DC	Seafood	1624 Q Street NW,WAshington, DC 20009	202.462.4265
38	Hank's Oyster Bar - Old Town	Seafood	1026 King Street,Alexandria, VA 22314	703.739.4265
6	Atlantic Grill Eastside	Seafood	1341 Third Ave,New York, NY 10021	212.988.9200
23	Kellari Taverna	Seafood	19 West 44th Street,New York, NY 10036	212.221.0144
33	Ocean Grill	Seafood	384 Columbus Ave,New York, NY 10024	212.579.2300

Fig. 3. A public Google Fusion table describing tap restaurants

4   Automated, Location-Aware GFT Clustering

Automatic clustering methods aim at determining **clusters of GFTs,** i.e. tables which describe the same real world object(s) and whose instances can therefore be merged. As a byproduct of this work, we are also able to detect GFTs that share properties and therefore can be joined.

Let us consider the table "Tap Restaurants" in Fig. 3, which describes restaurants belonging to a restaurant company in the US (most of which are located in New York City); when compared with the table "NYC coffee shop" of Fig. 1, we notice similarities between them, suggesting that the two tables should intuitively be part of the same cluster.

Names used in the two tables can indeed be mapped: "NYC Coffee shops" maps to "Tap Restaurants", "Text " maps to "Name", "Location" maps to "Address", and "Number" to "Number". The similarity between terms "NYC Coffee shops" and "Tap Restaurants" can be better appreciated if we consider YAGO2, as *cafe* has a hyponymy relation (*subclassOf*) with *restaurant*, and a synonymy relation (*means*) with *coffee shop* (see Fig. 4.) Moreover, the instances of the two tables overlap geographically (see Fig. 5.) Given the characteristics discussed above, we expect tables "NYC Coffee shops" and "Tap Restaurants" to be part of the same cluster.

Fig. 4. Entities coffee shop and cafe as they appear within the YAGO2 Web browser, see http://www.mpi-inf.mpg.de/yago-naga/

4.1 Clustering Algorithm

The *k-means* algorithm [McQueen, 1967] is an unsupervised clustering technique partitioning a set of n elements into k subsets, or clusters; the algorithm iterates on all items and assigns each items to the cluster with the nearest mean if a given similarity threshold is satisfied. Each cluster is characterized by a *centroid*, selected among the items of the cluster as the one that best generalizes the features of the whole set of cluster items. In our case, where items are GFTs and clusters are GFT sets, the centroid may be considered as a *super-table*, i.e. the most representative GFT (that is, the most "tightly connected") within the cluster.

More precisely, the k-means algorithm proceeds from an initial situation where the set of available clusters is empty and all items (GFTs) are "loose". As soon as the first table is randomly selected among the entire set of available tables, a one-table cluster is created and its centroid (super-table) is set to that unique table. As the algorithm proceeds, new tables are evaluated with respect to each cluster. Based on a well-chosen table similarity metric (see the following subsection for details) and on an empirically validated similarity threshold, the process decides whether a new "loose" table should belong to a cluster by evaluating the similarity between the candidate table and the centroid of each cluster. The designated cluster for the table at hand is the one maximizing such a similarity, provided that the similarity exceeds the threshold; in case no cluster satisfies the previous condition, a new cluster formed by the table itself is created. Note that similarity between a candidate table and a cluster is only computed once, i.e. with respect to the cluster centroid, making such a computation more tractable.

Fig. 5. Items from *"NYC Coffee shops"* (red markers) and *"Tap Restaurants"* (blue markers)

Whenever a table is added to a cluster, the cluster centroid is re-computed as the table having maximal average similarity score with respect to the other tables in the cluster. As the size of clusters increases, centroids tend to become stable.

Fig. 6 exemplifies the evolution of the clustering algorithm. Let us consider the cluster formed by tables A, B, and C where table C is the centroid, or super-table. In order to evaluate the inclusion of table X in the cluster, we compare it directly with table C. If table X's similarity with table C exceeds the predefined threshold, it is added to the cluster (Scenario A), otherwise a new cluster composed by table X alone is created (Scenario B).

4.2   Table Similarity Metrics

Similarity between two tables is measured by both schema and instance-specific properties. For what concerns schema elements (table and column names and types), we apply feature extraction techniques to the corresponding terms, by means of a simple lexical pre-processing (e.g., tokenization and stop-word removal). After such a processing, terms are described by set of representative words.

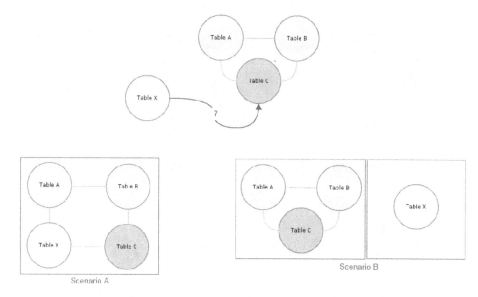

Fig. 6. An illustration of the clustering procedure

To evaluate **word similarity (WS)**, we use a linear combination of two types of similarity metrics: *syntactic* and *semantic* metrics; in particular, we measure

$$WS(W1,W2) = \square * SynScore(W1,W2) + \square * SemScore(W1,W2)$$

where:

- For SynScore, we use the *Levenshtein distance* metric [25], whereby distance depends on the number of substitution/insertion/deletion operations required to transform a string into another.
- For SemScore, we leverage the benefits of two well-known WordNet-based metrics, *Wu-Palmer* [24] and *Jiang-Conrath* [23]:
  $$SemScore(W1,W2) = \gamma * WuPalmer(W1,W2) + \delta * JiangConrath(W1,W2).$$

When applied to pairs of tables, word-based similarity is instrumental both for as a measure of **description similarity** DS and as a **header similarity** HS.

While the former is simply given by the word similarity of table names, the latter is computed by an iterative method that selects at each iteration the most similar name-type pairs among columns of the two tables; HS is the average word similarity of such pairs. A **cardinality corrector** (CC) takes into account the number of columns of a table (and gives lower values for tables with fewer attributes).

We have also developed a **spatial similarity metrics (SS)** applied to table columns that store geo-locations. The method first determines the enclosing spatial entity for all the values appearing in the column, where such entity can be of type city, county, state, or country; geocoding services such as *GeoNames*[2], *Yahoo! Placefinder*[3] and *Google Maps*[4] are used to convert spatial coordinates into appropriate values for the above entities. E.g., values of "Location" in Fig. 1 and "Address" in Fig. 3 are all enclosed within the city named "New York". The spatial similarity of two columns is a function of the granularity of the smallest enclosing geo-entity. Thus, two tables have SS=1 when they refer to the same city, SS=0.75 to the same county, SS=0.5 to the same state, SS=0.25 to the same country, SS=0 otherwise. An **overlap factor** (OF) takes into account the existence of equal item values within the two columns.

Finally, we obtain a global similarity metric by composing word-based similarity applied to table descriptions (DS) and headers (HS) and spatial similarity (SS) applied to table instances. The resulting **Global Table Similarity** (GTS) is defined as:

$$GTS(T1,T2) = DSW*DS(T1,T2) + HSW*HS(T1,T2) + SSW*SS(T1,T2)$$

where DSW, HSW and SSW are the weights given to description similarity, header similarity and spatial similarity, respectively. Similarly, a **Global Similarity Level (GSL)** indicates the threshold deciding when two tables under comparison should be merged within the same cluster; GSL compares to the score of candidate tables for union in [13].

4.3   Experiments

We have experimented with a set of ~8K randomly selected GFTs. Having defined as **significant** a cluster composed by two or more tables, we were able to obtain ~70-80 such clusters, covering roughly 9-10% of the initial tables. We have experimented with a number of weighting schemes and similarity thresholds, finally obtaining satisfactory performance with the values DSW = 0.2, HSW = 0.1, SSW = 0.7 and a threshold GSL of 0.5. These allowed us to obtain 64 interesting clusters from the initial dataset, some of which are illustrated later. Only in a limited subset of 3-4 clusters (~5%), we were able to identify data both relating to similar *entities* (e.g., restaurants, shops) and located in the same area: we believe this is due to the intrinsic sparseness of the data sources and to the size of our initial dataset.

Examples of interesting clusters that we found in the ~8K randomly selected GFTs include real estate offers in Austin from various sources, clusters of schools and educators in New Jersey, crossing real estate offers in the Chicago area with homicides and "wards" about consequences of minor offenses that citizens could suffer, e.g. due to illegal parking. To show that GFTs are not geographically constrained to North America, Fig. 7 shows a cluster, composed by four GFTs, groups entities related to leisure activities in Sao Paulo area. A first table, named "Pontos de Cultura Estado SP" (ID: 1391071), describes some cultural and recreational spots and associations related to music, theater, arts and popular events organization. A second table, named "Mapa das Rodas de Samba SP" (ID: 1243618) describes interesting place where to listen to Samba music. Other tables in the cluster describe bus routes in the same area.

---

[2] www.geonames.org
[3] developer.yahoo.com/placefinder
[4] maps.google.com

Table 1. Cluster functionality as a function of several parameters

Corrective Factors			Weights			Semantic Weights		Word Similarity Weights		
CC	OF	GSL	DSW	HSW	SSW	γ	δ	α	β	Relevant Clusters
0,8	1	0,65	0,4	0,1	0,5	0,5	0,5	0,3	0,7	41
1	0,8	0,4	0,4	0,1	0,5	1	0	0,3	0,7	76
1	1	0,5	0,2	0,1	0,7	1	0	0	1	83
1	1	0,5	0,2	0,1	0,7	0,7	0,3	0,3	0,7	64

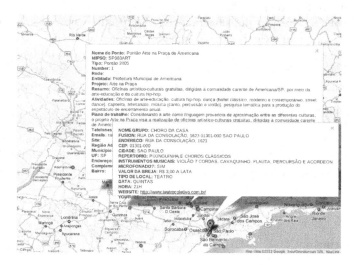

Fig. 7. Cluster describing leisure activities in the Sao Paulo Area, Brazil

5   Games with a Purpose

The Games with a Purpose (GWAP) technique, introduced by [16], is a methodology to encourage humans to perform computational activities by providing them with the classic incentives of playing. GWAPs are generally proposed as a solution for tasks otherwise difficult for machines to perform. Indeed, GWAPs are generally devised when they require skills in which users outperform their silicon counterparts, such as intuition, classification or judgment [11]. These notably include tasks dealing with natural language such as tagging and knowledge representation [12].

We believe that applying the GWAP technique in the Fusion Tables context could offer a number of advantages. First, the automatic clustering-based algorithm would hardly be as sophisticated as a human when it comes to the point of appreciating the similarities in meaning between tables. Moreover, group thinking and the participation of a large number of users may lead to new and unexpected clustering solutions, especially when more than one solution can be judged correct. To summarize, the combination of GWAP techniques with the automatic clustering method described above may lead to solutions taking the best from both human and algorithmic computation. For these reasons, we next propose a number of GWAP formulations that aim at improving the quality of GFTs in terms of table and column names significance.

5.1 Column Name Guesser

A relevant number of tables in GFTs database do not have meaningful names, either (or both) in terms of title or schema (such as *Sheet1, New Table, Text*, etc.). This is obviously a loss of potentially useful information, especially when such information is the only source of useful features to understand their semantics.

Column Name Guesser is a *collaborative output-agreement* game aiming to solve this issue. Here, users in pairs are presented a full table; they can see all data instances but not the column names. The game instructs players to suggest names for one column at a time, advancing to the next only when both players have entered the same name (not necessarily at the same time). Columns can also be marked as *"not useful"*: as an example, in Figure 8, the column number provides just an ordinal numbering of the shops that could be erased from the table without losing useful information. Users have a limited amount of time to complete as much columns as they can. In the following example, after five seconds, both players agree on the column name "Name" for the highlighted column.

The time limitation and the shared interest of finding a common solution to get points ensure a good degree both of answers quality and player enjoyment. The output accuracy may be further improved by the addition of *taboo input*: some column names may be known to be correct but not completely satisfying. Those won't be accepted by the game so as to motivate users in finding better solutions.

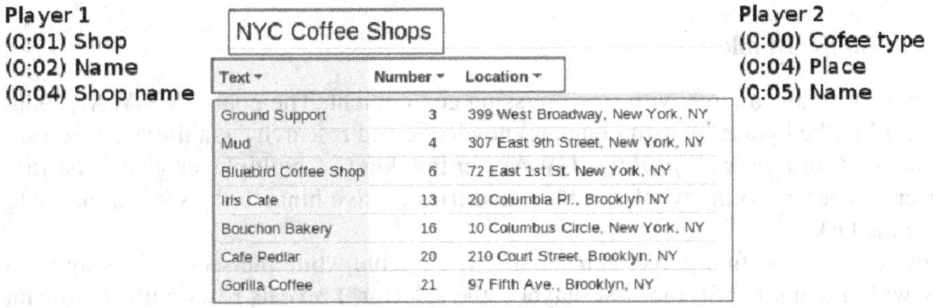

Fig. 8. Column Name Guesser

Opponent	Location	Date	Result	Team Website
Western New England College	John J Burns Park - Massapequa Park, NY, 11762	3/5/11	W, 18-8	http://www.wnecgoldenbears.com/index.aspx?tab=lacrosse&path=mlax
Denison University	Denison University - 100 West College Street, Gran...	4/30/11	W, 14-2	http://www.denison.edu/athletics/mens/lacrosse/index.html
Haverford College	Haverford College, Haverford PA 19041	2/19/11	W, 11-4	http://www.haverford.edu/athletics/lacrossem/
Frostburg State University	Frostburg State University - 101 Braddock Rd Frost...	4/6/11	W, 16-4	http://www.frostburgsports.com/index.aspx?tab=lacrosse&path=mlax
Tufts University	Johnny Unitas Stadium - Towson, MD	3/23/11	L, 14-13	http://www.gotuftsjumbos.com/sports/mlax/index
St. Mary's College	St. Mary's College of Maryland - College Dr, Lexin...	4/9/11	W, 17-4	http://www.smcmathletics.com/sports/mlax/index
Roanoke College	Roanoke College - 221 College Lane Salem, VA 24153	3/16/11	W, 16-6	http://maroons.roanoke.edu/index.aspx?path=mlax
York College	York College of Pennsylvania - 441 Country Club Ro...	4/12/11	W, 19-3	http://www.ycpspartans.com/sports/mlax/index
Salisbury University	Salisbury University - 1101 Camden Avenue, Salisbu...	4/16/11	W, 16-12	http://www.suseagulls.com/sports/mlax/index

Fig. 9. Table Name Hunt

5.2   Table Name Hunt

The table in Fig. 9 has good column names and meaningful instances but no title. By looking at instances, we understand that they report a number of match results, so we can assume that the table has to do with matches between teams. By visiting the URLs in the instances we find out that those are lacrosse matches and since we have just the opponent column, we may guess that are all matches of the same team: a Google lookup confirms the idea. At the end of the process we can give a much more significant name to the table: "Stevenson MD men lacrosse team – matches from February to April 2011". A similar process may be devised in order to improve instance values based on the table's description and on the values of other instances, correcting e.g. misspelled items or directly replacing them with more meaningful content.

The process of finding a good table name is somehow similar to the classic treasure hunt game: players have to find something and bring witnesses of their discovery. In the GWAP case, users ending up with a solution enter their table name and where they took the information. Such information may be used as hints for other players that are stuck in finding a solution.

We can define this game as an *asynchronous output-optimization* GWAP. It's a single player game since every player plays individually but it is community based because his reward will be proportional to how many other users find its hint useful. The resulting game should at the same time be challenging and enjoyable for the players since it requires intuition and good web surfing skills.

5.3   Fill the Blanks

Suppose we have a table with some missing cell content. The goal of a GWAP could be to fill in the blanks by using human knowledge and research capabilities. To do so, we devised an *inversion-problem* GWAP; in this kind of multiplayer game, the first player has access to the whole problem and tries to give hints to the second player to solve the task.

In our case, the first player can see the whole table while the second is assigned a row with a blank to fill; the first player ("the selector") reveals rows with significant content to the second player ("the guesser") to let him understand which type of data has to be entered. As an example, suppose we have the table in Fig. 10.

Row	Movie name	Director	Genre	Release Year
1	Pulp Fiction	Quentin Tarantino	Thriller	1994
2	The Green Mile	Frank Darabont	Drama	1999
3	Forrest Gump		Drama	1994
4	The Godfather	Francis Ford Coppola	Crime	1972
5	The Tourist	Florian Henckel von Donnersmarck	Action	2010

Fig. 10. Fill the Blanks

The guesser sees only row number 3 and no column names; the selector decides to reveal row number 1 that can now be seen also by the guesser. With his knowledge, or by surfing the web, player 2 understands that the blank field should contain the director's name of the movie and fills in the cell accordingly. For each cell filled, both players are given the same reward based on the time taken to enter the solution. If the guesser cannot fill the cell with one hint, the selector can reveal another row by losing some points.

The game is challenging for both roles: while the guesser needs to have good knowledge or good surfing skills, the guesser has a much more complicated job. In fact, since revealing more than one row costs points, he/she has to choose a row that best describes the content of the missing cell (e.g. director in row no.5 is not known as the others). Moreover, as the game goes, the players get to know each other and the selector can refine his choices based on the knowledge of the other player. To ensure enjoyability, the game should allow players to swap their role after some rounds. High scores can be shown to motivate players to play again.

5.4   Trading Tables

This GWAP has the purpose of encouraging users in improving tables and finding new clusters. Trading Tables is a complex GWAP composed of different game phases: users are given a limited amount of credits to "buy" new tables that can improve clusters content. Tables can also be bartered giving the user a greater incentive to "improve" them (e.g. by renaming their schema) to get good trades. The final goal for the player is to create good clusters of tables that can be sold on the market where other players can buy it. This market acts just like stock exchange: users can buy stocks of a cluster to bet on their success. At the end of the selling period, if the table is more valuable than when the user bought the stocks, he/she gets credits that can be used to buy new tables and to build new clusters.

6   Conclusions

We have outlined the importance of GFTs as a potential source of precious structured information, which however is hard to use due to its heterogeneity and dispersion. We have abstracted and partially experienced some methods for making sense of GFTs: 1) A registration method that allows to semi-automatically register GFTs; 2) An automatic clustering method that allows to group tables that have similar schemas and instances; 3) A number of GWAP formulations that allow us to "manually correct" tables in order to improve the automatic understanding of their meaning. In future work, we will continue our research on these three fields in order to get to an end-to-end processing of GFT, from discovery to query as a service.

References

[1] Baeza-Yates, R., Raghavan, P.: Chapter 2: Next Generation Web Search. In: Ceri, S., Brambilla, M. (eds.) Search Computing. LNCS, vol. 5950, pp. 11–23. Springer, Heidelberg (2010)

[2] Bozzon, A., Brambilla, M., Catarci, T., Ceri, S., Fraternali, P., Matera, M.: Visualization of Multi-domain Ranked Data. In: Ceri, S., Brambilla, M. (eds.) Search Computing II. LNCS, vol. 6585, pp. 53–69. Springer, Heidelberg (2011)

[3] Bozzon, A., Brambilla, M., Ceri, S.: Crowdsearcher. In: Proc. WWW 2012, Lyon (to appear, 2012)

[4] Bozzon, A., Brambilla, M., Ceri, S., Fraternali, P.: Liquid Query: Multi-Domain Exploratory Search on the Web. In: Proc. WWW 2010, pp. 161–170 (2011)

[5] Bozzon, A., Brambilla, M., Ceri, S., Quarteroni, S.: A Framework for Integrating, Exploring, and Searching Location-Based Web Data. IEEE Internet Computing 15(6), 24–31 (2011)

[6] Braga, D., Ceri, S., Daniel, F., Martinenghi, D.: Optimization of multi-domain queries on the Web. Proc. VLDB 1(1), 562–573 (2008)

[7] Brambilla, M., Campi, A., Ceri, S., Quarteroni, S.: Semantic Resource Framework. In: Ceri, S., Brambilla, M. (eds.) Search Computing II. LNCS, vol. 6585, pp. 73–84. Springer, Heidelberg (2011)

[8] Cai, D., Yu, S., Wen, J., Ma, W.: Block-based Web Search. In: Proceedings of SIGIR (2004)

[9] Fensel, D., Musen, M.: Special Issue on Semantic Web Technology. IEEE Intelligent Systems (IEEE IS) 16(2)

[10] Google Fusion Tables, http://tables.googlelabs.com/

[11] Gonzalez, H., Halevy, A., Jensen, C., Langen, A., Madhavan, J., Shapley, R., Shen, W., Goldberg-Kidon, J.: Google fusion tables: web-centered data management and collaboration. In: Proceedings of the 2010 International Conference on Management of Data, SIGMOD 2010, Indianapolis, USA, June 06 - 10, pp. 175–180 (2010)

[12] Gonzalez, H., Halevy, A., Jensen, C., Langen, A., Madhavan, J., Shapley, R., Shen, W.: Google Fusion Tables: Data Management, Integration, and Collaboration in the Cloud. In: Proceedings of the ACM Symposium on Cloud Computing, SOCC (2010)

[13] Das Sarma, A., Fang, L., Gupta, N., Halevy, A., Lee, H., Wu, F., Xin, R.: Finding Related Tables. In: Proc. ACM-SIGMOD (to appear, 2012)

[14] Macqueen, J.: Some methods for classification and analysis of multivariate observations. In: Proceedings of the 5th Berkeley Symposium on Mathematical Statistics and Probability, vol. 1, pp. 281–297. University of California Press, Berkeley (1967)

[15] WordNet, http://wordnet.princeton.edu/

[16] Von Ahn, L.: Games With A Purpose. Computer 39(6), 92–94 (2006)

[17] Chen, L.J., Wang, B.-C., Zhu, W.-Y.: The design of puzzle selection strategies for ESP-like GWAP systems. IEEE Transactions on Computational Intelligence and Games 2(2) (2010)

[18] Chan, K.T., King, I., Yuen, M.-C.: Mathematical Modeling of Social Games. In: Proceedings of ICCSE 2009. IEEE (2009)

[19] Franklin, M.J., et al.: CrowdDB: answering queries with crowdsourcing. In: Proceedings of the 2011 International Conference on Management of Data (SIGMOD 2011), pp. 61–72. ACM, New York (2011)

[20] Marcus, A., et al.: Crowdsourced Databases: Query Processing with People. In: Conference on Innovative Data Systems Research, Asilomar, CA, pp. 211–214 (2011)

[21] Parameswaran, A., Polyzotis, N.: Answering Queries using Databases, Humans and Algorithms. In: Conference on Innovative Data Systems Research 2011, Asilomar, CA, pp. 160–166 (2011)

[22] Hoffart, J., Suchanek, F.M., Berberich, K., Lewis Kelham, E., de Melo, G., Weikum, G.: YAGO2: Exploring and Querying World Knowledge in Time, Space, Context, and Many Languages. In: Proc. WWW 2011, pp. 229–232 (2011)

[23] Jiang, J., Conrath, D.: Semantic Similarity Based on Corpus Statistics and Lexical Taxonomy. In: Proc. International Conference on Research in Computational Linguistics, Taiwan, (1997)

[24] Wu, Z., Palmer, M.: Verb Semantics and Lexical Selection. In: Proc. 32nd Annual Meeting of the Association for Computational Linguistics, pp. 132–138 (1994)

[25] Levenshtein, V.: Binary codes capable of correcting deletions, insertions and reversals. Soviet Physics Doklady 10, 707–710 (1966)

[26] Ullman, J.: Information Integration using Logical Views. In: Afrati, F.N., Kolaitis, P.G. (eds.) ICDT 1997. LNCS, vol. 1186, pp. 19–40. Springer, Heidelberg (1996)

[27] Lenzerini, M.: Data Integration: A Theoretical Perspective. In: Proc. ACM-PODS, pp. 233–246 (2002)

Materialization of Web Data Sources

Alessandro Bozzon, Stefano Ceri, and Srđan Zagorac

Dipartimento di Elettronica e Informazione – Politecnico di Milano
{bozzon,ceri,zagorac}@elet.polimi.it

Abstract. Recent years witnessed an exponential increase in the number of data services available on the Web. Many popular Web sites, including social networks, offer API for interacting with their information, and open data initiative such as the Linked Data project promise to achieve the vision of the Web of data. Unfortunately, access to Web data is typically limited by the constraints imposed by the query interface, and by technical limitations such as the network latency, or the number and frequency of allowed daily service invocations. Moreover, several sources may independently publish data about the same real-world objects; in such case, their combined use for assembling all available information about those objects requires duplicate removal, reconciliation and integration. This paper describes various data materialization problems, defining properties such as source coverage and data alignment of the materialized data, and then focuses on a specific problem, the reseeding of data access methods by using available information from previous calls in order to build a materialization of maximum size.

1   Introduction

Data integration and materialization is a classic data management problem: thousands of existing systems and applications deal with some sort of data integration and materialization [7-9]. This problem is particularly hard to solve in the case of Web Applications, as the access to data resources is constrained by the use of given APIs possibly undergoing severe non-functional requirements such as speed, scalability, and availability, which often preclude real-time access. Such a scenario is typical for Search Computing (SeCo) applications, which perform search service integration for multi-domain queries over Web data; search services return *paginated* and *ranked* result lists.

Access to the Web data repositories is typically constrained by the query interface, which may limit the set of accessible data in a single service invocation to a subset of the whole corpus. Moreover, a data provider may impose additional access limitations, e.g., in the number and frequency of service invocations. Indeed, the quality of a search process depends on these constraints: when addressing queries, users expect good results provided in a timely and reliable way, and response delay or the unavailability of the allocated data sources ultimately causes a degraded user experience. Therefore, the need arises for systems and methods devoted to the (transient or persistent) materialization of Web data sources, that guarantees the

S. Ceri and M. Brambilla (Eds.): Search Computing III, LNCS 7538, pp. 68–81, 2012.

possibility of executing search integration applications upon materialized data rather than the original data sources.

Several solutions rely on transparent caching mechanisms for query results [4] but their ability to foster reuse among several queries is limited by their typical storing policy, where cached items (i.e., set of query results) are associated to a query-dependent hash value. Data integration systems working on constrained Web data sources like SeCo, instead, have to be able to exploit the result of past queries also to calculate the response to different, future queries that might be presented to the engine, thus limiting (or avoiding) the invocation of the original services while guaranteeing properties such as coverage and alignment w.r.t. the original data. Therefore, the materialization of Web data sources is a multi-objective problem, for which an optimal solution may be hard or impossible to achieve. The goal of this paper is provide a characterization of the materialization problem for multi-domain search queries addressed to Web data sources. We focus on the challenges provided by the data surfacing activity, i.e. the usage of the results of queries to build the materialization of a large portion of a data source.

The remainder of the paper is organized as follows: Section 2 presents background work on data materialization. In Section 3 and Section 4 we define a service description model devoted to the problem of Web data materialization, and that takes into account the properties required to conduct and evaluate the performance of a materialization system. Section 5 introduces a reference materialization process, categorizing its application to multi-domain queries into four materialization scenarios. We then focus on the problem of materializing the results of a single search service, for which we provide a formalization, and a set of materialization strategies. Finally, in Section 6 we describe the implementation of a system for the materialization of the results of single services, and we evaluate the performance of the proposed materialization strategies upon a real world data set. Section 7 draws some conclusions and paves the way for future research activities.

2   Related Work

In many Web data integration systems, data access limitations due to schema normalization or data distribution are addressed using *view materialization* [7]: the data sources are described as views over a mediated schema, and results of queries are materialized by storing the tuples of the view in the database or any persistent storage medium. A full materialization of a query over certain schema is also known as an *equivalent rewrite* of a query, and it is considered as one of the main dimensions in the problem of answering queries using views [8]. Index structures can be built on the materialized views, thus providing much faster access to the materialized data.

In this paper, as in most data materialization scenarios, we assume that access to data is constrained, and specifically that each data source may be accessed via one or more access patterns, characterized by given input and output parameters. Given an access pattern a, we define V_a as the set of its materialized views v_a, where each v_a is calculated according to a unique combination of values for the input parameters.

By specifying in input all the distinct combinations of values allowed by an access pattern, we create a *full materialization* of the data source over the specified access pattern - which is the portion of the data source made visible through APIs. In general, a full materialization cannot be built, e.g. due to the lack of input values or to the excess of required resources.

In most cases, the domain of the input attributes is not completely known, but it is possible to exploit a dictionary of keywords, or the values produced by the query results to generate legal input values [10] [13]; in particular, a "reseed" occurs whenever the input values to be used for given calls extracted from the results of previous calls. In general, the materialization that can be built by exploiting the entire set of available input data is strictly included into the full materialization, and the graph of connections linking the input data to the output often exhibits the presence of components, or "data island" [12]. The reseeding problem has been considered by Calì, Calvanese and Martinenghi in [3], tackling a setting where data sources can be accessed in limited ways due to the presence of input parameters. Methods used in that paper adopt recursive evaluation even in non-recursive queries, and use functional and inclusion dependencies for improving the access to data sources. Our work shares several assumptions with [3], but also considers the additional problems brought by the invocation limitations of the queried Web services.

Recently, there have been efforts to integrate a vast amount of structured data found on the Internet in the form of HTML tables [2] and by surfacing information hidden behind web forms [10]. However, the proposed approaches do not address the materialization of data provided through search interfaces, where results are ranked and paginated for the purposes of efficient multi-domain query answering.

3   Service Representation in SeCo

The description of the properties required to perform materialization of Web search services is based on the multi-layered model used in the *Service Description Framework* [5] of SeCo. Search services are typically registered in a service repository that describes the functional (e.g. invocation end-point, input and output attributes) information of data end-points. Figure 1 shows an example of *Service Description* for a movie search application. Next, we describe its features bottom-up, thereby using the same approach that is used for registering services in the system.

At a physical level, search services are registered as *Service Interfaces* (SI), a concrete representation of the service that provides a service identifier, a set of input parameters and a set of output parameters, and a set of *ranking* attributes specify the ordering imposed on the service results. For instance, the *SDF* in Figure 1 contains four service interfaces working on two data sources that contain information about movies, respectively "IMDB" and "Google Movie". Two of them query the data source and require as input the *genre* of the movie, while two require the name of an *actor*. As output, services return information about the movies that match the query condition (i.e. movies of a given genre, or movies acted by a given actor).

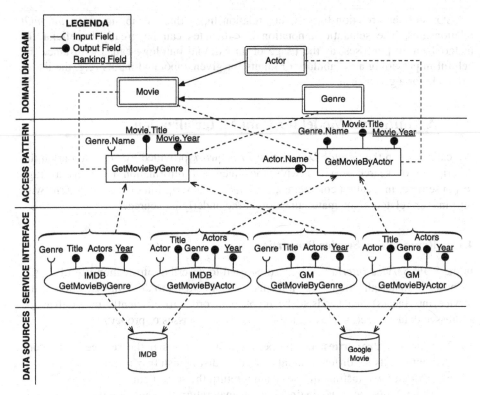

Fig. 1. An Example of Service Description Framework for a Movie Search Application

At the *logical level*, services are described in terms of data retrieval patterns, or *Access Patterns* (AP). Each AP is related to one or more SI that share the same invocation signature (input, output, and ranking attributes), and each input and output parameter of a SI is mapped to exactly one attribute of the AP; for instance, in the *GetByMovieActor* access pattern includes the *IMDB GetMovieByActor* and the *IMDB GetMovieByActor*. Access patterns are linked at a logical level through a *connection pattern*, a description of the pairwise attribute relations that enable the logical connections between data sources, so to enable join operation between their invocations during search.

To enrich the description of search services, AP are annotated with *entities*, properties and relationships of existing external knowledge bases (KBs) or ontologies, so to define a *conceptual level* called *Domain Diagram*. The purpose of this annotation is twofold: on the one hand, to provide a common ground for unifying the terminology between APs (attributes in the Aps are denoted by prefixing their name with the name of the entity they refer to, e.g. *Movie.title*) and SIs; on the other hand, to support the query process by providing a richer description of the objects (and object instances) addressed by the SDF. Currently, SeCo uses YAGO ontology [11] within its data model. YAGO merges Wikipedia and WordNet, while enforcing a hierarchy of *data types* to which all objects in SDF are associated. It also defines a number of *core relationships* such as *type*, *subclassOf*, *domain* and *range*. Lastly,

YAGO defines relationships over relationships thus enabling *subrelationOf* relationships. The semantic annotation of attributes can be greatly beneficial for materialization purposes, as the usage of an external ontology can, for instance, be helpful in providing a vocabulary of inputs for given annotated inputs (e.g. the list of ZIP code for a given city).

4   A Multi-level Model for Data Materialization

We capitalize on the *Service Description Framework* provided by SeCo to enrich the description of search services with non-functional information (such as average response time, invocation constraints, etc.) and the description of access patterns with information related to the materialization of the underlying sources.

4.1   Representing Service Properties

In the SDF, *Service Interfaces* can also be used to describe information useful for the purposes of materialization. Such information can be used to drive the selection of the service interface(s) that needs to be invoked in order to efficiently materialize the addressed data source(s). We distinguish three main classes of properties:

- **Uniqueness Properties**, i.e. properties that indicates if the service will return disjoint results for different inputs. We then distinguish two cases:
  o *Unique:* two distinct queries cannot return the same item.
  o *WithDuplicates:* two distinct queries may return the same item.
- **Performance Properties**, i.e. metrics that describe a service in terms of:
  o *Pagination*: indicates if the service returns results in chunks or globally. Search services (e.g. the Google Movie search service) typically return results in pages (chunks), and the service consumer must perform several invocations on order to exhaust the query result set.
  o *Maximum Result Size*: indicates the maximum number of items that can be returned by a single query.
  o *Maximum Chunk Size*: indicates the maximum number of items that are returned in each chunk.
  o *Response Time Statistics*, measuring end-to-end response time (e.g. average response time for each chunk).
- **Service Level Agreement** properties, i.e. properties that specify the level/quality of service offered by the data source service provider, including:
  o *Daily Invocation Limits*, i.e. the maximum number of allowed service invocations per day (or time unit).
  o *Chunk Invocation Limits*, i.e. the allowed number of consecutive chunk extractions.
  o *Invocation Access Delay*, i.e. an invocation delay superimposed by the remote service.
  o *Access Key* – i.e. a client identification value that is needed in order to access the remote source and enforce the SLA agreements.

4.2   Properties of the Materialized Data

The description of access patterns can be extended so to include a set of properties related to their materialization, which define how the materialized data relates to the data offered by the addressed sources, or to real-world data used as input for the materialization process.

- **Coverage Relative to the Full Materialization.** This property denotes the ratio between the number of items in the materialization and the number of items in the full materialization. Coverage can be further refined into a **query-specific coverage** expresses such ratio relative to the portion of data in the source that satisfy the query. E.g., an application may be interested in greater coverage of data which satisfy the query "Location = New York".
- **Coverage Relative to World's Entities**, which is quite hard to evaluate, denotes the ratio between the number of materialized items and the number of real world's items. Using multiple data sources describing the same real world's entities can enhance this coverage. For instance, several services offering New York's "evening events" can be queried in order to produce a more comprehensive materialization. It requires duplicate elimination across different data sources.
- **Alignment.** This property is satisfied when the materialization contains the same data as the data source; we regard as "consistent" a time when the source and materialization are aligned. **Query-specific alignment** expresses alignment relative to a given query. When full, real-time alignment cannot be maintained, materializations can be further characterized by: 1) *delay*, which indicates the maximum allowed time interval since the last consistent time; and 2) *max-inconsistency*, which indicates how many items can differ between the source and the materialization.
- **Redundancy.** A measure of the amount of duplicates in the materialization. It can be due to the presence of multiple sources, but also of a single source accessed via a service with duplicates. Duplicate removal in the first case may be harder due to the presence of value conflicts (e.g., distinct values for the same real world object).
- **Diversity.** This property measures how the items collected in the materialization represent the variety of data provided by the data sources according to some set of item attributes. E.g., in the case of events in New York, it may be more interesting to include events of a different nature rather than all the jazz concerts.
- **Accuracy.** A measure of semantic correctness and precision of the query answers obtained from the materialized data corpus compared against the same query answers from the actual data source.
- **Ranking Preservation.** A measure of the ability of the system to preserve the original ranking of results obtained from the materialized data corpus, compared against the same query answer from the actual data source.

The listed materialization properties allow the measurement of materialization's "quality", which can be used as a goal function for the data materialization process, described in the following section.

5   Characterizing Data Materialization in a Multi-domain Query Environment

5.1   The Materialization Process

According to the model presented in the Section 4, we define a data materialization process for multi-domain queries as a sequence of three main tasks: 1) *input discovery*, 2) *query generation*, and 3) *data surfacing*. In a typical materialization process, the three tasks are performed cyclically, as depicted in Figure 2.

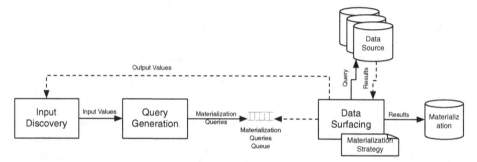

Fig. 2. The Data Materialization Process

The **input** values **discovery** phase consists in creating a list of values for each input attribute of the services to be queries. We can identify three input discovery strategies: 1) The *Dictionary input strategy*, where an existing dictionary of relevant input terms is used to generate values for the input attributes of the queries; semantic annotations of attributes help in dictionary selection. For example, if the input attribute required by the service is annotated as *City*, then its values can be extracted from a Knowledge Base about cities, possibly constrained by the values of other inputs (e.g., *Country*). 2) The *Reseeding input strategy*, where the input is selected from results obtained from the results of previous queries. 3) The Query *logs input strategy*, where existing query logs are used to populate the input attributes of the queries.

A materialization process can adopt one or more of the previously defined strategies, so to drive the creation of the queries used to materialized the targeted data sources: for instance, a materialization process can start with a *dictionary* input strategy, and then be fed with the new values provided by the *reseeding* strategy.

The **query generation** phase is devoted to the generation of the input values combinations used to populate the *materialization queries queue*, which contains a list of queries to be executed. The number of generated queries is bound by the Cartesian product of input lists, but constraints on correlations between input values may reduce the number of legal inputs; some background knowledge could limit the validity of some input combinations: for instance, if a service requires as input a *Country* and *City* inputs, then the inputs <*Italy, Los Angeles*> would not be allowed.

Finally, the **data surfacing** phase is in charge of selecting which materialization query, among the list of available ones, will be addressed to a search data service, thus retrieving the results and include them in the data materialization. When the reseeding input strategy is used for one of the input attributes, this task is intertwined with the input discovery phase.

5.2   Materialization Scenarios

When considering a set of data sources and service interfaces, as in the example of Figure 1, several data materialization scenario can emerge. For instance, an application might require the (full) materialization of a data source over a specific service interface (and related access pattern); in other scenarios, one might be interested in materializing the whole data source by exploiting all its available services (e.g., the whole IMDB database); finally, an application might aim at collecting a comprehensive view on the information related to one or more domains (e.g. all the movie ever released). According to the requirements of the underlying application, four classes of data materialization scenarios, can be identified:

- **Single Pattern, Single Service (SPSS):** in this scenario, the materialization is performed on a single service with a given access pattern.
  Duplicate elimination is only required if the service is not unique, and no value conflicts are possible (since data is extracted from the same service).
- **Single Pattern, Multiple Services (SPMS):** the scenario addresses a configuration where the materialization is performed on several services (from different data sources) that insist on the same access pattern. Here the goal is to maximize the coverage of a given domain by exploiting different information sources. For instance, one might want to collect a comprehensive list of actors by querying a movie service (e.g. IMDB) and Wikipedia (which also contain alternative arts actors). The SPMS configuration requires a duplicate reconciliation method dealing with value conflicts among the involved sources.
- **Multiple Patterns, Single Service (MPSS):** the scenario considers the materialization of a set of sources connected by a schema with interacting APs as described in Fig. 3, where the output values of an AP can feed the input values of another AP; each AP is mapped to a single service. The problem may reduce to a **single data source (MPSS-1)** with multiple APs. Figure 3 represents an instance of the MPSS-1 problem if we assume in that the two APs are on the same underlying data service, and the goal is to maximize the materialization of the data source. In general, duplicates may be found and must be eliminated, but no value conflicts are possible.
- **Multiple Patterns, Multiple Services (MPMS):** in this scenario, the materialization is performed on a set of sources connected by a schema where each AP can be mapped to multiple services. The problem may reduce to a **single data source (MPMS-1)** with multiple APs. This problem requires a duplicate identification method dealing with value conflicts.

5.2.1 Influence of Access Limitations on the Materialization Process

As the access to a data source is only possible through the access limitation imposed by Access Patterns (APs), each materialization query call requires filling the AP's input fields. To achieve coverage, the domains of all legal values for such fields must be known. Such knowledge could be known in advance when, for instance, a field insists on an enumerable value set, possibly of small size (e.g. the set of movie *genres*). Otherwise, input seeding can be seen as an <u>incremental process</u> driven by the materialization queries, where the knowledge about the input fields' domains is accumulated during this process when queries are executed and output fields are retrieved.

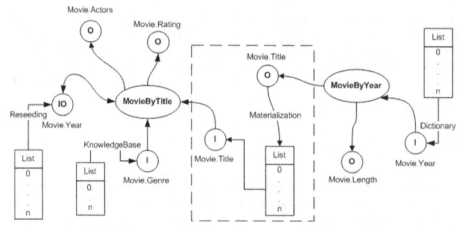

Fig. 3. Example of schema of the materialization problem

The impact of a materialization scenario on the input discover phase can be fully appreciated by considering the two APs represented in, **MovieByTitle** (which requires as input the Movie's *Title, Genre, and Year*) and **MovieByYear** (which requires as input the movies' *Year*); the former service has useful information, such as the *Actors* and the *Rating*, but requires very specific input. Instead, the latter service has a simple input domain, consisting of the *Year* of issuing (e.g. 2011); with such input, it produces a list of titles. Movie *Genres* are few, and thus an input generator that already knows the Title and is set on the current Year can iterate over all possible genres to generate the input for the former service, extracting all the information about actors and ratings of current Year movies.

5.2.2 Strategies for Data Surfacing

Data surfacing involves the selection of the next query to be executed among the ones available in the *materialization queries queue*. Such a selection is performed according to a *materialization strategy*, i.e. a logic devoted to the maximization of a given set of metrics (e.g., the quality metrics defined in Section 4) in order to optimize the query selection task. We next describe some materialization strategies for the SPSS materialization scenario, whose performance is evaluated in Section 6. We leave the formalization of the other scenarios to an extended version of this paper.

Let us consider a single service s described by an access pattern AP; AP has a set of input attributes I_i associated with a domain D_i, with $i = 1..n$, and a set of output attributes O_j associated with a domain D_j, with $j = 1..m$. In order to show the reseeding, we assume that $D_i = D_j$ for some i, j, i.e. that the domain of some input and output attributes is the same. Consider $D = D_1 \times ... D_n$ as the cross product of the input domains, and let $k \in D$ be a combination of input values for the AP. A paginated query q_k^p is a query addressed to the service s using the combination k of input values, and $1 \leq p \leq MaxNumChunks$ indicates the chunk currently queried. We define $r_k^p \subseteq R$ as the set of tuples in the source that satisfies a query q_k^p, where R represents all the items of the source to be materialized. The *input discovery* step of the materialization process builds, at materialization set-up time, the initial input combinations $C \subset D$, e.g. by retrieving them from a dictionary; then, new combinations of C can be found by using the values in results r_k^p of queries that are progressively computed. The materialization M is built as the union of the r_k^p; note that $M \subseteq R$, and in general M is much smaller than R due to the access limitations to the data source. With a single service, the union operation is sufficient for duplicate elimination.

The definition of a materialization strategy is influenced by the chunking of query answers, which requires multiple service calls to fully collect a query's result, and by the distribution of values for the input attributes, as distinct inputs produce uneven numbers of returned results, thus introducing skews in the materialized result set. These factors call for data surfacing strategies that are capable of balancing between the need for coverage and diversity.

In order to define few simple data surfacing strategies, let us model the sequence of queries produced by a data surfacing strategy as a tree QRT(V,E), where all the nodes except the root correspond to queries; the root is directly connected to queries q_k^1 with $k \in C$, and we do not further consider how nodes q_k^1 are ordered. In this context, a materialization strategy consists of interleaving of tree generation and tree traversal steps. Three generation occurs as follows:

- If the current query q_k^p has not exhausted the results and a new chunk can be retrieved, then q_k^{p+1} is generated as a child of q_k^p
- If the current query q_k^p has generated new combinations h which are not present in C, then new nodes q_h^1 are generated and C is set to $C \cup h$; the insertion of nodes q_h^1 in the tree may occur according to two insertion policies:
  - *Child insertion policy*: nodes q_h^1 are created as children of q_k^p, possibly on the left of q_k^{p+1};
  - *Sibling insertion policy*: nodes q_h^1 are left-appended as children of the root.

Once new queries are appended to the tree, the materialization strategy must select the next query in the tree to execute. Related works [12] perform a similar selection process by exploiting a cost model that associates a weight to each edge in the tree, so to find an optimal selection of queries that minimizes the total cost of traversal (a *Weighted Minimum Dominating Set* problem). In this work, we instead exploit classical *breadth-first* and *depth-first* tree tranversal algorithms. We apply them to the two variants of insertion policies, thus obtaining four materialization strategies, which yield to different performances in terms of coverage and diversity. An analysis of the performance of the proposed materialization strategies is provided in the following section.

6   Evaluation of the Four Data Surfacing Strategies

To support the materialization process, we designed and develop a materializer module within the broader SeCo framework [14], represented in Figure 4. The module relies on the descriptions stored with the existing SeCo service mart repository, and utilizes the existing SeCo QP (query processor) API implementation.

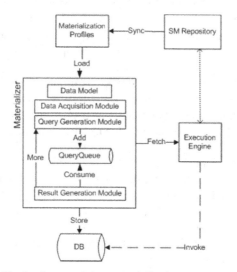

Fig. 4. The implemented data materialization architecture

The materialization module contains:

- *Materialization Profiles* repository, which contains the *service and materialization properties* of the Service Description Framework Service Interfaces and Access Patterns.
- *Data Acquisition* module, which implements the input discovery strategies (e.g. dictionary, reseeding and query log data acquisition), guided by the data model.
- *Query Generation* module, which generates the queries to be executed and adds them to a data structure PQ representing the pending queries to be executed.
- *Result Generation Module*, which extracts the next query from the query queue and launches its execution.

The materialization module is driven by a **materialization controller**, which is in charge of determining the order of execution for the queries produced during the *Query Generation* step, by traversing the data structure of pending queues according to a given materialization strategy.

We evaluated the efficiency of the materialization strategies described in Section 5 in terms of **domain coverage** for each attribute w.r.t. the number of queries required to achieve a given coverage value. The goal is to assess the ability of each materialization strategy to quickly explore the data- and domain- space of a data source. To perform the evaluation, we created a database composed of ~1M real estate offers crawled from an existing Real Estate Web site. Experiments were performed by considering the access pattern **realEstateByLocation,** which takes a real estate type and a geographical location as the input attributes.

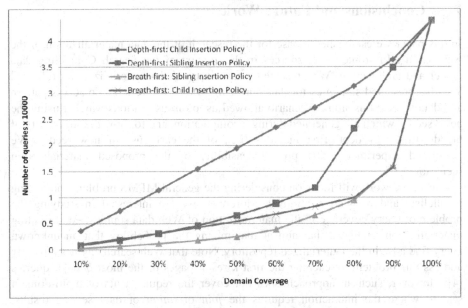

Fig. 5. Experimental Results for SPSS

The *real estate type* input attribute was populated using a dictionary strategy, which used a static, pre-populated list of attribute values such as 'rental' or 'for sale' as the input dictionary. The *location* input attribute was populated by using a reseeding strategy; moreover a matching location output attribute returning locations was mapped as an appropriate input attribute value provider. A domain of postal codes found in the collected real estate database was used as location input attribute domain. The domain size of the postal code reseeding input attribute was approximately 11000, a randomly selected subset of which was used as a starting seed dictionary.

For each of the materialization (result generation) strategies 10 runs were performed; to avoid biases in the evaluation, the input attribute conforming to the reseeding input strategy were initialized at each run by a randomly selected subset *initID* of size 100. The resulting domain coverage increase had been averaged between runs for each strategy and observed in 10% increments (w.r.t. the overall domain size). Figure 5 provides the results of our comparison. Breadth-first algorithms are able to retrieve a wider coverage on the input by requiring less service invocations. For the tested scenario, the first breadth-first algorithm is able to achieve a 65% coverage of the input domain after 5000 queries (a values in line with the daily limit imposed by several Web data source API provider), thus requiring 25% less queries than the second best breadth-first algorithm and 50% less queries than the best performing depth-first algorithm and almost a 5 fold improvement over the worst, depth-first based algorithm. The depth first algorithm, instead, proves very unsuited for the goal at hand. The experimental results match our intuition.

7   Conclusions and Future Work

In this paper we established a base for the research of the data materialization of the web based API fronted data sources in the context of the Search Computing data model and architecture. We presented a taxonomy of the materialization problems. We also presented strategies for data surfacing in the case of a single access pattern and data source; this simple scenario allowed us to discuss various ways of using the new "seeds" which are generated during a computation, and to show the superiority of breadth-first over depth-first methods (i.e., of the early use of new seeds). We performed experiments that proved feasibility of the proposed materialization scenarios.

Our future work will focus on considering the general MPMS problem and adding parallelism and replication removal. Moreover, we are interested in studying the problem of query coverage in the materialization of Web data sources, i.e. providing materialization strategies that aim at maximizing the probability that an unknown query find a hit in the materialized repository. Note that Web search engines typically address this problem by caching the first k result pages of the most popular queries [4]. However, such an approach does not cover the requirements of multi-domain search, where the interaction requires the *join* or *union* of data service results, enabled, for instance, by exploratory search approaches [1]. Finally, in addition to data coverage, we will consider the problems of alignment, diversity and accuracy of the materialized data corpus.

References

[1] Bozzon, A., Brambilla, M., Ceri, S., Fraternali, P.: Liquid query: multi-domain exploratory search on the web. In: WWW 2010: Proceedings of the 19th International Conference on World Wide Web (2010)
[2] Cafarella, M.J., Madhavan, J., Halevy, A.: Web-scale extraction of structured data. SIGMOD Rec. 37, 55–61 (2009)
[3] Cali, A., Calvanese, D., Martinenghi, D.: Dynamic Query Optimization under Access Limitations and Dependencies. J. UCS 15(1), 33–62 (2009)

[4] Cambazoglu, B.B., Junqueira, F.P., Plachouras, V., Banachowski, S., Cui, B., Lim, S., Bridge, B.: A refreshing perspective of search engine caching. In: WWW 2010: Proceedings of the 19th International Conference on World Wide Web (2010)

[5] Bozzon, A., Brambilla, M., Ceri, S., Quarteroni, S.: A Framework for Integrating, Exploring, and Searching Location-Based Web Data. IEEE Internet Computing 15(6), 24–31 (2011)

[6] Dasgupta, A., Das, G., Mannila: A random walk approach to sampling hidden databases. In: Proceedings of the 2007 ACM SIGMOD International Conference on Management of Data (2007)

[7] Gupta, A., Mumick, I.S. (eds.): Materialized views: techniques, implementations, and applications. MIT Press, Cambridge (1999)

[8] Halevy, A.Y.: Answering queries using views: A survey. The VLDB Journal 10, 270–294 (2001)

[9] Halevy, A., Rajaraman, A., Ordille, J.: Data integration: The teenage years. In: Proceedings of the 32nd International Conference on Very Large Data Bases, pp. 9–16. VLDB Endowment (2006)

[10] Madhavan, J., Ko, D., Kot, L., Ganapathy, V., Rasmussen, A., Halevy, A.: Google's deep web crawl. Proc. VLDB Endowment 1(2), 1241–1252 (2008)

[11] Suchanek, F.M., Kasneci, G., Weikum, G.: Yago: A Core of Semantic Knowledge. In: 16th International World Wide Web Conference (WWW 2007), New York, USA (2007)

[12] Wu, P., Wen, J.-R., Liu, H., Ma, W.-Y.: Query selection techniques for efficient crawling of structured web sources. In: International Conference on Data Engineering (2006)

[13] Zerfos, P., Cho, J., Ntoulas, A.: Downloading textual hidden web content through keyword queries. In: Joint Conference on Digital Libraries, pp. 100–109 (2005)

[14] Bozzon, A., Braga, D., Brambilla, M., Ceri, S., Corcoglioniti, F., Fraternali, P., Vadacca, S.: Search computing: multi-domain search on ranked data. In: Proceedings of the 2011 ACM SIGMOD International Conference on Management of Data (SIGMOD 2011), pp. 1267–1270. ACM, New York (2011)

Natural Language Interfaces to Data Services

Vincenzo Guerrisi, Pietro La Torre, and Silvia Quarteroni

Dipartimento di Elettronica e Informazione, Politecnico di Milano
{guerrisi.vincenzo,latorre.pietro}@gmail.com,
quarteroni@elet.polimi.it

Abstract. Natural language interfaces to data services will be a key technology to access unstructured data repositories in a natural way. This involves solving the complex problem of recognizing relevant services given an ambiguous, potentially ungrammatical natural language question.

In this paper, we address the requirements of natural language interfaces to data services. While current approaches deal with single-domain questions, we study both rule-based and machine learning methods to address multi-domain questions to support conjunctive queries over data services. Our results denote high accuracy with both approaches.

1 Introduction

The recent expansion of data providers on the Web has made a variety of information increasingly available, for instance via REST APIs as in Google Fusion Tables[1] or search-specific languages such as the Yahoo Query Language[2]. To support complex Web queries, data sources are usually wrapped as *data services* specified by I/O parameters. Although Information Retrieval is gaining interest toward such services, the problem of interfacing with them is still largely under-investigated: while it is currently possible only for experts to write logical queries or set up query interfaces to data services, it is widely believed that natural language (NL) interfaces will be key to guarantee access to huge data repositories to a large body of non-expert users in a natural way.

Devising a NL interface to data services is an ambitious goal, as it involves resolving the ambiguity of free-text queries and performing an accurate mapping from the lexical level of the question to the semantic level needed to compose a logical query, i.e. a statement describing relevant data services and their join criteria, constraints and selection conditions. In this paper, we illustrate how this problem is tackled in the context of the Search Computing project (SeCo) [2], that aims at powerful result composition and ranking infrastructures given multi-domain queries. The SeCo framework relies on a semantic annotation derived from data services with the aid of a reference external knowledge base whose useful entities and relationships are "projected" onto a domain representation (see Section 2).

Given such a representation, we address the requirements of query analysis in the context of natural language interfaces to data services (Section 3). As related work is

---

[1] google.com/fusiontables
[2] developer.yahoo.com/yql

S. Ceri and M. Brambilla (Eds.): Search Computing III, LNCS 7538, pp. 82–97, 2012.

centered on single-domain questions and rule-based approaches (Section 4), we study robust methods to address multi-domain questions, a requirement in the SeCo framework in order to support conjunctive queries over data services (Section 5). Our approaches are evaluated in Section 7 using a variety of datasets illustrated in Section 6. Finally, Section 8 draws conclusions and discusses future work.

2 A Semantic Description of Data Services

We build upon the two-facet service representation in SeCo [3], where a Service Description Framework interacts with a Semantic Annotation Framework.

In the Service Description Framework, services are represented at different levels of abstraction. At the lowest level, a **service interface** directly wraps a service call interface; at a higher level of abstraction, one or more service interfaces refer to a common **access pattern** described in terms of domain entities. Finally, the top conceptual view includes a collection of **service marts** that serve as hubs for access patterns referring to the same types of entities. While Section 2.1 illustrates these in detail, we here focus on the Semantic Annotation Framework.

In the Semantic Annotation Framework, domain entities and relationships are represented in a common **domain diagram** ($\mathcal{DD}$) where each item is modeled after a concept in a reference **knowledge base** ($\mathcal{KB}$). We represent $\mathcal{DD}$ as an Entity - Relationship diagram composed of modeled items – i.e. *entities* and *attributes* of entities – and binary *relationships* between entities. Entity and attribute names are extracted from the terminology of $\mathcal{KB}$; each $\mathcal{DD}$ item refers to a unique entity K within $\mathcal{KB}$.

The main function of $\mathcal{KB}$ is to provide a common ground for unifying the terminology of service interfaces in the aim of disambiguation during service registration and natural language querying; indeed, each entity or attribute in $\mathcal{DD}$ is required to correspond to exactly one $\mathcal{KB}$ entity.

In SeCo, we adopt YAGO [19] as a reference $\mathcal{KB}$ due to its extensive coverage of virtually any domain (around 3 million facts, i.e. predicates about entities). Moreover, YAGO has been acquired semi-automatically from Wikipedia[3] and WordNet[4], two resources frequently used by natural language processing toolkits. Section 5.4 illustrates a number of information extraction methods taking advantage of YAGO relationships.

2.1 Service Description Framework

In the Service Description Framework, **access patterns** (APs) are the key element to convert the user's question into a logical query. An AP describes a data retrieval method in terms of domain items: indeed, it is specified by a set of input fields and a set of output fields, whereby each field has a *semantic type* coinciding with the attribute of a $\mathcal{DD}$ entity. Addressing a user query therefore involves determining the most suitable AP to represent the user's need and finding values for its input fields. In addition to its input and output fields, an AP is further specified by:

---

[3] wikipedia.org
[4] wordnet.princeton.edu

– A *focus*, i.e. the main $\mathcal{DD}$ entity appearing in its output's semantic types;
– A *functional name* (e.g. *GET Restaurant BY Location*), taking into account its focus and the semantic types of its I/O fields;
– A set S of *service interfaces* for which there exists a one-to-one mapping at the field level with respect to the AP itself.

Access patterns are grouped by focus under the same **service mart**. This is important for query analysis, as the identification of a relevant service mart is the first step towards choosing a suitable AP (see Section 3).

2.2 Query Analysis in SeCo

The service framework is progressively populated by mapping new service interfaces made available by data providers into access patterns expressed in terms of relevant $\mathcal{DD}$ items. As the registration process is outside the scope of this chapter, we here assume the service framework to be static and focus on its querying.

Services registered in the SeCo framework can be queried in a variety of ways, including via graphical user interfaces or via textual input [1]. The processing of a query over data services is organized according to three steps that progressively "formalize" the semantics of application-level queries at the conceptual, logical and physical level, mapping their terms into objects of the Service Description Framework. As illustrated in Figure 1, the following process takes place:

1. *service mart selection*: the user query is analyzed to identify relevant service marts;
2. *access pattern selection*: a suitable access pattern is chosen for each service mart given the constraints found in the query;
3. *service interface selection*: a service interface is chosen for each access pattern to route the query to the appropriate data service.

Note that as SeCo supports the composition and concatenation of different data services, APs can be combined in a variety of ways by exploiting the matches between their I/O fields. Two APs whose output fields have a non-empty intersection (in terms of matching semantic types) may be joined in a *parallel* fashion, while two APs such that the input fields of one have a non-null intersection with the output fields of the other may be joined in a *serial* connection. In this case, phase 2 entails the formulation of constraints concerning the involved I/O fields. The result of this is an AP combination (or *solution*) where the input is the union of the inputs of the corresponding APs, the output is the union of the outputs of the corresponding APs, and a number of constraints determines which of the I/O fields are bound to have matching values due to AP joins.

A logical query specifying relevant service marts, access pattern solution and service interfaces is the final outcome of the query process.

3   Natural Language Query Analysis

With respect to handling other query formats, addressing a natural language query over the service framework outlined in Section 2 involves the difficulty of generalizing over text by mapping the question into a logical query. Given the general scheme outlined in Figure 1, natural language query analysis consists of the following three-step process:

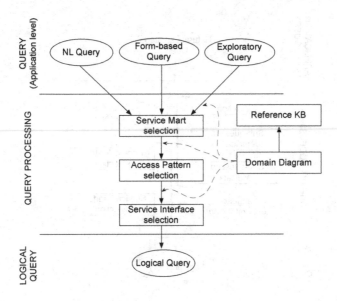

Fig. 1. Top-down query processing steps over the Service Description Framework

1. in *service mart selection*, the user's intent conveyed by the question is categorized in terms of relevant service marts available in the service description framework;
2. in *access pattern selection*, refinement operations allow to obtain the I/O fields of APs related to the selected service mart; these in turn determine their eligibility;
3. finally, in *service interface selection*, AP fields are mapped into lower-level service interface parameters to complete query specification.

Service Mart Selection is certainly the most crucial phase from a linguistic perspective as it involves three phases (see Figure 2):

1. *focus extraction*, i.e. the identification of a question's salient noun(s)/noun phrase(s);
2. *question segmentation*, i.e. the segmentation of an arbitrarily complex, multi-domain question q into N subqueries $q_i, i \in \{1, .., N\}$, each corresponding to a focus;
3. *(sub)question classification*, i.e. the categorization of each (sub)question according to a predefined taxonomy. Formally, this is the mapping of each q_i into a class c_i from the set of all query classes C, such that each c_i corresponds to a service mart in the SDF – or *other* in case the input is uninterpretable or out of the SDF scope.

Access Pattern Selection relies upon two processes. *Solution computation* is the combinatorial operation of identifying all valid AP combinations given the service marts selected at the previous step (see Section 2.2). Then, *language understanding* extracts and interprets relevant (sub)question terms in the light of the APs involved in each solution; as a result, a number of AP input fields become bound (e.g. the city of a restaurant search), generating constraints for the logical query.

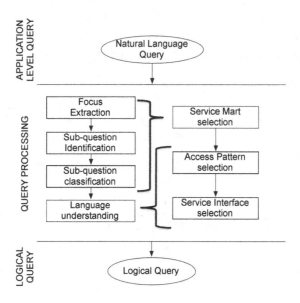

Fig. 2. General overview of natural language query analysis in SeCo

Finally, a weighted scoring function ranks each solution by considering how many output fields it offers, how many of its input fields remain unbound after language understanding, and how many field values are constrained by AP join conditions. The top scoring solution is then identified and its APs are used for service interface selection.

Service Interface Selection. Once APs have been chosen, suitable corresponding service interfaces are identified. In the current SeCo implementation, service interface selection offers no challenge from the NLP viewpoint as service interface I/O fields are currently bound to corresponding AP fields: we therefore omit this phase in the chapter.

Example. Let us exemplify the NL query analysis process by considering the question "Where are a cheap hotel and a Japanese restaurant near Covent Garden?". First, we can identify its two syntactic foci as *a cheap hotel* and *a Japanese restaurant*; both noun phrases can be reduced to their syntactic heads *hotel* and *restaurant* using e.g. the rules in [4]. The question can then be segmented into two subquestions q_1 = "Where are a cheap hotel" and q_2 = "a Japanese restaurant near Covent Garden" based on its lexical and morphological properties.

While focus extraction and question segmentation are domain-independent tasks that could be solved via syntactic analysis alone, (sub)question classification is by nature dependent on the taxonomy of choice; for instance, the choice for q_1 and q_2 might fall on the *Hotel* and *Food* classes, respectively, which are bound one-to-one with available service marts. Note that there is an analogy between a service mart (i.e. an AP focus) and the syntactic focus of a natural language question; Section 5.3 illustrates a learning model taking account of this.

Finally, *cheap*, *Japanese* and *in Covent Garden* are constraints to be included in the logical query to narrow down service results; if applicable, *Covent Garden* should be set as the location of both the hotel and the food service used.

4 Related Work

Semantic Web and Data Services. In the Semantic Web area, natural language interfaces to ontologies have been proposed in a number of studies as an alternative to keyword-based interfaces or interfaces based on query languages [5,10]. Generally speaking, methods in this field attempt to perform an exact mapping of the NL query into a logical formula in order to access knowledge, structured in e.g. RDF triples. Typical approaches in this direction involve a combination of statistical techniques (syntactic parsing) and semantic operations to identify ontology concepts in the input [11,6,20].

With respect to the above approaches, we aim at solving a different problem: not only we expect search engine-style, potentially ungrammatical interaction, but we also deal with a variety of heterogeneous data sources for which there is *a priori* no reference ontology. For these reasons, we cannot assume to have fully parsable queries or a consistent, stable ontology-like structural representation/domain lexicon. When it comes to data services, even fewer attempts have been made involving natural language interfaces: for instance, [16] propose a mapping of natural language query blocks to services using predefined workflow templates; this is however far away from the SeCo goal of supporting queries over flexible combinations of data services computed "on-the-go".

From Focus Extraction to Full NLP. A widely adopted method for the analysis of NL queries over ontologies is *focus extraction*, i.e. the identification of the question's salient term in the purpose of matching it to a relevant ontology concept. For instance, the method in [6] (henceforth *Daml*) identifies the focus as the first pre-preterminal node [5] of the sentence syntactic parse tree that is tagged as a noun or noun phrase (NP). For instance, the question "Where are a cheap hotel and a Japanese restaurant near Covent Garden?" would be annotated as in Figure 3, hence the algorithm identifies *a cheap hotel* as the question focus since its pre-preterminal is the first occurring NP in the sentence's syntactic tree. The approach in [14] (henceforth *Li*) exploits the chunked textual annotation obtained via a shallow parser: the rightmost noun phrase chunk before any prepositional phrase or adjective clause is marked as the syntactic focus. For instance, the above question, chunked as in Figure 4, would have focus *a Japanese Restaurant*.

It may be noted that both methods are designed for single-focus queries, making them unfit to locate the two foci in the example (*cheap accommodation* and *a Japanese restaurant*). The fact that they are rule-based and dependent on the deep annotation of text structure makes them struggle in capturing the semantics of queries with multiple foci, a task that however is the fundamental pre-requisite in SeCo as the identification of relevant data services depends on a correct identification of NL query foci.

Indeed, when it comes to identifying a relevant data service given question terms, we can take advantage of a large body of literature in the Question Answering field that has

---

[5] A node is a pre-preterminal if all its children are preterminals, i.e. nodes with one child which is itself a leaf. In Fig. 3, the pre-preterminal of *Where* is WHADVP.

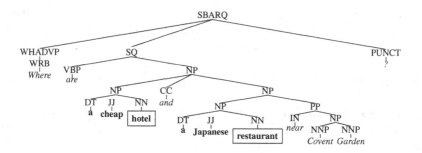

Fig. 3. Syntactic parse tree of "Where are a cheap hotel and a Japanese restaurant near Covent Garden?". Foci are in boldface with focus heads boxed.

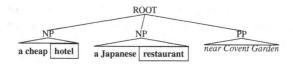

Fig. 4. Shallow syntactic parse tree of "Where are a cheap hotel and a Japanese restaurant near Covent Garden?"

effectively applied machine learning approaches joined with lexical and shallow syntactic features to *question classification* [15]. We pursue a similar direction in Section 5.3, as our classification problem is analogous; however, in this case we first need to account for questions characterized by multiple foci, i.e. to deal with the problem of splitting questions based on the span of their foci and then matching each sub-question to a data service class (*question segmentation*).

Finally, the identification of relevant query attributes in order to route the query to the most appropriate service is an information extraction problem; different methods exist for this, for example using open-domain tools (e.g. Named Entity recognizers) for the identification of instances of generic entities or applying rule-based methods for domain-specific extraction. We illustrate a number of these approaches in Section 5.4.

5   Natural Language Models for Query Analysis

We now illustrate the natural language processing methods applied in SeCo at each phase of the NL query analysis process outlined in Section 3.

5.1   Focus Extraction

As illustrated in Section 4, a number of focus extraction methods exploit regularities in the syntactic structure of natural language queries [6,14]. In particular, the syntactic analysis of submitted questions is carried out using two different kinds of structure, i.e. deep syntactic trees, and shallow parsing. However, as anticipated earlier, these methods yield good results when dealing with single focus queries, but are ineffective at handling questions with multiple foci, as illustrated in our experiments (Sec. 7). This suggests that relying too heavily on question syntax becomes more challenging as data quality deteriorates (as e.g. in Web queries) and the complexity of the question increases.

To contrast this issue, we propose to combine the extraction of lexical and morphological annotations with the learning of robust discriminative classifiers. We train machine learning classifiers to determine whether each word w in the question is a focus syntactic head (focus head, in brief) or not. As a learning algorithm, we adopt first-order linear-chain Conditional Random Fields (CRFs), a category of probabilistic learners frequently used for labeling and segmenting structured data[6] [13]. In this context, we study different combinations of four features (validated in Section 7.1):

1. word unigrams situated within an interval of n words centered on the current word: $[-n, n]$, $n \leq 2$ (case $n = 0$ corresponds to the current word w only);
2. word Part-of-Speech (POS) tags taken in the same interval[7];
3. word bigrams, i.e. sequences of two consecutive words comprising the current word w (i.e. taken in the interval $[-1, 1]$ with respect to w);
4. POS bigrams in the same interval.

5.2 Question Segmentation

The segmentation of a question q into its subqueries q_i, $i \in \{1, .., n\}$ is not trivial. As an example, the simplest approach that splits q based on its conjunctions may lead to unintended results if the latter connect terms that belong to the same segment ("bed and breakfast"). For these reasons, we also investigate a machine learning approach to question segmentation that consists in learning a binary classifier that, given a word w, determines whether w is situated at the beginning of a new segment or not. An intuitive criterion to make this distinction appears to be the word neighborhood: for instance, the absence of a previous word is a useful indicator for the beginning of a segment. POS tags are also potentially useful features, as e.g. a conjunction (CC tag) is a strong indicator of the presence of a new sub-query. To leverage the above criteria, we adopt the features devised for focus extraction (see Section 5.1) – i.e. word and POS unigrams and bigrams – to build a binary CRF classifier for sub-question identification. Our results are reported in Section 7.2.

5.3 (Sub)Question Classification

Starting from a multi-domain question and given a taxonomy of available services as labels (e.g. *Cinema*, *Hotel*), the goal of question classification is to map each subquery q_i of a question q to its most likely label c_i.

The (sub)question classification problem is different from the problem of labeling a question word w as "focus" or "subquestion starter" in various respects: not only we are dealing with a multi-classification problem, the boundaries of q_i are known from

---

[6] CRFs are undirected graphical models that define a conditional probability distribution over label sequences given a particular observation sequence, rather than a joint distribution over both label and observation sequences.

[7] Obtained via the OpenNLP toolkit, opennlp.sourceforge.net

previous steps (this task relies heavily on an accurate segmentation of q), and finally long-distance relationships between words are potentially useful.

We therefore conduct the classification task using a different discriminative approach, i.e. the learning of Support Vector Machine classifiers (SVMs), based on the set of previously split questions. A binary classifier is built for each question class, and results are combined according to a one-vs-all regime in order to assign the strongest label c_i to each subquery q_i. To account for data sparsity given the potentially high number of labels, we only study two types of features:

1. the bag-of-words (BOW) feature, consisting of all the words in q_i (stemmed following [17] for sparsity reduction);
2. the FOCUS feature, representing q_i's focus head.

As explained in Section 7.3, these are combined by summing linear kernel functions.

5.4   Intent Modifier Extraction

The final step in understanding the user question is the identification of relevant terms expressing constraints for the logical query – *intent modifiers*; these include locations, dates, proper nouns and (optionally) other domain-specific attributes. Recognizing intent modifiers guides the choice of a specific access pattern over another: for instance, identifying a location instance in a question classified as *Cinema* might result in choosing to route the query to an AP returning cinemas based on their location rather than one returning cinemas based on movie titles.

SeCo scenarios cover heterogenous domains and applications encompassing a wide variety of entity types; we focused on the effective recognition of the generic types of entities using domain-independent approaches. We here illustrate our location extraction models as a representative case of intent modifier extraction: locations are not only among the most widespread named entities, but also the most challenging as they often require disambiguation, e.g. distinguishing between New York as a city or a state.

An obvious choice for location recognition is to use statistical NER systems, such as LingPipe[8]: however, these identify entities at a coarse-grained level, hence cities, countries or states fall under the generic label "Location". Therefore, additional methods may be needed to refine the classification.

We also considered methods based on lexicon lookup, building gazetteers based on instances extracted from GeoNames[9] for both cities and countries, addressing the identification of these entities by looking for exact or approximate matching (for the latter case, we consider an edit distance-based similarity exceeding 0.75 as a match).

The disambiguation issue is addressed by the use of *wikifiers*, i.e. tools that annotate phrases in text in terms of relevant Wikipedia page by disambiguating amongst alternatives based on the distribution of hyperlinks to Wikipedia pages. Our choice fell on TagMe [7], due to its robustness to short and badly structured text; we connected annotations output by TagMe to entities in the YAGO reference knowledge base [19] (most of which refer to Wikipedia via the *hasWikipediaURL* property) in order to e.g. identify entities of type *yagoGeoEntity* as locations.

---

[8] `alias-i.com/lingpipe`
[9] `geonames.org`

To evaluate the methods outlined in this section, we have used a number of datasets described in Section 6; evaluation results are reported in Section 7.

6 Experimental Datasets

To align with the literature, we experiment with a number of single-domain query sets; moreover, in order to validate our algorithms for focus extraction on multi-domain queries, we produced an ad-hoc dataset.

6.1 Single-Domain Query Datasets

To experiment with focus identification in single-domain queries and compare to previous work, we adopt the well-known **GeoQuery** and **RestQuery** datasets[10]. These contain queries dealing with geographical entities and restaurant search, respectively; such queries have been manually created for the purpose of validating the mapping of natural language to logical query languages [9]. In particular, [6] resulted in a manual annotation of foci in 200 GeoQuery queries, which is the reference in our focus extraction experiments (Section 7.1).

In addition, to experiment with spontaneous Web user queries on a topic compatible with the SeCo project, we collected a dataset, **Y!Answer**, that consists of 50 questions retrieved from the Dining Out section of Yahoo! Answers[11]. These genuine user queries are often ungrammatical or syntactically ill-formed: they exhibit ellipsis ("Sri Lankan ethnic restaurant in UK?") and/or colloquial style ("What is the ultimate place to go with your date in winter London, not that pricy also :)?"). Thus, they form a good candidate dataset to investigate the possible shortcomings of syntax-based methods, otherwise found to be useful in more controlled corpora such as GeoQuery and RestQuery.

6.2 The SeCo-600 Multi-domain Query Dataset

Finally, in order to validate our algorithms (including question classification) on multi-domain queries, we produced an ad-hoc dataset, **SeCo-600** [18]. The corpus contains 600 spontaneous *multi-domain* user queries collected to fit SeCo scenarios, i.e. dealing with one of the following SeCo service marts: *Food, Cinema, Movie, Hotel, Event, Point of Interest (POI)*. Each query has been manually split into sub-queries; in turn, each sub-query has been manually tagged according to:

- its syntactic focus head (following the rules in [4]),
- one of seven classes, representing a SeCo service mart or *Other* if none applicable,
- intent modifiers drawn from the SeCo domain such as cities, ratings, titles.

The relative frequency of each class in SeCo-600 is reported in Table 4.

As SeCo-600 has been acquired from spontaneous user queries, it offers a variety of syntax, ranging from keyword-style queries ("nice hotel paris cheap events of design", "movies with Sean Connery shown in Medusa cinemas") to full-fledged natural

---

[10] cs.utexas.edu/users/ml/nldata.html
[11] answers.yahoo.com

language containing anaphora ("where could i find a wellness center in palermo and a mcdonald close to *it*?"). Moreover, as no control was exerted on query formulation, SeCo-600 contains both single-focus and multi-focus queries in different domains. In particular, 321 questions are single-focus, 254 have two foci and 15 have three foci. Note that focus extraction on this corpus is challenging as among the single-focus questions, 88 have nested intents (NI), i.e. implicit sub-requests for non-focal entities that concur in the formulation of the final result (e.g. "Are there [cinemas]$_{FOCUS}$ in Montreal that show [comedy movies]$_{NI}$ tonight?").

All question corpora have been automatically annotated with linguistic word-level features, i.e. Part-of-Speech tags, shallow syntactic chunks and syntactic parse trees using the OpenNLP framework. This ensures a fair comparison of the different models experimented in Section 7.

7   Experiments

In our NL query analysis experiments, we use all four corpora to evaluate focus extraction, while the subsequent phases are only validated on the multi-domain, multi-focus SeCo-600 corpus. The accuracy of all tasks is evaluated in terms of F1 measure, a standard information retrieval metric combining precision (P) and recall (R): $F1 = \frac{2(P*R)}{(P+R)}$. While the performance of rule-based systems is computed over the original datasets, machine learning experiments are conducted in 10-fold cross-validation to ensure the consistency of our results.

7.1   Focus Extraction

To get baseline figures for our focus extraction methods, we re-implemented the *Daml* [6] and *Li* [14] approaches and evaluated them first on the single-domain corpora for which they were designed, then on Y!Answer and finally on the SeCo-600 corpus.

As reported in Table 1, we note that method *Daml* [6] yields the best results on well-formed queries as found in e.g. GeoQuery, due to their regular structure; however, performance degrades compared to other methods on more complex corpora such as RestQuery and especially Y!Answer, which is collected from spontaneous Web queries. Method *Li* [14] tends to perform better on unstructured data such as the Y!Answer questions, due to its use of more shallow features (shallow parsing) compared to *Daml*, which relies on the sentence full parse. As expected, both methods yield poor results on SeCo-600 due to their design for single-focus questions. Indeed, even if they achieve a good precision (70.2% for *Daml* and 77.7% for *Li*), their inability to handle multi-focus questions results in 48% and 53.2% recall, respectively.

Table 1. Focus extraction F1 of rule-based approaches on four query datasets

Method	GeoQuery	RestQuery	Y!Answer	SeCo-600
Daml [6]	88.0%	89.0%	63.0%	57.0%
Li [14]	67.3%	98.0%	66.0%	63.1%

In our machine learning experiments, we used the CRF++ toolkit [12] to learn different CRF models by combining the features described in Section 5.1. A general observation concerning our models is that the baseline CRF model, i.e. the one adopting only the current word as a feature, is not sufficient by itself to outperform rule-based approaches in single-focus queries (see Table 2, row 1). This is especially true in the case of Y!Answer, where the heterogeneity of terms makes it difficult to identify foci by only considering the words. However, the linear chain topology of CRFs – a more "local" model relying less on a deep understanding of the syntax – shows its benefits in the multi-focus case (SeCo-600), where its accuracy largely exceeds the *Li* method.

Table 2. Focus extraction results: F1-measure of different CRF models

CRF Model	GeoQuery	RestQuery	Y!Answer	SeCo-600
W [0,0]	**80.4 ± 8.2**	**93.9 ± 2.0**	**39.9 ± 7.1**	**85.3 ± 3.0**
W [-2,2]	93.3 ± 4.6	98.6 ± 2.4	65.5 ± 8.5	92.4 ± 2.2
POS [0,0]	04.0 ± 6.3	48.5 ± 12.9	07.4 ± 9.3	69.9 ± 5.0
POS [-2,2]	93.3 ± 5.5	98.1 ± 3.5	74.7 ± 6.5	87.7 ± 3.0
2−W [-1,1]	88.5 ± 7.0	93.8 ± 3.5	10.1 ± 9.5	67.5 ± 4.7
W+POS [0,0]	82.1 ± 6.5	94.8 ± 2.6	58.8 ± 5.9	88.9 ± 2.7
W+POS [-2,2]	**95.1 ± 3.9**	**98.6 ± 2.4**	**77.5 ± 7.1**	**94.0 ± 1.5**

Table 2 also reports the results of CRF models with additional feature combinations. By widening the "window" of examined word unigrams, we find that the performance of our classifier progressively increases by around 10% relative in most cases (models W [-1,1] and W [-2,2]); this suggests the usefulness of considering the word neighborhood in the model. A similar finding is registered for POS tags, which in the case of the Y!Answer corpus allow us to reach an even higher result that words in the classification task (POS [-2,2] reaches 74.7% F1). It is therefore intuitive to evaluate word bigrams, however these do not yield better results than word unigrams in the same interval (Table 2, row 5). We then experiment with models joining our two best individual features, i.e. words and POS tags; our best results are obtained when combining them in the [-2,2] window centered around the current word (Table 2, last row).

To conclude, it is evident that the best CRF model is more successful than rule-based models across datasets, thanks to its robustness and the use of shallow features and their combinations, which best suit ungrammatical contexts.

7.2 Question Segmentation

As mentioned earlier, a correct identification of question subqueries plays an important role in finding the right set of services required to retrieve a relevant answer. In this section we analyze our approach to question segmentation using a CRF binary classifier. In Table 3, we show the performance of the segmentation algorithm on the only multi-focus corpus at our disposal, SeCo-600, by comparing different feature combinations.

Due to the relatively simple nature of the problem, the current word alone (W[0,0]) starts from a high F1, setting the baseline to 89.1 ± 3.5 %. By widening the unigram window up to the two previous and following words, we have a slight improvement

Table 3. Segmentation results: F1-measure of different CRF models on SeCo-600

CRF Model	F1 (%)	CRF Model	F1 (%)
W[0,0]	**89.1 ± 3.5**	POS[0,0]	88.8 ± 3.5
W[-2,2]	92.2 ± 2.7	POS[-2,2]	90.8 ± 3.0
2−W[-1,1]	70.3 ± 4.9	2−POS[-1,1]	90.5 ± 3.2
W+POS[-1,1]	**94.1 ± 3.0**	W+POS[-2,2]	93.6 ± 2.9

(see Table 3, W[-2,2]); in contrast, bigrams do not seem to yield an improvement over unigrams, suggesting the latter carry sufficient semantic information to solve the segmentation problem. Similar findings can be encountered for POS unigrams and bigrams, as illustrated in the second column of Table 3. As previously done for focus extraction, we then experiment with word and POS combinations, reaching our best results with W+POS[-1,1], which exceeds the baseline word model by 5% points.

7.3   (Sub-)Question Classification

To experiment with question classification, we used the SVM-light toolkit [8] to learn different combinations of linear kernel functions with SVMs using the SeCo-600 dataset.

We first experimented with manually segmented subqueries in order to evaluate only the classification task regardless of the question segmentation issue. As a general comment, our results are very encouraging as, despite the small training dataset, the overall classification F1 reaches 89.5% with the BOW feature and 92.7% with the addition of foci (see Table 4). A more detailed analysis suggests that:

1. class *Other* denotes a low accuracy as it is chosen whenever questions are too heterogeneous to be mapped to the remaining classes;
2. as the word *place* is strongly connected to the POI class, expressions such as "places where to eat" are erroneously classified as *POI*;
3. if a query about a specific entity type contains constraints involving other services (e.g. a cinema in proximity of a hotel), constraint terminology may lead to a wrong prediction (*Hotel* class).

The classifier trained with both BOW and FOCUS as features denotes better performance on most service classes, especially for *Cinema*, and shows a slight increase also in the *Overall* case by reaching 92.7%. As shown in Table 4, for *Hotel* and *Food*, the impact of FOCUS is negligible, while the only class resenting from this is *POI*. This can be explained by noting that, as mentioned above, *POI* often corresponds to a variety of foci: indeed, it is more affected by lexical ambiguity than the other classes, as its foci are often expressed with deliberately ambiguous terms in order to find more results.

However, the real benchmark of sub-question classification is its application in cascade to automatic segmentation. To evaluate the results of this task with respect to the reference annotation where question boundaries may vary, we align question class hypothesis *at the word level* with reference word labels available in the annotated SeCo-600 corpus. Label sequence alignment is evaluated by using `sclite`[12].

---

[12] Cf. NIST Speech Recognition Scoring Toolkit, `itl.nist.gov/iad/mig/tools/`

Table 4. Question Classification F1 on SeCo-600 (+ stands for sum of kernels)

Class	Frequency	BOW	BOW+FOCUS	Class	Frequency	BOW	BOW+FOCUS
Hotel	22.8%	89.8 ± 8.6	90.4 ± 8.1	*Event*	10.6%	95.8 ± 6.5	96.1 ± 6.0
Food	19.4%	96.2 ± 4.2	96.7 ± 3.7	*Cinema*	12.6%	84.5 ± 12.6	97.3 ± 4.2
Other	15%	89.9 ± 7.6	92.0 ± 6.6	*Movie*	8.3%	86.1 ± 15.3	95.1 ± 7.7
POI	11.3%	82.2 ± 10.7	80.7 ± 11.9	*Overall*		$\mathbf{89.5 \pm 4.2}$	$\mathbf{92.7 \pm 3.1}$

Table 5 shows the results obtained by joining the best segmentation model found in Section 7.2 (W+POS [-1,1]) with question classifiers trained using both BOW and BOW + FOCUS as models. Alignment accuracy with respect to the reference annotation[13] is reported both at the granularity of full questions and sub-questions. Question accuracy reaches 91.8% in BOW and BOW+FOCUS alike, subquestion accuracy reaches 83.4 $\pm$ 4.5% with BOW and 82.8 $\pm$ 3.4% with BOW + FOCUS. Although the performance of the latter model is not significantly inferior to BOW, we note that the former does not provide the expected improvement, either: this may be attributed to automatic segmentation errors, after which the contribution of focus extraction may be less effective. Also note that accuracy decreases when measured at the sub-question granularity with respect to question-level accuracy: indeed, erroneous alignment occurring with multi-focus questions makes errors count at least double at the sub-question granularity.

Table 5. Question Classification accuracy on automatic segmentation - SeCo-600

Instance granularity	Total instances	BOW	BOW+FOCUS
Question	600	91.8 ± 0.0	91.8 ± 0.0
Sub-question	888	83.4 ± 4.5	82.8 ± 3.4

7.4 Intent Modifier Extraction

Intent modifier extraction results for instances of *Location* are reported in Table 6. We note that while approaches based on general-purpose statistical NER systems such as LingPipe result in an F1 around 65% and the GeoNames-based approach has similar error rates, the TagMe approach described in Section 5.4 yields slightly higher results leading to the best score of 69.4%: this may be reconnected to the higher recall offered by a robust method referring to Wikipedia as a source of relevant entities.

Table 6. Intent Modifier extraction on the SeCo-600 corpus: *Location* entity

Method	Precision	Recall	F1
Lexicon lookup (edit distance threshold = 0.75)	79.0%	54.7%	64.7%
Statistical NER (Lingpipe)	71.0%	60.2%	65.2%
TagMe + YAGO validation (rho = 0.1)	**74.4%**	**65.0%**	**69.4%**

---

[13] We report alignment accuracy as returned by `sclite`, i.e. inverse error rate, instead of F1.

8 Conclusions

In this chapter, we address the requirements of natural language interfaces to data services. We build on the service framework developed in the context of the SeCo project [2] to support complex, multi-domain queries on data services. We investigate the basic requirements and methods for analyzing *natural language* queries over data service combinations using the afore-mentioned service framework.

Since related work highlights the shortcomings of rule-based approaches and deep syntactic analysis for the interpretation of multi-domain queries, we propose machine learning models based on Conditional Random Fields and Support Vector Machines and use a number of linguistic features to train classifiers to approach the above problems. Our results denote very high accuracy on all query analysis tasks, exceeding state-of-the-art results on well-known datasets and performing well on an ad-hoc multi-domain question dataset we have collected. In future work, we will continue our research on natural language query processing over data services by performing an end-to-end evaluation of query analysis in the SeCo project.

Acknowledgments. Work partly funded by the Search Computing project, EC IDEAS grant no. 227793.

References

1. Bozzon, A., Brambilla, M., Ceri, S., Della Valle, E., Quarteroni, S.: Understanding web data sources for search and exploration. In: IJCAI Workshop on Discovering Meaning on the Go in Large Heterogeneous Data (LHD 2011), p. 67 (2011)
2. Bozzon, A., Braga, D., Brambilla, M., Ceri, S., Corcoglioniti, F., Fraternali, P., Vadacca, S.: Search computing: Multi-domain search on ranked data. In: Proceedings of SIGMOD (2011)
3. Brambilla, M., Campi, A., Ceri, S., Quarteroni, S.: Semantic Resource Framework. In: Ceri, S., Brambilla, M. (eds.) Search Computing II. LNCS, vol. 6585, pp. 73–84. Springer, Heidelberg (2011)
4. Collins, M.: Head-driven statistical models for natural language parsing. Ph.D. thesis, University of Pennsylvania (1999)
5. Damljanovic, D., Agatonovic, M., Cunningham, H.: Natural Language Interfaces to Ontologies: Combining Syntactic Analysis and Ontology-Based Lookup through the User Interaction. In: Aroyo, L., Antoniou, G., Hyvönen, E., ten Teije, A., Stuckenschmidt, H., Cabral, L., Tudorache, T. (eds.) ESWC 2010, Part I. LNCS, vol. 6088, pp. 106–120. Springer, Heidelberg (2010)
6. Damljanovic, D., Agatonovic, M., Cunningham, H.: Natural language interfaces to ontologies: Combining syntactic analysis and ontology-based lookup through the user interaction. In: Proceedings of LREC (2010)
7. Ferragina, P., Scaiella, U.: Tagme: on-the-fly annotation of short text fragments (by wikipedia entities). In: Proceedings of CIKM 2010, pp. 1625–1628. ACM, New York (2010)
8. Joachims, T.: Making large-scale support vector machine learning practical, pp. 169–184. MIT Press, Cambridge (1999)
9. Kate, R., Mooney, R.: Using string-kernels for learning semantic parsers. In: Proceedings of ACL, pp. 913–920. ACL (2006)

10. Kaufmann, E., Bernstein, A.: How Useful Are Natural Language Interfaces to the Semantic Web for Casual End-Users? In: Aberer, K., Choi, K.-S., Noy, N., Allemang, D., Lee, K.-I., Nixon, L.J.B., Golbeck, J., Mika, P., Maynard, D., Mizoguchi, R., Schreiber, G., Cudré-Mauroux, P. (eds.) ASWC 2007/ISWC 2007. LNCS, vol. 4825, pp. 281–294. Springer, Heidelberg (2007)
11. Kaufmann, E.: Talking to the Semantic Web - Query Interfaces to Ontologies for the Casual User. In: Cruz, I., Decker, S., Allemang, D., Preist, C., Schwabe, D., Mika, P., Uschold, M., Aroyo, L.M. (eds.) ISWC 2006. LNCS, vol. 4273, pp. 980–981. Springer, Heidelberg (2006)
12. Kudo, T.: CRF++: Yet another CRF toolkit (2005), crfpp.sourceforge.net
13. Lafferty, J., McCallum, A., Pereira, F.: Conditional random fields: probabilistic models for segmenting and labeling sequence data. In: Proc. ICML, pp. 282–289 (2001)
14. Li, X.: Understanding the semantic structure of noun phrase queries. In: Proceedings of ACL, pp. 1337–1345. ACL (2010)
15. Li, X., Roth, D.: Learning question classifiers. In: Proceedings of ACL (2002)
16. Lim, J., Lee, K.: Constructing composite web services from natural language requests. Web Semantics: Science, Services and Agents on the World Wide Web 8(1), 1–13 (2010)
17. Porter, M.: An algorithm for suffix stripping. Program: Electronic Library and Information Systems 14(3), 130–137 (1980)
18. Quarteroni, S., Guerrisi, V., La Torre, P.: Evaluating multi-focus natural language queries over data services. In: Proceedings of LREC (2012)
19. Suchanek, F., Kasneci, G., Weikum, G.: Yago: a core of semantic knowledge. In: Proceedings of WWW, pp. 697–706. ACM (2007)
20. Wang, C., Xiong, M., Zhou, Q., Yu, Y.: PANTO: A Portable Natural Language Interface to Ontologies. In: Franconi, E., Kifer, M., May, W. (eds.) ESWC 2007. LNCS, vol. 4519, pp. 473–487. Springer, Heidelberg (2007)

Mobile Multi-domain Search
over Structured Web Data

Atakan Aral[1], Ilker Zafer Akin[2], and Marco Brambilla[2]

[1] Department of Computer Engineering,
Istanbul Technical University, Istanbul, Turkey
`aralat@itu.edu.tr`
[2] Dipartimento di Elettronica e Informazione, Politecnico di Milano, Milano, Italy
`ilker.akin@mail.polimi.it, mbrambil@elet.polimi.it`

Abstract. So far, web search applications have been primarily designed for access through personal computers, because this represented by far the most widespread usage scenario. However, the wider and wider adoption of web-enabled smartphones, tablets and embedded devices are opening completely new scenarios for applying search technologies in everyday life of people. In this paper we propose an approach and a concrete architecture for optimizing exploratory search tasks on mobile devices. Our claim is that new search paradigms may let users conduct the search on small devices without being hampered by the limitations of the devices themselves. Even better, appropriate solutions may also exploit the advantages of such devices for further improving the overall search experience.

Keywords: Web search, mobile application, multi-domain search, search computing, exploratory search.

1 Introduction

Nowadays search is the key activity of web browsing. While basic text-based search had been acceptable until recently, technological advances such as broadband internet connectivity, device mobility and trends such as Web 2.0 and semantic web have led to higher expectations in the users. Web integrates to our daily life more than ever with the introduction of smart phones and tablet PC's. The Web has become pervasive in the everyday life of people, and search seems to remain one of the main information finding paradigms. However, search on mobile systems also has different focus and peculiar requirements with respect to search on traditional computing systems. Mobile search allows users to search for information anywhere and anytime, moreover search experience can be enriched with location data which is made available by most mobile devices. On the other hand, factors such as screen size and input method complicate the search process. It is essential for search to evolve to keep up with the mobile migration that offers both new opportunities and threats. The paramount difference is that people typically look for utility information on concepts and on geo-located entities, more than web pages.

S. Ceri and M. Brambilla (Eds.): Search Computing III, LNCS 7538, pp. 98–110, 2012.
© Springer-Verlag Berlin Heidelberg 2012

In this paper, we aim to propose an exploratory search paradigm specifically targeted to design and implementation of search applications for mobile settings. The issues discussed here cover roughly four areas: mobile application design, multi-domain search, exploratory search and enhanced presentation of results.

Multi-domain search is about handling data coming from different semantic fields of interest, so as to accomplish complex information seeking tasks.

Exploratory search proposes that user should be aided in formulating his/her interest, in exploring most relevant and credited information sources and in correlating the elements of those sources. These can be accomplished by asking the user to choose a topic then specialize on the topic and information sources step by step, and finally asking for input data specific to that sub-topic. It is also possible to offer results from related topics during or after the search process in order to allow user enhance the query. Exploratory search comes into prominence especially while using mobile devices as it allows constructing more complex queries with less textual input and in shorter duration.

A natural outcome of multi-domain and exploratory search is the requirement of more advanced ways of presenting the results to the user and of interacting on such results. Result sets from different semantic fields should be treated differently and presented through different interface elements such as maps, lists or tables. Moreover, these elements should also allow users to filter and sort results according to various criteria as well as further specify their query.

Our focus is the exploration of applicable solutions for recent and innovative ideas on web search including mobile search, multi-domain search and exploratory search. We also intend to demonstrate how such solutions can work together in order to enhance and ease search process for complex needs on mobile devices and what kind of user interface elements can be used to support them. Moreover, a practical application of the discussed solutions is presented to clarify technical issues.

This paper is structured as follows: Section 2 summarizes the related work in the fields addressed by our study; Section 3 explains our proposed ideas for the topics explained here as well as illustrating how these ideas were implemented in a web based mobile application. Finally, remaining two sections conclude the solutions and discuss future research directions respectively.

2   Related Work

Web search is a thoroughly researched field. In this section, we mainly focus on describing the basic studies in three sub-fields: multi-domain exploratory search, search computing, and mobile application design.

2.1   Multi-domain and Exploratory Search

Multi-domain queries are defined as queries that are over more than one semantic fields of interest [1]. Some domain-specific search engines exist but they are applicable to only one domain. Multi-domain search engines, on the other hand, intend to automatically combine the results of domain-specific searches and provide answers originating from various domains. Without multi-domain search, only expert users can access such an answer by conducting individual searches on different domain-specific search engines and manually combining findings, which is an exhausting and time-consuming work.

A Model for the search process by a multi-domain search engine is described by Bozzon et al. [2]. It begins with query submission, proceeds with query computation and ends with result visualization. In query computation phase, which is on our focus in this sub-section, search engine first needs to identify one or more domains referred in the query. In their approach, domains are predefined and each domain has a set of attributes to define it. In addition, there are domain-specific sub-engines for each domain and they are invoked when a query is identified to be related to that domain. Thus, a multi-domain search engine can be considered as an integration of many domain-specific search engines.

Marchionini [3] introduced the idea of exploratory search which "blends querying and browsing strategies from retrieval that is best served by analytical strategies". He categorized search activities into three overlapping groups: (1) Lookup search where the user simply needs "fact retrieval" or "question answering" and the returned answers are discrete and well-structured; (2) Learn search that returns objects in various media forms and used for cognitive processes such as examining, comparing and making judgments; (3) Investigate search that takes longest time and includes critical assessment of results. While current systems are quite adequate in answering lookup search queries, latter two groups require more human participation. Exploratory search aims to include more human interaction into the search process by means of interactive user interfaces.

In a recent application of exploratory search [4], user begins the search process with an initial topic and then progressively develops it by discovering his/her needs and exploring additional related information. To achieve this, user selects the initial topic from a list and inputs a query. Then, among the top ranked results displayed for that query, user chooses the one he/she is most interested in and the system offers additional related topics to explore. Development of the result set continues with the topic the user selected and this time results are ranked considering previously chosen results as well.

A new paradigm called, Liquid Query [1] is proposed for multi-domain and exploratory search over structured information sources. It aims to allow searchers to develop their query by adding another search service, requesting more results specifically from a certain search service, ordering or filtering results, changing the visualization type etc. in order to get closer to the desired information step by step. While the user makes such changes in the query, result set dynamically accommodates to the modified query.

2.2   Search Computing

Goal of the Search Computing (SeCo) Project is to construct a platform to address multi-domain queries by integrating various search services [5]. SeCo provides an alternative to the conventional web crawling and indexing techniques of horizontal search engines that are not adequate for multi-domain search [1].

Architecture of the SeCo system, described by Brambilla and Ceri [6], contains two activity flows: (1) Registration flow is used by administrators and responsible for the addition and configuration of domains and search services, (2) Execution flow is used by final users and processes the queries. As the domains and related search services are entered by the administrator, and they are chosen by users, automatically identifying domains from the user query is not a concern in SeCo applications.

Two-tier (client and server tiers) and three-layer structure of the SeCo is explained by Bozzon et al. [4] and Campi et al. [7]. At the conceptual level, web objects or domains are represented by Service Marts which hide the underlying physical structure and provide a simple interface. A Service Mart has a name and both atomic and repeating attributes. Each attribute can be input or output depending on which Access Pattern is used at the logical level. A Service Mart may have multiple Access Patterns. Finally, there are Service Interfaces at the physical level and they mapped to specific concrete data sources. As an example, Cinema Service Mart may have name, address, city, country atomic attributes and movies repeating group. Name attribute may be an input value in one access pattern to allow user search by name. Same attribute can also be an output value in another Access Pattern where the user searches by address, city and country inputs. Under each Access Pattern there may be multiple Service Interfaces which are mapped to search services (such as IMDb.com or Yahoo! Movies) supporting that combination of inputs and outputs. Another notion to allow combination of Service Marts is Connection Patterns. A Connection Pattern is characterized by two coupled Service Marts and the logical connection between their attributes. A Cinema and a Restaurant can be related in a Connection Pattern according to their geographic proximity by having the same values for country, city and address attributes.

2.3   Search Interfaces and Mobile Applications

In her book [8], Hearst provided a comprehensive background research about mobile search interfaces and proposed dynamic term suggestion, query anticipation and spoken queries to overcome input difficulty in mobile devices. In addition, presenting alternative visualization methods for certain types of results (for example, map for results containing location data) is encouraged.

In addition to the mobile device issues, multi-domain search adds other challenges to the visualization problem [9]. One important factor is that, search results do not have to correspond to a web page and it may be a combination of objects from the web. As a consequence, result set for multi-domain query can be highly dimensional. Scheme of their proposed solution for these problems can be summarized in four steps: (1) Most relevant dimension is chosen. (2) Best visualization method for that dimension is identified. (3) All dimensions that are applicable for that method are visualized. (4) Repeat for the remaining dimensions. They exemplify their approach with map view for geo-referenced objects,

timeline view for time-located objects, and other methods when suitable interval
dimensions are not available.

Church et al. [10] examined seven mobile search engines and argued that
simply applying traditional query-based search and list-based result presentation
in mobile cases is not optimal. They proposed an approach aiming to generate
shorter but more informative result snippet texts by making use of terms from
previous queries that have led to the selection of that result. They also evaluated
their approach on a user base and validated usefulness of it. In our approach we
take into careful consideration the conceptual results highlighted by this study.

3   Mobile Exploratory Search over Multi-domain Data

In this section, we discuss our solution to the problem of search over structured
web data performed on mobile devices, with the aim of increasing usability and
functionality of mobile search.

3.1   Requirements

The peculiar aspect of this research is that most of the changes in the requirements apply on the non-functional requirement side, while the functional ones
basically remain unchanged with respect to traditional exploratory search and
visualization of structured Web data.

First requirement we want to satisfy is that the application should work on
mobile devices such as smart phones and tablet computers. Compatibility for
most kinds of devices and multiple browsers is also a desired feature.

In terms of multi-domain and exploratory search requirements, the application
should be able to search for combinational results from multiple semantic fields
in an incremental fashion and should guide the user during query development.

User should be able to visualize search results in multiple, customized perspectives in order to determine the best result for him/her. Moreover, the application
should also be capable of storing linked results from various semantic fields and
presenting to the user clearly.

Finally, the user interface should be as natural as possible since the main
target of the application is the end user. It should be straightforward enough
to search in a domain, examine the results, and combine them with another
domain. Visualizations and navigation paradigms must fit with the limited size
of the screen and with the interaction paradigms of mobile systems. In particular,
despite of the need of combining concepts, the system must allow the user to
see lists of instances of one entity at a time, select one instance and continue
the exploration by aggregating additional items to the selected one. Multiple
exploration paths, that could be possible in an extended user interface for a PC
screen, should be disabled in this case.

Actors, their actions and dependencies are described by the Use Case diagram
in Figure 1.

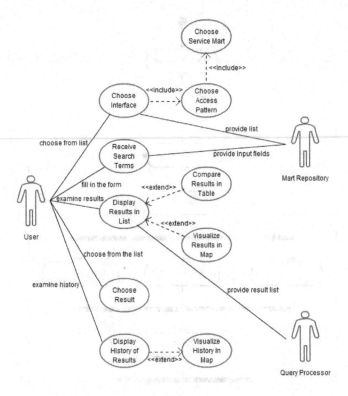

Fig. 1. Use Case diagram summarizing the scenarios for mobile exploratory search

3.2   Interaction Paradigm

The overall picture of the user interaction upon the application can be considered as a potentially unlimited loop of connected domain-specific searches. The user searches for a result from a single domain, selects one item of interest at the current step, and then moves to selecting an item from a connected domain. Obviously, previously chosen results from other domains affect the extraction of the current result set.

More in detail, the interaction paradigm proceeds as follows described in Figure 2 and comprises the following macro-phases:

1. As a first step the user decides which domain his initial search belongs to, by which input he will search and which information source will be used. The notions of Service Marts, Access Patterns and Service Interfaces defined in Search Computing are used in the application in a top-down approach: the search process starts by identifying the initial domain by choosing a Service Mart from the list. Next steps are choosing an Access Pattern for that selected Service Mart and subsequently a Service Interface for the chosen Access Pattern.
2. Then, the user enters the input data according to the expected input parameter for the selected Service Interface and thus submits the initial query.

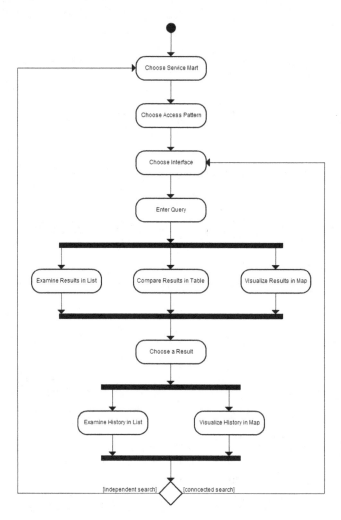

Fig. 2. Activity diagram summarizing the interaction paradigm for the mobile exploratory search application

Indeed, instead of presenting a generic free-text field for specifying the search criteria, every Access Pattern has its own structured input parameters. For instance, an Access Pattern to search for restaurants by location should typically have at least street, city and country input attributes and they are displayed as separate input fields.

3. Once the query is performed, the results are shown to the user, who in turn examines the result set, possibly compares two or more items in detail or looks at the results in a map, and finally decides which result is the most interesting for him.

4. After the user selects a result from the result set, exploration towards other domains can begin. The user is presented with the domains related with

the initial domain as defined in Connection Patterns. It is possible to add these domains to the query by following the same steps as the initial domain. However, results of the query on the new domain will also depend on the results selected from the existing domains and the pairwise Connection Pattern definitions between existing domains and the additional domain.

5. The same operations should be carried out at each step until the user includes all the domains to the query and is satisfied with the chosen results. In this way, user may combine as many domains as he desires and improve his query one domain at a time.

6. In between each step, the user is presented with an overview of the ongoing multi-domain search. This overview is stored for later reference or modification until the user discards it to launch a new search. This enables full fledged navigation of the exploration history.

To illustrate this mechanism with a sample query, let us assume that the user wants to answer question: "Where can I find a Cinema in Paris that has Titanic on display with a good, nearby Chinese restaurant". One way to build up the query is to start with the movie domain. Movies can be searched by title using the related Access Pattern and Search Interface. Once Titanic is found, user may add Cinema domain through a Connection Pattern. This Connection Pattern would allow to list cinemas that has Titanic on display. User should also enter Paris as the city input to filter results. After the user decides which cinema to go, he/she may add another domain for the restaurants possibly connected to cinema by distance. Chinese kitchen can be used an input, while rating should be the ranking criteria to display "good" restaurants only. Final step of the search would be to choose the best restaurant from the list. One should note that, these example steps are only one to find the best solution.

Notice that the above described interaction paradigm, also shown in Figure 2, implies strong limitations with respect to the full potentials of exploration that could be exploited in complex search interfaces:

- At every exploration step, the user is shown only homogeneous results coming from *only one* domain of interest. No combinations, aggregations or heterogeneous results can be seen.
- At every exploration step, the user can select *only one* item of interest.
- At every exploration step, the user can select only one exploration path along the connections starting from the last entity explored.
- Alternatively, the user can either (i) restart the exploration from scratch or (ii) move back in the exploration history in one of the previous steps.

These limitations aim at coping with the size of the mobile screens, with the expected simplicity of the interaction paradigms, and with the pragmatic attitude of the user that typically has simpler information needs while on the move.

For completeness, Figure 2 shows the detailed navigation map supported by our approach.

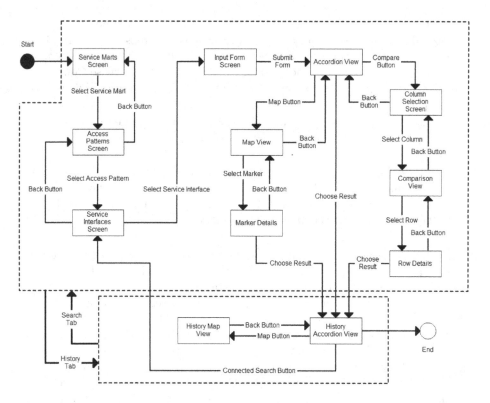

Fig. 3. Statechart diagram of the application, describing all the detailed user interaction steps

3.3 Presentation of Results

Screen size and resolution limitations preclude usage of wide tables to display all output attributes of results. Number of these attributes, hence columns of the table, can easily exceed 10 for most domains. However, showing this kind of data structure is not viable on small devices. Therefore, we define the concept of "main output attribute", defined for each domain and pointing to the most important output attribute of the domain. Instances of such attribute should be self-explaining, should carry commonly understood meaning for users and should more or less uniquely identify the results. Some examples of main output attribute are: *Title* for *News* domain, *Street address* for *Real estate domain*, *Name* for *Restaurant* domain, and so on.

Three result views, that can be seen in Figure 4, are offered and implemented to tackle the visualization issue.

Default view for all domains is the *accordion view* which can be seen from Figure 4(a). It allocates one line space for each results and displays only their main output attribute and score. When the user wants to know more about a result, it is possible to tap on the record to slide down values of all output attributes. Accordion view lets the user to see maximum number of results in

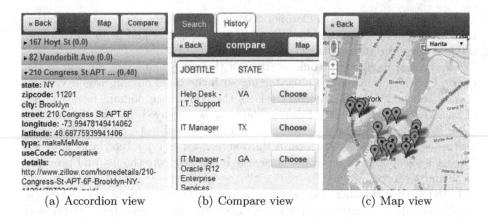

(a) Accordion view   (b) Compare view   (c) Map view

Fig. 4. Screen captures from the application for three result views

a small screen with the possibility of accessing details without screen change. It can also be used for multi-domain data in the list called history where the results selected from different domains are displayed.

While accordion view gives all details about one result at a time, it does not let user display details of multiple results at the same time. Such functionality is especially useful when the user needs to compare results according to certain criteria, for instance to compare the prices of a real estate result set. *Comparison view* is available for all domains as a secondary presentation method as seen in Figure 4(b). When the user switches to comparison view, he/she is first presented with a list containing the names of all output attributes for that domain. User chooses which attribute to use in comparison and the second screen is displayed. Second screen consists of a 2-column table for main attribute and selected comparison attribute. Each record of the result set occupies one row of the table. Comparison view cannot be used for multi-domain data as the output attributes of different domains would not always fit.

Map view (Figure 4(c)) is only available for domains with location data i.e. those with latitude and longitude information in their output attributes. In map view, each result is represented with a marker on a map initially centered and zoomed to make maximum number of results visible. If the user device provides GPS location information, another marker for the user position is added. It is possible to scroll, zoom in and out in map view using multi-touch gestures like swipe, pinch or double tap. Similar to the accordion view, map view can also be used for multi-domain data in history list as long as at least one of the domains containing location data. Domains without location data shall not be displayable using the map view.

4 An Example Scenario

This section aims at demonstrating the interaction process by listing the exploration steps performed to answer a sample multi-domain query such as: "Find a good database conference in October 2012 in Milan, Italy, with accommodation in a 5-star hotel with reasonable price". (The reader may find it useful to follow the flow from the statechart diagram given in Figure 3.)

The typical navigation would start with the most significant domain of the query: Conference, although also starting with the hotel domain would yield to a good solution as well. The user selects the conference domain from the list of Service Marts and a list of Access Patterns is displayed. Let us assume that there is an Access Pattern to query conferences by subject and date. Once the user selects that Access Pattern, a third screen for Service Interfaces is given. The user selects one of the conference search engines from the list and proceeds to the next screen.

In the input form where the user is asked for the search criteria, the user enters "Database" and "October" into the subject and date fields respectively and submits the form. Results for the first query are then displayed in the accordion view ranked by rating. User may also visualize results in a map or compare results in the comparison view to find the top conferences in Milan. When the user is decided about the conference, he chooses it by tapping on the related button.

Every time user chooses a result, the history tab is activated. In history tab, user may see an accordion list of previously selected results from each domain. Only one result from each domain can be chosen and the rows of the accordion list contain domain names. When a row is expanded, buttons for connected domains are listed in addition to the details of the result. User taps on a button to initiate the connected search and add another domain. Let us assume that there is a Connection Pattern between conference and hotel domains by location. Once clicked, the input form for the second search is displayed and connected fields (latitude, longitude, city, etc.) are automatically filled with the data coming from the selected conference. The user enters star preference and price range and submits the form. Again, the user chooses the preferred hotel through one of the three view modes, and therefore the history tab is displayed. In the history tab, the user may remove a domain, add a new connected domain, or visualize all the results on the map until he/she is content with the outcome. In this scenario, the query concludes here, with the selected conference and hotel stored in the history list.

5   Implementation

Web search, as the name suggests, conventionally carried out in web pages through a browser instead of standalone applications. This allows users to visit web pages linked among the results in the same context and without switching to the browser. We follow the convention in order to ensure that the user searches in a natural way on their mobile browsers. [1]

---

[1] More about the technical details can be found in the M.Sc. thesis by Akin and Aral [11].

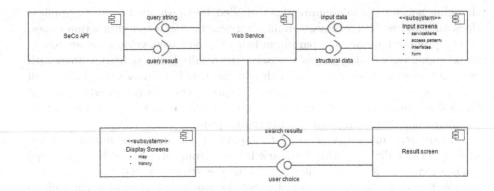

Fig. 5. Component diagram of the application

At the purpose of validating the concepts described in this paper, we implemented our exploratory search application as a web application optimized for mobile devices and browsers. This choice is motivated by the need of avoiding development of multiple device-specific native applications, as well as by the possibility of exploiting the new opportunities provided by HTML5 and client-side technologies such as JavaScript, AJAX, and CSS. These technologies allow web-based applications to make use of most features of mobile devices like GPS -based geo-location, camera, and other sensors. Moreover, web-based mobile applications work cross-device, which redeems developers from the complexity of developing native applications for each device.

A domain specific language for developing mobile web applications called mobl [12] is chosen to speed up building the application. Mobl is a statically typed language that integrates all aspects of the application: data modeling, user interfaces, application logic, graphical styling and interaction with web services. Mobl projects generate static HTML5, JavaScript, and CSS files as output. The generated application is standard-compliant and therefore is supported by most mobile devices and browsers.

The application is organized in four main subsystems, as reported in Figure 5: the set of input screens, where users can submit their selections in terms of Service Marts, Access Patterns, and Service Interfaces, as well as the inputs required by the invoked search services; a set of result screens, comprising the accordion and comparison view; a set of display screens, currently covering the map and history visualizations; and the Web Service invocation module, which interacts with the Search Computing APIs for retrieving the list of available services and for querying them.

6   Conclusion and Future Work

This paper proposes a solution for multi-domain search and exploratory search performed on mobile devices. The study mainly focused on addressing the changing non-functional requirements implied by the move to mobile applications and devices. These aspects mainly concern interface and interaction issues.

The proposed application paradigm helps the user to develop complex multi-domain queries, with the aim of exploring the results from credited sources with ease and possibly associate them with one another. It increases the usability of exploratory search in mobile devices with respect to full-fledged interfaces meant for desktop usage and exploits the strengths of the mobile devices interaction paradigms by channeling them to the search process.

Effectiveness and convenience of the approach has been preliminarily evaluated by informally collecting feedback from a group of users of the prototype application. The feedback collected during the study allowed to improve the approach and led to the current state of the work. Future works will include empirical analysis studies to quantitatively evaluate ease of use, user satisfaction, precision, recall, and reproducibility of the results through surveys and semi-automated methods.

References

1. Bozzon, A., Brambilla, M., Ceri, S., Fraternali, P.: Liquid Query: Multi-Domain Exploratory Search on the Web. In: 19th International Conference on World Wide Web, pp. 161–170. ACM, New York (2010)
2. Bozzon, A., Brambilla, M., Comai, S.: A Characterization of the Layout Definition Problem for Web Search Results. In: Meersman, R., Dillon, T., Herrero, P. (eds.) OTM 2010. LNCS, vol. 6428, pp. 150–159. Springer, Heidelberg (2010)
3. Marchionini, G.: Exploratory search: from finding to understanding. Communications of the ACM 49(4), 41–46 (2006)
4. Bozzon, A., Brambilla, M., Ceri, S., Quarteroni, S.: A Framework for Integrating, Exploring, and Searching Location-Based Web Data. IEEE Internet Computing 15(6), 24–31 (2011)
5. The Search Computing Project, Politecnico di Milano, http://www.search-computing.eu/
6. Brambilla, M., Ceri, S.: Engineering Search Computing Applications: Vision and Challenges. In: 7th Joint Meeting of the European Software Engineering Conference and the ACM SIGSOFT Symposium on the Foundations of Software Engineering, pp. 365–372. ACM, New York (2009)
7. Campi, A., Ceri, S., Maesani, A., Ronchi, S.: Designing Service Marts for Engineering Search Computing Applications. In: Benatallah, B., Casati, F., Kappel, G., Rossi, G. (eds.) ICWE 2010. LNCS, vol. 6189, pp. 50–65. Springer, Heidelberg (2010)
8. Hearst, M.A.: Search User Interfaces. Morgan Kaufmann, Cambridge University Press (2009)
9. Bozzon, A., Brambilla, M., Catarci, T., Ceri, S., Fraternali, P., Matera, M.: Visualization of Multi-domain Ranked Data. In: Ceri, S., Brambilla, M. (eds.) Search Computing II. LNCS, vol. 6585, pp. 53–69. Springer, Heidelberg (2011)
10. Church, K., Smyth, B., Keane., M.T.: Evaluating Interfaces for Intelligent Mobile Search. In: International Cross-disciplinary Workshop on Web Accessibility, pp. 69–78. ACM, New York (2006)
11. Akin, I.Z., Aral, A.: Development of Mobile Search Applications over Structured Web Data through Domain Specific Modeling Languages. M.Sc. Thesis, Politecnico di Milano (2011)
12. Mobl, Delft University of Technology, http://www.mobl-lang.org/

Clustering and Labeling
of Multi-dimensional Mixed Structured Data

Marco Brambilla and Massimiliano Zanoni

Politecnico di Milano, Dipartimento di Elettronica e Informazione, 20133 Milano, Italy
{mbrambil,zanoni}@elet.polimi.it

Abstract. Cluster Analysis consists of the aggregation of data items of a given set into subsets based on some similarity properties. Clustering techniques have been applied in many fields which typically involve a large amount of complex data. This study focuses on what we call multi-domain clustering and labeling, i.e. a set of techniques for multi-dimensional structured mixed data clustering. The work consists of studying the best mix of clustering techniques that address the problem in the multi-domain setting. Considered data types are numerical, categorical and textual. All of them can appear together within the same clustering scenario. We focus on k-means and agglomerative hierarchical clustering methods based on a new distance function we define for this specific setting. The proposed approach has been validated on some real and realistic data-sets based onto college, automobile and leisure fields. Experimental data allowed to evaluate the effectiveness of the different solutions, both for clustering and labeling.

1 Introduction

Nowadays, users can access a huge amount of information through the Internet, much more than that one can examine in an entire lifetime. In this scenario, users have to face the problem of information overload. A large part of data is not available as indexed documents and web pages, but it is hidden in the so-called *Deep Web*[1]. Deep web refers to contents hidden behind HTML forms; normally made up of domain specific databases, dynamic content, unlinked content, private web, contextual web, limited access content, scripted content, non-HTML/text content. Information in the deep Web basically consists of multi-domain structured data, which is hard to integrate and consume, due to its size, diversity and heterogeneity. One possible way to tackle these difficulties in accessing deep Web data is to apply knowledge discovery techniques for clustering the available items and therefore making it easier for users to quickly identify the areas of interest for them.

Data clustering is a categorization technique that can be defined as a method of creating groups of objects, called *clusters*, in such a way that objects in one cluster are very similar and objects in different clusters are different. Data Clustering is a so-called *unsupervised* data mining technique since the requester is not precisely aware of which and how many clusters he is looking for, what plays a role in forming these clusters, and how it does that. Clustering is a very broad problem, which can be applied to many fields. For that reason it has been addressed extensively. Despite there is no uniform definition for data clustering and there could exist a specific set of effective methods

S. Ceri and M. Brambilla (Eds.): Search Computing III, LNCS 7538, pp. 111–126, 2012.

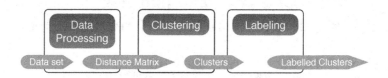

Fig. 1. Clustering Overall Scheme

for each problem family to solve [2]. Data clustering is widely used in web search: it is typically applied to documents and web pages in order to group items by typology[1].

This work is a first attempt in applying clustering techniques to multi-domain structured data generated as query result sets over deep Web structured content. In particular, we will investigate the possibility to automatically produce meaningful labeling in order to capture concepts enclosed in clusters. The work can therefore be subdivided into two main steps: *clustering* and *labeling*. Given that the clustering process has the purpose to agglomerate similar objects, the choose of the appropriate similarity metric for specific settings is a crucial and, generally, a not easy task. In this work we will look into how metrics can be defined for multi-domain structured data, we will study how this impacts on the quality of the clustering and, finally, we will automatically produce labels for the generated clusters and evaluate them.

The rest of the paper is organized as follows. Section 2 presents an overview on the main techniques used for clustering and labeling with a particular attention to mixed data and documents. Some theoretical backgrounds will also be introduced. Section 3 presents the overall clustering and labeling method. Section 4 presents some experimental results and in Section 5 discusses our conclusions.

2   Background and Related Works

Figure 1 summarizes the main steps involved in the clustering process:

- **Data Processing:** it aims at representing data through a set of highly descriptive and discriminant descriptors (*features*). Often, given the different nature of the data that are involved, a standardization process that could produce comparable data is needed.
- **Similarity Function:** data are grouped according to their similarity. The definition of the most effective similarity function is an important factor for the overall quality of the clustering result.
- **Clustering:** data are grouped according to the chosen similarity function. The quality of the clustering algorithm is evaluated using *validity indexes*.
- **Semantic Labeling:** highly descriptive and meaningful labels are inferred for each generated cluster.

The following subsections will explain more in deep each step, with special attention to the specific issues associated with the application of clustering techniques to multi-domain search results, namely labeling and mixed data type management.

---

[1] http://search.carrotsearch.com/

2.1 Data Format and Processing

Data clustering algorithms are strictly related to the characteristics of the involved data sets. For that reason, understanding scale, normalization, and proximity is very important in interpreting the results of clustering algorithms. In particular, data items can differ by type: numerical, nominal, textual and time-series. Subdivisions in numerical data type refers to the degree of quantization in the data and can be binary, discrete or continuous. Nominal data, also called categorical, include a set of labels. Time-series can be considered as a particular case of continuous numerical features. *Textual data* defined as a sequence of words that compose complex phrases. If the set of features used to represent objects is not type-consistent, referring data is called *mixed-data*.

2.2 Similarity

The previously mentioned clustering process aims to group similar data objects: for this purpose, a *similarity function*, or *similarity index*, for each data type is needed. Let $\mathbf{x} = (x_1, x_2, ..., x_d)$ and $\mathbf{y} = (y_1, y_2, ..., y_d)$ be two d-dimensional data objects. Then the similarity coefficient between $\mathbf{x}$ and $\mathbf{y}$ obviously depends on how close their values are, considering all attributes, and will be some function of their attribute values, i.e., $s(\mathbf{x}, \mathbf{y}) = s(x_1, x_2, ..., x_d, y_1, y_2, ..., y_d)$. The inverse of the similarity function is the *dissimilarity function*, or *distance function*, defined as: $d(\mathbf{x}, \mathbf{y}) = d(x_1, x_2, ..., x_d, y_1, y_2, ..., y_d)$.

Similarity needs to be calculated in different ways based on the data types it involves. To define the most suitable similarity function between **categorical data objects** in unsupervised learning is an important data mining problem. While it is easy to compute the closeness for numeric attributes, it becomes difficult to capture this notion for categorical attributes. The most used dissimilarity measure [2] is a simple, well-known measure called *simple matching distance* that is based on boolean value set to 1 if two categorical feature values are the same and to 0 if they are not. The dissimilarity between two items is then calculated as the sum of the distances for each feature. Since the distance is actually a function of the distribution of values, the distance function should also take into account the significance of attributes [3].

Discover similarity metrics on **numerical features** has been extensively addressed in the past. However, the choice of the optimal metric is strictly dependent on the application context and it is not an easy task. Many similarity metrics have been introduced [4]. Some of the most used ones are: *Euclidean distance*, *Manhattan distance*, and their generalization called *Minkowski distance*.

In many applications, the need arises to deal with data described by an **heterogeneous set of mixed descriptors**. In order to overcome this problem, two strategies that have been adopted in literature:

– *Data Standardization*: according to these strategy, any data converges to a chosen type through a set of specific conversions. A usual conversions process is to convert nominal attribute values into numeric integer values. Numeric distance measures are then applied for computing similarity between object pairs [2]. Another popular methods is based on the application of a binary coding scheme.

– *General Metric Definition*: in this approach, data is not converted, but a general metrics able to perform similarity over a set of different features is defined. Many works have been presented in literature [5].

2.3 Clustering

Clustering methods aim at partitioning a set of objects into clusters in the way that objects in the same cluster are more similar to each other than objects in different clusters according to some defined criteria. The criteria involved in clustering process is generally based on a (dis)similarity measure between objects. Clustering methods are divided in two categories: *Hard Clustering* and *Soft Clustering (Fuzzy Clustering)*. In Hard clustering each element can belong to only one cluster. In soft or fuzzy clustering, instead, each data object can belong to different categories with some grade of belonging.

Both hard and soft clustering methods are categorized in two different categories: *partitional* and *hierarchical* [4]. Partitional methods attempt to divide the data-set into non-overlapping groups. The partitional k-means algorithm is one of the most used partitional clustering algorithms [6]. In hierarchical clustering, clusters are defined according to containment hierarchies of nested clusters. In this work we will use both hard partitional and hard hierarchical clustering techniques. We will not take into account soft clustering techniques.

K-means [2] is one the most used clustering methods. In this algorithm, the number k of clusters is assumed to be fixed and known a priori. The algorithm is based on the minimization of an error function as follows. It proceeds, for a given initial set of k cluster seed points, by allocating the remaining data to the nearest clusters. At each step a new set of seed points is determined as the mean (centroid) for each cluster and the membership of the clusters is changed according to the error function. The iterative process stops when the error function does not change significantly or the membership of the clusters no longer changes. Some variants of the k-means algorithm exist. The **k-modes** algorithm [7], specifically designed for nominal data types. An integration of k-means ad k-modes called **k-prototype** [5] has been proposed in order to perform clustering of mixed data (numerical and categorical). More recently, [8] proposed to cluster pure numeric subset of attributes and categorical attributes differently and [9] proposed an algorithm for clustering mixed data called Squeezed algorithm.

Hierarchical algorithms divide a data set into a sequence of nested partitions, according to two possible strategies: *divisive hierarchical* and *agglomerative hierarchical*. In a divisive approach, the algorithm proceeds starting with one large cluster containing all the data points in the data set and continues splitting it into more and more detailed clusters; in an agglomerative hierarchical algorithm, the algorithm proceeds starting with elementary clusters, each containing one data point, and continues merging the clusters. Due to their high computational complexity that make them very time-consuming, divisive algorithm are not extensively adopted in applications that deal with large data sets. Some new techniques have been proposed to improve the scalability of hierarchical clustering [10] [11] [12].

2.4   Clusters Validation

Since clustering algorithms produces clusters that are not known a priori, the final partition of data requires some kind of evaluation in most applications. We call *cluster validity index* [2] the measure of the quality of a clustering scheme. Cluster validity can be checked according to two kinds of criteria: *external criteria* and *internal criteria*. External criteria are based on the evaluation of the results compared with a pre-specified data organization, which is imposed to reflect our intuition about the clustering structure of the data set. Internal criteria attempt to evaluate the results of clustering in terms of quantities that involve the vectors of the data set themselves. They are based on the idea that a cluster algorithm should search for clusters whose members are close to each other (maximize the *compactness* – minimize the distance intra-cluster) and well separated (maximize the *separateness* – maximize the distance inter-cluster).

The *silhouette method*[13] is the internal criterion used in this work. For a given cluster, $X_j, j = 1, ..., k$ the silhouette assigns the i-th member $x_{ij}, i = 1, ..., n_j$ of cluster X_j a quality measure (*silhouette width*):

$$S_{ij} = \frac{b_i - a_i}{\max(a_i, b_i)} \tag{1}$$

where a_i is the average distance between x_{ij} and all other members in X_j and b_i denotes the minimum of average dissimilarity of x_{ij} to all objects in other clusters. It can be seen that s_{ij} has a value between -1 and $+1$, where s_{ij} equals 1 means that s_{ij} is in the proper cluster. Additionally, when using hierarchical clustering techniques, the *cophenetic correlation coefficient* can be used as a measure of correlation between distances in the hierarchical tree and natural distances between data. In particular, it expresses the correlation between the dissimilarity matrix P and the cophenetic matrix P_c, where the matrix P_c is defined in such a way that the element $P_c(i, j)$ represents the proximity level at which the two data points x_i and x_j are found in the same cluster for the first time.

2.5   Web Document Clustering

Especially in the Web context, dealing with multi-modal data often means to deal with documents, i.e., long texts, which need to be manipulated in a special manner. Many document clustering techniques exist in literature [14]. In particular some effective methods and tools that attempt to semantically group documents produced as result of a search engine interrogation have been proposed.[2,3]

Document clustering techniques have to face different issues than classic clustering approaches, such as computational efficiency, possibility of overlapping clustering, complex labeling. The outcomes of a document clustering system may provide items from optimal clusters [15] or may leave to the user the ability to choose the groups of interest in an interactive manner [16].

One of the most used data representation model for document clustering is the so-called *Space Vector Model* (VSM) [17], where every document d is represented as a

---

[2] http://www.carrot2.org
[3] http://www.vivisimo.com

vector $[w_{t_0}, w_{t_1}, ..., w_{t_m}]$, where $t_0, t_1, ..., t_m$ is a global set of words (features) and w_{t_i} expresses the weight (importance) of feature t_i to document d. The distance function adopted in VSM is usually cosine similarity, which is used in many clustering algorithms: [18] used the very popular agglomerative hierarchical clustering (AHC), with an average-link merge criterion.

Recently, the concept of *semantic clustering* that uses ontology in order to describe relations between words has been introduced; for instance, [19] applies a conceptual description to a partitional clustering algorithm and [20] determines cluster descriptions as conjunctions of attributes selected among those that describe the clustered objects.

However, no study have been conducted yet that takes into account clustering techniques performed on multi-modal data type that include a document descriptor. In our work we propose a method for this problem, based on SVM text representation.

2.6   Labeling

Labeling is the process that applies knowledge discovery techniques to capture the knowledge embedded in grouped data in order to define a meaningful, highly representative label for each cluster, which, at the same time, is not a good representative for the other clusters. It is obvious that representative labels are those that are frequent in the cluster and rare in the others. In our study we need to consider two different classes of labeling problem: *text clusters labeling* and *categorical clusters labeling*.

The most known method for text clustering [21] is the Mutual Information method, defined as measure of the degree of dependence of two variables. In text clustering, each term is a possible candidate to be the cluster label and the Mutual Information associated to the term is the probability to be chosen as the delegate. In particular, given C as the membership propriety to a cluster (C=1 is a member, C=0 is not a member), and T as the presence of a specific term (T=1 the term is present, T=0 the term is not present), the mutual information of the two variables is defined as:

$$I(C,T) = \sum_{c \in 0,1} \sum_{t \in 0,1} p(C = c, T = t) log_2 \left(\frac{p(C = c, T = t)}{p(C = c)p(T = t)} \right) \qquad (2)$$

In this case, $p(C = 1)$ represents the probability that a randomly-selected document is a member of a particular cluster, and $p(C = 0)$ represents the probability that it is not. Similarly, $p(T = 1)$ represents the probability that a randomly-selected document contains a given term and $p(T = 0)$ represents the probability that it does not. The joint probability distribution function $p(C, T)$ represents the probability that two events occur simultaneously.

Other works used pre-defined ontology for the labeling process. In [19] authors combine the standard model-theoretic semantics to partitional clustering. In [22], instead, the authors propose an algorithm that integrates the text semantic to the incremental clustering process. The clusters are represented using semantic histogram that measures the distribution of semantic similarities within each cluster.

3   Overview of Our Approach

The approach we propose in this study aims at defining a framework that performs automatic clustering and labeling over results produced by a multi-dimensional mixed structured data source such as a multi–domain search engine. The main characteristics of this setting that should be considered are:

- structured data, with predefined schema;
- no prior information on the actual data domains and semantics;

In this work we use two of the main clustering algorithms, k-means and hierarchical, and we define a new distance function able to integrate categorical, numerical, and text data types, so as to accommodate the needs associated with the SeCo setting.

To demonstrate the feasibility of the approach and validate the associated outcomes, we applied our technique to three different scenarios. In the first and second scenarios only categorical and numerical attributes are considered. In particular, in the first scenario, categorical information is converted into numerical data; in the second scenario, the *Huang* general distance function for mixed data is used. In the third scenario categorical, numerical and textual attributed are considered and a new distance function is defined and used.

3.1   Data Format

The data types considered in this work are categorical, numerical and textual. We consider string attributes as textual attributes (i.e., documents) if the data set contains at least N_c characters. Otherwise, strings are considered as categorical attributes. Table 1 shows an extract of the whole set of attributes of the movie database. The whole list of attributes and data formats will be presented in Table 2.

Table 1. Example of Movies attribute data formats

Title	Release Year	Description	Duration	Price
Categorical	*Numerical*	*Textual*	*Numerical*	*Num.*
Sweet Home Alabama	2003	Melanie Carmichael an up and rising fashion designer in New York has gotten almost everything she wished for since she was little....	108	19.99
Love Wedding Marriage	2011	Mandy Moore stars as Eva a newlywed who has it all: a successful career as a top marriage counselor a hot husband....	151	24.98

For categorical attributes two different approaches have been used. In the first approach a categorical to numerical transformation is performed using binary coding method. The second approach uses a new general distance function defined in this study in order to integrate numerical, categorical and textual attributes. Normalization in the range $(0, 1)$ is performed for all numerical attributes.

3.2   A New Similarity Matrix for Mixed Data Type

In order to calculate the distance between heterogeneous data type, we defined a new dissimilarity function that integrates numerical, categorical and textual attributes. The distance between two elements $\mathbf{x}$ and $\mathbf{y}$ is defined as:

$$d(\mathbf{x}, \mathbf{y}) = \sum_{j=1}^{p}(x_j - y_j)^2 + \gamma \sum_{j=1}^{m}\delta(x_j, y_j) + \sum_{j=1}^{l}\omega(1 - \frac{\mathbf{x}_i^T \mathbf{y}_j}{\|\mathbf{x}_i\|\|\mathbf{y}_j\|}) \tag{3}$$

where γ is the weight associated to categorical attributes, ω is the weight associated to textual attributes, p is the number of numerical attributes, m is number of categorical attributes, l is the number of textual attributes. In our case, $\gamma = 1$ and $\omega = 1$, given that there is no prior information about attribute and relations between them. The first section of the function, which is relative to numerical and categorical attributes, is the general distance function for mixed data. The model used to represent textual data is the Vector Space Model and in particular the *Term frequency VSM model* (Section 2.5). As a consequence, the second part of the new distance function is the cosine distance function where $\mathbf{x}_i$ and $\mathbf{y}_j$ are two documents represented through the Vector Space Model. In order to pre-process textual attributes, tokenization, stop words analysis and stemming are performed for each document.

3.3   Clustering

The choice of the optimal clustering method requires to compare different approaches and select the best one. In our work we have chosen to use two different popular techniques: *k*-means e Hierarchical.

K-means has been used in all three presented scenario. In the first scenario all attributes are numerical and the classical *k*-means algorithm can be used. In the second scenario the *k*-prototype version of the *k*-means is used in order to integrate categorical and numerical data. In the third scenario the new distance function reported in eq. 3 has been used. In the latter case the new cost function to be minimized is defined as:

$$P(W, \mathbf{Q}) = \sum_{l=1}^{k}(P_l^r + P_l^c + P_l^t) \tag{4}$$

where

$$P_l^r = \sum_{i=1}^{n} w_{i,j} \sum_{j=1}^{p}(x_{i,j} - q_{l,j})^2 \tag{5}$$

$$P_l^c = \gamma \sum_{i=1}^{n} w_{i,j} \sum_{j=p+1}^{p+m} \delta(x_{i,j}, q_{l,j}) \tag{6}$$

$$P_l^t = \omega \sum_{i=1}^{n} w_{i,j} \sum_{j=p+m+1}^{p+m+l} 1 - \frac{\mathbf{x}_i^T \mathbf{y}_j}{\|\mathbf{x}_i\|\|\mathbf{y}_j\|} \tag{7}$$

Two shortcomings of the k-means algorithm are: (i) the need of prior information about the desired number of clusters; and (ii) the strict dependency of the final results quality to initial centroids, randomly chosen. In this work we adopted a greedy approach to discover the number of clusters k. The number of clusters that produce the best cluster division according to the Silhouette index is a candidate. Once the number of clusters k is obtained, in order to overcome the dependency of results on initial centroids, the k-means algorithm is repeated n_l times and the final clustering result is the one that produced the highest Silhouette value.

The *hierarchical algorithm*, used as agglomerative method, has been used in all the three considered scenarios. Even thought this approach is used in many applications it is still not clear the best criteria to choose the optimal linkage criteria. For that reason a greedy search method is used considering the cophenetic index as quality index. The algorithm is repeated iteratively using a different linkage criteria: Single-link method, Complete-link method, Group Average method, Centroid method, Ward method. The adopted criterion is the one that best represents data and distances between data, i.e., the one that produces the dendogram with the higher cophenetic value. In order to obtain the final clustering scheme, the produced dendogram must be cut at a specific level. The criterion used for deciding the level to cut is based on retrieving the number of cluster that produced the best clustering schema. The optimal number of clusters is the one that produces the highest Silhouette index.

3.4   Labeling Process

Labeling process is generally performed by choosing some instances of the attributes of clustered objects that can be highly representative for the most objects within the cluster. In our scenario three types of descriptors need to be considered: numerical, nominal and textual. Among all, textual attribute is the most informative with the risk of predominance over the other. To avoid it, labeling over text is performed independently from numerical and categorical attributes. A final merge is then performed.

While in most cases the labeling process means to find a unique representative label per cluster, in this work we have chosen to represent each cluster with a set of labels. This permits to produce a better characterization.

For numerical and nominal attributes, in order to evaluate the most suitable labeling paradigm for our scenario, we used two different approaches. The former uses Silhouette index in order to capture the ratio between intra-cluster and inter-cluster distance.

The second approach uses a new labeling scheme introduced in this work, which considers: the *strength* of the concept into a cluster; the cluster *compactness*; and the *spread* of a concept along clusters. In this approach numerical attributes are discretized into labels using a regular interval subdivision. The average value is used as label for the interval.

Concerning the labeling process on textual attributes we adopted the mutual information index, which has been extended with information relative to the terms frequencies of a term in the cluster (after the appropriate text cleansing). The new Mutual Information Index is defined as:

Table 2. Attribute list and relative data type for each dataset

Colleges	Type	Automobiles	Type	Movies	Type
Name	categorical	Make	categorical	Title	categorical
Category	categorical	Fuel Type	categorical	Genre	categorical
Tuition Out State	numerical	Aspiration	categorical	Release Year	numerical
Tuition In State	numerical	Number of Doors	categorical	Description	textual
Enrollment	numerical	Body Style	categorical	Audio Format	categorical
Acceptance	numerical	Drive Wheels	categorical	Video Format	categorical
		Engine Location	categorical	Editor	categorical
		Wheel Base	numerical	Duration	numerical
		Length	numerical	Price	numerical
		Width	numerical		
		Height	numerical		
		Weight	numerical		
		Engine Type	categorical		
		Number of Cylinders	categorical		
		Engine Size	numerical		
		Fuel System	categorical		
		Bore	numerical		
		Stroke	numerical		
		Compression Ratio	numerical		
		Horse Power	numerical		
		Peak RPM	numerical		
		City MPG	numerical		
		Highway MPG	numerical		
		Price	numerical		

$$I(C,T) = f_t \sum_{c \in 0,1} \sum_{t \in 0,1} p(C = c, T = t) log_2 \left(\frac{p(C = c, T = t)}{p(C = c)p(T = t)} \right) \tag{8}$$

where f_t is the number of occurrences of the term in the cluster, C is the cluster and T is the term. For each cluster, the set of labels inducted from the all attributes are then merged together through a union set operation.

4 Experiments and Results

In this section we present the experimental settings and the results of our tests, both with respect to the clustering methods and the labeling techniques.

4.1 Datasets

Used datasets includes data retrieved from the real world. In particular we used three databases:

- Colleges (from the SeCo data repositories): The dataset contains the description attributes about a set of colleges located in the US. The data schema contains 5 numerical attributes and 2 categorical attributes. Its extension comprises 420 elements.

Table 3. Clustering Results for the three experimental scenarios (automobile, college, and movies)

	Automobile		College		Movies
	Binary	General Distance	Binary	General Distance	General Distance
k-means	6 clusters	5 clusters	6 clusters	5 clusters	3 clusters
	0.29	0.23	0.40	0.23	0.21
Hierarchical	5 clusters	3 clusters	5 clusters	3 clusters	2 clusters
	0.27	0.31	0.40	017	0.24

- Automobiles (from UCI Irvine University Repository[4]): The collection contains datasets from the real world used for data mining purposes. We considered the dataset about automobiles. The data schema includes 16 numerical attributes and 10 categorical attributes. The total number of instances are 105.
- Movies (from Amazon[5]): This dataset consists of movies extracted from the Amazon database. Movies attributes includes title and description considered as textual attributes. The schema comprises 3 numerical attributes, 4 categorical attributes, and 2 textual attributes. The total number of instances are 46.

The whole list of attributes and the relative data format,such as determined by the system, for each dataset, is listed in table 2.

4.2 Clustering Evaluation

In order to test the proposed clustering approach two different experiments have been performed and for each experiment both k-means and hierarchical clustering methods have been applied. The purpose of the experiments is to test the effectiveness of the new similarity function.

The first experiment has been conducted using Automobile and College datasets performing a conversion from categorical to numerical attributes. The second experiment has been still conducted on Automobile and College datasets but using the general mixed function proposed in section 3.2(eq.3). Results of the experiments are shown in Table 3.

As shown in Table 3 the first approach, in which categorical attributes are converted in numerical attributes using a binary schema, seems to perform better, even if results are very close. This is due to the uniformity of attribute guarantee by the conversion. General distance could perform better with some prior information on attributes. The second experiment has been conducted on Amazon Movies dataset. Given the impossibility to convert the text attributes using a binary scheme, in the experiment we only use the new proposed distance function. Even in this test the use of the proposed general distance function resulted to be effective.

Notice that in all the scenarios, the performances of the two clustering techniques are similar. However, k-means is very computational efficient, but strictly dependent

---

[4] http://archive.ics.uci.edu/ml/
[5] http://www.amazon.com

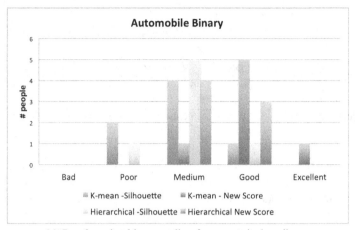

(a) Results using binary coding for categorical attributes

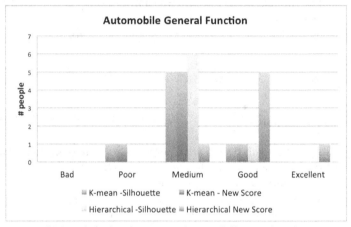

(b) Results using the proposed general distance function

Fig. 2. Results of labeling for Automobile dataset

on the number of clusters and the initial set of centroid. Hierarchical methods are not dependent on initial condition, but is a very time-consuming approach.

4.3 Labeling Evaluation

The labeling process have been performed for each of the produced clustering scheme. In order to test its effectiveness, such as introduced in section 3.4, the proposed method is compared with a more classic approach based on the Silhouette index. Given the novelty of the application of an automatic labeling process on multi-domain data objects that include textual attributes, we came up with the impossibility to retrieve an appropriate ground through. For that reason the validation test have been performed in a subjective manner. The produced labeling schema have been evaluated by seven human testers who have been asked to grade the quality of all produced labeling scheme evaluating the representativeness of labels with respect to data present in the clusters. The evaluation results for the three scenarios are shown in Figure 2, Figure 3, and Figure 4 respectively. As stated in section 4.2, due to the presence of the text attribute, it has been not possible to perform a data standardization process in the context of Amazon Movies dataset. For that reason the results of automatic labeling for Movie dataset over the binary scheme has been omitted.

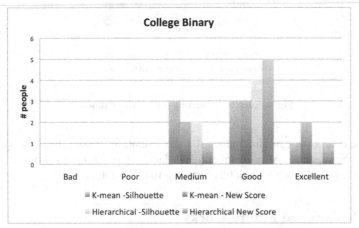

(a) Results using binary coding for categorical attributes

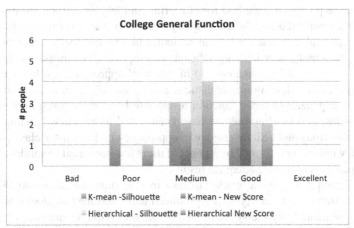

(b) Results using the proposed general distance function

Fig. 3. Results of labeling for College dataset

As the results show, evaluators graded well the new labeling scheme based on general distance function in almost all tests. In particular, given a clustering scheme, the labeling method defined in this work have been better evaluated in respect to the corresponding scheme that use the Silhouette method.

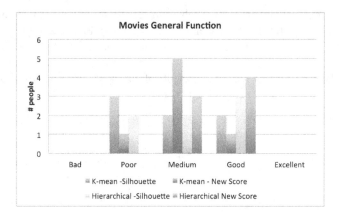

Fig. 4. Results of labeling for Movies dataset

From the charts we can also induce the strict relation existing between quality of clustering schema and quality of labeling. In fact, esters tended to propose a higher grade to clusters with high Silhouette clustering Index (Table 3).

5 Conclusions and Future Works

In this paper we proposed a method for clustering and labeling structured mixed data returned as the result of a multi-domain query over deep Web information. In order to integrate categorical, numerical a textual attributes in a unique method, a new general distance function and a new labeling schema are proposed. The proposed method for clustering, performed using k-means and hierarchical approach, have been evaluated using the Silhouette Index in three realistic scenarios and using datasets from the real world. The new general distance function resulted to be effective even in presence of textual attributes. The labeling method have been tested using a new labeling schema proposed in this study and a Silhouette-based approach, which is a more classic method. A subjective validation performed by a panel of users has been used to validate labeling schema, which proved to give adequate results.

Further developments of the work will take into account incrementality. Since result sets of search engines are typically produced and consumed in blocks, which are generated incrementally by the system based on the user requests and according to optimization strategies, the application of clustering techniques has to face the problem of not having the entire set of data available upfront; in other words, it has to deal with data-sets in continuous evolution. For that reason, an important characteristic should be considered is *incrementality*. Incremental clustering techniques provide the ability to follow up the large scale of information generated every day, without the need to often re-cluster the entire dataset again.Even if in this work we don't address incrementality as a requisite, some choices have been made to guarantee the future application of incremental methodologies. This which will be addressed by applying some incremental k-means and incremental agglomerative hierarchical methods proposed in literature.

A second future development will consider clustering of composite objects, i.e., elements with subparts belonging to different domains. We also plan to exploit ontological information, both as a-priori knowledge on the datasets and for semantic similarity calculation.

Finally, another further development will concern the definition of automatic methods for retrieving a-priori information and statistics from data sets, so as to increase the quality of clustering and labeling.

References

1. Singh, M.P.: Deep web structure. IEEE Internet Computing 6, 4–5 (2002)
2. Gan, G., Ma, C., Wu, J.: Data Clustering: Theory, Algorithms, and Applications. SIAM, Society for Industrial and Applied Mathematics (2007)
3. Ahmad, A., Dey, L.: A method to compute distance between two categorical values of same attributein unsupervised learning for categorical data set. Pattern Recognition Letters 28(1), 110–118 (2007)
4. Duda, R., Hart, P.: Pattern Classification and Scene Analysis. John Wiley and Sons, New York (1973)
5. Huang, Z.: Extensions to the k-means algorithm for clustering large data sets with categorical values. Data Mining and Knowledge Discovery 2, 283–304 (1998)
6. Macqueen, J.: Some methods for classification and analysis of multivariate observations. In: Proceedings of the 5th Berkeley Symposium on Mathematical Statistics and Probability, vol. 1, pp. 281–297. University of California Press, Berkeley (1967)
7. Huang, Z.: A fast clustering algorithm to cluster very large categorical data sets in data mining. In: Proceedings of the SIGMOD Workshop on Research Issues on Data Mining and Knowledge Discovery, Dept. of Computer Science, The University of British Columbia, Canada (1997)
8. Luo, H., Kong, F., Li, Y.: Clustering Mixed Data Based on Evidence Accumulation. In: Li, X., Zaïane, O.R., Li, Z.-h. (eds.) ADMA 2006. LNCS (LNAI), vol. 4093, pp. 348–355. Springer, Heidelberg (2006)
9. He, Z., Xu, X., Deng, S.: Scalable algorithms for clustering large datasets with mixed type attributes. International Journal of Intelligence Systems 20, 1077–1089 (2005)
10. Zhang, T., Ramakrishnan, R., Livny, M.: Birch: An efficient data clustering method for very large databases. In: SIGMOD Conference (1996)
11. Ankerst, M., Breunig, M., Kriegel, H., Sander, J.: Optics: ordering points to identify the clustering structure. In: ACM SIGMOD International Conference on Management of Data (1999)
12. Karypis, G., Han, E., Kumar, V.: Chameleon: A hierarchical clustering algorithm using dynamic modeling. IEEE Computer 32(8), 68–75 (1999)
13. Rousseeuw, P.: Silhouettes: A graphical aid to the interpretation and validation of cluster analysis. Journal of Computational and Applied Mathematics 20, 53–65 (1987)
14. Carpineto, C., Osinski, S., Romano, G., Weiss, D.: A survey of web clustering engines. ACM Computing Surveys 41 (2009)
15. Liu, X., Croft, B.W.: Cluster-based retrieval using language models. In: Proceedings of the 27th International ACM SIGIR Conference on Research and Development in Information Retrieval, vol. 1, pp. 186–193. ACM Press (2004)
16. Heart, M.A., Pedersen, J.O.: Reexamining the cluster hypothesis: scatter/gather on retrieval results. In: Proceedings of the 19th ACM International Conference on Research and Development in Information Retrieval, pp. 76–84. ACM Press (1996)

17. Salton, G., Wong, A., Yang, C.S.: A vector space model for automatic indexing. Comm. ACM 18, 613–620 (1975)
18. Everitt, B.S., Landau, S., Leese, M.: Cluster Analysis, 4th edn. Oxford Press (2001)
19. Esposito, F., Fanizzi, N., d'Amato, C.: Partitional Conceptual Clustering of Web Resources Annotated with Ontology Languages. In: Berendt, B., Mladenič, D., de Gemmis, M., Semeraro, G., Spiliopoulou, M., Stumme, G., Svátek, V., Železný, F. (eds.) Knowledge Discovery Enhanced with Semantic and Social Information. SCI, vol. 220, pp. 53–70. Springer, Heidelberg (2009)
20. Stepp, R.E., Michalski, R.S.: Conceptual clustering of structured objects: A goal-oriented approach. Artificial Intelligence 28(1), 43–69 (1986)
21. Manning, C., Raghavan, P., Schutze, H.: Introduction to Information Retrieval. Cambridge UP, Cambridge (2008), Cluster Labeling Stanford Natural Language Processing Group (2009)
22. Gad, W.K., Kamel, M.S.: Incremental clustering algorithm based on phrase-semantic similarity histogram. In: Proceedings of the Ninth International Conference on Machine Learning and Cybernetics, Qingdao (2010)

Visualizing Search Results: Engineering Visual Patterns Development for the Web*

Rober Morales-Chaparro, Juan Carlos Preciado,
and Fernando Sánchez-Figueroa

Quercus Software Engineering Group, Universidad de Extremadura
{robermorales,jcpreciado,fernando}@unex.es

Abstract. Visualization is a key concept when presenting search results. Sometimes a bad visualization leads to a wrong decision. In many cases the building of a visual representation for a given set of data is fixed a priori by the developer with no chance for the user to adjust or change it. The fact is that not all the users have the same interests on the same data. In this work we present a Domain-Specific Language to develop visual patterns that allows the user choosing the desired visualization for a given data search result. An example is used to drive the explanations.

Keywords: Search Computing, Human Computer Interaction, Data Visualization, Web Engineering, Model Driven Engineering, Domain-Specific Languages.

1 Introduction

Available data on the Internet is growing up more and more every day, with heterogeneous formats and sources. This fact makes the users need more and better ways to access the data they are interested in. The data resulting from a query need to be explored, analyzed, interpreted or even communicated to/with other people. For these actions data visualization is a key concept [1].

However, building visualizations is not an easy task. The designer has to face different problems that can be grouped at two different levels. On the one hand, the technological level, that involves those issues related to changing rendering technologies (such as the recent emergence of HTML5), different visualization devices (smart phones, tablets,...), heterogeneous data sources (query languages, APIs,...) and so on. This is a recurrent problem in Software Engineering. On the other hand, the human or social factors level that mainly involves issues related to the accuracy of the visualization to the user expectations according to the context (user profile, company interests, colleague interests, market tendencies, social tendencies, etc). This is an emerging problem in Business Intelligence systems.

The visualization of a search result should take into account both levels. The visualization could be rendered in different platforms and devices and make

---

* This work has been supported by the Spanish Contract MIGRARIA - TIN2011-27340 funded by Ministerio de Ciencia e Innovación and Gobierno de Extremadura.

S. Ceri and M. Brambilla (Eds.): Search Computing III, LNCS 7538, pp. 127–142, 2012.

use of the best technologies available at a given moment. Moreover, the same information should be shown in different ways attending to the user changing context.

As a solution to both problems in [2] it was briefly presented a data-driven and user-driven process for data visualization. The technological problems are solved by using a Model Driven Development (MDD) approach while the human problems are overcoming by letting the user to drive and customize the presentation just to obtain the information in the most appropriate way.

In this paper we give details of that process, focusing on the modeling of visualizations. The modeling is done through a Domain Specific Language (DSL). Far from giving all the details of the DSL, the paper shows its main pillars and illustrates its use through a driving example. The models obtained can be reused among different applications and can generate code for different technologies, platforms and/or devices. Besides, models generate code that allows the users to adjust a given visualization by changing the predominant dimension. This way, the user can move from one visualization to another, taking as input the same search results. The process provided is in the scope of exploratory and analytical visualization. Other kinks of visualizations such as collaborative or narrative are out of the scope of this research work.

The rest of the paper is as follows. Section 2 shows a motivating example. Section 3 outlines the global approach while section 4, 5 and 6 will detail the main phases of the proposal (data sources, visualization modeling and application building). Finally, related work, and conclusions and future work will be shown in sections 7 and 8.

2   Motivating Example

On-line sports betting is becoming more and more popular and any help to take the right decision when wagering is welcome. Let us suppose that Ernest wants to bet some money on the final score of Sunday's morning match, which will face *F.C. Barcelona* and *Real Madrid C.F.* To get some data which can help him in taking the decision, he visits some online gambling sites and digital newspapers, that display scores, and other statistics, for the latest few times both teams faced, e.g. Figs. 1 and 2. The data shown in both figures are sparse, poorly organized, tangled and badly visualized, so it is useless for him.[1,2]

Since Ernest needs more (and better displayed) data to take a good decision, he decides to make a query to a specialized search engine. Once he has invoked the query, the system answers with a results representation, shown in Fig. 3. The visualization provided obeys to a visual pattern selected by the search engine developer, for this specific kind of query. Observing this chart, one can see that, recently, local team mostly gets one goal a match, and away team usually gets two. Ernest can interpret that the most predictable result is a 1-2 away win.

---

[1] https://stats.betradar.com/s4/#8_2311818,9_headtohead
[2] http://www.marca.com/2012/01/17/multimedia/graficos/1326989967.html

However, that representation does not keep visual track of the time of the day in which the matches were played. From Ernest point of view, this piece of data can be relevant. He would have liked to obtain the visualization shown in Fig. 4 where the time of the match plays a relevant role in the graphic. Using the new visualization, the most expectable result is 2-0 home win, since Ernest can now keep in mind that the Sunday game is at 12 PM. *Depending on the visualization used,* he had bet on the home win or quite the opposite. The problem comes from the fact of determining a priori the kind of visualization to be used, without any possibility of adjusting or changing it. Why not presenting the data according to Ernest's profile and letting him to drive the visualization according to his expectations?

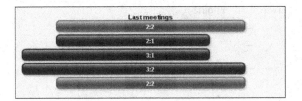

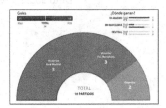

Fig. 1. Latest head to head scores presented by a well-known betting site

Fig. 2. Previous results published by a sports newspaper

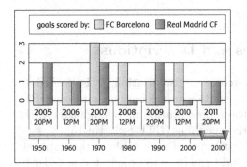

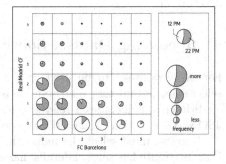

Fig. 3. Original visualization

Fig. 4. Alternative visualization

Next we show briefly the whole process that supports this possibility and its different phases, giving more details on the modeling of visualizations.

3   Proposed Process

Fig. 5 shows an overview of the system choreography. The entry point is the user, who makes a query to the search engine which uses the data sources to fulfill the request. The user is offered a default visualization of the results (chosen by the modeler or the system itself). Besides that, the user can change from one pattern to another looking for fulfilling his expectations, since the visualization get the patterns from a server different from the search engine.

To render visualizations, the server uses the visualization patterns developed by the modelers with the help of a reasoner system that reads data description and searchs for similar situations in the past. For this purpose a Domain Specific Language (DSL) has been defined. That DSL allows that a generator produces final code from the models that connects with the data, executes transformations over them and outputs the final result.

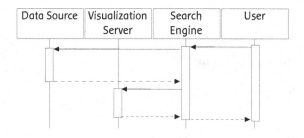

Fig. 5. System overview

Next, the different phases of the process are shown, starting with the data description.

4   Specifying Dataset Sources and Descriptions

For every data-set to be used as a source in a visualization, it is needed to select some parameters. The first one is the data source location that is an URL. Additionally, it includes a reference to the representation metalanguage (XML, JSON, YAML, CSV, XLS, ODS,...) or the encoding (UTF-8, Latin-15,...).

Then, we must select the name and attributes of each table of the data-set. Each attribute has several details: **name** and **type** have to be selected in order to make a successful connection and further reference at run-time. Other meta-data can be specified as well, to improve system comprehension of the source (and drive the automatic selection as much as possible). Those extra meta-data can include the **description**, the **null** (indication of allowed blank values); etc.

A possible data description for our example is provided as a reference below. Additionally a set of sample data is provided in Table 1:

Source http://search.example.com/results?home=FCB&away=MAD
    Encoding UTF-8
    Representation JSON
Table: Results

Year: integer *(Final year of the season)*
Hour: string
Home: integer *(Goals by home team)*
Away: integer *(Goals by away team)*

Table 1. Sample data: three value columns for every match

Year OID	FCB integer	RMC integer	Hour string
⋮	⋮	⋮	⋮
2005	1	2	20PM
2006	1	1	12PM
2007	3	2	20PM
2008	2	1	12PM
2009	0	2	20PM
2010	2	1	12PM
2011	1	1	20PM

5 Model-Driven Development of Visualization Patterns

The aim of this section is showing how the developer models a structured work-flow that transforms the data into retinal variables, to build data-based visualizations. This can be achieved using a Domain-Specific Language which is the main contribution of the present work and that will be detailed during this section.

First, the theoretical foundations of the DSL will be briefly introduced. Then, the native library description will guide us to the creation of the patterns behind Figs. 3 and 4, as a practical example of the use of the DSL.

5.1 Foundations

Three key concepts make up the DSL core.

Nodes Compute, Streams Communicate. The language is based on nodes which receive one or many inputs, and transform them into one or many outputs performing some computations. Outputs are connected to inputs again, using typed streams, favouring the chained execution of nodes. One can think on streams as metaphoric pipes, or as electronic circuit paths, if desired.

Nodes Inputs Are Strict-Typed. Conversion operations between values of different types will be provided for convenience when possible, but essentially node outputs can be used as input of other nodes *only* if they are of the same type. This feature allows modules having the same inputs and outputs to be interchangeable. This will make straightforward interchanging visual patterns if they receive the same input.

Nodes Do the Job as Soon as They Can. Node execution order is not constrained. The only restriction here is that "a node is not executed before all of its inputs are ready". This allows the modeler to think in the pattern as a dependency tree, not as a step-by-step task list, which would require more abstraction.

The most relevant grammatical details of the DSL are:

Modularity and Translation Units. Every concatenation of elements can be packed as a module. This makes the modules reusable (and shareable) inter- and intra-projects. One module is stored in a file and one file only contains one module.

Persistence. Modules are stored in text-based files that conform to a formal grammar. An additional graphic level is provided to help the modeler in several further tasks: communication, documentation, learning,...

5.2   DSL Toolbox, through a Running Example

A native library is provided for convenience. Having a basic set of types and operations improves future compatibility and provides a better developer experience. Every new pattern can use the elements declared in the native library, whose main compartments are next described. In this section we will explain the native library and, also, how a pattern can be developed using that DSL. The graphic of Fig. 3 will be used as an example target. Like every visualization, it has an underlying structure (see Fig. 10) that helps to take decisions. We will be shelling it step by step. Native types are split into three categories. The modeler can create new types based on existing ones.

Lexical Types. Mainly oriented to classify data from external sources. `Bool`, `Integer`, `Float`, `String`. Among these, lexical types can be enriched indicating the space density: categorical, ordinal or quantitative. The unit behind numeric values is also selectable.

Visual Types. Intended to represent retinal variables. Most of the general-purpose languages do not support as primitives those concepts. `Position`, `Size`, `Angle`, `Color`, `Shape`, `Texture`.

Structural Types. Minded to combine, group, and encapsulate other data. `Sequence`s are intended to be a list of values of the same type. `Tuple`s are dictionaries, a key-driven storage of heterogeneous values.

Native types constant values can be expressed in a simple textual way since they have specifications of literals. So, visually they appear as mere text. Next, we explain native operations that are also categorized for a better understanding of their purpose.

Getters and Setters. Read and/or write the attributes of the tuples. Visually, they are represented by a box with a pair of brackets.

Builders. Intended to create new instances of objects assigning values to the needed attributes. The native library provides builders for basic types, but mostly they are used to generate shapes.

Invocations of builders are, visually, mere boxes with an icon upon the labeled input slots.

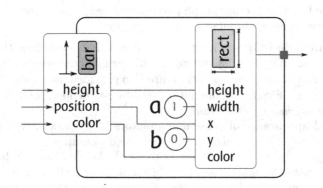

Fig. 6. Reusable pattern example that builds one bar

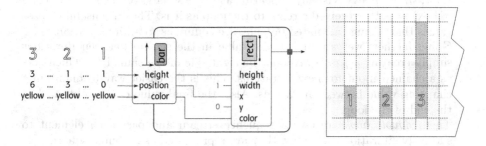

Fig. 7. Expected first invocations of the Fig. 6 bar pattern. At left, first input values. At right, firts output bars.

With the previously explained tools, we can start developing the pattern behind Fig. 3. The selected starting point is a single bar pattern, that will build one bar every time it is invoked. The first thing to do to develop it will be to discover the geometrical relationships behind it. This will help us to drive a result-oriented implementation. In this case, we will follow the description on Fig. 10, based on a two dimensional coordinate system. Every bar is basically a rectangle, and there are two invariants for every bar: $width = 1$ (**a**) and $y = 0$ (**b**). So the main task of the pattern, shown in Fig. 6, is including a *rectangle* builder primitive. Facts a and b are explicitly implemented on the pattern using constants. Also, variable values (height, x position and color) are taken from the declared inputs, while the pattern outputs the built shape.

We provide in Fig. 7 a simulation for an execution of the pattern repeated three times. At run-time, expected first input values for the pattern (shown at left) will build some of the first bars, of the first series of Fig. 10 (labeled in Fig. 7 as 1,2 and 3). Note, as example, how the first bar of the first series is at position 0, is 1 unit height, and is *yellow*. Next bars of the same series will be built using the remaining data from those input streams.

To continue building the bar graph pattern we need to know more operations. Let us continue seeing manipulators, loops and hooks:

Basic Manipulation Operations. Here we can find operations that manipulate strings: *split, join, substring,...* and regular expressions: *test, match, replace,...* Algebraic basic operations are also provided: *add, subs, times, quotient, modulo,...* Finally, accumulators and statistical operators: *size, average, maximum, variance, count, sum,...*
The visual appearance of these manipulators is a yellow small box labeled with the name or the symbol of the performed operation.

Loops. Designed for performing operations on all the elements of a list or to do repetitive tasks. Visually, they are big blank boxes, allowing us to include more operations inside them. To pass a stream inside the box in order to be used by inner operations, we need to introduce hooks.

Hooks. They are the holes on a loop where we can pass streams in and get values out.
First, *simple hooks* (visually appearing as single squares on the left or bottom of box) pass the received stream to the loop as it is. They are useful to pass values that, being calculated outside, are commons to all its iterations.
Going further, we can change the value in the stream between iterations simply creating a *paired hook* on the right side of the same box, which acts as a chained input for next iterations. This is the easier way to maintain a changing value between iterations. Also, the final value can be obtained at the end of the loop.
Then, *double hooks* receive a sequence stream and pass each element to successive iterations. Visually, they are represented as a double square.
We can sequence the output of any inner operation, getting outside a sequence of all outputs computed by that operation, iteration over iteration. This is achieved by the *sequencer hooks*, visualized as squares on the right side of the loop and labeled with a (+) plus sign.

Let's continue building up the bar graph pattern using the recently learned concepts. Now we'll draw *one series* reusing the bar sub-module. From Fig. 10 we gather the following requirements.

c. For each numerical value of the series there will be a bar with its height being the value.
d. Every bar of the same series has the same color.
e. Inside a data series, the bars are spaced a known number of units.

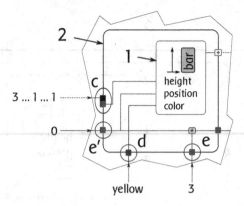

Fig. 8. Excerpt of a pattern representing the iteration over the values of one series. Outside values are the expected input values for the first series.

In Fig. 8 we can see the loop (2) that iterates over the value list using a double hook. Inside the loop, for every value we build one bar (1) invoking the recently developed bar pattern as sub-module. Each bar pattern invocation receives (c) the iterated value as input, from the double hook. Label **d** indicates that the series color is passed as it is through a simple input hook since it is the same for all the bars of the same series.

Bar separation enforces the use of two new input hooks. One of them represents the proper separation between bars of the same series (e) that can be calculated outside this simple excerpt. The other is a chained hook, starting at a provided point (e') that represents the position of the first bar. This value is modified inside the loop, iteration over iteration, to compute the position for every new bar. In this small example we can also see a sequencer hook on the top right corner, that creates a sequence with every output of the bar pattern invocations. That is, it outputs a sequence of every created bar.

A small new item of the native library will be finally explained in order to help us completing the pattern.

Mapping and Conversion. They transform data from a known value space to another. Several models are provided to describe most of native types, since there exist many descriptions of them.

For instance, a color stream can be packed (and unpacked) using CYMK, HSL or RGB. Also, we can build angles based on degrees, grads or radians; or positions using coordinate (x, y) pairs or polar $r\theta$ ones. We can use them, for instance, to map a value with a known minimum and maximum to a color scale. These operations can generate a visual representation of the mapping itself, a *legend* or an *axis*.

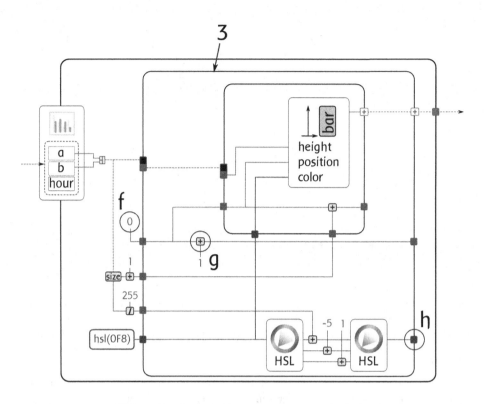

Fig. 9. Barchart implementation using the DSL

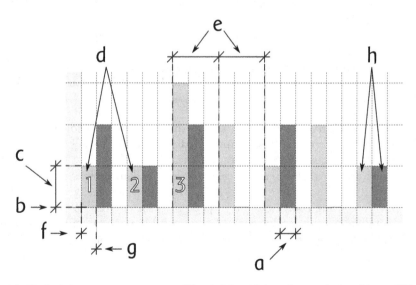

Fig. 10. Underlying geometry seen at Fig. 3. Identifying those relationships will help us to develop the pattern using the DSL.

With this concept we can finish the running pattern. The final step of the development is on Fig. 9. The two inputs of the pattern a and b have been sequenced to do the same operations for both (in a loop) since we want to generalize and draw the two series in the same way. Then, the loop (3) receives the built sequence as an input. Note that this pattern does not use the last input value (*hour*), so it gets not visualized, which exposed the problem found by Ernest on the motivating example.

Once explained the required execution flow, the final details will be explained together. The first bar of the first series starts at $x = 0$ (f), so we use a constant for that. Series spacing (g) requires that the starting of one series is one step right of the previous one. Besides, bar color (h) is different between series. We do the task decomposing the color using a mapping of the HSL model. Then we change separately the hue, saturation and luminosity, and finally package the color again. Finally, we chain on a hook the value of the color to be used in the next iteration.

Please note that we have not implemented some minor details of the pattern, in order to keep it simplest: these details include the legends and filters. The native library also provides a basic set of native patterns. that include the pie, scatter, lines and bar graphs.

Lastly, Fig. 11 shows the implementation of the pattern for Fig. 4. Without getting into details that time, let us show you how a pivot is invoked over the input data to properly aggregate counts grouping by result. The labeling of that operation is inspired on [3]. As previously noted in [4], data projections are very important to most of visualizations since they can reduce the number of dimensions. The reader must note that inputs are exactly of the same *type* of the pattern of Fig. 9, which was the only requirement for them to be interchangeable by the user, as our architecture allows.

Next we will explain the way these models can be rendered on a browser.

6 Rendering the Generated Visualizations on the Web

The aim of this section is explaining some of the decisions taken during the system development, such as the main technologies used for developing the DSL, the interpreter and the visualization rendering.

6.1 Development Time

The main relationships between artifacts are described in Fig. 12. The language grammar has been developed using the EBNF notation with the support of the XText[3] Eclipse project. An example of grammar can be seen on Listing 1, which shows a textual representation of the bar pattern developed in Fig. 6. We have chosen XText because it provides automatic and customizable generation of a full editor with syntax-coloring, validation and auto-completion input. Also, it

---

[3] https://www.eclipse.org/Xtext/

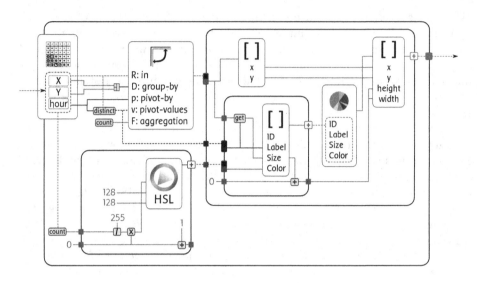

Fig. 11. Implementation for Fig. 4

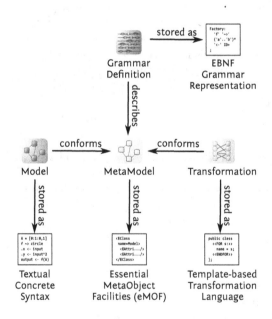

Fig. 12. Artifacts relationships

generates an EMF[4] meta-model for every grammar. This meta-model is essential since it represents not only the key part of the DSL conception, but also the needed starting point to develop a GMF[5]-based graphical editor. Required model-to-text transformations have been developed using XTend[6], which is fully integrated with XText and with the tool-chain provided by Eclipse.

6.2   Supporting the System at the Server

The concepts of node and stream together with native data types, among others, have been implemented through a Java library. This library performs the computation of each node whenever the data inputs are available. The library uses the standard I/O for representing the patterns input and outputs. However, for the communication with the visualization server (Fig. 5) HTTP is used by means of an API REST. This makes necessary a middleware in charge of attending the requests and forwarding them to the interpreter. The chosen middleware has been Apache[7]. The serialization of data used as inputs and outputs is performed using YAML[8], which is a super-set of the well-known JSON. For example, YAML allows references in the document (relational anchors), which are necessaries for the correct serialization of graphs.

6.3   Visualizing the Patterns at the Client

The final output of a visualization pattern is an abstract representation of the image. The browser will be in charge of rendering it. This allows having different engines depending on the device or the platform. Currently it has been developed using JavaScript, which is widely extended thanks to the intensive use of AJAX. As seen in Fig. 9, the final size is not taken into account by the patterns in any way. This is because the process of rendering has an automatic scale-and-center subsystem that does the needed computations to show the graph in the final desired area. The final result of that process is a SVG[9] mark-up image that can be embedded in a HTML5 Web page at run time. Choosing SVG is due to it being supported by all the browsers and standardized by W3C. The `canvas` API of HTML5 has been avoided due to the difficulties for accessing the image once it has been drawn. On the contrary, SVG allows to access practically each point of the graphic, to manipulate the graphic from the code and, thus, making easier the interaction with the user.

---

[4] https://www.eclipse.org/emf/
[5] https://www.eclipse.org/modeling/gmp/
[6] https://www.eclipse.org/xtend/
[7] http://www.apache.org/
[8] http://yaml.org/spec/
   http://www.mangoost-airsoft.ru/products_files/spec.pdf
[9] http://www.w3.org/Graphics/SVG/

```
 1 module "bar"
 2
 3 require "standard.vml"
 4
 5 input
 6   height: Integer, position: Position, color: Color
 7
 8 Builder b -> Rectangle
 9 {
10   height <- input.height
11   width <- 1
12   x <- input.position
13   y <- 0
14   color <- input.color
15 }
16
17 output <- b.out
```

Listing 1. Bar pattern representation using textual syntax of the DSL

7 Related Work

In this section we will review some relevant work about data visualization development. This will be split in academic and technological, and later on Web-or desktop-based.

7.1 Academic

The problem of making the visualizations development easier has been taken into account since the early taxonomy of Bertin [5]. We should mention Mackinlay for the visionary concept of data-driven automation of pattern selection [6]; Shneiderman for his data-based taxonomy [7]; and Tufte for his inspiring and valuable work [8] on static visualization techniques. Since Fowler published his inspiring book about DSLs [9] a lot of new small languages have been arising, to cover the most varied domains. Stencil [10] is a promising computational architecture claiming that it enables a rapid development of visualizations. Until now this approach has not graphical representation. Some academic researches inside Search Computing world have included also a visualization perspective, like [11] and [12], but these approaches do not focus on enabling user to interchange the patterns.

Our DSL is able to target several platforms and their render engine can evolve together with the technologies without compromising the core concepts or the already developed patterns. Also, giving a formal specification, by means of a grammar, provides some extra advantages: it allows for better sharing and modularization, and it makes easier automating some jobs of the modeler.

7.2   Technological

Web. Recently, JavaScript revolution over the Web concept has made possible a storm of new libraries or technologies. We will cite the most relevant for this work. *three.js*[10] is a JavaScript library to create 3D Scenes on the browser. *VVVV.js*[11] is a Web-based runtime that executes interactive programs specified using a graphical-only syntax. *Raphaël*[12] is also a library, intended to make easier to the developer creating and managing Web vector graphics. *Protovis*[13] [13] was born following also that idea (of making an abstraction layer for SVG). However, currently their team is working on *d3.js*[14] [14] which is more focused on accessing directly to the graphics –allowing better interaction– instead of creating a new tier (in a similar way that *jQuery*[15] did some years ago to make easier the direct access to the HTML DOM). *Unveil.js*[16] is also a library that creates a layer of abstraction combining SVG with canvas API[15]. Google has made a cloud and service-oriented approach to the Web visualizations called Chart Tools[17] that can be invoked from any Web page using JavaScript.

However, these works have technological orientation and they do not fit the target of being independent. Also, they present some lack of abstraction to facilitate development to non-programmers.

Desktop -oriented technologies have also arisen around visualization hype. Processing[18] is one of them, basically a language to develop interactive systems. It has a port called *Processing.js*[19] that compiles the code for publishing on Web environments. Microsoft Excel[20] has graphic creation features, very limited, but cited here for its widespread use. Tableau[21] is a program that also allows for data-based graphic creation. These approaches have little or none entailment with the Web.

8   Conclusions and Future Work

Data visualization is a key concept when representing search results and is gaining momentum in Business Intelligence environmens. However, data visualization development is not an easy task. It has to face problems at two different levels: technological and human/social. The work presented in this paper tries to solve

---

[10] http://mrdoob.github.com/three.js/
[11] http://vvvvjs.quasipartikel.at/
[12] http://raphaeljs.com/
[13] http://mbostock.github.com/protovis/
[14] http://mbostock.github.com/d3/
[15] http://jquery.com/
[16] https://github.com/michael/unveil
[17] https://code.google.com/intl/en/apis/chart/
[18] http://processing.org/
[19] http://processingjs.org/
[20] http://office.microsoft.com/es-es/excel/
[21] http://www.tableausoftware.com/

both problems by following a Model Driven approach. The paper has shown, through a driving example, the main pillars of a DSL for modeling reusable visual patterns. The use of the DSL adds comprehensibility and, although its use could appear quite complex, it is not more complex than using whatever imperative language to develop the graphic. From a computational point of view the use of the DSL favors a potential parallelization of tasks.

Future work includes the definition of an expert system to suggest the most suitable visualization pattern for a given data-set based on metadata and other social information such as how these data have been seen in the past by other colleagues, among others. Developing a debugger with the possibility of seeing patterns working with real data and populating more and more the pattern library are also in our roadmap.

References

1. Brooks, M.G.: The Business Case for Advanced Data Visualization (2008)
2. Morales-Chaparro, R., Preciado, J.C., Sánchez-Figueroa, F.: Data-Driven and User-Driven Multidimensional Data Visualization. In: Harth, A., Koch, N. (eds.) ICWE 2011. LNCS, vol. 7059, pp. 159–166. Springer, Heidelberg (2012)
3. Cunningham, C., Graefe, G.: PIVOT and UNPIVOT: Optimization and Execution Strategies in an RDBMS. In: Data Base, pp. 998–1009 (2004)
4. Gray, J., Chaudhuri, S., Bosworth, A., Layman, A., Reichart, D., Venkatrao, M., Pellow, F., Pirahesh, H.: Data Cube: A Relational Aggregation Operator Generalizing Group-By, Cross-Tab, and Sub-Totals (1997)
5. Bertin, J.: Semiologie Graphique: Les Diagrammes, Les Reseaux, Les Cartes (1967)
6. Mackinlay, J.: Automating the design of graphical presentations of relational information. ACM Transactions on Graphics 5(2), 110–141 (1986)
7. Shneiderman, B.: The eyes have it: A task by data type taxonomy for information visualizations. In: Proceedings of IEEE Visual Languages (1996)
8. Tufte, E.R., Howard, G.: The visual display of quantitative information, vol. 16. Graphics Press, Cheshire (1983)
9. Fowler, M.: Domain Specific Languages. Programming the Memory Heirarchy, vol. 1, pp. 99–105. Addison-Wesley Professional (2010)
10. Cottam, J.A.: Design and implementation of a stream-based visualization language. PhD thesis (2011)
11. Clarkson, E., Desai, K., Foley, J.: ResultMaps: visualization for search interfaces. IEEE Transactions on Visualization and Computer Graphics 15(6), 1057–1064 (2009)
12. Bozzon, A., Brambilla, M., Catarci, T., Ceri, S., Fraternali, P., Matera, M.: Visualization of Multi-domain Ranked Data. In: Ceri, S., Brambilla, M. (eds.) Search Computing II. LNCS, vol. 6585, pp. 53–69. Springer, Heidelberg (2011)
13. Heer, J., Bostock, M.: Declarative language design for interactive visualization. IEEE Transactions on Visualization and Computer Graphics 16(6), 1149–1156 (2010)
14. Bostock, M., Ogievetsky, V., Heer, J.: D^3: Data-Driven Documents. IEEE Transactions on Visualization and Computer Graphics 17(12), 2301–2309 (2011)
15. Aufreiter, M.: Web-based Information Visualization. Master's thesis (2011)

Extending SPARQL Algebra to Support Efficient Evaluation of Top-K SPARQL Queries

Alessandro Bozzon[1], Emanuele Della Valle[1], and Sara Magliacane[1,2]

[1] Politecnico di Milano, P.za L. Da Vinci, 32. I-20133 Milano, Italy
[2] VU University Amsterdam, The Netherlands

Abstract. With the widespread adoption of Linked Data, the efficient processing of SPARQL queries gains importance. A crucial category of queries that is prone to optimization is "top-k" queries, i.e. queries returning the top k results ordered by a specified ranking function. Top-k queries can be expressed in SPARQL by appending to a SELECT query the ORDER BY and LIMIT clauses, which impose a sorting order on the result set, and limit the number of results. However, the ORDER BY and LIMIT clauses in SPARQL algebra are result modifiers, i.e. their evaluation is performed only after the evaluation of the other query clauses. The evaluation of ORDER BY and LIMIT clauses in SPARQL engines typically requires the process of all the matching solutions (possibly thousands), followed by a monolithically computation of the ranking function for each solution, even if only a limited number (e.g. $K = 10$) of them were requested, thus leading to poor performance.

In this paper, we present $\mathcal{S}$PARQL-$\mathcal{R}$ANK, an extension of the SPARQL algebra and execution model that supports ranking as a first-class SPAR-QL construct. The new algebra and execution model allow for splitting the ranking function and interleaving it with other operations. We also provide a prototypal open source implementation of $\mathcal{S}$PARQL-$\mathcal{R}$ANK based on ARQ, and we carry out a series of preliminary experiments.

1 Introduction

SPARQL [16] is a W3C recommendation that specifies a query language as well as a protocol for Linked Data (LD). An ever-increasing number of SPARQL endpoints allows to query the published LD, thus calling for efficient SPARQL query processing. An important category of queries that is prone to optimization is the ranking, or "top-k", queries, i.e. queries returning the top k results ordered by a specified ranking function.

Simple top-k queries can be expressed in SPARQL by appending to a SELECT query the ORDER BY and LIMIT clauses, which impose an order on the result set, and limit the number of results. Practitioners willing to issue top-k queries using complex ranking functions have been forced to create ad-hoc extensions such as project functions whose results can be used in the ORDER BY clause. This has lead to the inclusions of projection functions in the SPARQL 1.1 [9]

S. Ceri and M. Brambilla (Eds.): Search Computing III, LNCS 7538, pp. 143–156, 2012.

working draft. Listing 1.1 provides an example of SPARQL 1.1 top-k query on a BSBM [3] dataset[1].

SPARQL engines supporting SPARQL and SPARQL 1.1 typically manage ORDER BY and LIMIT clauses are result modifiers that alter the solution generated in evaluating the WHERE clause before returning the result to the user. The semantics of modifiers imposes to take a solution as input, manipulate it, and generate a new solution as output. Specifically, an order modifier puts the solutions in the order required by the ordering clauses that are either ascending (indicated by ASC() that is also assumed as default) or descending (indicated by DESC()). The limit modifier defines an upper bound on the number of returned results; it allows to slice the result set and to retrieve just a portion of it. For instance, the query in Listing 1.1 is executed according to the query plan in Figure 1.a: solutions matching the WHERE clause are drawn iteratively from the RDF store until the whole result is materialized; then, the ordering function is evaluated monolithically, and the top 10 results are returned.

```
1  SELECT ?product ?offer ((?avgRateProduct + ?avgRateProducer) AS ?score)
2  WHERE {
3    ?offer bsbm:product ?product .
4    ?product bsbm:avgRate ?avgRateProduct ;
5           bsbm:producer ?producer .
6    ?producer bsbm:avgRate ?avgRateProducer.
7  }
8  ORDER BY DESC(?score)
9  LIMIT 10
```

Listing 1.1. "Example of a top-k query on BSBM"

As a result the performances of SPARQL top-k queries can be very poor when a SPARQL engine elaborates thousands of matching solutions and computes the ranking for each of them, even if only a limited number (e.g. ten) were requested. Moreover, the ranking predicates can be expensive to compute and, therefore, they should be evaluated only when needed and on the minimum possible number of results. It is clear that it may be beneficial in these cases to **split** the evaluation of the ranking projection function in ranking atoms, and **interleave** the evaluation of these ranking atoms with joins and boolean filters as shown in Figure 1.b.

Contribution. In a previous work [4], we presented a first sketch of $\mathcal{S}$PARQL-$\mathcal{R}$ANK algebra, and we applied it to the execution of top-k SPARQL queries on top of virtual RDF stores through query rewriting over a rank-aware RDBMS. In this paper, we propose a consolidated version of $\mathcal{S}$PARQL-$\mathcal{R}$ANK algebra and a general rank-aware execution model that can be applied to state-of-the-art SPARQL engine built on top of both RDBMS and native triple stores.

We provide an open source implementation of $\mathcal{S}$PARQL-$\mathcal{R}$ANK extending ARQ[2]) and we carry out some preliminary experiments.

Organization of the Paper. In Section 2, we provide an introduction of SPARQL as presented in [15]. In Section 3, we show how we extended [15]

---

[1] For simplicity, we assume the average rates to be materialized in the dataset.

[2] The code is available at `http://sparqlrank.search-computing.org/`

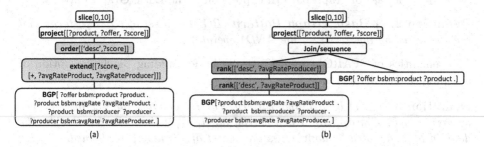

Fig. 1. Examples of (a) standard and (b) $\mathcal{S}$PARQL-$\mathcal{R}$ANK algebraic query plan for the top-k SPARQL query in Listing 1.1

introducing a ranking model for SPARQL queries and proposing new algebraic operators of $\mathcal{S}$PARQL-$\mathcal{R}$ANK. In Section 4 we briefly discuss an incremental execution model supporting $\mathcal{S}$PARQL-$\mathcal{R}$ANK. In Section 5, we report on the preliminary results of the experiments we carried out comparing ARQ 2.8.9 with our rank-aware version. In Section 6, we present the related work. Finally, in Section 7, we elaborate on future works.

2   An Introduction to SPARQL Algebra

The features of SPARQL, taken one by one, are simple to describe and to understand. However, the combination of such features makes SPARQL a complex language whose semantics can only be fully understood through an algebraic representation. Several alternative algebraic models were proposed. Hereafter, we discuss the formalization presented in [15], focusing on the WHERE clause.

In SPARQL, the WHERE clause contains a set of *graph pattern* expressions that can be constructed using the operators OPTIONAL, UNION, FILTER and concatenation via a point symbol "." that means AND. Formally, a graph pattern expression is defined as:

Definition 1. *Assuming three pairwise disjoint sets I (IRIs), L (literals) and V (variables), a **graph pattern expression** is defined recursively as:*

1. *A tuple from $(I \cup L \cup V) \times (I \cup V) \times (I \cup L \cup V)$ is a graph pattern and in particular it is a triple pattern.*
2. *If P_1 and P_2 are graph patterns, then $(P_1 \, . \, P_2)$, $(P_1 \ OPTIONAL \ P_2)$ and $(P_1 \ UNION \ P_2)$ are graph patterns.*
3. *If P is a graph pattern and R is a SPARQL built-in condition, then $(P \ FILTER \ R)$ is a graph pattern.*

A SPARQL built-in condition is composed by elements of the set $I \cup L \cup V$ and constants, logical connectives $(\neg, \wedge, \vee)$, ordering symbols $(<, \leq, \geq, >)$, the equality symbol $(=)$, unary predicates like bound, isBlank, isIRI and other features.

An important case of graph pattern expression is the Basic Graph Pattern:

Definition 2. *A **Basic Graph Pattern** (BGP) is a set of triple patterns that are connected by the "." (i.e., the AND) operator.*

The semantics of SPARQL queries uses as basic building block the notion of mapping that is defined as:

Definition 3. *Let P be a graph pattern, $var(P)$ denotes the set of variables occurring in P. A **mapping** μ is a partial function $\mu : V \to (I \cup L \cup BN)^3$. The domain of μ, denoted by $dom(\mu)$, is the subset of V where μ is defined.*

The **relation between** the notions of **mapping, triple pattern and basic graph pattern** is given in the following definition:

Definition 4. *Given a triple pattern t and a mapping μ such that $var(t) \subseteq dom(\mu)$, $\mu(t)$ is the triple obtained by replacing the variables in t according to μ. Given a basic graph pattern B and a mapping μ such that $var(B) \subseteq dom(\mu)$, we define $\mu(B) = \cup_{t \in B} \mu(t)$, i.e. $\mu(B)$ is the set of triples obtained by replacing the variables in the triples of B according to μ.*

Using these definitions, [15] defines the semantics of SPARQL queries as an algebra. The main algebra operators are Join ($\bowtie$), Union ($\cup$), Difference($\backslash$) and Left Join ($\bowtie$). The authors define the semantics of these operators on **sets of mappings** denoted with Ω. The evaluation of a SPARQL query is based on its translation into an algebraic tree composed of those algebraic operators.

The simplest case is the **evaluation of a basic graph pattern** defined as:

Definition 5. *Let G be an RDF graph and P a Basic Graph Pattern. The evaluation of P over G, denoted by $[\![P]\!]_G$, is defined by the set of mapping:*

$$[\![P]\!]_G = \{\mu|\; dom(\mu) = var(P) \text{ and } \mu(P) \subseteq G\}$$

If $\mu \in [\![P]\!]_G$, μ is said to be a solution for P in G.

The evaluation of more complex graph pattern is compositional and can be defined recursively from basic graph pattern evaluation by mapping the graph expressions to algebraic expressions.

Noteworthy, in SPARQL, the OPTIONAL and UNION operators can introduce unbound variables; it is known that the problem of verifying, given a graph pattern P and a variable $?x \in var(P)$, whether $?x$ is bound in P is undecidable [2], but an efficiently verifiable syntactical condition can be introduced. Hereafter, we propose such a syntactic notion of *certainly bound* variable, defined as:

Definition 6. *Let P, P_1 and P_2 be a graph patterns. Then the set of **certainly bound variables** in P, denoted as $CB(P)$, is recursively defined as follows:*

1. if t is a triple pattern and $P = t$, then $CB(P) = var(t)$;

---

[3] BN is the set of blank nodes.

2. *if* $P = (P_1 \cdot P_2)$, *then* $CB(P) = CB(P_1) \cup CB(P_2)$;
3. *if* $P = (P_1 \ UNION \ P_2)$, *then* $CB(P) = CB(P_1) \cap CB(P_2)$;
4. *if* $P = (P_1 \ OPTIONAL \ P_2)$, *then* $CB(P) = CB(P_1)$;

The above definition recursively accumulates a set of variables that are certainly bound in a given graph pattern P because: they appear in graph pattern expressions that do not contain the OPTIONAL or UNION operators (rules 1 and 2), or they appear both on the left and on the right side of a graph pattern containing the UNION operator (rule 3), or they appear only in the left side of graph pattern expression that contains the OPTIONAL operator (rule 4)[4].

3   The $\mathcal{SPARQL}$-$\mathcal{RANK}$ Algebra

In this section, we progressively introduce: *a*) the basic concept of ranking criterion, scoring function and upper bound that characterised rank-aware data management [12], *b*) the concept of *ranked set of mappings*, an extension of the standard SPARQL definition of a set of mappings that embeds the notion of *ranking*, *c*) the new $\mathcal{SPARQL}$-$\mathcal{RANK}$ algebraic operators, and *d*) the new $\mathcal{SPARQL}$-$\mathcal{RANK}$ algebraic equivalences.

3.1   Basic Concepts

$\mathcal{SPARQL}$-$\mathcal{RANK}$ supports top-k SPARQL queries that have an ORDER BY clause that can be formulated as a scoring function combining several ranking criteria. Given a graph pattern P, a **ranking criterion** $b \colon \mathbb{R}^m \to \mathbb{R}$ is a function defined over a set of variables $?x_j \in var(P)$. The evaluation of a ranking criterion on a mapping μ, that is, the substitution of all of the variables $?x_j$ with the corresponding values from the mapping, is indicated by $b[\mu]$. A criterion b can be the result of the evaluation of any built-in function (having an arbitrary cost) of query variables.

A **scoring function** on P is an expression of the form $\mathcal{F}$ defined over the set B of ranking criteria. As typical in ranked queries, the scoring function $\mathcal{F}$ is assumed to be **monotonic**, i.e., a $\mathcal{F}$ for which holds $\mathcal{F}(x_1, \ldots, x_n) \geq \mathcal{F}(y_1, \ldots, y_n)$ when $\forall i : x_i \geq y_i$. In order for a scoring function to be evaluable, the variables in $var(P)$ that contribute in the evaluation of $\mathcal{F}$ must be bound. Since OPTIONAL and UNION clauses can introduce unbound variables, we assume all the variables in $var(P)$ to be *certainly bound*, i.e. variables that are certainly bound for every mapping produced by P (see also Definition 6 in Section 2). An extension of $\mathcal{SPARQL}$-$\mathcal{RANK}$ toward the relaxation of the *certainly bound variables* constraint is part of the future work and will be discussed in the conclusions of the paper.

Listing 1.1 provides an example of the scoring function $\mathcal{F}$ calculated over the ranking criteria *?avgRateProduct* and *?avgRateProducer*. We note that *?avgRateProduct* and *?avgRateProducer* are certain bound variables, as the query

---

[4] We omit discussing FILTER clauses since they cannot add any variable, granted that the variables occurring in a filter condition (P FILTER R) are a subset of $var(P)$.

contains no OPTIONAL or UNION clauses. The result of the evaluation is stored in the *?score* variable, which is later used in the ORDER BY clause.

Overall, a key property of $\mathcal{SPARQL\text{-}RANK}$ is the ability to retrieve the first k results of a top-k query before scanning the complete set of mappings resulting from the evaluation of the WHERE clause. To enable such a property, the mappings progressively produced by each operator should flow in an order consistent with the final order, i.e., the order imposed by $\mathcal{F}$. When the evaluation of a SPARQL top-k query starts on the Basic Graph Patterns the resulting mappings are unordered. As soon as some $\mathcal{B} = \{b_1, \ldots, b_j\}$ (with $j < |B|$) of the ranking criteria can be computed (i.e., when $var(b_j) \subseteq dom(\mu)$), an order can be imposed to a set of mappings Ω by evaluating for each $\mu \in \Omega$ the **upper bound** of $\mathcal{F}[\mu]$ as:

$$\overline{\mathcal{F}}_\mathcal{B}[\mu] = \mathcal{F}\left(\begin{array}{ll} b_i = b_i[\mu] & \text{if } b_i \in \mathcal{B} \\ b_i = max(b_i) & \text{otherwise} \end{array} \forall i \right)$$

where $max(b_i)$ is the application-specific maximal possible value for the ranking criterion b_i. $\overline{\mathcal{F}}_\mathcal{B}[\mu]$ is the upper bound of the score that μ can obtain, when $\mathcal{F}[\mu]$ is completely evaluated, by assuming that all the ranking criteria still to evaluate will return their maximal possible value. We can now formalize the notion of *ranked set of mappings*.

Table 1. $\Omega'_{b_1} \bowtie \Omega''_{b_2}$

	?p	?pr	?a1	?a2	b_1	b_2	$\overline{\mathcal{F}}_{\{b_1 \cup b_2\}}$
μ_1	p1	pr3	4.0	4.5	0.80	0.90	1.70
μ_3	p3	pr4	2.0	3.5	0.40	0.70	1.10
μ_2	p2	pr2	2.0	3.0	0.40	0.60	1.00

Table 2. Ω'_{b_1}

	?p	?a1	b_1	$\overline{\mathcal{F}}_{\{b_1\}}$
μ_1	p1	4.0	0.80	1.80
μ_2	p2	2.0	0.40	1.40
μ_3	p3	2.0	0.40	1.40

Table 3. Ω''_{b_2}

	?pr	?a2	b_2	$\overline{\mathcal{F}}_{\{b_2\}}$
μ_1	pr3	4.5	0.90	1.90
μ_3	pr4	3.5	0.70	1.70
μ_2	pr2	3.0	0.60	1.60

A **ranked set of mappings** $\Omega_\mathcal{B}$, with respect to a scoring function $\mathcal{F}$, and a set $\mathcal{B}$ of ranking criteria, is the set of mappings Ω augmented with an order relation $<_{\Omega_\mathcal{B}}$ defined over Ω, which orders mappings by their upper bound scores, i.e., $\forall \mu_1, \mu_2 \in \Omega : \mu_1 <_{\Omega_\mathcal{B}} \mu_2 \iff \overline{\mathcal{F}}_\mathcal{B}[\mu_1] < \overline{\mathcal{F}}_\mathcal{B}[\mu_2]$.

The monotonicity of $\mathcal{F}$ implies that $\overline{\mathcal{F}}_\mathcal{B}$ is always an upper bound of $\mathcal{F}$, i.e. $\overline{\mathcal{F}}_\mathcal{B}[\mu] \geq \mathcal{F}[\mu]$ for any mapping $\mu \in \Omega_\mathcal{B}$, thus guaranteeing that the order imposed by $\overline{\mathcal{F}}_\mathcal{B}$ is consistent with the order imposed by $\mathcal{F}$.

Note that a set of mappings on which no ranking criteria is evaluated ($\mathcal{B} = \emptyset$) is consistently denoted as $\Omega_\emptyset$ or simply Ω.

Table 1 depicts a subset of ranked set of mappings

$$\Omega_{\{?avgRateProduct, ?avgRateProducer\}}$$

(the ranking criteria are represented as b_1 and b_2 respectively) resulting from the evaluation of

$$\overline{\mathcal{F}}_{\{?avgRateProduct, ?avgRateProducer\}}$$

of the query in Listing 1.1, where mappings $\mu_i \in \Omega$ are ordered according to their upper bounds. When there are ties in the ordering, we assume an arbitrary deterministic tie-breaker function (e.g., by using the hash code of the lexical form of a mapping).

3.2 $\mathcal{S}$PARQL-$\mathcal{R}$ANK Algebraic Operators

Starting from the notion of *ranked set of mappings*, $\mathcal{S}$PARQL-$\mathcal{R}$ANK introduces a new *rank operator* ρ, representing the evaluation of a single ranking criterion, and redefines the Selection (σ), Join ($\bowtie$), Union ($\cup$), Difference($\backslash$) and Left Join ($\bowtie$) operators, enabling them to process and output ranked sets of mappings. For the sake of brevity, we present ρ and $\bowtie$, referring the reader to [4] for further details.

The *rank operator* ρ_b evaluates the ranking criterion $b \in B$ upon a ranked set of mappings Ω_B and returns $\Omega_{B \cup \{b\}}$, i.e. the same set ordered by $\overline{\mathcal{F}}_{B \cup \{b\}}$. Thus, by definition $\rho_b(\Omega_B) = \Omega_{\{B \cup b\}}$. Tables 2 and 3 respectively exemplify the evaluation of ?*avgRateProduct* – to shorten, b_1 – an additional ranking criterion ?*avgRateProduct2* – b_2 – over the ?product bsbm:avgRate ?avgRateProduct and ?product bsbm:avgRate ?avgRateProduct2 triple patterns. Moreover, the tables show the evaluation of the upper bounds $\overline{\mathcal{F}}_{\{b_1\}}$ and $\overline{\mathcal{F}}_{\{b_2\}}$.

The extended $\bowtie$ operator has a standard semantics for what it concerns the membership property [15], while it defines an order relation on its output mappings: given two ranked sets of mappings Ω'_{B_1} and Ω''_{B_2} ordered with respect to two sets of ranking criteria B_1 and B_2, the join between Ω'_{B_1} and Ω''_{B_2}, denoted as $\Omega'_{B_1} \bowtie \Omega''_{B_2}$, produces a ranked set of mappings ordered by $\overline{\mathcal{F}}_{B_1 \cup B_2}$. Thus, formally $\Omega'_{B_1} \bowtie \Omega''_{B_2} \equiv (\Omega' \bowtie \Omega'')_{B_1 \cup B_2}$. Table 1 exemplifies the application of the $\bowtie$ operator over the ranked set of mappings of Tables 2 and 3.

3.3 $\mathcal{S}$PARQL-$\mathcal{R}$ANK Algebraic Equivalences

Query optimization relies on algebraic equivalences in order to produce several equivalent formulations of a query. The $\mathcal{S}$PARQL-$\mathcal{R}$ANK algebra defines a set of algebraic equivalences that take into account the order property. The rank operator ρ can be pushed-down to impose an order to a set of mappings; such order can be then exploited to limit the number of mappings flowing through the physical execution plan, while allowing the production of the k results. In the following we focus on the equivalence laws that apply to the ρ and $\bowtie$ operators:

1. **Rank splitting** $[\Omega_{\{b_1, b_2, ..., b_n\}} \equiv \rho_{b_1}(\rho_{b_2}(...(\rho_{b_n}(\Omega))...))]$: allows splitting the criteria of a scoring function into a series of rank operations ($\rho_{b_1}, ..., \rho_{b_n}$), thus enabling the individual processing of the ranking criteria.
2. **Rank commutative law** $[\rho_{b_1}(\rho_{b_2}(\Omega_B)) \equiv \rho_{b_2}(\rho_{b_1}(\Omega_B))]$: allows the commutativity of the ρ operand with itself, thus enabling query planning strategies that exploit optimal ordering of rank operators.

3. **Pushing ρ over** $\bowtie$ [if Ω' does not map all variables of the ranking criterion b, then $\rho_b(\Omega'_{B_1} \bowtie \Omega''_{B_2}) \equiv \rho_b(\Omega'_{B_1}) \bowtie \Omega''_{B_2}$; if both Ω' and Ω'' map all variables of b, then $\rho_b(\Omega'_{B_1} \bowtie \Omega''_{B_2}) \equiv \rho_b(\Omega'_{B_1}) \bowtie \rho_b(\Omega''_{B_2})$]: this law handles swapping $\bowtie$ with ρ, thus allowing to push the rank operator only on the operands whose variables also appear in b.

The new algebraic laws lay the foundation for query optimization, as discussed in the following Section. We refer the reader to [4] for the complete set of equivalences.

4   Execution of Top-K SPARQL Queries

In common SPARQL engines, a query execution plan is a tree of physical operators as iterators. During the execution of the query, mappings are drawn from the root operator, which draws mappings from underlying operators recursively, till the evaluation of a Basic Graph Pattern in the RDF store. The execution is incremental unless some blocking operator is present in the query execution plan (e.g., the ORDER BY operator in SPARQL).

In Section 3, we remove the logical barriers that make ranking a blocking operator in SPARQL. $\mathcal{SPARQL}$-$\mathcal{RANK}$ algebra allows for writing logic plans that split ranking and interleave the ranking operators with other operators evaluation. Thus, it allows for an incremental execution of top-k SPARQL queries. In the rest of the section, we first describe the $\mathcal{SPARQL}$-$\mathcal{RANK}$ incremental execution model and how to implement physical operators; then, we report on our initial investigations on a rank-aware optimizer that uses the new algebraic equivalences.

4.1   Incremental Execution Model and Physical Operators

The $\mathcal{SPARQL}$-$\mathcal{RANK}$ execution model handles ranking-aware query plans as follows:

1. physical operators incrementally output ranked sets of mappings in the order of the upper bound of their scores;
2. the execution stops when the requested number of mapping have been drawn from the root operator or no more mapping can be drawn.

In order to implement the proposed execution model, algorithms for the physical operators are needed. Some algorithms are trivial, e.g., selection that rejects solutions that do not satisfy the FILTER clauses while preserving the mapping ordering. For the non-trivial cases, e.g., ρ and $\bowtie$, many algorithms are described in the literature: MPro [7] and Upper [5] are two state-of-the-art algorithms useful for implementing the ρ operator, whereas the implementation of $\bowtie$ can be based on algorithms such as HRJN (hash rank-join) and NRJN (nested-loop rank-join) described in [13,11].

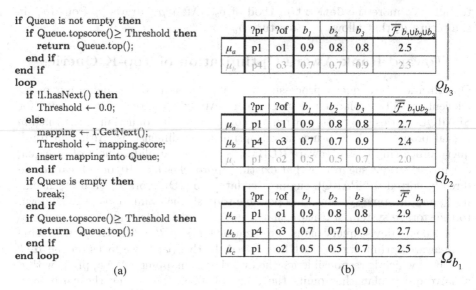

```
if Queue is not empty then
    if Queue.topscore()≥ Threshold then
        return Queue.top();
    end if
end if
loop
    if !I.hasNext() then
        Threshold ← 0.0;
    else
        mapping ← I.GetNext();
        Threshold ← mapping.score;
        insert mapping into Queue;
    end if
    if Queue is empty then
        break;
    end if
    if Queue.topscore()≥ Threshold then
        return Queue.top();
    end if
end loop
```

(a)

	?pr	?of	b_1	b_2	b_3	$\overline{\mathcal{F}}_{b_1 \cup b_2 \cup b_3}$
μ_a	p1	o1	0.9	0.8	0.8	2.5
μ_b	p4	o3	0.7	0.7	0.9	2.3

ϱ_{b_3}

	?pr	?of	b_1	b_2	b_3	$\overline{\mathcal{F}}_{b_1 \cup b_2}$
μ_a	p1	o1	0.9	0.8	0.8	2.7
μ_b	p4	o3	0.7	0.7	0.9	2.4
μ_c	p1	o2	0.5	0.5	0.7	2.0

ϱ_{b_2}

	?pr	?of	b_1	b_2	b_3	$\overline{\mathcal{F}}_{b_1}$
μ_a	p1	o1	0.9	0.8	0.8	2.9
μ_b	p4	o3	0.7	0.7	0.9	2.7
μ_c	p1	o2	0.5	0.5	0.7	2.5

Ω_{b_1}

(b)

Fig. 2. Example of the rank operator algorithm

In Figure 2.a, we present the pseudo code of our implementation for the rank operator ρ. In particular, we show the GetNext method that allows a downstream operator to draw one mapping from the rank operator.

Let b be a scoring function not already evaluated (i.e., $b \notin B$). When $\mathcal{SPARQL}$-$\mathcal{RANK}$ applies ρ_b on a ranked set of mappings Ω_B flowing from an upstream operator, the drawn mappings from Ω_B are buffered in a priority queue, which maintains them ranked by $\overline{\mathcal{F}}_{B \cup \{b\}}$. The operator ρ_b cannot output immediately each drawn mapping, because one of the next mappings could obtain a higher score after evaluation. The operator can output the top ranked mapping of the queue μ, only when it draws from a upstream operator a mapping μ' such that

$$\overline{\mathcal{F}}_{B \cup \{b\}}[\mu] \geq \overline{\mathcal{F}}_B[\mu']$$

This implies that $\overline{\mathcal{F}}_{B \cup \{b\}}[\mu] \geq \overline{\mathcal{F}}_B[\mu'] \geq \overline{\mathcal{F}}_B[\mu'']$ for any future mapping μ'' and, moreover, $\overline{\mathcal{F}}_B[\mu''] \geq \overline{\mathcal{F}}_{B \cup \{b\}}[\mu'']$. None of the mappings μ'' that ρ_b will draw from Ω_B can achieve a better score than μ.

In Figure 2.b, we present an example execution of a pipeline consisting of two rank operators ρ_{b_3} and ρ_{b_2} that draws mappings from Ω_{b_1}. It is work to notice that the proposed algorithm concretely allows for splitting the evaluation of Ω_{b_1,b_2,b_3} in $\rho_{b_3}(\rho_{b_2}(\Omega_{b_1}))$ by applying the algebraic equivalence law in Proposition 1. Thus, it practically implements the intuition given in Figure 1.b.

When an operator downstream to ρ_{b_3} wants to draw a mapping from ρ_{b_3}, it calls the GetNext method of ρ_{b_3} that recursively calls the GetNext method of ρ_{b_2} that draws mapping ranked by $\overline{\mathcal{F}}_{b_1}$ from Ω_{b_1}. ρ_{b_2} has to draw μ_a and μ_b from Ω_{b_1}, before returning μ_a to ρ_3. At this point, ρ_3 cannot output μ_a yet, it needs to call once more the `GetNext` method of ρ_{b_2}. After ρ_{b_2} draws μ_c from Ω_{b_1}, it can return μ_b that allows ρ_{b_3} to return μ_a.

5   Toward Rank-Aware Optimization of Top-K Queries

Optimization is a query processing activity devoted to the definition of an efficient execution plan for a given query. Many optimization techniques for SPARQL queries [18] exist, but none account for the introduction of the *ranking* logical property, which brings novel optimization dimensions. Although top-k query processing in rank-aware RDBMS is a very consolidate field of research, our investigations suggest us that existing approaches like [10] or [14] cannot be directly ported to SPARQL engines, as data in a RDF storage can be "schema-free", and, in some systems, it is possible to push the evaluations of BGP down to the storage system, a feature that is not present in RDBMS.

In order to devise query plans optimization for $\mathcal{S}$PARQL-$\mathcal{R}$ANK queries, some rank-aware optimizations must be advised. In this paper we focus on the *rank* operator, which is responsible for the ordering of mappings. We apply it within a naïve query plan that omits the usage of joins, thus losing the cardinality reduction brought by join selectivity; we just consider the evaluation of a single BGP, and the subsequent application of several rank operators to order mappings as they are incrementally extracted from the underlying storage system.

Notice that data can be retrieved from the source according to one ranking criterion b_i: in a previous work [4] we exploited a rank-aware RDBMS as a data storage layer offering indexes over ranking criteria. In such a case, additional ranking criterion are applied by serializing several rank operators. On the other hand, in this work we focus on native triple stores, namely, Jena TDB.

To have an initial assessment of the performance increase brought by the $\mathcal{S}$PARQL-$\mathcal{R}$ANK algebra with this naïve query plan, we extended the Jena ARQ 2.8.8 query engine with a new *rank* operator. We also extended the Berlin SPARQL Benchmark (BSBM), a synthetic dataset generator providing data resembling a real-life e-commerce website: we defined 12 test queries and, to exclude from the evaluation the time required for the run-time calculation of scoring functions, we materialized four numeric values for *Products*, *Producers* and *Offers*, each representing the result of a scoring function calculation.

Our experiments were conducted on an AMD 64bit processor with 2.66 GHz and 2 GB main memory, a Debian distribution with kernel 2.6.26-2, and Sun Java 1.6.0.

Table 4 reports the average execution time for the test queries, calculated for $k \in (1, 10, 100)$ on a 1M triple dataset. Notably, the performance boost of our prototype implementation with 1 variable queries (Q1, Q4, Q7, Q10) is at least one order of magnitude, regardless of optimizations. The good performances of the simple implementation techniques is justified by the co-occurence of the ranking function evaluation and sorting operation, which greatly reduce the number of calculation to be performed.

Table 4 also highlights queries where the performance of our prototype are comparable to ARQ. For instance, the poor (or worse) performance offered by

Table 4. Query Execution Time for Dataset=1M and score functions $b_1 \to$ avgScore1, $b_2 \to$ avgScore2, $b_3 \to$ numRevProd, $b_4 \to$ norm(price)

Query	Rank $\mathcal{F}$			SPARQL ARQ			SPARQL-RANK Extended ARQ		
				1	10	100	1	10	100
Q1. Product	b_1			142	143	141	35	36	71
Q2. Product	b_1	b_3		255	256	244	126	364	381
Q3. Product	b_1	b_2	b_3	269	268	267	354	629	711
Q4. Product, Producer	b_2			173	170	170	45	47	171
Q5. Product, Producer	b_1	b_3		261	273	259	101	138	304
Q6. Product, Producer	b_1	b_2	b_3	295	293	293	300	388	612
Q7. Product, Offer	b_1			3863	3779	3854	467	461	948
Q8. Product, Offer	b_1	b_2		5705	5849	5847	907	936	1365
Q9. Product, Offer	b_1	b_2	b_3	6612	6485	6817	2933	5062	8933
Q10. Product, Producer, Offer	b_2			4026	4089	4055	509	520	494
Q11. Product, Producer, Offer	b_1	b_3		6360	6229	6359	1279	1337	1576
Q12. Product, Producer, Offer	b_1	b_2	b_4	8234	8165	8111	2304	3149	6137

Q2 and Q3 are due to the low correlation of the applied scoring functions, that, when split, require the system to perform several reordering on sets of ranked mappings. Finally, Q12 shows how the on-the-fly calculation of scoring predicates (b_4) still leads to better performance for our prototype.

This discussion calls for investigating more advanced, cost-based, optimization techniques that include join (or rank-join) operators, which can provide better performance boost due to join selectivity. Moreover, it would be interesting to try and estimate the correlation between the order of intermediate results imposed by multiple pipelined scoring functions evaluations. This is the subject of our future work. An extensive description of the settings and result of our experiment can be found at sparqlrank.search-computing.org, together with the latest results of this research work.

6   Related Work

Our work builds on the results of several well-established techniques for the efficient evaluation of top-k queries in relational databases such as [12,10,13,19] where efficient rank-aware operators are investigated, and [14] where a rank-aware relational algebra and the RankSQL DBMS are described.

The application of such results to SPARQL is not straightforward, as SPARQL and relational algebra have equivalent expressive power, while just a subset of the relational optimizations can be ported to SPARQL [18]. Moreover, the schema-free nature of RDF data demands dedicated random access data structures to achieve efficient query evalutation; however, rank-aware operators typically rely on indexes for the sorted access; this can be expensive if naively done in native RDF stores, but cheaper in virtual RDF stores.

Our work contributes to the stream of investigations on SPARQL query optimization. Existing approaches focus on algebraic [15,18] or selectivity-based optimizations [21]. Despite an increasing need from practitioners [6], few works address SPARQL top-k query optimization.

Few works [8,20] extend the standard SPARQL algebra to allow the definition of ranking predicates, but, to the best of our knowledge, none addresses the problem of efficient evaluation of top-k queries in SPARQL. Straccia [22] describes an ontology mediated top-k information retrieval system over relational databases, where user queries are first rewritten into a set of conjunctive queries that are translated in SQL queries and executed on a rank-aware RDBMS [14]; then, the obtained results are merged into the final top-k answers. AnQL [24] is an extension of the SPARQL language and algebra able to address a wide variety of queries (including top-k ones) over annotated RDF graphs; our approach, instead, requires no annotations. Another rank-join algorithm, the Horizon based Ranked Join, is introduced [17] and aims at optimizing twig queries on weighted data graphs. In this case, results are ranked based on the underlying cost model, not based on an ad-hoc scoring function as in our work. The SemRank system [1] uses a rank-join algorithm to calculate the top-k most relevant paths from all the paths that connect two resources specified in the query. However, the application context of this algorithm is different from the one we presented, because it targets paths and ranks them by relevance using IR metrics. Moreover, the focus is not on query performance optimization.

7   Conclusion

In this paper, we presented $\mathcal{S}$PARQL-$\mathcal{R}$ANK, a rank-aware SPARQL algebra for the efficient evaluation of top-k queries. We introduced a new rank operator ρ, and extended the semantics of the other operators presented in [15]. To enable an incremental processing model, we added new algebraic equivalences laws that enable splitting ranking and interleaving it with other operators. In order to prototype an engine able to benefit from $\mathcal{S}$PARQL-$\mathcal{R}$ANK algebra, we extended both the algebra and the transformations of ARQ. We also run some preliminary experiments using our prototype on an extended version of the BSBM. The results show a significant performance gains when the limit k is in the order of tens, and hundreds of results.

As future work we plan to study additional optimizations techniques by, for instance, estimating the correlation between the order imposed by different scoring functions, and applying known algorithms to estimate the optimal order of execution of multiple rank operation obtained by splitting a complex ranking function. We also have preliminary positive results on a simple cost-base optimization techniques that uses rank-join algorithms [13,11] in combination with star-shaped patterns identification [23]. In addition, we plan to perform an exhaustive comparison with the 2.8.9 version of the Jena ARQ query engine, which recently included an ad-hoc optimization for top-k queries, where the ORDER BY and LIMIT clauses are still evaluated after the completion of the other operations, but they are merged into a single operator with a priority queue that contains k ordered mappings. Finally, we outlook potential extensions of $SPARQL\text{-}RANK$ in dealing with SPARQL 1.1 federation extension and with the evaluation of SPARQL queries under OWL2QL entailment regime.

References

1. Anyanwu, K., Maduko, A., Sheth, A.: SemRank: ranking complex relationship search results on the semantic web. In: WWW 2005, pp. 117–127. ACM (2005)
2. Buil-Aranda, C., Arenas, M., Corcho, O.: Semantics and Optimization of the SPARQL 1.1 Federation Extension. In: Antoniou, G., Grobelnik, M., Simperl, E., Parsia, B., Plexousakis, D., De Leenheer, P., Pan, J. (eds.) ESWC 2011, Part II. LNCS, vol. 6644, pp. 1–15. Springer, Heidelberg (2011)
3. Bizer, C., Schultz, A.: The Berlin SPARQL Benchmark. Int. J. Semantic Web Inf. Syst. 5(2), 1–24 (2009)
4. Bozzon, A., Della Valle, E., Magliacane, S.: Towards and efficient SPARQL top-k query execution in virtual RDF stores. In: 5th International Workshop on Ranking in Databases (DBRANK 2011) (August 2011)
5. Bruno, N., Gravano, L., Marian, A.: Evaluating Top-k Queries over Web-Accessible Databases. In: ICDE, p. 369. IEEE Computer Society (2002)
6. Castagna, P.: Avoid a total sort for order by + limit queries. JENA bug tracker, https://issues.apache.org/jira/browse/jena-89
7. Chang, K.C.-C., Hwang, S.-W.: Minimal probing: supporting expensive predicates for top-k queries. In: SIGMOD Conference, pp. 346–357. ACM (2002)
8. Cheng, J., Ma, Z.M., Yan, L.: f-SPARQL: A Flexible Extension of SPARQL. In: Bringas, P.G., Hameurlain, A., Quirchmayr, G. (eds.) DEXA 2010, Part I. LNCS, vol. 6261, pp. 487–494. Springer, Heidelberg (2010)
9. Harris, S., Seaborne, A.: SPARQL 1.1 Working Draft. Technical report, W3C (2011), http://www.w3.org/TR/sparql11-query/
10. Hwang, S.-W., Chang, K.C.-C.: Probe minimization by schedule optimization: Supporting top-k queries with expensive predicates. IEEE Transactions on Knowledge and Data Engineering 19(5), 646–662 (2007)
11. Ilyas, I.F., Aref, W.G., Elmagarmid, A.K.: Supporting Top-k Join Queries in Relational Databases. In: VLDB, pp. 754–765 (2003)
12. Ilyas, I.F., Beskales, G., Soliman, M.A.: A survey of top-k query processing techniques in relational database systems. ACM Comput. Surv. 40(4) (2008)
13. Ilyas, I.F., Shah, R., Aref, W.G., Vitter, J.S., Elmagarmid, A.K.: Rank-aware Query Optimization. In: SIGMOD Conference, pp. 203–214. ACM (2004)
14. Li, C., Soliman, M.A., Chang, K.C.-C., Ilyas, I.F.: RankSQL: query algebra and optimization for relational top-k queries. In: SIGMOD 2005, pp. 131–142 (2005)
15. Pérez, J., Arenas, M., Gutierrez, C.: Semantics and complexity of SPARQL. ACM Trans. Database Syst. 34(3) (2009)
16. Prud'hommeaux, E., Seaborne, A.: SPARQL Query Language for RDF W3C Recommendation (January 2008), http://www.w3.org/TR/rdf-sparql-query/
17. Qi, Y., Candan, K.S., Sapino, M.L.: Sum-Max Monotonic Ranked Joins for Evaluating Top-K Twig Queries on Weighted Data Graphs. In: VLDB, pp. 507–518 (2007)
18. Schmidt, M., Meier, M., Lausen, G.: Foundations of SPARQL query optimization. In: ICDT 2010, pp. 4–33. ACM, New York (2010)

19. Schnaitter, K., Polyzotis, N.: Optimal algorithms for evaluating rank joins in database systems. ACM Transactions on Database Systems 35(1), 1–47 (2010)
20. Siberski, W., Pan, J.Z., Thaden, U.: Querying the Semantic Web with Preferences. In: Cruz, I., Decker, S., Allemang, D., Preist, C., Schwabe, D., Mika, P., Uschold, M., Aroyo, L.M. (eds.) ISWC 2006. LNCS, vol. 4273, pp. 612–624. Springer, Heidelberg (2006)
21. Stocker, M., Seaborne, A., Bernstein, A., Kiefer, C., Reynolds, D.: SPARQL basic graph pattern optimization using selectivity estimation. In: WWW, pp. 595–604. ACM (2008)
22. Straccia, U.: SoftFacts: A top-k retrieval engine for ontology mediated access to relational databases. In: SMC, pp. 4115–4122. IEEE (2010)
23. Vidal, M.-E., Ruckhaus, E., Lampo, T., Martínez, A., Sierra, J., Polleres, A.: Efficiently Joining Group Patterns in SPARQL Queries. In: Aroyo, L., Antoniou, G., Hyvönen, E., ten Teije, A., Stuckenschmidt, H., Cabral, L., Tudorache, T. (eds.) ESWC 2010, Part I. LNCS, vol. 6088, pp. 228–242. Springer, Heidelberg (2010)
24. Zimmermann, A., Lopes, N., Polleres, A., Straccia, U.: A general framework for representing, reasoning and querying with annotated semantic web data. CoRR, abs/1103.1255 (2011)

Thematic Clustering and Exploration
of Linked Data

Silvana Castano, Alfio Ferrara, and Stefano Montanelli

DI - Università degli Studi di Milano
Via Comelico, 39 - 20135 Milano
{silvana.castano,alfio.ferrara,stefano.montanelli}@unimi.it

Abstract. Now that a huge amount of data is available in the Linked
Data Cloud, the need of effective exploration and visualization techniques is becoming more and more important. In this paper, we propose
aggregation and abstraction techniques for thematic clustering and exploration of linked data. These techniques transform a basic, flat view
of a potentially large set of messy linked data for a given search target,
into a high-level, thematic view called *in*Cloud. In an *in*Cloud, thematic
exploration is guided by few *essentials* auto-describing their *prominence*
for the search target and by their reciprocal *proximity* relations.

1 Introduction

The linked data paradigm promoted a new way of exposing, sharing, and connecting pieces of data, information, and knowledge on the Semantic Web, based
on URIs (Universal Resource Identifier) and RDF (Resource Description Framework) [3]. After an initial success due to the strenuous participation of common
users in publishing data following the recommended linked data practices, a
huge amount of data is now available in the Linked Data Cloud. For this reason, the capability to enforce techniques for effective search, exploration, and
visualization is becoming crucial [12,13,15,18].

One of the most challenging issue is to provide effective browsing solutions
capable to deal with the inherent flat organization of linked data and to manage the existing huge-sized repositories storing millions of RDF triples. Suitable
techniques are thus required in order to provide a thematic layer on top of the
linked data graph, and to mine and explicitly represent key concepts and semantic relations spread and immersed in a, generally huge, set of linked data coming
from one or more linked data repositories.

In this paper, we propose aggregation and abstraction techniques to transform
a basic, flat view of a potentially large set of messy linked data, into an *in*Cloud,
that is, a high-level, thematic view enabling a more effective, topic-driven exploration of the same dataset. Through aggregation techniques, we identify thematic
clusters of semantically related linked data in a (even large) collection representing the flat answer to a search target. Through abstraction techniques, we mine
suitable *essentials* capturing the theme dealt with by a linked data cluster and its

S. Ceri and M. Brambilla (Eds.): Search Computing III, LNCS 7538, pp. 157–175, 2012.

relevance for the search target, as well as proximity relations reflecting reciprocal degree of closeness between cluster essentials.

We motivate the role of *in*Clouds through a real example of linked data collection extracted from the Freebase repository considering the city of Seattle as search target (Section 2). After presenting the state of the art in the field (Section 3), we will describe the construction of an *in*Cloud through aggregation and abstraction techniques (Sections 4 and 5). Then, we discuss the use of *in*Clouds for enabling different thematic exploration modalities of the underlying linked data collection (Section 6). Concluding remarks are finally provided (Section 7).

2   InClouds for Linked Data Exploration

In this section, we introduce a motivating example that shows a typical situation where the user has to face several different problems in order to satisfy her search target. Moreover, we show how *in*Clouds provide a valid solution to this situation.

2.1   Motivating Example

In a conventional scenario, the user interested in exploring a linked data repository to satisfy a certain search target usually has to face a long and loosely-intuitive browsing activity. This is due to the inherent flat organization of linked data repositories where the URIs of interest for a given target frequently require the user to follow more than one property link before being explored. In particular, the user exploration is typically characterized by the following interaction pattern:

- Submission to the repository of a *search target* (t), namely a keyword (or a list of keywords) that describes the subject of interest for the search. An example of search target is the name of the US city Seattle.
- Selection of the *seed of interest* (s), namely an URI that represents the "point of origin" for the exploration about the search target. The seed of interest is chosen from the list of URIs returned by the repository as a reply to the search target. In the Freebase linked data repository[1], an example of seed for our target is the URI /en/seattle.
- Exploration of the URIs reachable from the seed with the aim to get access to more information about the search target. This requires the user to submit appropriate queries to the repository to extract the seed properties and the URIs directly linked to s through these properties. An example of MQL query for the Freebase repository to extract the tourist attractions directly connected to the seed $s = $ /en/seattle through the property /travel/travel_destination/tourist_attractions is:

```
[{ ''id'' : ''/en/seattle''
   ''type'' : ''/travel/travel_destination''
''.../tourist_attractions'' : {}}]
```

---

[1] http://www.freebase.com/

In this query, Seattle is taken into account as a "travel destination". However, other properties of Seattle are available with respect to other types associated with the URI /en/seattle, such as for example Seattle as a business location, or Seattle as a sports team location. Moreover, each URI returned as a result of the query execution can be a subject of new exploration queries in order to access to the properties of each tourist attraction of Seattle. Thus, the exploration step can be recursively applied to the visited URIs to progressively discover further URIs at higher distance from the seed according to the user choices and interests.

Due to the huge number of linked data that is usually concerned with a search target, a lot of exploration steps are required to build a (more or less) comprehensive picture of the available information about the target. As an example, in Figure 1, we show the set of linked data extracted from Freebase for the target Seattle. In this example, we considered the seed $s = $ /en/seattle, we explored the complete set of directly linked URIs and some selected URIs at distance $d = 2$ from s. As it is clear from this simple example, exploring such a flat and huge collection of data is cumbersome. First, because the representation is flat

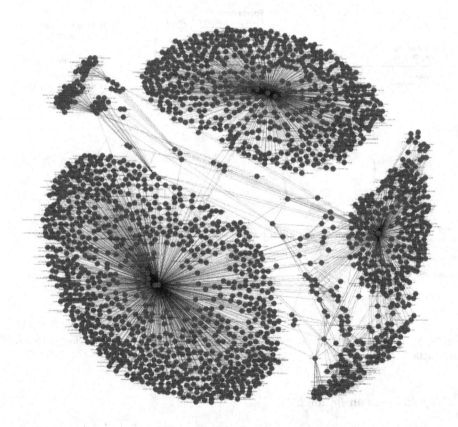

Fig. 1. A graph of linked data extracted from the Freebase repository for the search target Seattle

and it is impossible to immediately understand whether some URIs are more important than others. Moreover, possible sets of URIs addressing the same/similar argument about the target are neither highlighted nor grouped.

2.2   InClouds as a Solution

The solution we propose is to transform the basic, flat view of linked data like the one in Figure 1, into an *in*Cloud view (see Figure 2 providing a high-level, thematic view of the same data.

The *in*Cloud is defined as a graph $iC = (CL, PR)$, where a node $Cl_i \in CL$ represents a *cluster* of interrelated linked data and an edge $Pr_k(Cl_i, Cl_j) \in PR$ represents a relation of *proximity* between clusters Cl_i and Cl_j, respectively. Moreover, each node $Cl_i \in CL$ is labeled with an *essential*, namely a concise and convenient summary of the theme content of the cluster represented by Cl_i.

An example of *in*Cloud for the seed $s =$ /en/seattle is shown in Figure 2.

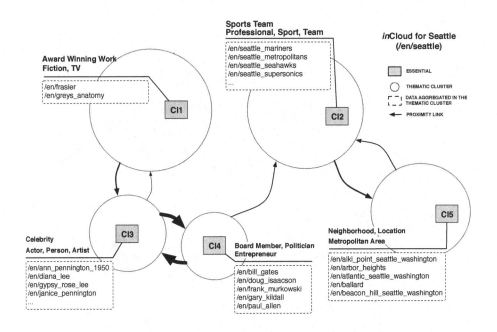

Fig. 2. An example of *in*Cloud extracted from the Freebase repository for the seed /en/seattle

Graphically, in an *in*Cloud:

- a circle-box represents a *a cluster*, namely a group of linked data (shown in the dashed box) focused on a specific theme/argument/topic related to the considered seed (e.g., the set of sports teams located in Seattle (cluster Cl_2)

or the set of celebrities from Seattle (Cluster Cl_3). Clusters in an *in*Cloud are also characterized by a *prominence value* denoting their level of importance for the seed in the framework of the overall *in*Cloud. The size of the cluster circles is proportional to their prominence, thus the most prominent cluster in the *in*Cloud of Figure 2 is Cluster Cl_1;

- a square-box represents an *essential*, namely a concise and convenient summary of the thematic content of a cluster at a glance (e.g., Award Winning Work, Fiction, TV used to summarize the content of Cluster Cl_1);
- an arrow represents a proximity relation between clusters/essentials, namely a closeness relationship between the themes/topics their represent. The arrow thickness denotes the degree of proximity between the two clusters/essentials connected by the arrow.

2.3   InCloud Construction

The process of *in*Cloud construction is illustrated in Figure 3. This process is articulated in two main phases, namely, *thematic cluster aggregation* and *in*Cloud *abstraction*. Thematic cluster aggregation is executed to group semantically related linked data using similarity metrics. *in*Cloud abstraction is then applied to synthesize the *in*Cloud elements out of the thematic clusters. In particular, starting from an initial linked data graph $\mathcal{G}_s$ extracted for the seed s, we produce an augmented graph $\mathcal{G}_s^+$, by adding similarity links between linked data dealing with the same topic/theme. Clustering techniques are subsequently applied to produce thematic clusters of linked data out of $\mathcal{G}_s^+$. Finally, cluster essentials, prominence values and proximity relations are derived through suitable abstraction techniques. The aggregation phase and the abstraction phase are described in Section 4 and Section 5, respectively.

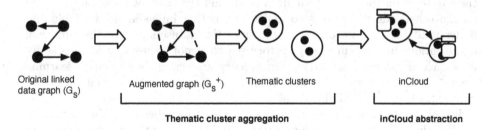

Original linked data graph (G_s)   Augmented graph (G_s^+)   Thematic clusters   inCloud

Thematic cluster aggregation   inCloud abstraction

Fig. 3. The *in*Cloud construction process

The *in*Cloud construction process is conceived to be coupled with the conventional query interfaces of the existing linked data repositories. Indeed, *in*Clouds can directly built on top of the dataset $\mathcal{G}_s$ extracted for the seed s to provide a more effective presentation of the dataset itself. The expected usage of *in*Clouds is that the user submits to the linked data repository a certain seed s of interest and the resulting *in*Cloud is visualized as the starting point for subsequent exploration. This means that, in a typical setting, we expect that the *in*Cloud construction can be performed *on-the-fly*, upon specification of the seed s. The capability to support the on-the-fly construction of an *in*Cloud mainly depends on the size of the linked data set acquired from the repository. In a typical scenario, we assume that the user specifies a query with single a seed of interest to be submitted to a single linked data repository. In this case, the process of *in*Cloud construction can be configured to dynamically tune the distance d parameter that controls the range/number of linked data to acquire[2]. This way, the set of acquired linked data can be limited in size (i.e., up to some hundreds of linked data entities) and the execution time required for the *in*Cloud construction can be estimated up to few seconds in the worst case. We believe that this is an acceptable awaiting time for an interactive web user for visualizing the *in*Cloud and for starting its exploration activity.

3   State of the Art

The main goal of *in*Clouds is to enable an easier access to linked data contents both for collecting information and for obtaining a more intuitive, high-level view of the linked data contents available for a given target of interest. The state of the art on these topics is related to *linked data exploration* and *linked data visualization*.

3.1   Linked Data Exploration

The high-level description of search activities proposed in [17], intended to introduce the notion of *exploratory search*, can be used as a framework to discuss linked data exploration as a specific case of web exploration. According to the author, exploratory search has two main goals: on one side, the goal is to bridge the gap between the user information needs and the data available on the Web; on the other side the goal is to make information immediately available and understandable in spite of the largeness of the datasets and of their internal organization. In particular, exploratory search is not focused on lookup activities such as information retrieval and query answering, but more on learning from data and investigating their internal relations, in order to generate more knowledge from the available data.

In this context, a key point is the searching user behavior. In particular, in [2] authors suggest two main criteria for understanding the problems that can decrease user satisfaction during exploration: i) the level of goal abstraction, that is the distance between the user understanding of the domain of interest and the operators available in the specific data repository where data are searched; ii) the search moves, that are the number of search steps required to achieve the search goals. In case of linked data, the complexity and number of data available about a given target of interest as well as the flat structure of the linked data graph, where all the URIs are equally relevant, affect the level of goal abstraction,

---

[2] In usual scenarios, a distance $d = 2$ is a good trade-off to obtain a sufficient number of linked data about s and a well-sized RDF graph.

because users, that are typically interested in few general topics, have instead to deal with a variety of specific data. Moreover, users are also required to perform a high number of search moves (i.e., queries) in order to obtain a satisfactory number of object descriptions.

When linked data are directly consumed by a user, this happens typically through a web interface, such as for example Wikipedia or the Freebase web site. About the user behavior when performing a web search activity, an interesting experimental analysis has been presented in [26]. An interesting result in this work is that about one third of user interaction with a web search system is with the search result page, while the remainder is with pages obtained through browsing activities performed starting from the search result page. As a consequence, authors stress the fact that is important for a exploration system to support users with browsing, understanding, and topic coverage functionalities, capable of providing a sort of "guided tour" of the data contents already during the first interaction between the user and the web contents (i.e., the linked data in our case).

The problem of supporting topic-based and thematic access to data has been addressed also in the Kosmix system [21]. Kosmix has the goal of creating a topic page representing the main topics available in a set of web search results, together with a list of related topics suggesting further areas to explore. Something similar is also provided by the Freebase web interface, where linked data are grouped according to their types. However, the usage of data types as a criterion for aggregating results is not sufficient to support an effective thematic exploration of linked data, because topics and themes are often corresponding to resources that are classified under different types.

3.2   Linked Data Visualization

A further relevant problem in the context of linked data is their visualization and, more in general, the visualization of semantic web resources in a more intuitive way. Visualization approaches can be mainly classified into two different categories, according to the way RDF datasets are visualized and navigated [8]. The first kind of visualization consists in browsing a labeled oriented graph, while the second one consists in displaying RDF properties as browsable facets of a node.

Graph-oriented visualization approaches exploit the concept relations in the RDF graph and provide some kind of entity aggregation. For example, in [14], authors propose a tool for a visual navigation and exploration of Freebase. Given a topic of interest, the tool produces its graph-based representation, where nodes are associated with an icon representing the type of the node, as defined in Freebase, and edges are labeled with the name of the corresponding relationships. Moreover, related topics of the same type are combined in aggregated nodes, and a textual description of each selected node is provided. In [18], a tool that helps users in exploring DBpedia is presented, not only via directed links in the RDF dataset, but also via newly discovered knowledge associations and visual navigation. Moreover, it exploits aggregation techniques in order to combine related topics in unified nodes, providing also a textual description of each node. LESS [1] is an approach providing a set of web-based templates to define visual representations of Linked Data. LESS templates may take as input one or more data sources via SPARQL queries. The resulting visual output can be embedded as formatted HTML into web pages or can be produced in form of RSS. The main drawback of graph-oriented visualization approaches is that they do not scale to large datasets [10], even if some efficient graph compression techniques for potentially huge graphs have been recently proposed [23].

Faceted browsing [27] has been widely adopted for many RDF dataset, spanning from DBpedia to DBLP. In faceted browsing the information space is partitioned using the "facets", which represent the important characteristics of an information element. The goal of faceted browsing is to restrict the search space to a set of relevant resources, by selecting, manually or automatically, the most important facets and values. The facet theory can be directly mapped to navigation in RDF data: information elements are RDF subjects, facets are RDF predicates and the values are the RDF objects. An implementation for faceted navigation of arbitrary RDF data is presented in [19], where important facets are identified by automatically ranking the predicates that best represent and most efficiently navigate the dataset. In [11], authors present a faceted browser for Wikipedia. The system enables users to ask complex queries against the Wikipedia knowledge, by exploiting the Wikipedia infoboxes (i.e., the set of most relevant facts of an article displayed as a table of attribute-value pairs in the article Wikipedia page). In [28], a hierarchically faceted search implementation is described. Here, the facet values that are shown to the user are selected not only on the bases of their relevance with respect to the specific query, but also on the bases of their general importance. Marbles retrieves information about resources of interest by querying Sindice. Sindice [24] ranks resources (i.e., RDF triples) retrieved by SPARQL queries exploiting external ranking services (as Google popularity) and information related to hostnames, relevant statements, and the dimension of the information sources. Marbles improves the user experience by presenting the resources as property-value pairs in a table. Different colors are used to distinguish the sources of the retrieved information, which are presented as a list of URIs. Sig.ma (Semantic Information MAshup) [25] retrieves and integrates Linked Data, starting from a single URI, by querying the Semantic Web and applying machine learning to the data found. Results are presented as a orderable list of verified resources and links to potentially relevant information on the query subject; users may confirm or reject the relevance of each resource.

Faceted browsing improves usability over current interfaces and RDF visualizers as it provides a better information lookup with respect to keyword searches. Nevertheless, faceted interfaces are domain-dependent, do not allow to navigate through relations different from the ones explicitly represented in the dataset, and they become difficult to use for the users as the number of presented facets grows, since aggregation techniques are usually not used as a visualization support facility.

3.3 Contribution of Thematic InClouds

In Table 1, we summarize the main differences between *in*Clouds and raw linked data. With respect to issues related to linked data exploration, the contribu-

Table 1. Comparison between linked data and *in*Clouds

Linked data	inClouds
Resulting structure: graph	Resulting structure: graph
Aim: connect different RDF descriptions of the same object	Aim: thematically organize the relevant web resources for a target entity
One general graph (connecting different repositories)	One graph for each target entity
Directed graph	Directed graph
Unweighted graph	Weighted graph
The nodes can be URIs or literals	The nodes are clusters of web resources
The edges can be labeled with properties or with owl:sameAs	The edges are labeled with the value of proximity between clusters
No distinction between the nodes	Each node has a different prominence
Only descriptions referred to the same object are connected	Clusters are connected by different proximity relations reflecting different levels of closeness/similarity of their contents

tion of thematic *in*Clouds is twofold. One one side, *in*Clouds rely on the use of similarity evaluation and thematic clustering techniques to address the learning phase. On the other side, essentials abstraction and prominence evaluation contribute to enforce the investigation phase. Indeed, we start from the flat and complex data structure typically obtained from a lookup search over the linked data with the purpose to obtain a high-level and thematic view of the same data with the aim to simplify data understanding and to enable intuitive search and browsing functionalities. In particular, our approach to thematic exploration of linked data can be seen as a solution for the exploratory search known as *topic exploration* [4].

With respect to issues related to linked data visualization, our contribution regards the combined use of data similarity, proximity, and prominence techniques for *in*Cloud construction. In particular, the proposed techniques allow the different themes/topics to directly emerge from the original data and their mutual linkage, by suggesting also an intuitive visualization of data contents in terms of cluster essentials, prominence, and proximity.

4 Thematic Clusters Aggregation

The goal of the aggregation phase is to transform an initial set of linked data into a number of thematic clusters. The starting point is a RDF graph $\mathcal{G}_s$ containing the linked data about a certain seed s of interest automatically extracted from a linked data repository $\mathcal{R}$. Appropriate extraction queries are defined to this end according to the language (e.g., SPARQL, MQL) supported by the repository $\mathcal{R}$. These queries generally enforce the following extraction/filtering operations:

- *Extraction of properties and corresponding values within a distance $\leq d$ from the seed s.* We consider that an URI in the repository $\mathcal{R}$ is concerned with the seed s if there is a property path of length $\leq d$ between the URI and s. The distance d can be dynamically changed and it has an impact on the number of extracted linked data and thus on the size of the resulting RDF graph.
- *Extraction of the URI types.* For each URI within a distance $\leq d$ from the seed s, we extract the list of types (i.e., classes) the URI belongs to. The appropriate property of the repository $\mathcal{R}$ is exploited to this end (e.g., the property type in Freebase).
- *Filtering of non-relevant properties.* Loosely meaningful properties of a repository, like the property *image* of Freebase, can be excluded from the resulting RDF graph since they are poorly useful in providing information about s.

The query result is the graph $\mathcal{G}_s = (N_s, E_s)$ where a node $n \in N_s$, called *linked data entity*, can be an URI, a literal, or a type value that satisfy the query selection, and an edge $e(n_i, n_j) \in E_s$, called *property link*, represents a property relationship of $\mathcal{R}$ between the nodes $n_i, n_j \in N_s$.

Based on the RDF graph $\mathcal{G}_s$, linked data aggregation is articulated in two main steps, namely *similarity evaluation* and *thematic clustering*.

4.1   Similarity Evaluation

This step has the goal to analyze the graph $\mathcal{G}_s$ and to generate an *augmented linked data graph* $\mathcal{G}_s^+$ where a *similarity link* is added between each pair of matching linked data entities in N_s. To this end, the level of affinity between the entities of N_s is evaluated as follows. Given two linked data entities n_i, $n_j \in N_s$, the *linked data affinity* $\sigma(n_i, n_j) \in [0, 1]$ denotes the level of similarity of n_i and n_j based on the commonalities of their *terminological equipments*. Each linked data entity $n \in N_s$ is associated with a terminological equipment $\mathsf{Term}_n = \{term_1, \ldots, term_m\}$ where $term_j$, with $1 \leq j \leq m$, is a term appearing in the label of a node adjacent to n in $\mathcal{G}_s$, or a term appearing in the label of n itself. Before inclusion in a terminological equipment, each term is submitted to a normalization procedure for word-lemma extraction and for compound-term tokenization [7,22].

The affinity σ of two linked data entities n_i, $n_j \in N_s$ is calculated as the Dice coefficient over their terminological equipments as follows:

$$\sigma(n_i, n_j) = \frac{2 \cdot |\ term_x \sim term_y\ |}{|\ \mathsf{Term}_{n_i}\ | + |\ \mathsf{Term}_{n_j}\ |}$$

where $term_x \sim term_y$ denotes that $term_x \in \mathsf{Term}_{n_i}$ and $term_y \in \mathsf{Term}_{n_j}$ are matching terms according to a string matching metric that considers the structure of the terms $term_x$ and $term_y$. For σ calculation, we employ our matching system HMatch 2.0, where state-of-the-art metrics for string matching (e.g., I-Sub, Q-Gram, Edit-Distance, and Jaro-Winkler) are implemented [5]. A similarity link $e\left(n_i, n_j\right)$ is established between the linked data entities n_i and n_j iff $\sigma(n_i, n_j) \geq th$ where $th \in (0,1]$ is a matching threshold denoting the minimum level of similarity required to consider two linked data entities as matching entities.

4.2   Thematic Aggregation

This step has the goal to analyze the graph $\mathcal{G}_s^+$ obtained through similarity evaluation and to identify/mine a set CL of thematic clusters. Given a graph $\mathcal{G}_s^+$, a cluster $Cl_i = \{(n_1, f_{i1}), \ldots, (n_h, f_{ih})\}$ is a set of linked data entities $n_1, \ldots, n_h \in N_s$ that are more similar to each other than to the other entities of N_s. Each entity n_j belonging to Cl_i is associated with a corresponding frequency f_{ij} which denotes the number of occurrences of n_j in Cl_i.

Clusters are determined by exploiting the graph $\mathcal{G}_s^+$ and by detecting those node regions that are highly interconnected through property/similarity links. The problem of thematic aggregation is analogous to the problem of cluster calculation, also known as *module*, *community*, or *cohesive group*, in graph theory. For this reason, for thematic aggregation, we rely on a clique percolation method (CPM) [20]. The CPM is based on the notion of *k-clique* which corresponds to a complete (fully-connected) sub-graph of k nodes within the graph $\mathcal{G}_s^+$. Two k-cliques are defined as *adjacent k-cliques* if they share $k-1$ nodes. The CPM determines clusters from k-cliques. In particular, a cluster, or more precisely, a k-clique-cluster, is defined as the union of all k-cliques that can be reached from each other through a series of adjacent k-cliques. As a consequence, a typical k-clique-cluster is composed of several cliques (with size $\leq k$) that tend to share many of their nodes. Since the cliques of a graph can share one or more nodes, we observe that a node can belong to several clusters, and thus clusters can overlap. In our approach, we employ the CPM implemented in the CFinder tool[3]. Although the determination of the full set of cliques of a graph is widely believed to be a non-polynomial problem, CFinder proves to be efficient when applied to graphs like those considered in our approach. Such an algorithm is based on first locating all complete subgraphs of $\mathcal{G}_s^+$ that are not part of larger complete subgraphs, and then on identifying existing k-clique-clusters by carrying out a standard component analysis of the clique-clique overlap matrix [9]. As a result, CFinder produces the full set CL of k-clique-clusters existing in the graph $\mathcal{G}_s^+$ for all the possible values of k.

---

[3] Available at http://www.cfinder.org/

5   InCloud Abstraction

The goal of the abstraction phase is to build an *in*Cloud, namely a high-level view on top of linked data clusters by synthesizing them through essentials. *in*Cloud clusters are also featured by a level of prominence and by proximity relations that denote the level of overlapping of the different clusters.

5.1   Essential Abstraction

An essential Ess_i is a concise and convenient summary expressing the theme/topic of a thematic cluster Cl_i and it is defined as a pair of the form $Ess_i = (C_i, D_i)$ where C_i is the category associated with Cl_i and D_i is a descriptor associated with Cl_i. A category C_i is a set composed by the labels of the most frequent types of the linked data entities in Cl_i, while a descriptor D_i is a set composed by the most frequent terms in the terminological equipments of the entities in Cl_i. If more than one most equally-frequent type and/or term exist, they are all inserted in C_i and D_i, respectively. In the example of Figure 2, the cluster Cl_4 corresponds to a very focused theme expressed by the essential categories Board Member, Politician (the most frequent types of the entities in the cluster) and by the essential descriptor Entrepreneur (the most frequent term in the terminological equipments of the entities in Cl_4). In cases where many entities are equally frequent in a cluster, the abstracted essential is less focused and contains more terms. This is the case for example of the cluster Cl_3 of Figure 2, representing persons, actors, and artists from Seattle.

5.2   Prominence Evaluation

Clusters (and related essentials) in an *in*Cloud are differently relevant with respect to the original search target. In order to represent this fact, we introduce the notion of prominence of a cluster, namely a value $P_i \in [0, 1]$. The higher P_i is, the higher is also the prominence of Cl_i in the *in*Cloud. In our approach, the level of prominence of a cluster is higher when the cluster is very focused on its theme and its contents are homogeneous. In particular, we formalize two cluster properties that are *variability* and *density*.

The variability v_i is the degree of overlap among the cliques of the cluster Cl_i. Variability v_i is measured by a coefficient of variation, which is the ratio between the standard deviation of the linked data entity frequencies in Cl_i and the arithmetic mean of those frequencies, as follows:

$$v_i = \frac{1}{\overline{f}} \sqrt{\frac{1}{N_i - 1} \sum_{j=1}^{N_i} (f_{ij} - \overline{f})^2}$$

where $\overline{f}$ denotes the arithmetic mean value of frequency values, and $N_i = |Cl_i|$ denotes the cardinality of Cl_i, namely the number of linked data entities contained in Cl_i. According to this definition, high values of v_i denote a low degree of overlap in the cliques of the cluster Cl_i, while low values of v_i denote a high degree of overlap in the Cl_i cliques.

The density d_i of a cluster Cl_i is the degree of interconnection among the linked data entities of Cl_i. The density coefficient $d_i = 2 \cdot R_i / N_i (N_i - 1)$ is the ratio between the number R_i of links in the cluster Cl_i and the maximum number of possible links. According to this definition, high values of d_i denote a high degree of interconnection among the cluster Cl_i entities, while low values of d_i denote a low degree of interconnection. The prominence P_i of a cluster Cl_i is calculated on the basis of its variability and density as follows:

$$P_i = \frac{2 \cdot (1 - v_i) \cdot d_i}{(1 - v_i) + d_i}$$

According to this approach, most prominent clusters are those which are more focused and homogeneous with respect to their theme. We graphically represent cluster prominence by drawing circles proportional to the prominence values of the corresponding clusters. In our example of Figure 2, clusters Cl_1 and Cl_2 are more prominent (larger circles) because they are more focused and homogeneous. On the opposite, clusters like Cl_3, which collect several entities of different types are considered less prominent (smaller circle). However, other options are possible for the evaluation of prominence in case of specific application needs. A first option is to consider a cluster to be more prominent as it is more close to the seed s of interest. In this case, the prominence P_i of a cluster Cl_i is evaluated by taking into account the average value of similarity between the linked data entities in the cluster Cl_i and s, weighted by the frequency of each entity n_i in Cl_i, as follows:

$$P_i = \frac{\sum_{j=1}^{N_i} \sigma(n_j, s) \cdot f_{ij}}{\sum_{j=1}^{N_i} f_{ij}}$$

Another option is to consider the prominence P_i of a cluster Cl_i as proportional to the cardinality N_i of Cl_i and to the size k_i of the smaller clique in Cl_i, as follows: $P_i = 2 \cdot N_i \cdot k_i / N_i + k_i$.

5.3   Proximity Relations

A proximity relation $Pr_k(Cl_i, Cl_j) \in PR$ is characterized by a proximity degree X_{ij}, which represents the level of overlap between the entities of Cl_i and Cl_j. In particular, the degree of proximity $X_{ij} = | Cl_i \cap Cl_j | / | Cl_i |$ is proportional to the number of linked data entities common to Cl_i and Cl_j over the number of linked data entities in Cl_i. The greater the level of overlapping between Cl_i and Cl_j, the higher the degree of their proximity relation. Proximity relations are graphically represented by arrows with thickness proportional to the proximity degree. In Figure 2, we can see how proximity relations connect those clusters that are more semantically related to each other, such as Cl_3 and Cl_4 which both contains famous people from the city of Seattle.

6   Thematic Exploration Modalities

In this section, we describe the exploration modalities envisaged for *in*Clouds and we discuss the *in*Cloud settings when shifting from typical settings to exploration in-the-large scenario.

6.1   Thematic Exploration through InClouds

An *in*Cloud enables the thematic exploration of the underlying linked data according to different modalities that can be switched on according to the specific user preferences. Possible exploration modalities supported through *in*Clouds are *exploration-by-essential*, *exploration-by-prominence*, and *exploration-by-proximity*. In Figure 4, we show examples of the exploration modalities based on the *in*Cloud of Figure 2.

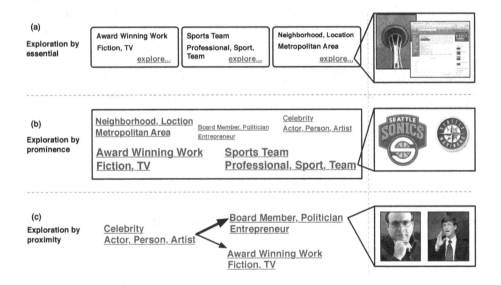

Fig. 4. Examples of exploration modalities supported through *in*Clouds

Exploration-by-Essential. This is the most intuitive exploration modality and it is based on cluster essentials. A user exploits the essentials of the *in*Cloud clusters to get a comprehensive overview of the available themes. An essential can be considered as a sort of instantaneous picture of the associated cluster and linked data therein contained, thus allowing the user to rapidly choose the most preferred one for starting the exploration. Once selected the essential of interest, a preview of the linked data contained in the associated cluster is show to the user for final data visualization. In the example of Figure 4(a), the available *in*Cloud essentials are shown as boxes to explore. A preview of the contained linked data is shown for the essential about neighborhood, location, metropolitan area of Seattle. By selecting this essential, the user can explore the linked data about points of interest and tourist locations in the metropolitan area of Seattle.

Exploration-by-Prominence. This modality allows the user to organize the exploration according to the prominence values associated with the *in*Cloud clusters. The idea is to support the user in browsing throughout the clusters according to their relative importance with respect to the *in*Cloud and thus to the underlying linked data. In this modality, both categories and descriptors of the cluster essentials are shown in a sort of tag-cloud, where the font size of each element is proportional to the associated prominence within the *in*Cloud. By selecting a term of interest in the tag-cloud, a preview of the linked data featured by the selected term are shown to the user. As discussed in Section 5, different criteria can be used to calculate the prominence value of an *in*Cloud. The capability to switch from one criterion to another allows the user to dynamically re-organize the tag-cloud in light of a different notion of cluster prominence. In the example of Figure 4(b), most prominent categories and descriptors of the *in*Cloud essentials are provided. A preview of the linked data associated with the category sports team, professional, sport, team are shown as an example of possible user exploration.

Exploration-by-Proximity. This modality enables the user to move from one cluster to another by exploiting the proximity relations. When a user is exploring a certain cluster, the proximity relations provide indication of its fully/partially overlapping neighbors, thus suggesting the possible exploration of clusters that are somehow related in content. This modality can be coupled either with exploration-by-essential and exploration-by-prominence. Once that an element of interest is selected for exploration by the user, the links to other related clusters are shown. Linked clusters are represented through their essentials in the form of boxes or tag-clouds depending on the active exploration modality, namely exploration-by-essential and exploration-by-prominence, respectively. The degree of proximity that features each proximity relation is used to rank the possible exploration paths from one cluster to the others. In particular, the thickness of each link is proportional to the proximity degree between the two considered clusters. In the example of Figure 4(c), the currently selected essential is about the topic Celebrity. The essentials board members and politicians and award winning fiction TV works are suggested as possible exploration paths due to the fact that they are the two essentials in the *in*Cloud connected with the celebrity cluster with the highest degree of proximity.

6.2   InCloud Settings in-the-Large Scale

When moving from the typical *in*Cloud setting to a large-scale scenario, the construction process should be extended to consider the multi-repository exploration and the multi-seed extraction requirements.

Extension to Multi-repository Exploration. For a more complete visualization of the available linked data about a certain search target, multiple RDF repositories can be queried to originate a unique and comprehensive inCloud view of their contents. In the conventional Linked Data Cloud[4], the property owl:sameAs is used to denote when a linked data entity n_i belonging to a certain RDF repository $\mathcal{R}$ and another entity n_j belonging to a different repository $\mathcal{R}'$ refer to the same real-world object. In a multi-repository scenario, the construction of the graph $\mathcal{G}_s$ can take into account the owl:sameAs relations as a sort of "natural join" operation. The idea is to start the construction of $\mathcal{G}_s$ by querying an initial repository $\mathcal{R}$ and to exploit the owl:sameAs relations to extend the linked data extraction to other RDF repositories. In particular, the URIs connected by a owl:sameAs relation are collapsed in a unique linked data entity of $\mathcal{G}_s$ and the extraction/filtering operations described in Section 4 are applied to the whole set of linked data extracted by the considered RDF repositories.

Extension to Multi-seed Extraction. In some cases, the user can be interested in exploring the available linked data about more than one seed of interest. In this framework, the inCloud construction process can be used to build a comprehensive thematic picture that takes into account all the seeds of interest. In a multi-seed scenario, the starting point is a set of seeds $S = \{s_1, \ldots, s_k\}$. The graph $\mathcal{G}_s$ is built by executing the extraction/filtering operations of Section 4 for each element $s_i \in S$. Depending on the seeds of interest, one or more portions of the graph $\mathcal{G}_s$ can be disjoint from the rest of the graph. In particular, when the seeds in S are about completely different arguments, a separate independent cluster is generated through aggregation for each $s_i \in S$. In such a limit case, the usefulness of the inCloud mechanism for exploration is in the capability of providing an effective synthetic essential for each seed $s_i \in S$ and in calculating the relative prominence of each seed with respect to the others.

Linked data exploration in-the-large can require the execution of thematic aggregation techniques over a starting RDF graph $\mathcal{G}_s$ containing a huge number of nodes (e.g., thousands of linked data entities). The clique percolation method we use for cluster calculation best performs when a small-medium number of nodes in the graph $\mathcal{G}_s$ is considered (e.g., hundreds of linked data entities). For example, in our tests, the CPM over a graph $\mathcal{G}_s$ containing 200 nodes takes an execution time of 200ms (considering a matching threshold th=0.9). For linked data exploration in-the-large, when 1.000 (or more) nodes are considered, two possible solutions can be envisaged. First, more efficient clustering algorithms, like hierarchical clustering, can be exploited (see [6] for further details). Second, in-the-large scale, we note that the execution time required for the inCloud construction can imply an excessive awaiting time for the web user (up to some minutes). This means that when the web user specifies more than one seed of interest to be submitted to one or more repositories, the resulting inCloud is always prepared off-line, in a batch manner. In other words, in this case, inCloud

---

[4] http://linkeddata.org/

construction and exploration are asynchronous processes. In this direction, for supporting synchronous exploration in-the-large, a number of *in*Clouds can be pre-calculated to satisfy most frequently-asked topics of interest and/or most popular domains. In this case, the aggregation techniques are executed off-line to prepare the thematic clusters, while the abstraction techniques can be executed on-line, at the query time, to customize the *in*Cloud presentation according to the user preferences about the metric for prominence calculation.

7 Concluding Remarks

In this paper, we presented techniques for building *in*Clouds as high-level views of linked data enabling their thematic exploration.

Ongoing work is focused on finalizing the development of a web application fully covering the steps of linked data aggregation and abstraction required for *in*Cloud construction. By exploiting an initial prototype implementation, we run some experiments concerning user evaluation of *in*Clouds based on standard user-oriented evaluation methods for interactive web search interfaces and systems [16]. Initial results are promising and *in*Clouds are seen by real users as a valid support to the satisfaction of users information needs [6]. In this context, some experimental results have already been collected by focusing on evaluation of *in*Clouds with respect to matching/clustering accuracy and user-perceived quality of data cloud organization [6]. In particular, we run an experiment with a group of 18 students of the Databases course of the Master Degree in Computer Science held at the University of Milan. The students had a similar background on linked data and Semantic Web, mainly based on some classes delivered on these topics in the course. Students where required to work on three test cases corresponding to different kinds of initial seeds of interest and *in*Clouds involving different datasources, including Freebase and DBpedia. In particular, we asked each student to compare *in*Clouds with respect to conventional web tools for accessing the linked data contents, such as the web interfaces of Freebase and Wikipedia. The main goal of the experiment was to collect a feedback concerning the effectiveness and advantages of our approach for linked data exploration. The answers were positive. For about the 75% of the users, *in*Clouds provide relevant and sufficient information about the data of interest and the perceived quality of the thematic organization is generally good. Moreover, the majority of the involved students reported that *in*Clouds provide an advantage in terms of effectiveness and usability with respect to conventional web tools for linked data exploration.

Future research activity regards the extension of the *in*Cloud approach to consider additional kinds of web data contents, like microdata, microblogging posts, and news. The idea is to propose *in*Clouds as a comprehensive exploration tool considering also actual, up-to-date social web information about the search target for possible fruition in the framework of event-promoting applications.

References

1. Auer, S., Doehring, R., Dietzold, S.: LESS - Template-Based Syndication and Presentation of Linked Data. In: Aroyo, L., Antoniou, G., Hyvönen, E., ten Teije, A., Stuckenschmidt, H., Cabral, L., Tudorache, T. (eds.) ESWC 2010, Part II. LNCS, vol. 6089, pp. 211–224. Springer, Heidelberg (2010)
2. Aula, A., Russell, D.M.: Complex and Exploratory Web Search. In: Information Seeking Support Systems Workshop (ISSS 2008), Chappel Hill, NC, USA (2008)
3. Bizer, C., Heath, T., Berners-Lee, T.: Linked Data - The Story So Far. Int. Journal on Semantic Web and Information Systems 5(3), 1–22 (2009)
4. Bozzon, A., Brambilla, M., Ceri, S., Fraternali, P.: Liquid Query: Multi-Domain Exploratory Search on the Web. In: Proceedings of the 19th International Conference on World Wide Web, pp. 161–170 (2010)
5. Castano, S., Ferrara, A., Montanelli, S.: Matching Ontologies in Open Networked Systems: Techniques and Applications. In: Spaccapietra, S., Atzeni, P., Chu, W.W., Catarci, T., Sycara, K. (eds.) Journal on Data Semantics V. LNCS, vol. 3870, pp. 25–63. Springer, Heidelberg (2006)
6. Castano, S., Ferrara, A., Montanelli, S.: Structured Data Clouding across Multiple Webs. Information Systems 37(4), 352–371 (2012)
7. Varese, G., Castano, S.: Building Collective Tag Intelligence through Folksonomy Coordination. In: Bessis, N., Xhafa, F. (eds.) Next Generation Data Technologies for Collective Computational Intelligence. SCI, vol. 352, pp. 87–112. Springer, Heidelberg (2011)
8. Deligiannidis, L., Kochut, K., Sheth, A.: Rdf data exploration and visualization. In: Proc. of the ACM 1st Workshop on CyberInfrastructure: Information Management in eScience, New York, USA (2007)
9. Everitt, B.S.: Cluster Analysis, 3rd edn. Edward Arnold, London (1993)
10. Frasincar, F., Telea, R., Houben, G.: Adapting Graph Visualization Techniques for the Visualization of RDF Data. In: Visualizing the Semantic Web. Springer, Heidelberg (2006)
11. Hahn, R., Bizer, C., Sahnwaldt, C., Herta, C., Robinson, S., Bürgle, M., Düwiger, H., Scheel, U.: Faceted Wikipedia Search. In: Abramowicz, W., Tolksdorf, R. (eds.) BIS 2010. LNBIP, vol. 47, pp. 1–11. Springer, Heidelberg (2010)
12. Halb, W., Raimond, Y., Hausenblas, M.: Building Linked Data for both Humans and Machines. In: Proc. of the WWW Int. Workshop on Linked Data on the Web (LDOW 2008), Beijing, China (2008)
13. Hirsch, C., et al.: Interactive Visualization Tools for Exploring the Semantic Graph of Large Knowledge Spaces. In: Proc. of the IUI Int. Workshop on Visual Interfaces to the Social and the Semantic Web, Sanibel Island, USA (2009)
14. Hirsch, C., Hosking, J., Grundy, J.: Interactive visualization tools for exploring the semantic graph of large knowledge spaces. In: Proc. of the Workshop on Visual Interfaces to the Social and the Semantic Web, VISSW 2009 (2009)
15. Hogan, A., Harth, A., Passant, A., Decker, S., Polleres, A.: Weaving the Pedantic Web. In: Proc. of the WWW Int. Workshop on Linked Data on the Web (LDOW 2010), Raleigh, NC, USA (2010)
16. Leclercq, A.: The perceptual evaluation of information systems using the construct of user satisfaction: case study of a large french group. ACM SIGMIS Database 38(2), 27–60 (2007)
17. Marchionini, G.: Exploratory Search: from Finding to Understanding. Communications of the ACM 49(4), 41–46 (2006)

18. Mirizzi, R., Ragone, A., Di Noia, T., Di Sciascio, E.: Semantic Wonder Cloud: Exploratory Search in DBpedia. In: Proc. of the ICWE 2nd Int. Workshop on Semantic Web Information Management (SWIM 2010), Vienna, Austria, pp. 138–149 (2010)
19. Oren, E., Delbru, R., Decker, S.: Extending Faceted Navigation for RDF Data. In: Cruz, I., Decker, S., Allemang, D., Preist, C., Schwabe, D., Mika, P., Uschold, M., Aroyo, L.M. (eds.) ISWC 2006. LNCS, vol. 4273, pp. 559–572. Springer, Heidelberg (2006)
20. Palla, G., Derényi, I., Farkas, I., Vicsek, T.: Uncovering the Overlapping Community Structure of Complex Networks in Nature and Society. Nature 435, 814–818 (2005)
21. Rajaraman, A.: Kosmix: High-Performance Topic Exploration using the Deep Web. Proceedings of the VLDB Endowment 2(2), 1524–1529 (2009)
22. Sorrentino, S., Bergamaschi, S., Gawinecki, M., Po, L.: Schema Normalization for Improving Schema Matching. In: Laender, A.H.F., Castano, S., Dayal, U., Casati, F., de Oliveira, J.P.M. (eds.) ER 2009. LNCS, vol. 5829, pp. 280–293. Springer,
Heidelberg (2009)
23. Tian, Y., Hankins, R., Patel, J.: Efficient aggregation for graph summarization. In: Proc. of the 6th ACM SIGMOD International Conference on Management of Data, SIGMOD 2008 (2008)
24. Tummarello, G., Delbru, R., Oren, E.: Sindice.com: Weaving the Open Linked Data. In: Aberer, K., Choi, K.-S., Noy, N., Allemang, D., Lee, K.-I., Nixon, L.J.B., Golbeck, J., Mika, P., Maynard, D., Mizoguchi, R., Schreiber, G., Cudré-Mauroux, P. (eds.) ASWC/ISWC 2007. LNCS, vol. 4825, pp. 552–565. Springer, Heidelberg (2007)
25. Tummarello, G., et al.: Sig. ma: Live Views on the Web of Data. Web Semantics: Science, Services and Agents on the World Wide Web 8(4), 355–364 (2010)
26. White, R.W., Drucker, S.M.: Investigating Behavioral Variability in Web Search. In: Proceedings of the 16th International Conference on World Wide Web, pp. 21–30 (2007)
27. Yee, K., Swearingen, K., Li, K., Hearst, M.: Faceted metadata for image search and browsing. In: Proc. of the SIGCHI Conference on Human Factors in Computing Systems (2003)
28. Yitzhak, O., Golbandi, N., Har'el, N., Lempel, R., Neumann, A., Koifman, S., Sheinwald, D., Shekita, E., Sznajder, B., Yogev, S.: Beyond basic faceted search. In: Proc. of the International Conference on Web Search and Web Data Mining, WSDM 2008 (2008)

Support for Reusable Explorations
of Linked Data in the Semantic Web

Marcelo Cohen and Daniel Schwabe

Pontifical Catholic University of Rio de Janeiro
R. M. S. Vicente 225
Gávea, Rio de Janeiro, RJ, Brazil
mcohen21@gmail.com, dschwabe@inf.puc-rio.br

Abstract. The Linked Data cloud growth is changing current Web application development. One of the first steps is to determine whether there is information already available that can be immediately reused.

A recurring problem being faced in this process is finding and understanding information in such repositories, especially because often their structure is unknown beforehand. Thus, users typically have to explore the data until they understand its structure, then they are able to formulate operations to extract the desired information, and finally they have to combine the results and make them available to other users.

We provide an environment which allows non-technically savvy users, but who understand the problem domain, to accomplish these tasks. They employ a combination of search, query and faceted navigation in a direct manipulation, query-by-example style interface. In this process, users can reuse solutions previously found by other users, which may accomplish sub-tasks of the problem at hand. It is also possible to create an end-user friendly interface to allow them to access the information. Once a solution has been found, it can be generalized, and optionally made available for reuse by other users.

Keywords: RDF, exploratory search, exploration, ontology, semantic web, reuse, interface, set-based navigation.

1 Introduction

The availability of Linked Open Data in the WWW has increased tremendously[1]. Currently, when building a new application, it is becoming increasingly common to first explore available data that can be leveraged to enhance and complete one's own data to provide the desired functionality. The BBC Music website[2] is one visible example of this approach, combining MusicBrainz and DBPedia with their own data.

Even though it is engineered to be processed by programs, it is still common that human beings need to explore these datasets, especially when they are previously unknown. In such cases, experts typically explore the repository to make sense out of

---

[1] http://linkeddata.org
[2] http://www.bbc.co.uk/music

S. Ceri and M. Brambilla (Eds.): Search Computing III, LNCS 7538, pp. 176–190, 2012.
© Springer-Verlag Berlin Heidelberg 2012

the available data, to eventually be able to formulate queries that will support their tasks. Existing interfaces range from basic RDF browsers such as Tabulator [3], Zitgist data viewer [3], Marbles[4], ObjectViewer[5] and Openlink RDF Browser[6], to query generators such as NITELIGHT [14] and iSPARQL[7], to faceted browsers [11] [5] and set-based interfaces [6].

In previous work [2], we presented Explorator, a model for representing information processing by users in exploratory tasks, and its associated tool, which provides a browser interface supporting this model. Explorator is based on the metaphor of direct manipulation of information in the interface, with immediate feedback of user actions.

Our experience with Explorator [1] has shown that to be effectively used, it is necessary for users to understand the RDF model. Even for these users, once a solution was found, it was not possible to generalize it, and to save it for reuse later. These two mechanisms are essential to enable a community of users around datasets of interest, so that more experienced users can find and share solutions with less experienced ones.

In many situations, notably browsing applications, it is sufficient that the designer, once having found the solution for a given information seeking task, to make it available for other users. In this case, it should be possible to present an end-user facing interface that hides the underlying data and operations, and has the look-and-feel of a traditional web application.

In this paper we present RExplorator[8], a significant extension of Explorator that allows

1. Parameterized interlinked operations, forming a graph of operations;
2. Saving these graphs for reuse;
3. he user to define new operators;
4. the user to define end-user friendly interfaces.

In the remainder of this paper, section 2 discusses related work, section 3 summarizes Explorator and provides a running example, section 4 describes RExplorator, section 5 discusses evaluation, and section 6 draws some conclusions.

2   Related Work

2.1   Browsing

As already mentioned, there are several tools that allow users to conveniently access the Semantic Web as we currently access the (data) web. In summary, these tools allow the user to manipulate raw RDF data but do not provide a user-friendly way to ask questions. The user is limited to visualizing the result as aggregate data.

---

[3] http://dataviewer.zitgist.com/
[4] http://beckr.org/marbles
[5] http://objectviewer.semwebcentral.org/
[6] http://demo.openlinksw.com/rdfbrowser/index.html
[7] iSparql can be accessed at http://demo.openlinksw.com/isparql/
[8] Available at http://www.tecweb.inf.puc-rio.br/rexplorator

Any processing is done manually, and the user has a limited way to rearrange, group or filter the data [15]. The browsing model is suitable to visualize the information but does not have a proper model of exploration, restricting the user exploration to navigation between nodes (resources) of an RDF graph, sequentially.

2.2   Faceted Navigation

A popular approach to overcome this simple "graph traversal mode" limitation of RDF browsers, or even classic WWW (http+html) browsers is the use of faceted navigation. S.R.Ranganathan first proposed information classification in facets in 1930. This concept was first applied to information categorization in libraries and bookstores. In the Semantic Web, facet navigation has been used to provide users with a friendlier way to filter RDF data as provided in tools such as FacetMap[9], Longwell[10,] BrowseRDF [11], Flamenco[11,] Gfacet [4], Humboldt [7], Exhibit [6], /facet [5], and Visor [13]. Faceted navigation enables users, with minimal knowledge of the RDF model, to explore an unstructured (in the sense of being schema-less) RDF database without a priori knowledge of the data domain. For example, for a collection of people, users could filter them by selecting their interest, age, eye color, or nationality properties without knowing the existence of these properties in advance.

These tools differ in several aspects: how the facets are specified (in some cases they are computed automatically); how the facets are presented to users; and which operations can be applied to filtering items. For example, users can filter all books written by a Spanish author in Gfacet, but this is not possible in Longwell. Also, some tools extend operations in the model, allowing pivoting [7], joins [11], and union or intersection between items being faceted. Visor enables the creation of spreadsheets from linked data by allowing users to explore the underlying data with multi-pivoting, i.e., using several starting points and exploiting existing relations to explore the data.

From this discussion, we can observe that the underlying models for current faceted navigation systems have some limitations. Most of them do not allow the user to explore an arbitrary SPARQL endpoint or limits the user to explore one remote endpoint. Their facet specification models do not address several useful scenarios that we will discuss further, and their facet generation or ranking algorithms do not take into consideration user's goals, past history or preferences. Finally, none of these systems allows any kind of generalization once a useful set of exploratory steps has been found, as well as sharing them with other users.

3   Summary of Explorator and a Running Example

3.1   Summary of Explorator

Explorator is an environment that allows users to explore a set of RDF repositories by direct manipulation of its contents, following a set-based metaphor. The user starts by

---

[9] http://www.facetmap.com/
[10] http://simile.mit.edu/wiki/Longwell
[11] http://flamenco.berkeley.edu/

either executing a full-text search, or by executing pre-defined queries (e.g., "All RDF Classes" or "All RDF Properties"). It is also possible to simply take a URI and de-reference it. In all cases, the results are always sets of triples.

The user explores the repositories by executing operations that take as operands sets of resources, and return new sets. The usual set operations, union, intersection and difference are available. In addition, there is the SPO operator, which corresponds to a match operation over <s, p, and o> triple patterns (e.g., <s, *, *>, <s, p, *>, for given *s* and *p* values, which are URIs). This match is executed against all enabled RDF triple repositories. Thus, <s, *, *> corresponds to the SPARQL query

```
SELECT ?s ?p ?o WHERE  { ?s ?p ?o. Filter (?s = s )} .
```

In reality, the SPO operator has been defined to operate on sets of resources instead of individual ones, by taking the union of the triples resulting from individual match operations as described above.

Since each new operation takes its parameter from existing sets, the end result is a graph of inter-related operations, where the inputs of one are outputs of others. This is analogous to an Excel spreadsheet, where each cell has formulas that reference the value of other cells, forming a graph of interdependent formulas.

In the next section we illustrate how this set manipulation metaphor can be used in a simple scenario.

3.2   A Running Example

Consider two simple tasks to be carried out over the so-called "Dogfood" data server[12], containing collected publication information for several conferences related to the Semantic Web. We assume the user has no prior knowledge about the contents of this repository. The tasks are to

1. Find all publications of a given author
2. Find co-workers of a given researcher, and their publications.

For task 1, the user has to

1. Find a class that represents persons
2. Find the desired person, "a".
3. Find a property "p" that relates a person to publications,
4. Find all triples of the form <a p ?pub> and collect all objects from these triples.

In Explorator, this is achieved by first clicking on "Menu"-> All RDF Classes", noticing class Person, mousing over it to click on "All Instances", which reveals a set of all Persons. Double-clicking on a Person (e.g. "Steffen Staab"), a new box appears with all details for this resource (i.e., all triples with this resource as subject). Looking at the details, one notices the property "made", which relates Person to Publications.

---

[12] http://data.semanticweb.org

To get all publications by a Person, one may click on the "Selected Person Details" box, and click on the "S" operand position at the top; click on the "made" box and click on the "P" operand position at the top, and then clicking on the "=" ("compute") operator at the top. Figure 1 shows the results after these steps.

Fig. 1. All Persons, Details of a selected Person, and Publications of selected Person, in RExplorator

Fig. 2. Co-Workers of a Selected Person

For task 2, the user has to

1. Find a class that represents persons
2. Find the desired person, "a".
3. Find a property "p" that relates a person to an institution;
4. Find all triples of the form <a p ?i> and collect all objects from these triples.
5. For each collected resource "r" (which are institutions), find all triples of the form <?per p r>, and collect the subjects of these triples.
6. For each collected resource, use the solution found in task 1.

Figure 2 show steps 1-5 of these tasks in RExplorator. Step 6 is discussed later.

4   Rexplorator

RExplorator extends Explorator by

1. Allowing operations to be parameterized;
2. Allowing the results of a query to be fed as input of another query, thus forming graphs of interconnected operations;
3. Allowing keeping such graphs as separate workbenches, while enabling interconnection of graphs across workbenches;
4. Allowing the designer to import previously defined query graphs into the current workbench;
5. Allowing the designer to define additional operators beyond the set operations provided;
6. Allowing the designer to define interfaces oriented towards end users, hiding details and customizing the look-and-feel.

RExplorator's metamodel is shown in Figure 3, which supports the implementation of these features. Some of these aspects will be elaborated as we explain these added functionalities in the coming sub-sections.

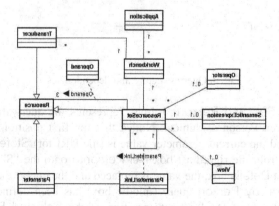

Fig. 3. RExplorator's meta-model

4.1   Parameterized Queries

The original Explorator metaphor lets users compose operations incrementally, seeing the results at each composition step. Each new query takes its operands from existing query results. In the end, one may regard this set of inter-related operations as a graph, similar to an Excel spreadsheet. However, the operations are all grounded, which would be akin to not having any variables in the formulas of the analogous spreadsheet. Thus, the first generalization made was to allow operations to have its operands parameterized, and to propagate values trough the graph of operations when the value of the parameter is changed. This is equivalent to introducing variables in the expression that denotes the operation.

Consider step 4 in task 1, finding all publications of a Person. In Explorator, this is achieved by selecting an instance of Person (e.g., "Steffen Staab in box "All Persons") in Figure 1, setting it as the subject parameter, selecting the relation "make" as the property parameter, and clicking on the "=" operator to find all triples of the form <<url for Steffen Staab> made ?o> .Clicking on the 🖉 icon in each box, as shown in Figure 4 reveals the actual operations and their dependencies .

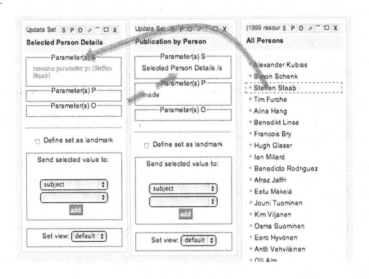

Fig. 4. Query structure and dependencies

The first box, Selected Person Details, represents the query that finds out all triples with a given Person as subject. Notice that the first position, "S", has been parameterized, and the current parameter value is (the URI for) Stefen Staab. If we drag any person from the rightmost box (All Persons) onto the "S" position in the Selected Person Details box, the value is replaced and the query re-evaluated.

The Publication by Person query (middle box) has been defined as taking its "subject" parameter from the "subject" position of the Selected Person Details query. Therefore, if a new value is plugged into the "S" position in the Selected

Person Details query, it is automatically propagated to this query, which triggers its reevaluation.

4.2   Workspace Organization

RExplorator organizes the workspace into workbenches. The idea is that each workbench represents a task, or a use case in traditional Software Engineering methods. A user may save workbenches for later reuse, and share it with other users as well.

To reuse a workbench, the user opens the Workbenches menu (see Figure 5, where he has the option of copying an existing shared workbench into the current workspace. Once this copy has been placed in the workspace, its contents may be modified as if the user had entered it, just like any other graph of operations. It is also possible to log into RExplorator (using OpenID), in which case workbenches can be saved between sessions.

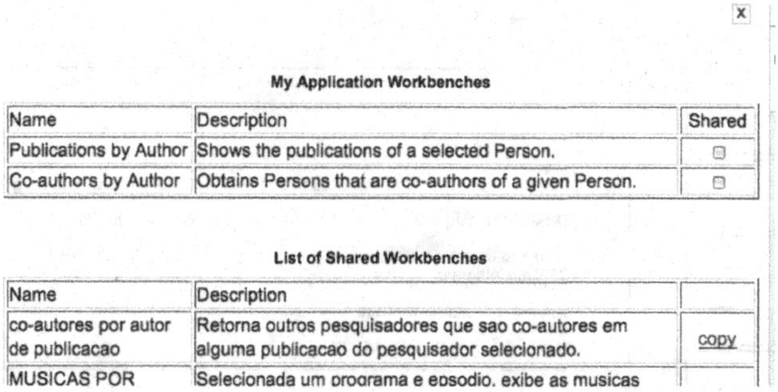

My Application Workbenches

Name	Description	Shared
Publications by Author	Shows the publications of a selected Person.	☐
Co-authors by Author	Obtains Persons that are co-authors of a given Person.	☐

List of Shared Workbenches

Name	Description	
co-autores por autor de publicacao	Retorna outros pesquisadores que sao co-autores em alguma publicacao do pesquisador selecionado.	copy
MUSICAS POR	Selecionada um programa e episodio, exibe as musicas	

Fig. 5. Saved workbenches dialog

In RExplorator a workspace contains several workbenches, similar to the way an Excel a workspace contains several worksheets (see Figure 6), where there may be cross-references between operations within separate workbenches. For example, workbench Co Workers by Person contains the Co Workers query, which can be interconnected to the "Publication by Person" query in the similarly named workbench.

+ Giuseppe Vizzari	Universität Koblenz-Landau

CREATE NEW | REMOVE CURRENT | Co Workers by Person | Publications by Person

Fig. 6. Detail of workspace organization in workbenches

4.3   End-User Interfaces

The development interface of Rexplorator is best suited to allow users to explore RDF repositories, and requires understanding the RDF model. Our experience with Explorator has shown that non-technical people have difficulties in reasoning over this model. There are several approaches to overcome this difficulty, one of which is to allow expert users to provide end-user friendly interfaces – called the Application Interface - to solutions found while exploring datasets. As the community of users of a repository (or set of repositories) grows, solutions to common tasks are gradually developed, and these solutions should be shared within the community.

The Application Interface is exhibited when the user clicks on the "Go to Application" button in RExplorator's interface. Figure 7 shows an example of a non-technical user-friendly interface, where one can click on a person's name in the left column, and see that person's list of publications. This interface is generated by a combination of views, which are defined using the "views" menu option; generic, pre-defined views are initially available for reuse.

Views make full use of CSS, which is also defined in a separate view that can be customized to change the look-and-feel of the generated interface.

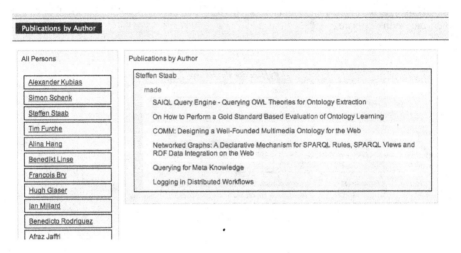

Fig. 7. User-friendly interface with All Persons and Selected Person Co-Workers

Figure 8 shows an alternative format for the same view presented in Figure 7, using a different CSS stylesheet.

The Application Interface is defined in two parts – a view (and associated CSS stylesheets), and an association between the sets in the developer workbench and the defined views. For each set definition, it is possible to assign a particular view to be used in rendering its result. Consider the "Publications by Author" workbench. Figure 9 shows how each set (operation) may have its results exposed in the Application Interface by choosing a view from the dropdown menu next to " Set view", which lists all the views defined for the workbench.

An example of a view definition can be seen in Figure 10, which defines the rendering of an Index (i.e., a list of links to other resources). Views make use of a library of built-in helper functions that allow referring to set elements and their properties, such as *uri* and *render_resource*. Helper functions may also be defined by the developer as needed, but require knowledge of the RExplorator meta-model.

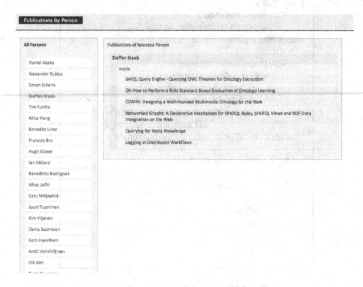

Fig. 8. Alternative formatting for the view in **Figure 7**, using CSS

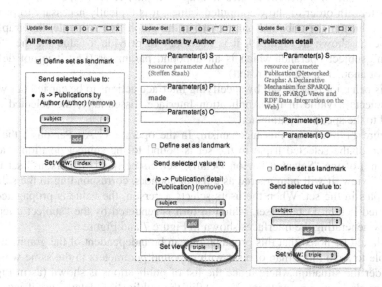

Fig. 9. Operations can be made visible in the Application Interface by setting a view

```
<div class="set menu _set" id = "<%=uri(resourceset)%>"
fixed="true">
    <div class="menutitle">
        <span class="menutitle_span"><%=
resourceset.explorator::name  %></span>
    </div>
    <div class="menuresources">
        <ul class="menuresources_ul">
            <% groupBy(:s, true).each do |resource| %>
            <li class="menuresource">
                <span class="menuresource_span">
                    <a class="menuresource_a
_menulink" id="<%= uri(resource)%>" position="s">
                        <%=
render_resource(resource)  %>
                    </a>
                </span>
            </li>
            <% end %>
        </ul>
    </div>
</div>
```

Fig. 10. Example of a view - Index

In addition to the Application Interface structure, it is necessary to also define its behavior. The workbench defines a graph of inter-related operations, containing parameters. In order to show computed values, it is typically necessary to provide an initial value for the unbound parameters in the graph. For example, the graph in the workbench shown in Figure 9, it is necessary to provide a value for the "Selected Person" subject operand, which is an unbound parameter (i.e., it is not defined in terms of another operation's result).

This behavior is achieved by specifying interface actions to be carried out when the user selects a value in the Application Interface. Essentially, the selected value is bound to the specified parameter.

Figure 11 illustrates this mechanism. In the operation "All Persons", the subject position of the selected triple in the set is bound to the subject position (parameter "Person") of the "Selected Person Details" set. Since the "All Persons" set uses the "Index" view, it will be rendered as a list of anchors, corresponding to the subjects of the triples in the set. When the users selects a person, the value is propagated to the "Selected Person Details" set, which in turn is rendered by the "subject after" view, thereby generating the interfaces shown in Figure 7 and Figure 8.

It should be noted that this propagation can be independent of the graph, since it is possible to have more than one set with unbound parameters in the same workbench. Consider the situation where, once the list of publications is shown (as in Figure 7), the user clicks on one of them. To exhibit the publication details, it suffices to send the value (in this case, the "o" position of the "Publications of Selected Person" set, which is the publication's URI) to the "subject" position of the "Selected Publication Details", as shown in Figure 11. The resulting interface is shown in Figure 12.

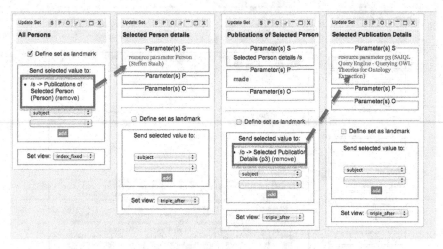

Fig. 11. Specifying the propagation of values in the Application Interface

4.4   User-Defined Operators

The original Explorator tool provides built-in set operators to manipulate the resource (triple) sets, besides the SPO query operator. While useful, they do not cover all possible computations one may want to perform over sets of resources. RExplorator provides a mechanism for the designer to define new operators.

Since operators work on sets of triples, a natural kind of function is the "list", "iterator" or "map" function commonly found in functional languages such as Lisp, Python, and Ruby, among others. In RExplorator, operators take two sets of triples as input and produce a set of triples as output.

As an example, one may want to filter a result set that contains datatype properties (e.g., rdf:label) according to a string value passed as a parameter. The Ruby code snippet below shows the definition of an operator that takes a resource set and a string as input parameters, and selects those triples whose object position matches the string.

```
param_a.select    {   |triple|   triple[2].to_s.strip.downcase   ==
param_b[0].to_s.strip.downcase }
```

The careful reader will have noticed that this operator requires defining a special operand that accepts text input from the user, to be able to bind it to the second parameter. More generally, RExplorator provides a primitive, named *transducer*, to allow values from outside RExploraror to be used as operands. The simplest form of transducer is a form with a text input field.

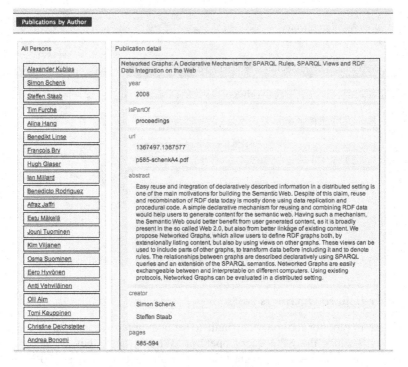

Fig. 12. Generated interface with Publication Detail

5   Evaluation

The main purpose of this paper is to present the underlying concepts in RExplorator, and their implementation in the running system. Nevertheless, we also discuss briefly a small qualitative study we carried out, to have a preliminary evaluation of RExplorator. We asked 5 persons with basic RDF knowledge to build simple applications using a repository describing cellular phone models. The tasks consisted of

1. Exhibiting all available models
2. Showing models that support MP3
3. Showing models grouped by supported band

First they were shown a short video with RExplorator's basic functionalities. Then they were allowed to experiment with RExplorator for a short time and have basic questions about its functioning answered, after which they were given one hour to accomplish the tasks.

Of the five people, three were able to successfully accomplish the tasks in less the allotted time; one completed the tasks but with a slightly incorrect solution; and one could not accomplish the task.

We consider these results to be positive, showing that the tool can be effective. The test subjects were given minimal instructions, and yet most were able to accomplish the tasks. It is clear that this interface is not for beginners, but once the developer has become familiar with it, it is quite effective.

These experiments also indicate that the authoring interface should be improved, for example using graphics to better represent the dependencies between sets.

6   Conclusions

The environment that has the closest functionality to RExplorator is DERI Pipes [3], which allows the definition of mash-ups by creating networks of interconnected operators, with strings, XML or RDF data flowing through them. The desired result is obtained by the composition of the operators.

By analogy, RExplorator can be seen as a network of interconnected operators, which can be queries, set operations or customized functions. The data that flows in this network are sets of triples.

Thus, the major difference is that it is oriented towards mash-up development, and as such its operators work at a lower abstraction level. Additionally, DERI Pipes does not provide an interface layer, and is not meant to be used together with an exploration environment.

One of the major focuses for future work is providing a graphical authoring interface that makes it easier to visually identify the inter-dependence of the various operations. It is not easy to readily understand the workings of a workbench by looking at its query definitions.

A second focus is the interface definition language. Presently, it uses HTML with embedded Ruby code, which uses functions of a library to help manipulating the underlying data. A simple extension would be to allow using Fresnel-style definitions for views [[12], but without the lens definition part, which is be given by the underlying workbench graph. More generally we plan to provide a higher-level definition language to make it easier for non-programmers to develop customized interfaces, using the work in [9][10].

Another interesting phenomenon that is developing is the formation of user communities around topics that have several repositories with RDF data available (see for example, the Bio Hackathon, http://hackathon3.dbcls.jp/). It is reasonable to expect that as users become more familiar with the data and formats of the various repositories, they will develop solutions for common tasks. We plan to enrich the RExplorator environment to allow it to support Communities of Practice that share solutions for recurring tasks over repositories of interest.

Acknowledgment. Daniel Schwabe was partially supported by a grant from CNPq.

References

[1] Araújo, F.C.S., Schwabe, D., Barbosa, D.J.S.: Experimenting with Explorator: a Direct Manipulation Generic RDF Browser and Querying Tool. In: Visual Interfaces to the Social and the Semantic Web, VISSW 2009, Sanibel Island, Florida (February 2009), http://www.smart-ui.org/events/vissw2009/index.html

[2] Araújo, F.C.S., Schwabe, D.: Explorator: A tool for exploring RDF data through direct manipulation. In: Proceedings of the Linked Data on the Web Workshop (LDOW 2009), Madrid, Spain, April 20. CEUR Workshop Proceedings (2009) ISSN 1613-0073, http://CEUR-WS.org/Vol-538/ldow2009_paper2.pdf

[3] Berners-Lee, T., Chen, Y., Chilton, L., Connolly, D., Dhanaraj, R., Hollenbach, J., Lerer, A., Sheets, D.: Tabulator: Exploring and Analyzing linked data on the Semantic Web. Decentralized Information Group. Computer Science and Artificial, Intelligence Laboratory. Massachusetts Institute of Technology, Cambridge (2006)

[4] Heim, P., Ziegler, J., Lohmann, S.: gFacet: A Browser for the Web of Data. In: Proceedings of the International Workshop on Interacting with Multimedia Content in the Social Semantic Web (IMC-SSW 2008), pp. S.49–S.58 (2008), http://gfacet.org/dbpedia/

[5] Hildebrand, M., van Ossenbruggen, J., Hardman, L.: /facet: A Browser for Heterogeneous Semantic Web Repositories. In: Cruz, I., Decker, S., Allemang, D., Preist, C., Schwabe, D., Mika, P., Uschold, M., Aroyo, L.M. (eds.) ISWC 2006. LNCS, vol. 4273, pp. 272–285. Springer, Heidelberg (2006)

[6] Huynh, D., Karger, D.: Parallax and companion: Set- based browsing for the data web, http://davidhuynh.net/media/papers/2009/www2009-parallax.pdf

[7] Kobilarov, G., Dickinson, I.: Humboldt: Exploring Linked Data. In: Linked Data on the WebWorkshop (LDOW 2008) at WWW 2008, Beijing, China (April 2008)

[8] Le Phuoc, D., Polleres, A., Morbidoni, C., Manfred Hauswirth, M., Tummarello, G.: Rapid semantic web mashup development through semantic web pipes. In: Proceedings of the 18th World Wide Web Conference (WWW 2009), Madrid, Spain (April 2009)

[9] Luna, A.M., Schwabe, D.: Ontology Driven Dynamic Web Interface Generation. In: Proceedings of the 8th International Workshop on Web Oriented Technologies (IWWOST 2009), San Sebastian, Spain, vol. 493, pp. 16–27. CEUR (2009) ISSN 1613-0073, http://ceur-ws.org/Vol-493/iwwost2009-luna.pdf

[10] Moura, S.S., Schwabe, D.: Interface Development for Hypermedia Applications in the Semantic Web. In: Proc. of LA Web 2004, Ribeirão Preto, Brasil, pp. 106–113. IEEE CS Pres (2004) ISBN 0-7695-2237-8

[11] Oren, E., Delbru, R., Decker, S.: Extending Faceted Navigation for RDF Data. In: Cruz, I., Decker, S., Allemang, D., Preist, C., Schwabe, D., Mika, P., Uschold, M., Aroyo, L.M. (eds.) ISWC 2006. LNCS, vol. 4273, pp. 559–572. Springer, Heidelberg (2006), http://browserdf.org/.

[12] Pietriga, E., Bizer, C., Karger, D.R., Lee, R.: Fresnel: A Browser-Independent Presentation Vocabulary for RDF. In: Cruz, I., Decker, S., Allemang, D., Preist, C., Schwabe, D., Mika, P., Uschold, M., Aroyo, L.M. (eds.) ISWC 2006. LNCS, vol. 4273, pp. 158–171. Springer, Heidelberg (2006)

[13] Popov, I.O., Schraefel, M.C., Hall, W., Shadbolt, N.: Connecting the Dots: A Multi-pivot Approach to Data Exploration. In: Aroyo, L., Welty, C., Alani, H., Taylor, J., Bernstein, A., Kagal, L., Noy, N., Blomqvist, E. (eds.) ISWC 2011, Part I. LNCS, vol. 7031, pp. 553–568. Springer, Heidelberg (2011)

[14] Russell, A., Smart, P.R., Braines, D., Shadbolt, N.R.: NITELIGHT: A Graphical Tool for Semantic Query Construction. In: Semantic Web User Interaction Workshop (SWUI 2008), Florence, Italy, April 5 (2008)

[15] Shneiderman, B.: Direct manipulation: a step beyond programming languages. IEEE Computer 16(8), 57–69 (1983)

A Survey on Proximity Measures
for Social Networks

Sara Cohen[1], Benny Kimelfeld[2], and Georgia Koutrika[3]

[1] Dept. of Computer Science and Engineering
Hebrew University of Jerusalem
Jerusalem, Israel
sara@cs.huji.ac.il
[2] IBM Research–Almaden
San Jose, CA 95120, USA
kimelfeld@us.ibm.com
[3] HP Labs
Palo Alto, USA
koutrika@hp.com

Abstract. Measuring proximity in a social network is an important task, with many interesting applications, including person search and link prediction. Person search is the problem of finding, by means of keyword search, relevant people in a social network. In user-centric person search, the search query is issued by a person participating in the social network and the goal is to find people that are relevant not only to the keywords, but also to the searcher herself. Link prediction is the task of predicting new friendships (links) that are likely to be added to the network. Both of these tasks require the ability to measure proximity of nodes within a network, and are becoming increasingly important as social networks become more ubiquitous.

This chapter surveys recent work on scoring measures for determining proximity between nodes in a social network. We broadly identify various classes of measures and discuss prominent examples within each class. We also survey efficient implementations for computing or estimating the values of the proximity measures.

1 Introduction

Online social networks have grown in popularity at an extraordinary pace over the last few years. In fact, social networks, such as Facebook, MySpace and Twitter, have become so widespread that they currently boast hundreds of millions of users. The graph structure defined by a social network encodes interesting and useful information about the social relations between users. Leveraging this data to effectively answer different types of queries is an interesting and challenging problem.

Abstractly, a social network is simply a graph of people. Edges indicate that one person (node) likes/trusts/recommends another. This graph may be undirected (e.g., as in Facebook) or directed (e.g., as in Twitter). In some scenarios

S. Ceri and M. Brambilla (Eds.): Search Computing III, LNCS 7538, pp. 191–206, 2012.
© Springer-Verlag Berlin Heidelberg 2012

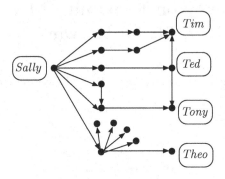

Fig. 1. Small fragment of a social network

edge weights are also desirable [44] to express the strength of a relationship, possibly by measuring the frequency of interactions between users. In addition, each node in a social network is typically associated with textual data, such as personal information, posts, etc.

The focus of this article is on surveying *proximity measures* for social networks. Intuitively, a proximity measure is a method of quantifying the degree of closeness between two given nodes s and t. Measuring proximity is an important aspect of several social network problems, including the following:

- *Person search* is the problem of finding, by means of keyword search, relevant people in a social network. Person search is an important type of query over a social network, as it is an aid in finding people of interest. In *user-centric person search*, the search query is issued by a person s participating in the social network, and the goal is to find people that possess two qualities: relevancy to the query, and relevancy to s herself. Proximity is highly important in ranking results of a user-centric person search, as nodes in close proximity to s are people (transitively) trusted by s. Hence, s can be less wary of entering into a real-life interaction (social or otherwise) with these people.
- *Link prediction* is the problem of predicting, using the graph structure of the network, the new relationships (i.e., edges) that are likely to be added in the near future. The ability to predict new edges for the network is useful for friend recommendation. It has been observed in the past that new social relations are likely to involve people who are already close one to another in a social network (e.g., triadic closure [37]). Thus, measuring proximity is an important aspect of solving the link prediction problem.

Now, consider the problem of measuring proximity in the social network of Figure 1. In this example, nodes have a name for easy reference. Suppose now that we would like to determine the proximity of Sally to each of the nodes Tim, Ted, Tony and Theo. This may occur as Sally poses a query for which these nodes are relevant (user-centric person search), or perhaps, we would like to determine which of these nodes is most likely to enter a relationship with Sally (link prediction).

Devising a general proximity measure in a large network is a difficult task, since many different properties of the network should be taken into consideration. For example, a shorter path from s to t should increase the proximity of t to s. According to this measure, Ted is closer to Sally than Tim (as the distance from Sally to Ted is 2, while the distance from Sally to Tim is only 3). The existence of multiple paths from s to t should again increase the proximity of t. According to this measure, Tony would be closer to Sally than Ted. Additional graph features might also affect proximity, such as the disjointedness of paths from s to t and the out-degrees of nodes on the paths from s to t.

Trying to combine such features raises interesting questions about how the four nodes should be ranked. *Should Tim be ranked above or below Tony?* Tim has more disjoint paths from Sally, but the paths are longer. *Should Theo be ranked above or below Ted?* The paths from Sally to Ted and to Theo are of the same length, but the path from Sally to Theo is more "diluted" by nodes with high out-degrees than the path from Sally to Ted.

This article surveys recent work on proximity measures for social networks. As there has been considerable work introducing a variety of proximity measures, we do not profess to exhaustively cover all measures that have been proposed in the past. Instead, we broadly identify various classes of measures (by their underlying intuition and motivation). In Section 2, for each class, we discuss prominent examples of proximity measures. Next, Section 3 considers the problem of implementing these measures over huge social networks, and surveys recent work on efficiently computing or estimating proximity measures.

We note that this chapter differs greatly from previous works, such as that of Liben-Nowel and Kleinberg [32] that focus on comparing the effectiveness of various proximity measures for link prediction. First, our focus is on general proximity measures (some of which may be useful for search but not for link prediction). Second, we do not present an empirical comparison of the measures, as clearly different measures may be useful for different proximity-related tasks. Finally, we extensively survey implementations of the various proximity measures, which is pivotal for a real-world system.

2 Ranking Functions

A social network is a directed graph $G(V, E, txt)$, where V is a set of nodes, called people, $E \subseteq V \times V$ is a set of edges and for all $v \in V$, $txt(v)$ associates v with textual content, such as personal information, posts and so forth. Unless otherwise stated, social networks are directed, and thus, allow for asymmetric social relations. An edge (u, v) indicates that u views v in a positive light, that is, u likes/trusts/recommends v. A small fragment of a social network appears in Figure 1. Note that most textual content has been omitted in this figure for simplicity in presentation.

In this article, we will consider functions $\text{prox}(s, t, G)$ that measure the proximity of t to s in graph G. In these ranking functions, greater values are preferable, that is, prox(s, t, G) > prox(s, t', G) implies that t is, in some sense, closer to s than t' in G. Such a function can be used in user-centric person search, in order to rank query results, and in link prediction, in order to suggest likely new links.

   In some contexts, the quality of a proximity ranking function can be measured. For example, datasets for measuring proximity with respect to link prediction are relatively easy to obtain (by recrawling a social network after some time has elapsed). However, there are no known benchmarks to test the quality of a proximity ranking function in the context of user-centric search. One might suppose that a proximity function proven to be superior for link prediction will also be superior for user-centric search. However, link prediction and user-centric search are quite different tasks. Conceptually, there is no reason to believe that a desired search result would also be a desired neighbor; indeed, an algorithm for link prediction may return none of the nodes matching a given set of keywords, as no corresponding link is predicted, and then provide no ranking at all for candidate answers. Moreover, while link prediction and benchmarks thereof typically capture relationships that already exist in real life, search is often about discovery beyond present knowledge.

   Due to the lack of test data, and to the fact that different measures may be useful in different contexts, in this article we make no pretense of comparing proximity measures and pointing out which one(s) are of highest effectiveness. Instead we take a classification-based approach. Specifically, our discussion in this section is based on classifying proximity measures by their underlying intuition and motivation. Thus, we discuss measuring proximity based on shortest paths (Section 2.1), node neighborhoods (Section 2.2), random walks (Section 2.3), network flow (Section 2.4) and network sampling (Section 2.5). Finally, we discuss a property-based approach to classifying proximity measures (Section 2.6).

2.1   Shortest Paths

Certainly the simplest notion of measuring proximity is to use the length of the *shortest path* from s to t for this purpose. In order to have a greater proximity value for closer nodes, we can define this function, called $rdist(s, t, G)$, simply as the reciprocal of the distance from s to t in G, that is,

$$rdist(s, t, G) \stackrel{\text{def}}{=} (dist(s, t, G))^{-1},$$

where $dist(s, t, G)$ is the length of the shortest path from s to t. (An alternative is to use $-dist(s, t, G)$, instead of the reciprocal.)

   The function $rdist(s, t, G)$ has the distinct advantage of being quite simple. Hence, efficiently computing this value over a dynamically changing and enormous social network is more feasible than for many of the other functions considered later. Computing $rdist(s, t, G)$ is discussed further in Section 3. On the other hand, $rdist(s, t, G)$ is oblivious to the structure of the social network, beyond edges on the shortest path. Hence, $rdist(s, t, G)$ is not very discriminating. As an example, Ted, Tony and Theo all have the same distance from Sally in Figure 1.

The *Katz measure* [29] captures the idea that the more paths that there are between s and t, and the shorter these paths are, the closer t is to s. Formally,

$$katz(s, t, G) \stackrel{\text{def}}{=} \sum_{l=1}^{\infty} \beta^l |\text{paths}_{s,t,G}^l| , \qquad (1)$$

where $\text{paths}_{s,t,G}^l$ is the set of all length-l paths from s to t in G and the constant β dampens by length to count short paths more heavily.

Since *katz* takes all paths from s to t into consideration, it is much more discriminating that $rdist(s, t, G)$. In Figure 1, Ted and Theo have the same proximity to Sally, according to *katz* while Tony has higher proximity (due to the extra path of length 3 from Sally to Tony).

2.2   Node Neighborhoods

Several proximity measures are based on the neighborhoods of nodes s and t. We use $\Gamma(x)$ to denote the set of (undirected) neighbors of x. Preferential attachment [34] is the simplest neighborhood-based measure, and defines the similarity of s and t simply by $|\Gamma(s)| \times |\Gamma(t)|$. Thus, with respect to preferential attachment, a node s will always be most similar to nodes t with high degree. Preferential attachment has been successfully used to model the growth of networks and has been shown to be useful for link prediction in citation networks [6].

By considering not only the sizes of the neighborhoods of s and t, but also their intersection, we can further analyze the similarity of s and t. Intuitively, if s and t have many common neighbors, then they are likely to be closely related. Several neighborhood-based proximity measures were surveyed by Liben-Nowell and Kleinberg [32], including: the number of common neighbors, $|\Gamma(s) \cap \Gamma(t)|$, Jaccard coefficient of neighbors

$$\frac{|\Gamma(s) \cap \Gamma(t)|}{|\Gamma(s) \cup \Gamma(t)|}$$

and an adaptation of the Adamic/Adar measure [1]

$$\sum_{v \in \Gamma(s) \cap \Gamma(t)} \frac{1}{\log(|\Gamma(v)|)} .$$

Note that the last measure uses the log function to weight rarer features more heavily. A variation of the Adamic/Adar measure, that reduces the punishment on large-degree common neighbors, by defining similarity as

$$\sum_{v \in \Gamma(s) \cap \Gamma(t)} \frac{1}{|\Gamma(v)|} ,$$

has been introduced [50] and has been shown to outperform Adamic/Adar on some networks.

The above proximity measures have proven useful for link prediction [32], especially since links tend to be added between close nodes. However these measures are inappropriate for person search. In particular all neighborhood-based measures (other than preferential attachment), give a score of 0 if s and t have no common neighbors. For person search, relevant answers may be much farther from s. Thus, it is even possible that no node within distance two from s even satisfies the textual part of the person query, and hence all nodes relevant to the query might receive a rank of zero using neighborhood-based proximity measures.

2.3   Random Walks

Ranking measures based on random walks, such as PageRank, have proven extraordinarily successful for search on the Web. Intuitively, the PageRank of a Web page t is a measure of the likelihood that a Web surfer, starting at a random page, randomly choosing outgoing links to click on (and occasionally teleporting to a random Web page), will reach t. More precisely, the PageRank of t is the stationary probability of t in a random walk that jumps to a random node in the graph with probability α at each step, and moves to a random neighbor with probability $1 - \alpha$.

PageRank is not immediately applicable to ranking proximity, as it measures the importance of a page t in the entire graph, and not with respect to another node s. A relevant adaptation of PageRank is that of *personalized PageRank* [26]. In this ranking function, there is a probability distribution Ω over the nodes of the graph. The personalized PageRank of t is the stationary probability of t in a random walk that jumps to a random node v in the graph with probability $\alpha \times \Omega(v)$ at each step, and moves to a random neighbor with probability $1 - \alpha$. Thus, personalized PageRank favors nodes with high probability according to Ω (as well as their neighbors, and neighbors' neighbors, etc.).

Rooted PageRank [31, 32], a special case of personalized PageRank, was considered for measuring proximity in a social network (in the context of link prediction). In rooted PageRank, there is a designated node s, called the root, for which $\Omega(s) = 1$, while $\Omega(v) = 0$, for all other nodes $v \neq s$. Thus, rooted PageRank, denoted $rPR(s, t, G)$, is the stationary probability of t in a random walk that *returns to* s with probability α at each step, moving to a random neighbor with probability $1 - \alpha$. Intuitively, this function gives a higher ranking to nodes t that are more easily reached from s when traversing G.

2.4   Flow in Networks

Koren et al. [30] developed sophisticated proximity measures for an *undirected and weighted* graph. They propose that proximity should be more sensitive to edges between low-degree nodes that show meaningful relationships and should take into account multiple paths between s and t. To define such a measure, they first consider *network flow* as a ranking function. The network flow from s to t grows as the number of paths from s to t increases, as intuitively required from a proximity measure. However, network flow is not sensitive to path lengths, and is bounded by the s-t-cut[1] capacity, both of which are undesirable.

To overcome the problems associated with network flow, Koren et al. [30] model the network as an electrical circuit. Intuitively, edges can be seen as resistors, with s having a voltage of 1, and t having a voltage of 0. Then, a series of linear equations can be used to estimate the currents of the network, and in particular, the current delivered from s to t, called the *effective conductance* [13]. They proposed *cycle-free effective conductance* as an improvement over effective conductance for measuring network proximity. This measure is quite intricate, and we present the main details here. (See [30] for full details.)

In a random walk, the probability to follow an edge from node u to node v is $w_{u,v}/\deg_u$ where $w_{u,v}$ is the weight of the edge from u to v and $\deg_u$ is the degree of u. Thus, the probability of a random walk following the path $\bar{v} = v_1, \ldots, v_n$ is simply the product of the probabilities of each transition in the path. The *cycle-free escape probability* from s to t is the probability that a random walk beginning at s will reach t without visiting any node more than once. Finally, the proposed measure of proximity, called *cycle-free effective conductance* is the product of the degree of s and the cycle-free escape probability from s to t.

2.5   Random Sampling

A rather different approach to measuring proximity comes from the field of communication networks, where the notion of *network reliability* was considered [10, 20]. In this measure, there is a fixed probability $p \in (0, 1)$. We denote by G^r a random subgraph of G that is obtained by removing each edge of G, independently, with probability $1 - p$. The reliability of G is the probability that G^r is connected. The greater the reliability of a network, the more likely it is that communication will be possible with all nodes, even in the presence of network failures.

Reliability is a global function of a graph. However, *two-terminal network reliability* [41] is the natural counterpart of this function for a given pair of nodes s and t. Thus, two-terminal network reliability measures the likelihood that there will be a path from s to t in a random subgraph, formally defined as

$$reliability_2\,(s, t, G) \stackrel{\text{def}}{=} \Pr\left[G^r \text{ has a path from } s \text{ to } t\right].$$

Obviously, the closer t is to s, and the more (independent) paths there are from s to t, the higher the two-terminal network reliability will be. This function has been considered for proximity ranking in user-centric person search [9].

Another sampling based function considered for person search [9] is that of *expected distance*. Intuitively, this function measures the expected distance from s to t, when each edge is removed with probability $1 - p$. Note that for this value

---

[1] Recall that an s-t-cut is a partition of the graph into two disjoint sets of nodes, one of which contains s and the other of which contains t. The capacity of the cut is the sum of weights of edges "split" by the cut.

to be well defined, there must be a number m, that is returned by the function, when no path from s to t exists.

Once again, we assume that there is a fixed probability $p \in (0, 1)$. In addition, we fix a parameter $m \in \mathbb{R}$. We will implicitly assume that m is larger than the number of nodes in the graph G. The m-bounded distance from s to t, denoted $\hat{\delta}_G(s, t)$, is defined by

$$\hat{\delta}_G(s, t) \stackrel{\text{def}}{=} \min\{dist(s, t, G), m\} .$$

Thus, if G has no path from s to t, then $\hat{\delta}_G(s, t) = m$. Note that if $s \neq t$, then $\hat{\delta}_G(s, t)$ is always in the interval $[1, m]$.

We denote by G^{r} a random subgraph of G that is obtained by removing each edge of G, independently, with probability $1 - p$. The expected m-bounded distance, denoted by $\overline{\delta_G}(s, t)$, is defined as follows.

$$\overline{\delta_G}(s, t) \stackrel{\text{def}}{=} \mathbb{E}\left[\hat{\delta}_{G^{\mathrm{r}}}(s, t)\right] .$$

That is, $\overline{\delta_G}(s, t)$ is the expected m-bounded distance from s to t in a random subgraph G^{r} of G. Finally, the proposed proximity ranking function is the reciprocal of $\overline{\delta_G}(s, t)$, namely

$$expd(s, t, G) \stackrel{\text{def}}{=} (\overline{\delta_G}(s, t))^{-1} .$$

2.6   Properties for Proximity Ranking Functions

In lieu of empirical comparison of proximity functions (which is not always currently possible due to lack of benchmarks), Cohen et al. [9] propose three simple properties that proximity functions $prox(s, t, G)$ should satisfy. They analyze a variety of functions with respect to these properties. Intuitively, the properties are based on the observation that certain graph transformations should only increase $prox(s, t, G)$, as these transformations, in a sense, make the relationship between s and t more significant. In a way, this is similar in spirit to the underlying premise of the family of TF-IDF ranking functions [33] for textual search and ranking. This premise requires that increasing term occurrences within a document, or decreasing term frequency within a corpus, should only increase the ranking of a document with respect to the given term.

One property of Cohen et al. [9] requires the following. Suppose that a node v lies on a simple path from s to t in G. Moreover, suppose that v has a single incoming and outgoing edge. Then, removing v from G (and directly connecting its incoming and outgoing neighbors) can only shorten paths from s to t without having additional effect on the graph. Thus, such a transformation should only cause $prox(s, t, G)$ to grow. Other properties of Cohen et al. [9] consider the effect expected when paths from s to t become more disjoint. These properties state that (under certain conditions) splitting a node into several nodes (while preserving existing paths) should again only increase $prox(s, t, G)$. We demonstrate these ideas in the following example.

Example 1. Let G be the graph of Figure 1, and let s be the node Sally. Removing the node on the path from Sally to Ted should raise Ted's score. Splitting the node with two incoming edges on the paths from Sally to Tony would result in the graph structure containing two disjoint paths from Sally to Tony (with lengths of two and three) and hence, should raise Tony's score.

Cohen et al. [9] analyzed the satisfaction of the given properties by different proximity measures, namely, shortest path, the Katz measure, rooted PageRank, reliability and expected distance. They showed that, of the measures considered, only those based on random sampling (reliability and expected distance) satisfied all properties *in the strong sense* (i.e., the graph transformation guaranteed the ranking the increase). As one example where other measures failed to strongly satisfy all properties, note that the Katz measure is oblivious to disjointness of paths. Hence, this measure does not increase given graph transformations making paths more disjoint. (For full details see [9].)

3   Efficiently Computing or Estimating Ranking Functions

Real-life social networks are often huge, easily containing hundreds of millions of members. Storing pairwise ranking values (for any chosen ranking function) is infeasible, due to its huge memory requirements. In addition, the dynamic nature of social networks, which are constantly changing and evolving, would seem to quickly make pre-computed ranking values obsolete. Therefore, answering person search queries or link prediction requires online computation (or estimation) of ranking functions. In this section, we reconsider the ranking functions introduced in Section 2, and survey recent algorithms for their efficient computation, or estimation.[2]

3.1   Shortest Paths

The first ranking function considered, $rdist(s, t, G)$, simply computes the reciprocal of the shortest distance from s to t. Thus, to compute this function, an algorithm for finding shortest paths in needed. Due to the simplicity of this function, and to the many applications using shortest paths, it is not surprising that this is the most well-studied ranking function.

Computing shortest paths is a well-studied problem, with many well-known solutions. For example, the single-source shortest path problem can be solved using breadth-first search in $O(|V| + |E|)$ for unweighted graphs, and can be solved using Dijkstra's algorithm [11] in time $O(|V|^2)$ (or $O(|V|log|V| + |E|)$ for sparse graphs) for weighted graphs. The all-pairs shortest paths problem can be solved using the Floyd-Warshall algorithm in time $O(|V|^3)$ [17]. It would therefore seem that this ranking function needs no further treatment.

---

[2] We do not discuss implementing neighborhood based proximity measures as these are typically straightforward.

The response time for a search is typically expected to be within a few milliseconds. However, in practice, the online computation of the above algorithms in huge social networks is simply too slow. For example, Potamias et al. [36] experimentally show that a standard PC requires a minute to compute a full breadth-first search (BFS) traversal of a network containing only four million nodes and 50 million edges. Hence, recent work has focused on significantly speeding up processing time by approximating the shortest path length, instead of its precise computation.

Several different methods have been introduced to estimate shortest path distances. One method is to choose a subset of the nodes, called *landmarks* [36] or *seeds* [42]. Instead of computing all-pairs shortest paths, the shortest path from each landmark to every other node in the graph is pre-computed and stored. When the distance from s to t is desired, this value is estimated using the distance of s and t to each of the landmarks. (In particular, the distance of s to t is at most the minimal sum of the distance of s to any landmark u, and the distance of u to t).

An interesting question is how to best choose the landmarks, so as to derive a good estimation of distances. To be precise, a set of landmarks *covers* a pair of vertices s, t if there exists at least one landmark in the set which lies on a shortest path from s to t. (Using such a landmark will yield the precise distance from s to t.) Potamias et al. [36] showed that selecting k landmarks so as to maximize the number of covered pairs is an NP-complete problem. However, they have presented and experimentally studied various strategies for landmark selection, and have shown their strategies to be quite effective and efficient in practice. Adding small path sketches to the information stored at the landmarks has been considered to allow shortest paths (and not just their lengths) to be computed and retrieved [23].

Efficiently finding the precise distance between two nodes (called point-to-point shortest paths) was studied by Goldberg and Harrelsons [22]. There, pre-computed landmarks are used as an upped bound for the actual distance. These bounds are leveraged to compute the exact distance, based on A^* search and using the triangle inequality, thereby defining a new class of algorithms, called *ALT algorithms* (for A^*, landmarks and triangle inequality). They show significant improvement on the number of neighbors traversed during computation, with respect to the state of the art.

Landmarks have also been used as a bootstrapping stage for *graph coordinate systems* [48, 49]. Intuitively, a graph coordinate system maps the nodes of a graph to coordinates in a Euclidean or hyperbolic space. Once such a mapping is available, shortest path estimation is easily achieved, by simply computing the distance between the coordinates corresponding to the nodes of interest. However, finding an effective mapping is a difficult problem.

The system architecture can have a significant impact on the speed of computing shortest paths. Katz and Kider [28] investigated the problem of computing all-pairs shortest paths on a Graphics Processing Unit (GPU). They present a highly parallel and scalable formulation of a transitive closure, and then use this to run the Floyd-Warshall algorithm on a GPU. A significant speedup is shown in comparison to runtime on a CPU.

Recently, Gao et al. [21] considered leveraging a relational database to compute shortest paths. For that purpose, they introduce the *FEM framework* with new operators that are suitable for the task at hand. Optimizations (such as use of new SQL features, and bi-directional set Dijkstra) are presented to further speed-up shortest path calculation. Finally, Xiao et al. [45] consider the problem of pre-indexing all shortest path distances. As storing all distances is not feasible, due to the amount of memory required, they focus on reducing the required memory size. To achieve this, they exploit graph symmetry (using graph automorphisms), and enable indexing at the *orbit level* instead of at the *node level*.

3.2   Katz Measure

While shortest path considers a single path from source to target, the Katz measure is a function of *all* source-to-target paths. Obviously, this makes computing, or estimating, $katz(s, t, G)$ a much more difficult task. There are very few works attempting to solve this problem.

One method of speeding up the computation of the Katz measure is to truncate the computation at paths of a specific, predetermined, length. Thus, the sum of Equation (1) will be computed only up to this predefined length (and not until infinity) [19, 43]. The wealth of work on enumerating shortest paths (e.g., [7,14,27,46,47]) can be leveraged to compute the truncated Katz measure.

Two new techniques, called *proximity sketches* and *proximity embeddings* were introduced by Song et al. [39] to efficiently estimate a family of proximity measures. Interestingly, they show that the Katz measures, rooted PageRank and escape probability can all be estimated efficiently, if the *proximity inversion problem* can be efficiently solved. The basic idea is that all three measures can be defined as functions of the adjacency matrix of the network, and thus, can be computed by matrix inversion. Proximity sketches and embeddings are introduced as dimension reduction techniques, so as to make sparser the matrix that must be inverted, and hence, allow its inversion to be efficiently achieved.

While Song et al. [39] compute the Katz measure for all pairs, Esfandiar et al. [15] focus on computing pairwise $katz(s, t, G)$, in order to reduce computation time. They introduce a technique that combines Lanczos iteration and a quadrature rule to compute the values of interest. (Their work can also be used to compute another proximity function, called *commute time*.)

3.3   Rooted PageRank

As discussed earlier, rooted PageRank is a special type of personalized PageRank ranking function, which, in turn, adapts the classical PageRank by changing its teleporting mechanism. In the previous section we discussed one method to efficiently estimate PageRank [39]. In this section, we consider other methods that have been developed for estimating personalized PageRank. We note that work on computing PageRank generally takes one of two approaches: using linear algebraic techniques or Monte Carlo methods. Unsurprisingly, this is also the case with personalized PageRank.

We start by discussing work that use *linear algebraic techniques* (as does the simple power iteration method for computing PageRank [35]). Jeh and Widom [26] explored the computation of personalized PageRank in a scalable manner. One of the crucial aspects of their algorithm is the assumption that the *preference set* (i.e., nodes to which teleporting is allowed) is always a subset of a given set of nodes H (called hubs). Unfortunately, for rooted PageRank, the set H is precisely all nodes in the network. Hence, the method presented of Jeh and Widom [26] reduces to a simple dynamic programming algorithm that provides no performance improvement over the standard power iteration method [35]. Sarlós et. al [38] improve upon that method by using *deterministic rounding* and *randomized sketching* techniques. Thus, their approach is for unrestricted on-line personalized PageRank.

In *Monte Carlo methods*, the basic idea is to approximate PageRank by directly simulating the corresponding random walks and then estimating the stationary distributions with the empirical distributions of the performed walks. Based on this idea, the following method for approximating personalized PageRank has been proposed [2, 18]. Starting at each node u, perform a number R of random walks, called *fingerprints*, each having a length geometrically distributed. They have shown that the frequencies of visits to different nodes in these fingerprints will approximate personalized PageRanks. Monte Carlo algorithms to compute personalized PageRank have also been studied [3, 4].

3.4   Effective Conductance

After introducing cycle-free effective conductance (CFEC), Koren et al. [30] provide an efficient method for approximating this value. In their approximation, they use only the most probable paths between a source node s and a target node t. The authors have experimentally found that path probability falls off exponentially, hence the low probability paths cannot sum to any significant value. Therefore, the k most probable simple paths are determined by some threshold. This is similar, in a sense, to the notion of truncating the Katz measure, discussed earlier.

Based on the above idea, the problem of cycle-free effective conductance estimation is mapped to the k shortest-simple-paths problem, a natural generalization of the shortest path problem, in which not one but several paths in order of increasing length are sought. They employ an algorithm for the computation of the k most probable paths [25] for the CFEC estimation. Typically, the algorithm stops when the probability of the unscanned paths drops significantly below that of the most probable path (e.g., below a factor of 10^{-6}).

3.5 Reliability and Expected Distance

The problem of computing expected distance seems to have not been studied in the past. Hence, its complexity, as well as methods for estimating this value, are currently unknown. Therefore, in this section we focus only on computing and estimating two-terminal network reliability.

It was shown [41] that exact calculation of two-terminal reliability for general networks is #P-complete. (Recall that #P is the class of the counting problems associated with the decision problems in NP.) Hence, precisely computing two-terminal reliability is likely to be highly intractable. Instead, there has been work focusing on computing upper and lower bounds to this measure, while avoiding the exponential computation likely to required by exact algorithms.

The difficulty of two-terminal reliability and its many interesting applications in networks have stimulated many different approaches to estimating two-terminal reliability. These include partitioning techniques [12], techniques based on the sum of disjoint products [5], and Monte-Carlo simulations [16]. Terruggia [40] surveys these approaches.

4 Conclusion

In this article we surveyed a variety of proximity measures for social networks. We also discussed the underlying principles guiding the development of these proximity measures (e.g., based on shortest paths, sampling, flow, random walks). Efficient algorithms for computing or estimating proximity measures were also surveyed. The tradeoffs of simplicity versus efficient computability are clearly apparent.

Only graph-based similarity measures were considered in this article. However, there additional types of information can be useful for determining similarity of nodes, when available. For example, [8] leverages tags on nodes for people search, and [24] takes a crowd-sourcing approach to determining node similarity.

There are many related problems that are still open. Development of benchmark data for user-centric person search is an important problem. Only such a benchmark can guide the development of proximity measures for user-centric person search. We also observe that many of the algorithms for computing (or estimating) proximity measures do not adapt well to changes in the social network. Since social networks are constantly changing and evolving, this is a critical issue. Finally, it would be interesting to adapt the proximity measures we discussed to weighted graphs, and to graphs with edge labels that represent different kinds of relationships such as "follower," "friend of" and "spouse of," and even ones carrying a negative sentiment like "warns about" and "denounces."

Acknowledgements. The research of Sara Cohen was partially supported by the ISF (Grant 143/09) and the Israeli Ministry of Science and Technology (Grant 3-6472).

References

1. Adamic, L., Adar, E.: How to search a social network. In: VLDB, pp. 217–225 (1987)
2. Avrachenkov, K., Litvak, N., Nemirovsky, D., Osipova, N.: Monte carlo methods in pagerank computation: When one iteration is sufficient. SIAM J. Numer. Anal. 45(2), 890–904 (2007)
3. Bahmani, B., Chakrabarti, K., Xin, D.: Fast personalized pagerank on mapreduce. In: SIGMOD Conference, pp. 973–984 (2011)
4. Bahmani, B., Chowdhury, A., Goel, A.: Fast incremental and personalized pagerank. PVLDB 4(3), 173–184 (2010)
5. Balan, A.O., Traldi, L.: Preprocessing minpaths for sum of disjoint products. IEEE Trans. Reliability 52(3), 289–295 (2003)
6. Barabasi, A.L., Jeong, H., Neda, Z., Ravasz, E., Schubert, A., Vicsek, T.: Evolution of the social network of scientific collaborations. Physica A 311(3-4), 590–614 (2002)
7. Brander, A., Sinclair, M.: A comparative study of k-shortest path algorithms. In: Proc. 11th UK Performance Engineering Workshop for Computer and Telecommunications Systems (1995)
8. Carmel, D., Zwerdling, N., Guy, I., Ofek-Koifman, S., Har'el, N., Ronen, I., Uziel, E., Yogev, S., Chernov, S.: Personalized social search based on the user's social network. In: Proceedings of the 18th ACM Conference on Information and Knowledge Management, CIKM 2009, pp. 1227–1236. ACM, New York (2009), http://doi.acm.org/10.1145/1645953.1646109
9. Cohen, S., Kimelfeld, B., Koutrika, G., Vondrák, J.: On principles of egocentric person search in social networks. In: First International Workshop on Searching and Integrating New Web Data Sources, Seattle, Washington (2011)
10. Davies, D., Barber, D.: Communication Networks for Computers. John Wiley, London (1973)
11. Dijkstra, E.W.: A note on two problems in connexion with graphs. Numerische Mathematik 1, 269–271 (1959)
12. Dotson, W.P., Gobien, J.O.: A new analysis technique for probabilistic graphs. IEEE Trans. Circuits and Systems 26(10), 855–865 (1979)
13. Doyle, P., Snell, J.: Random walks and electical networks. The Mathematical Association of America (1984)
14. Eppstein, D.: Finding the k shortest paths. SIAM J. Comput. 28(2), 652–673 (1998)
15. Esfandiar, P., Bonchi, F., Gleich, D.F., Greif, C., Lakshmanan, L.V.S., On, B.-W.: Fast Katz and Commuters: Efficient Estimation of Social Relatedness in Large Networks. In: Kumar, R., Sivakumar, D. (eds.) WAW 2010. LNCS, vol. 6516, pp. 132–145. Springer, Heidelberg (2010)
16. Fishman, G.S.: A comparison of four monte carlo methods for estimating the probability of s-t connectedness. IEEE Trans. Reliability 35(2), 145–155 (1986)
17. Floyd, R.W.: Algorithm 97: Shortest path. Communications of the ACM 5(6), 345 (1962)
18. Fogaras, D., Rácz, B.: Towards Scaling Fully Personalized PageRank. In: Leonardi, S. (ed.) WAW 2004. LNCS, vol. 3243, pp. 105–117. Springer, Heidelberg (2004)
19. Foster, K.C., Muth, S.Q., Potterat, J.J., Rothenberg, R.B.: A faster katz status score algorithm. Computational and Mathematical Organization Theory 7, 275–285 (2001)
20. Frank, H., Frisch, I.: Communication, Transmission and Transportation Networks. Addison Wesley, Reading (1971)

21. Gao, J., Jim, R., Zhou, J., Yu, J.X., Jiang, X., Wang, T.: Relational approach for shortest path discovery over large graphs. PVLDB 5(4), 358–369 (2012)
22. Goldberg, A., Harrelsons, C.: Computing the shortest path: A* search meets graph theory. In: SODA (2005)
23. Gubichev, A., Bedathur, S.J., Seufert, S., Weikum, G.: Fast and accurate estimation of shortest paths in large graphs. In: CIKM, pp. 499–508 (2010)
24. Guy, I., Perer, A., Daniel, T., Greenshpan, O., Turbahn, I.: Guess who?: enriching the social graph through a crowdsourcing game. In: Proceedings of the 2011 Annual Conference on Human Factors in Computing Systems, CHI 2011, pp. 1373–1382. ACM, New York (2011), http://doi.acm.org/10.1145/1978942.1979145
25. Hadjiconstantinou, E., Christofides, N.: An efficient implementation of an algorithm for finding k shortest simple paths. Networks 34, 88–101 (1999)
26. Jeh, G., Widom, J.: Scaling personalized web search. In: Proceedings of the 12th International Conference on World Wide Web, WWW 2003, pp. 271–279. ACM, New York (2003), http://doi.acm.org/10.1145/775152.775191
27. Katoh, N., Ibaraki, T., Mine, H.: An efficient algorithm for k shortest simple paths. Networks 12 (1982)
28. Katz, G.J., Kider Jr., J.T.: All-pairs shortest-paths for large graphs on the gpu. In: Graphics Hardware, pp. 47–55 (2008)
29. Katz, L.: A new status index derived from sociometric analysis. Psychometrika 18(1), 39–43 (1953)
30. Koren, Y., North, S.C., Volinsky, C.: Measuring and extracting proximity graphs in networks. TKDD 1(3) (2007)
31. Liben-Nowell, D., Kleinberg, J.M.: The link-prediction problem for social networks. In: CIKM (2003)
32. Liben-Nowell, D., Kleinberg, J.M.: The link-prediction problem for social networks. JASIST 58(7), 1019–1031 (2007)
33. Manning, C.D., Raghavan, P., Schtze, H.: Introduction to Information Retrieval. Cambridge University Press, New York (2008)
34. Mitzenmacher, M.: A brief history of generative models for power law and lognormal distributions. Internet Mathematics 1(2), 226–251 (2004)
35. Page, L., Brin, S., Motwani, R., Winograd, T.: The pagerank citation ranking: Bringing order to the web. Tech. rep., Stanford University (1998)
36. Potamias, M., Bonchi, F., Castillo, C., Gionis, A.: Fast shortest path distance estimation in large networks. In: CIKM (2009)
37. Rapoport, A.: Spread of information through a population with socio-structural bias i: Assumption of transitivity. Bulletin of Mathematical Biophysics 15(4), 523–533 (1953)
38. Sarlós, T., Benczúr, A.A., Csalogány, K., Fogaras, D., Ráz, B.: To randomize or not to randomize: space optimal summaries for hyperlink analysis. In: World Wide Web, pp. 297–306 (2006)
39. Song, H.H., Cho, T.W., Dave, V., Zhang, Y., Qiu, L.: Scalable proximity estimation and link prediction in online social networks. In: IMC (2009)
40. Terruggia, R.: A comparison of four monte carlo methods for estimating the probability of s-t connectedness. Thesis. Università degli Studi di Torino (2010)
41. Valiant, L.G.: The complexity of enumeration and reliability problems. SIAM J. Comput. 8(3), 410–421 (1979)
42. Vieira, M.V., Fonseca, B.M., Damazio, R., Golgher, P.B., de Castro Reis, D., Ribeiro-Neto, B.A.: Efficient search ranking in social networks. In: CIKM, pp. 563–572 (2007)
43. Wang, C., Satuluri, V., Parthasarathy, S.: Local probabilistic models for link prediction. In: ICDM, pp. 322–331 (2007)

44. Xiang, R., Neville, J., Rogati, M.: Modeling relationship strength in online social networks. In: Proceedings of the 19th International Conference on World Wide Web, WWW 2010, pp. 981–990. ACM, New York (2010), http://doi.acm.org/10.1145/1772690.1772790
45. Xiao, Y., Wu, W., Pei, J., Wang, W., He, Z.: Efficiently indexing shortest paths by exploiting symmetry in graphs. In: EDBT (2009)
46. Yen, J.Y.: Finding the k shortest loopless paths in a network. Management Science 17 (1971)
47. Yen, J.Y.: Another algorithm for finding the k shortest loopless network paths. In: Proc. of 41st Mtg. Operations Research Society of America 20 (1972)
48. Zhao, X., Salaa, A., Wilson, C., Zheng, H., Zhao, B.Y.: Orion: Shortest path estimation for large social graphs. In: Proceedings of the 3rd Workshop on Online Social Networks, WOSN (2010)
49. Zhao, X., Salaa, A., Zheng, H., Zhao, B.Y.: Efficient shortest paths on massive social graphs. In: Proceedings of 7th International Conference on Collaborative Computing: Networking, Applications and Worksharing, CollaborateCom (2011)
50. Zhou, T., Lü, L., Zhang, Y.C.: Predicting missing links via local information. The European Physical Journal B—Condensed Matter and Complex Systems 71(4), 623–630 (2009)

Extending Search to Crowds: A Model-Driven Approach

Alessandro Bozzon, Marco Brambilla, Stefano Ceri, and Andrea Mauri

Dipartimento di Elettronica e Informazione, Politecnico di Milano
{bozzon,mbrambil,ceri,mauri}@elet.polimi.it

Abstract. In many settings, the human opinion provided by an expert or knowledgeable user can be more useful than factual information retrieved by a search engine. Search systems do not capture the subjective opinions and recommendations of friends, or fresh, online-provided information that require contextual or domain-specific expertise. Search results obtained from conventional search engines can be complemented by crowdsearch, an online interaction with crowds, selected among friends, experts, or people who are presently at a given location; an interplay between conventional and search-based queries can occur, so that the two search methods can support each other. In this paper, we use a model-driven approach for specifying and implementing a crowdsearch application; in particular we define two models: the "Query Task Model", representing the meta-model of the query that is submitted to the crowd and the associated answers; and the "User Interaction Model", showing how the user can interact with the query model to fulfil her needs. Our solution allows for a top-down design approach, from the crowd-search task design, down to the crowd answering system design. Our approach also grants automatic code generation, thus leading to quick prototyping of crowd-search applications.

1 Introduction

While information retrieval systems are extremely good at query answering on information dispersed on the Web, people tend to trust opinions of human beings more than rankings provided by machines. The so-called "wisdom of the crowd" is already the de-facto dominant factor in determining the retrieval behaviour, as weights assigned by search systems to Web pages depend on their link popularity, and selected resources are usually associated with social recommendations. However, most human decisions are even more influenced by opinions of people; an off-line, informal process occurs to validate the "best" system-selected solutions, by consulting friends and experts. In current Web systems, the crowd-search activity, i.e. looking for opinion from friends or experts, is detached from the original search process, and is often carried out through different social networking platforms and technologies. Moreover, people manage different applications, different virtual identities and maybe also different devices: they send email, ask questions on Twitter, Facebook or any other social network, or ask to friends and people they know.

A recently introduced trend in search systems, called *crowdsearching*, aims at making the crowd consultation simpler and more efficient, by interconnecting search systems with humans [6, 21, 22]. Recent works (see Section 5) on crowd-based search

S. Ceri and M. Brambilla (Eds.): Search Computing III, LNCS 7538, pp. 207–222, 2012.

focus on simple and atomic task, while crowd-sourced search involve a wide range of scenario, from trivial decisions, like choosing where going to eat at dinner, to more complex activities, like organizing a travel or even buying a house. Thus, users need a way to manage and control the whole process, from the creation of the query and the selection of the target to the gathering of the results.

In our previous work [6] we have proposed CrowdSearcher, a system architecture with associated query and execution model that bridges conventional search experiences to crowdsearching and social network exploitation. The high-level system architecture is described in Figure 1: the user submits an initial query, which can be addressed either to a traditional exploratory search system or to a human search system. If the interaction starts on the conventional search system (e.g., a vertical search system for real estate, events, travels, businesses), such system interacts synchronously with data sources and produces several solutions (e.g. house offers, concerts, itineraries, restaurants, hotels). Then, users may open a CrowdSearcher interaction by selecting some of those objects and asking questions about them; input selection and preparation is performed by the user with the help of ad-hoc web applications or wrappers. In principle, even the results produced by conventional search engines, such as Google, could be used as input sources, although in such case the user should build the input manually by extracting structured information for each selected result item. As an alternative, the user can immediately start with a human search step; in this case, the query formulation and the inputs are directly provided by the user. At the end of the CrowdSearcher interaction, results are presented to the user, in a format that allows their acquisition by the search system, thereby enabling a seamless integration of the two search processes.

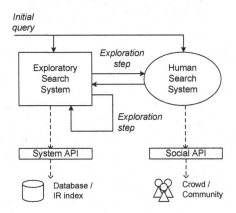

Fig. 1. Overview of the CrowdSearcher approach

An important design principle for CrowdSearcher is the independence of queries from the *crowdsearching engines*. This term denotes a broad class of solutions, spanning from classic crowdsourcing systems (such as Amazon Turk), to social platforms (such as Facebook, LinkedIn, Twitter), and even to emails and document sharing platforms, e.g. Google Tables. To achieve independence, we defined the *CrowdSearcher Query Language* as a mapping from an *Input Model*, including a dataset and structured queries, to an *Output Model*, which is obtained by modifying the dataset and by adding the answers to structured queries.

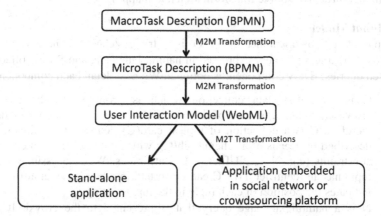

Fig. 2. Overview of the proposed MDD approach

In this paper we focus on the aspects related to the model-driven design of the crowd-search user interactions, spanning from the question definition to the engagement, dissemination, and ending in the response submission and collection. The main results presented in this paper are: 1) a metamodel of the crowd-sourced question; and 2) the models of the user interfaces needed for defining the questions and for responding. We define a top-down design approach, as sketched in Figure 2, which applies model-driven engineering (MDE) techniques for the specification of the crowd-sourced information collection task, its splitting and refinement, and its mapping to the Web user interaction specification. Task refinement and redesign are outside the scope of this work. The approach starts from the task description and applies model-to-model transformations to build the detailed task definitions (described e.g. in BPMN) and then the platform independent user interaction model (described in the domain-specific language WebML [3][4]). Then the final application is automatically generated by means of a model-to-text code generation transformation.

The paper is organized as follows. Section 2 defines the query language and its execution semantics on the system's architecture. Section 3 presents the query meta-model and user interaction models. Section 4 summarizes the related works for both the crowd-sourcing and the model-driven fields. Conclusions are in Section 5.

2   Formalization of CrowdSearch Interactions

2.1   Query Language

A CrowdSearcher query is a transformation of an input model into an output model, produced by crowdsearching or social networking engines interacting with people in real time; a mapping scheme selects the engines, the query representation for each engine, and the resources that should be used by the engine for answering the query. The model is very general so as to include many kinds of queries, although some transformations may not be supported by all engines. In most practical situations, however, queries will use a small subset of the input model, thereby producing the output model through a simple transformation and mapping.

2.1.1 Input Model

The input of a CrowdSearcher query Q^I is a triple <C,N,S> where C is a data collection, N is a textual query expressed in natural language, and S is a collection of structured queries. Every component is optional. We next detail each component.

- C is an initial data collection which is proposed to the crowd for crowdsearching. For ease of description, we use the relational model, and therefore C is a collection of tuples; card(C) denotes its cardinality. C is described by means of a schema sch(C), which contains the name, type, and constraints (e.g. NOT NULL) of C's attributes. We also assume that each tuple has an identifier TID. C can be sorted, in which case an attribute POS indicates the position of each tuple in the input sorting.
- N is a natural language query that is presented to the crowd. It can be mechanically generated, e.g. in relationship with specific structured queries, or instead be written by the user who starts the crowd search.
- S is a collection of structured queries that are asked to the crowd, relative to the collection C. Queries allow to express preferences about the elements of C, to rank them, cluster them, and change their content.

Preference queries correspond to typical social interactions (like, dislike, comment, tag); the other structured queries abstract simple and classical primitives of relational query languages that are common in human computation and social computation activities.

The **preference queries** include:

- Like query, counting the number of individuals who like specific tuples of C.
- Dislike query, counting the number of individuals who dislike specific tuples in C.
- Recommend query, asking users to provide recommendations about specific tuples in C.
- Tag query, asking users to provide either global tags or tags about specific attributes of sch(C).

The **rank queries** include:

- Score query, asking users to assign a score (in the 1..K interval) to tuples of C.
- Order query, asking users to order the (top K) tuples in C.

The **cluster queries** include:

- Group query, asking users to cluster the tuples in C into (at most K) distinct groups.
- OrderGroup query, asking users to cluster the tuples in C into (at most K) distinct groups and then order the (top M) tuples in each group.

- MergeGroup query, asking users to merge K sorted groups producing a single ordering.
- TopGroup query, asking users to cluster the tuples in C into (at most K) distinct groups and then select the top element of each group.

The **modification queries** include:

- Insert query, asking users to add tuples in C.
- Delete query, asking users to delete tuples from C.
- Correct queries, asking users to identify and possibly correct errors in the tuples in C.
- Connect query, asking users to match pairs of similar tuples.

2.1.2 Output Model

The output of a CrowdSearcher query Q^O is a tuple <C',S'> where C' is a data collection and S' is a collection of structured answers. It is produced by CrowdSearcher engines and delivered asynchronously. C' is the data collection which is returned to a user after a crowdsearching task. The schema Sch(C') is obtained by adding to Sch(C) attributes which are used as slots for the answers to the structured queries S in S', i.e.:

- A counter L of people whom like each tuple.
- A counter D of people who disliked each tuple.
- A score value S representing the average score given by people to each tuple.
- A list R of character strings of people who added recommendations to tuples.
- A list T of terms (simple or compound words) of people who tagged each tuple.
- A tuple identifier POS if the users ordered the tuples.
- A group identifier GID if the users clustered the tuples into groups.
- A group position GPOS if the users ordered the clusters (GPOS is repeated for each tuple in the cluster).

Tuples C' are obtained from tuples in C after insertions, deletions, and updates of tuples in S; S' is the set of answers to the queries in S, placed within the appropriate slots – the new attributes in Sch(C').

2.1.3 Mapping Model

The mapping model specifies how given search engines can be involved in producing the output of a given query Q. A Mapping M of a query Q is a quintuple <E, G, H, T, D> where:

- E is the crowd engine or engines to be used in the query.
- G is the crowd group that should interact with engine. This could be: the user's friends, specific subsets of the user's friends, geo-localized people, expert people, workers selected on a work platform, and so on. We denote as G(E) the subset of users in G that are accessible through a given crowd engine E.

- H represents constraints in the execution of a query Q; in particular, it indicates which conditions should hold for a query to be terminated. For instance, collecting at least K answers from H different users, or lasting for three minutes.
- T is a transformation process, which applies to a query Q and transforms it into smaller queries Q' such that answering Q' and then combining their results allows answering Q. A transformation is needed when the query Q is too complex to be directly proposed to a crowd engine.
- D is the set of templates used to present C and express structured queries for a given crowdsourced query. Templates are typically targeted to specific crowd engines; we denote as D(E) the subset of templates that can be submitted to a given engine E. Templates for displaying C have a style, e.g. textual, tabular, geo-referenced on a map, time-referenced on a time line, represented as the points of a Cartesian space, and so on.

2.1.4 Meta-model

The starting point of our MDE approach is the meta-model of the crowd-search domain, shown in Figure 3. The main element is the **Query** entity, that carries as attribute the accompanying question (in natural language) and the **queryType**, describing the action that should be performed in order to answer to the query. A **Query** is defined to a **Schema**, which in turn is described by several **Fields**.

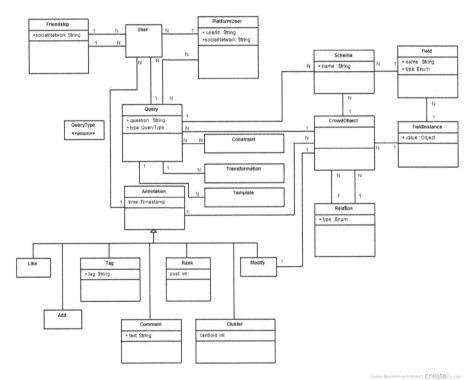

Fig. 3. The query task meta-model

Every query is associated to several **Crowd Objects** which in turn may be associated to several **Annotations** during the query answering process. **Annotations** are set by users, they inclue *Like* options, *Tags*, *Comments*; in addition, users can *Add* or *Modify* **Crowd Objects**. A **Query** is associated to a **Master User** (that is the author of the query), who is registered on many **Platforms** and may participate to many **Friendships** on the various **Social Networks**.

3   Model Driven Specification of the User Interaction of CrowdSearcher

The user interaction model describes the interface and navigation aspects of the crowdsearch application. Starting from the meta-model, a model transformation leads to a coarse user interaction model, that can be manually refined by the designer. The user interaction must cover 3 fundamental phases of the crowd-search process:

- The submission of the query (performed by the query master);
- The collection of the responses (performed by the responder);
- The analysis of the results (performed by the query master).

At the current stage, our research has identified the interaction patterns relevant for each phase, considering the various options of deployment platform; we report one possible outcome of the user interaction design in the case of a simple query task and of deployment on Facebook and Twitter social networking platforms.

Figure 4 shows the user interaction model for creating and submitting a query. In the *Create Query* page, the user specifies the textual question (e.g., "What's the best museum to visit in Milan?") and sets the query type (e.g.,"Like","Add", and so on). The user can also choose the type "open question", thus assuming that no items are needed in input for the responder to select/like and so on. In both cases, a **Query** instance is created, and its type is set. If the query does not have inputs, then the user is directly brought to the *Responder Selection* page.

If, on the other hand, the user chooses to build a structured question with inputs, then he is redirected to the *Define schema* page, where he can create a schema for inputs by assigning a general name to the input type and by defining its attributes in terms of name and type. By submitting the form, the application creates a new instance for the **Schema** entity and its associated **Fields**. Then the author of the query is brought to the *Add Instance* page, where he can add input objects following the schema previously defined. The specified instances of the inputs are created and linked to the query. Finally, in the *Responder Selection* page the query master can select the responders to the query: the list of possible responders is retrieved from the social network or crowdsourcing platforms by invoking the *GetFriendList* module[1]. Figure 5 exemplifies the internals of the *GetFriendList* module for a user interacting with Facebook and Twitter.

Then, the user can select the responders through the "Friends" multi-selection list in the page. Eventually, after viewing a preview of the created question, the user can

---

[1] A *Module* in WebML represent the factorization of a given business or presentation logic.

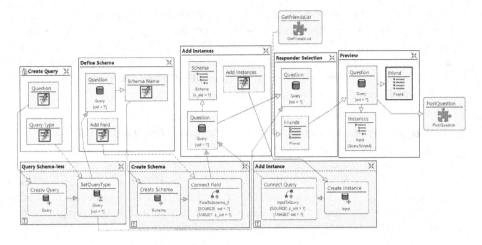

Fig. 4. User Interaction Model for Query Creation

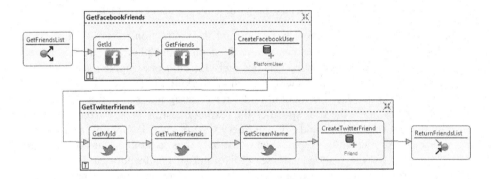

Fig. 5. Model for the Retrieval of friends list from social networks

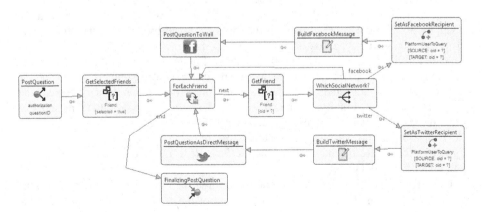

Fig. 6. Model for the Posting of questions to friends

post the query on the social platform by invoking the execution of the *PostQuestion* module. Figure 6 depicts the logic of the *PostQuestion* module, which iteratively create new messages to the involved users, according to their platform of existence.

Figure 8 shows the WebML Module for retrieving friend's lists. Note the use of WebML units specifically targeted to Facebook or Twitter, each invoking the relevant system's API. Figure 9 shows the WebML Module for publishing the query on Facebook and Twitter; the module gets as input the query ID and as a first step it extracts all the friends that were selected as query recipients. Then a case unit selects three cases (Facebook user, Twitter user, "else") and in first two cases the user is set as recipient of an interaction, which in the specific case is a message posted either on the Facebook wall or as a direct message in Twitter.

Figure 7 shows the user interaction model for the query answering activity, performed by a responder, based on the query structure defined by the asker. When accessing the application through the Responder Dashboard page, the responder is presented with a list of questions to answer. By clicking on a question, he is brought to the *Details* page, where he can provide his answer. The page shows the question text, plus the set of defined input instances (Input component in the Details page).

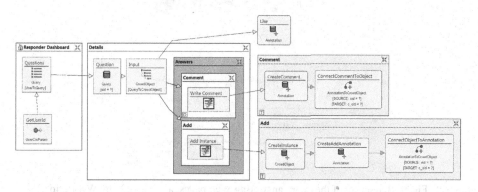

Fig. 7. Hypertext model for answering to a query

Depending on the type of the question (defined by the query master during the query creation phase), different concrete user interfaces can be shown: in the case of a "Like" question, the responder simply selects the preferred instances in the Input list; as a consequence, a set of Annotation objects of type Like are created corresponding to the "likes" of the user. In the case of "Comment" or "Add" question, the user is shown a form to respectively write a comment or add a new instance to the list. In the case of "Comment" questions, an Annotation object of *Comment* type (i.e. a an object with a single textual field) is created. The "Add" case is more complex, as a CrowdObject with the same schema of the input ones will be created. The object will be connected to an Annotation of type Add, that will identify this kind of objects from the ones belonging to the original input set.

Fig. 8. Rendering of the query creation Web pages, as generated by WebRatio

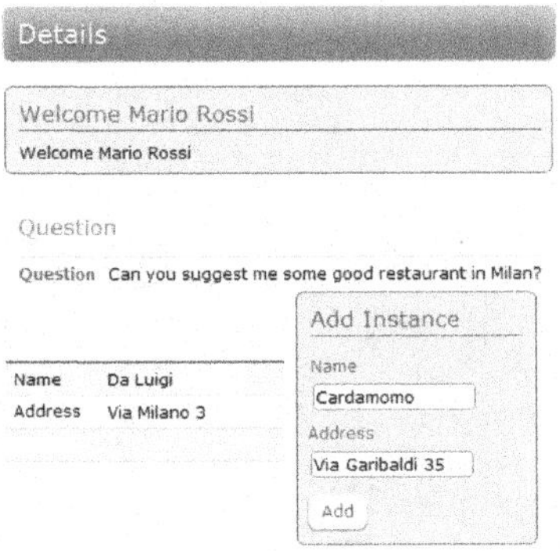

Fig. 9. Rendering of the query answering Web pages, as generated by WebRatio

Figure 11 shows a possible rendering of the query creation process defined in Figure 7. The application is automatically generated by using WebRatio [7], that is a modelling tool that allow automated code generation and fast application deployment starting from WebML models. The process consists of defining a question, then a schema, then adding instances to the query, then adding responders. Figure 12 shows the rendering of the page for adding instances of answers, generated from the WebML model of Figure 10.

4   Architecture

A **CrowdSearch System** implements the queries upon human and social platforms. The system instantiates query templates by importing information from search systems, sends queries to the social/crowd platform, gets a collection of responders involved, and gathers the results. The system acts in the context provided by a given social/crowd platform user, denoted as **query master**, who is instrumental to the crowdsourcing process by being responsible (and possibly covering costs) of tasks that are spawn to the crowd and by offering friends and colleagues as responders. Ultimately, the social/crowd platform must import a query through a dedicated interface, and this can be achieved by either a standalone system, or directly using the native APIs offered by each platform, or by embedding the query interface as a new application of the platform, as illustrated in Figure 10.

- With a **standalone approach,** the system uses the social platforms just as a repository of social data (e.g., the set of friends or experts) but it exposes its own UI.

- With a **native approach**, the system behaves as an external application that is directly using the native features of the social platform for creating queries and collecting results. This guarantees higher transparency but forces the query to be expressed using the native widgets of the platform, resulting sometimes less natural and explicit.

- With an **embedded application**, it is possible to use the social/crowd platform for embedding a crowdsearch-specific client that directly interacts with the crowdsearch system server. This option is the most powerful for supporting a description of the initial collection and of structured queries upon them; however, it requires users of the platform to install and load the embedded application. Embedding may occur either just in the context of the query master or also in the context of the master's friends or colleagues.

The adoption of each platform by the user may be subject to an **initialization process**. For instance, MechanicalTurk requires the master user to register and to give proof of being able to cover the costs of work tasks; with Facebook, the master user must initially install an application which authorizes the crowdsearch platform to communicate by using the master user's identity, and so on.

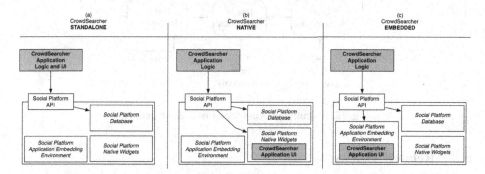

Fig. 10. Alternative configurations of a CrowdSearcher system

The crowdsearch system performs the platform and user selection in order to respectively define the crowd engine E to be used and the group of users G(E) that will be targeted, setting at the same time the constraints H on query termination.

Based on these choices and on the input model, the query is possibly split and routed to groups of users, and then a query template is generated by choosing among supported templates D(E). Examples of concrete deployments of the crowdsearch system are shown in Figure 11.

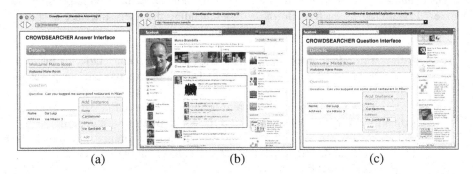

(a)   (b)   (c)

Fig. 11. Examples of standalone (a), embedded(b), and native (c) CrowdSearch deployments

The social platform users are then engaged by inviting them to reply to the question with their contribution. Finally, replies are collected by the crowdsearch system and manipulated for generating the final output model. The corresponding workflow is shown in Figure 12

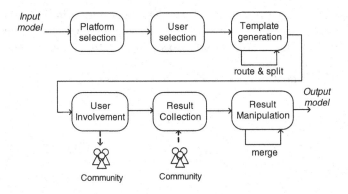

Fig. 12. Execution process for CrowdSearch queries

5   Related Works

Human computation is a computational paradigm where humans interact with computers in order to solve a computational problem, usually too hard to be solved by computers alone. Crowdsourcing is a means and a facilitator for achieving human computation, but the two concepts are not equivalent: crowdsourcing focuses on mechanisms for collecting information from the masses, while human computation focuses on problem solving. Involving human computation into problem solving imposes to address a completely new set of problems related to results quality: bias, spamming, independence of the workers, role of the social network structure.

For general crowdsourcing tasks, several works have studied the impact of the design dimensions (cost per task, number of tasks allowed, and so on) upon various metrics on the results (quality of the outcome, time to response, number of participants, and so on). They all agree that cost per task has little impact on the final quality, while it has on the time needed to obtain it (and participation in general) [34][35]. Optimization on time can be achieved by studying possible early acceptance/termination algorithms. Some heuristics can be defined for deciding how many workers are needed for every task [31]. In case of complex tasks, these can be split or associated with new microtasks that aim at validating the complex one [32]. Experiments show that the definition of the process itself can be delegated to the users, with a map-reduce approach, like in the case of Turkomatic [33]. Unfortunately, some practical aspects must be considered too: for instance, it has been shown that workers on Mechanical Turk pick tasks from "most HITs" or "most recent" queues [36]; and HITs in 3rd page and after are not picked by workers.

There are no widespread approaches tackling the problem of applying human computation to exploratory search scenarios [20]. The most common ways of collaborating in information seeking tasks are sending emails back and forth, using instant messaging (e.g. Skype) to exchange links and query terms, and using phone calls while looking at a Web browser [37]. The bottom line is that current capacity of users to exploit the actual potential of human computation for exploratory search is still very limited.

The CrowdSearcher approach directly compares with systems, such as CrowdDB [23], Turk [24], and Snoop [25]. There are, however, significant differences: the three systems all integrate with crowdsourcing engines (specifically Mechanical Turk) and not with social networks; they advocate transparent optimization, while we advocate conscious interaction driven by the query master; they involve users just in data completion, while we also involve users in other classical social responses, such as liking, ranking, and tagging

The novelty aspects of our approach with respect to the existing works include: independence with respect to the crowdsourcing platform (in particular, we allow to exploit indifferently a social network or a crowdsourcing marketplace of choice); model-driven design of tasks and user interactions; model-transformation based approach that partly automates the generation of some models, thus reducing the cost of designing new applications; and possibility of manually or automatically choosing the responders to a query task. Our work can be seen as an extended social question answering approach (as applied in Quora[2] and other platforms), where the asker has greater flexibility in defining and sharing his questions. Our work addresses the problem of defining crowdsourcing tasks at the modeling level, while existing approaches and tools typically allow for a programming approach to the problem (e.g., see TurkIt [2]).

---

[2] http://www.quora.com/

Our work is based on general purpose model-driven techniques and on our previous work on Web application design [9], on mapping business processes to user interaction models [8], as well as on the preliminary results presented in the CrowdSearcher approach [6]. From the implementation perspective, we rely on the WebRatio toolsuite [7], which provides code generation facilities for WebML models.

6   Conclusions and Future Works

In this paper we presented a model-driven approach for crowdsourcing responses to questions. We defined a meta-model of the query tasks and a user interaction model for building and answering to a query. Our current work addresses the problems of task splitting and automatic model transformations, so as to implement a model-driven approach to the design of the tasks, considering the structured crowdsourcing patterns identified in literature. For the future we plan to extend the coverage of the deployment to more social and crowdsourcing platforms and the integration of more responders from several platforms, thus enhancing platform interoperability.

References

[1] Amazon mechanical turk, https://www.mturk.com
[2] Turkit, http://groups.csail.mit.edu/uid/turkit/
[3] Webml, http://www.webml.org
[4] Ariely, D., Gneezy, U., Loewenstein, G., Mazar, N.: Large Stakes and Big Mistakes. Review of Economic Studies 75, 1–19 (2009)
[5] Bernstein, M.S., Little, G., Miller, R.C., Hartmann, B., Ackerman, M.S., Karger, D.R., Crowell, D., Panovich, K.: Soylent: a word processor with a crowd inside. In: Proceedings of the 23nd Annual ACM Symposium on User Interface Software and Technology, UIST 2010, pp. 313–322. ACM, New York (2010)
[6] Bozzon, A., Brambilla, M., Ceri, S.: Answering search queries with crowdsearcher. In Proceedings of the World Wide Web Conference (WWW 2012) (page in print, 2012)
[7] Brambilla, M., Butti, S., Fraternali, P.: WebRatio BPM: A Tool for Designing and Deploying Business Processes on the Web. In: Benatallah, B., Casati, F., Kappel, G., Rossi, G. (eds.) ICWE 2010. LNCS, vol. 6189, pp. 415–429. Springer, Heidelberg (2010)
[8] Brambilla, M., Ceri, S., Fraternali, P., Manolescu, I.: Process modeling in web applications. ACM Trans. Softw. Eng. Methodol. 15(4), 360–409 (2006)
[9] Ceri, S., Fraternali, P., Bongio, A., Brambilla, M., Comai, S., Matera, M.: Designing data-intensive Web applications. Morgan Kaufmann, USA (2003)
[10] Franklin, M.J., Kossmann, D., Kraska, T., Ramesh, S., Xin, R.: CrowdDB: answering queries with crowdsourcing. In: Proceedings of the 2011 International Conference on Management of Data, SIGMOD 2011, pp. 61–72. ACM, New York (2011)
[11] Kittur, A., Smus, B., Kraut, R.: CrowdForge: crowdsourcing complex work. In: Proceedings of the 2011 Annual Conference Extended Abstracts on Human Factors in Computing Systems, CHI EA 2011, pp. 1801–1806. ACM, New York (2011)

[12] Kulkarni, A.P., Can, M., Hartmann, B.: Turkomatic: automatic recursive task and workflow design for mechanical turk. In: Proceedings of the 2011 Annual Conference Extended Abstracts on Human Factors in Computing Systems, CHI EA 2011, pp. 2053–2058. ACM, New York (2011)

[13] Mason, W., Watts, D.J.: Financial incentives and the "performance of crowds". In: Proceedings of the ACM SIGKDD Workshop on Human Computation, HCOMP 2009, pp. 77–85. ACM, New York (2009)

[14] Parameswaran, A., Polyzotis, N.: Answering queries using humans, algorithms and databases. In: Conference on Inovative Data Systems Research (CIDR 2011). Stanford InfoLab (January 2011)

[15] Yan, T., Kumar, V., Ganesan, D.: Crowdsearch: exploiting crowds for accurate real-time image search on mobile phones. In: Proceedings of the 8th International Conference on Mobile Systems, Applications, and Services, MobiSys 2010, pp. 77–90. ACM, New York (2010)

[16] Garlandini, S., Fabrikant, S.I.: Evaluating the Effectiveness and Efficiency of Visual Variables for Geographic Information Visualization. In: Hornsby, K.S., Claramunt, C., Denis, M., Ligozat, G. (eds.) COSIT 2009. LNCS, vol. 5756, pp. 195–211. Springer, Heidelberg (2009)

[17] Fox, E.A., Hix, D., Nowell, L.T., Brueni, D.J., Wake, W.C., Heath, L.S., Rao, D.: Users, user interfaces, and objects: Envision, a digital library. Journal of the American Society for Information Science 44(8), 480–491 (1993)

[18] Takatsuka, M., Gahegan, M.: GeoVISTA Studio: A Codeless Visual Programming Environment For Geoscientific Data Analysis and Visualization. In: Computational Geoscience, vol. 28, pp. 1131–1144 (2002)

[19] Wattenberg, M.: Visual exploration of multivariate graphs. In: Proceedings of the SIGCHI Conference on Human Factors in Computing Systems - CHI 2006, pp. 811–819. ACM, New York (2006)

[20] Aula, A., et al.: How does search behaviour change as search becomes more difficult? In: Proc. 28th International Conference on Human Factors in Computing Systems, HCI, Atlanta, GA, USA, pp. 35–44 (2010)

[21] Doan, A., Ramakrishnan, R., Halevy, A.: Crowdsourcing Systems on the World-Wide Web. Communications of the ACM (April 2011)

[22] Yan, T., Kumar, V., Ganesan, D.: CrowdSearch: exploiting crowds for accurate real-time image search. In: Proc. 8th Int. Conference on Mobile Systems, Applications, and Services – MOBISYS, S. Francisco, CA, pp. 77–90 (2010)

[23] Franklin, M.J., et al.: CrowdDB: answering queries with crowdsourcing. In: Proceedings of the 2011 International Conference on Management of Data (SIGMOD 2011), pp. 61–72. ACM, New York (2011)

[24] Marcus, A., et al.: Crowdsourced Databases: Query Processing with People. In: Conference on Innovative Data Systems Research, Asilomar, CA, pp. 211–214 (2011)

[25] Parameswaran, A., Polyzotis, N.: Answering Queries using Databases, Humans and Algorithms. In: Conference on Innovative Data Systems Research 2011, Asilomar, CA, pp. 160–166 (2011)

[26] Baeza-Yates, R., Raghavan, P.: Next Generation Web Search. In: Ceri, S., Brambilla, M. (eds.) Search Computing. LNCS, vol. 5950, pp. 11–23. Springer, Heidelberg (2010)

[27] Marchionini, G.: Exploratory Search: from Finding to Understanding. Communications of the ACM, 41–46 (2006)

[28] Bozzon, A., Brambilla, M., Ceri, S., Fraternali, P.: Liquid Query: Multi-Domain Exploratory Search on the Web. In: WWW 2010, Raleigh, USA, pp. 161–170. ACM, New York (2010)

[29] Bozzon, A., et al.: Exploratory Search in Multi-Domain Information Spaces with Liquid Query. In: Proc. WWW 2011 - Demo, Hyderabad, India, pp. 189–192. ACM, New York (2011)

[30] Marcus, A., Wu, E., Karger, D., Madden, S., Miller, R.: Humanpowered Sorts and Joins. PVLDB 5(1), 13–24 (2011)

[31] Kumar, A., Lease, M.: Modeling Annotator Accuracies for Supervised Learning. In: Proc. Crowdsourcing for Search and Data Mining Workshop – CSDM, Hong-Kong, China (2011)

[32] Bernstein, M.S., et al.: Soylent: a word processor with a crowd inside. In: Proceedings of the 23nd Annual ACM Symposium on User Interface Software and Technology, pp. 313–322. ACM, New York

[33] Kulkarni, A.P., Can, M., Hartmann, B.: Turkomatic: Automatic Recursive Task and Workflow Design for Mechanical Turk. In: Proc. Extended Abstracts on Human Factors in Computing Systems - CHI EA, Vancouver, CA, pp. 2053–2058 (2011)

[34] Mason, W.A., Watts, D.J.: Financial Incentives and the "Performance of Crowds". In: KDD Workshop on Human Computation, Paris, France, pp. 77–85 (2009)

[35] Ariely, D., et al.: Large Stakes and Big Mistakes. Review of Economic Studies 76(2), 451–469 (2009)

[36] Chilton, et al.: Task search in a human computation market. In: ACM SIGKDD Workshop on Human Computation (HCOMP 2010), pp. 1–9. ACM Press, New York (2010)

[37] Morris, M.R.: A survey of Collaborative Web Search practices. In: Proc. SIGCHI Conference on Human Factors in Computing Systems, Florence, pp. 1657–1666 (2008)

BetterRelations: Collecting Association Strengths for Linked Data Triples with a Game

Jörn Hees[1,2], Thomas Roth-Berghofer[2,3], Ralf Biedert[2],
Benjamin Adrian[2], and Andreas Dengel[1,2]

[1] Computer Science Department, University of Kaiserslautern, Germany
[2] Knowledge Management Department, DFKI GmbH, Kaiserslautern, Germany
[3] School of Computing and Technology, University of West London, UK
{firstname.lastname}@dfki.de

Abstract. The simulation of human thinking is one of the long term goals of the Artificial Intelligence community. In recent years, the adoption of Semantic Web technologies and the ongoing sharing of Linked Data has generated one of the world's largest knowledge bases, bringing us closer to this dream than ever. Nevertheless, while associations in the human memory have different strengths, such explicit association strengths (edge weights) are missing in Linked Data. Hence, finding good heuristics which can estimate human-like association strengths for Linked Data facts (triples) is of major interest to us. In order to evaluate existing approaches with respect to human-like association strengths, we need a collection of such explicit edge weights for Linked Data triples.

In this chapter we first provide an overview of existing approaches to rate Linked Data triples which could be valuable candidates for good heuristics. We then present a web-game prototype which can help with the collection of a ground truth of edge weights for triples. We explain the game's concept, summarize Linked Data related implementation aspects, and include a detailed evaluation of the game.

1 Introduction

Since its introduction in 2001 the Semantic Web [1] has gained much attention. In recent years, especially the Linking Open Data (LOD) project contributed many large, interlinked and publicly accessible RDF datasets, generating one of the world's largest, decentralized knowledge bases [2]. The accumulated amount of Linked Data has many applications and can already be used to answer structured questions (e.g., the DBpedia [3] dataset can easily be used to compile a list of musicians who were born in Berlin).

Nevertheless, it currently is unclear how to rank result sets—not even those of simplistic (descriptive) queries—by importance as considered by an average human. For example, asked to describe (What/Who is ...?) a *topic* such as "Facebook", nearly all humans will explain that it "is an online social network", but only few will tell us that "Chris Hughes is one of its co-founders". In the remainder of this chapter, we will hence call the fact "Facebook has subject online social

S. Ceri and M. Brambilla (Eds.): Search Computing III, LNCS 7538, pp. 223–239, 2012.

networking" more *important* than "Facebook has key person Chris Hughes" wrt. the topic "Facebook". Despite the fact that this importance relation is surely user and context dependent, we want to focus on an average human's view, leaving the application of user and context models to future work. In terms of [4] our definition of importance balances formality, stability and sharing scope mostly by focusing on a wide sharing scope and being applicable to cross-domain datasets such as DBpedia.

In contrast to this human view, triples in Linked Data, which are (subject, predicate, object)-statements, also called *facts*, are facts in a logical sense. Like logical axioms, they all are of the same "importance", none being more valuable than another. Given a *topic* (e.g., `dbpedia:Facebook`) there is no easy way to order its more than 100 related facts in DBpedia by importance. This leads to problems, for example when a user requests a concise description[1] of a resource.

A collection of such importance information would allow us to ask machines not only to give us all known facts related to a resource in an arbitrary order, but also to rank this information by importance, allowing us to constrain the number of results to the most important ones (e.g., the top 10).

Aside from concise descriptions the applications of a method to rank facts about a given topic from Linked Data are manifold. With regard to Artificial Intelligence this would provide a basis for human-like reasoning on Linked Data (e.g., using spreading activation approaches [5] for semantic search [6] with meaningful edge weights) and enable us to drastically reduce the search space to only those concepts strongly associated with the current context by an average human. Another immediate benefit from annotating Linked Data triples with association strengths is the possibility of feedback for automated extraction processes, e.g., the one underlying DBpedia. One could investigate, which extraction rules yield high and which ones yield low strengths, facilitating a quality assurance process.

Besides these immediate benefits, such a collection of association strengths would also allow us to investigate whether currently used approaches to rank Linked Data (e.g., based on network analysis approaches, such as PageRank [7] and HITS [8], trying to model how much activation flows from one concept to another, or based on semantic similarities, such as estimated by word co-occurrences on websites) truly model how we associate thoughts. If this is the case, the heuristics could be used to bootstrap the acquisition of associations strengths for Linked Data triples, else such a dataset would be a valuable prerequisite to develop heuristics to estimate triple importances.

Despite all the benefits a collection of Linked Data triples rated by human association strengths would have, it suffers from the typical knowledge acquisition bottleneck. Collecting such strength values is prone to subjectivity, it is extremely monotonous and tedious, and it is difficult for humans to reliably and objectively assess the absolute strength value of a triple. Furthermore, the immense amount of Linked Data would cause great expenses if people were to be paid for rating even a small part thereof.

---

[1] Description as in SPARQL DESCRIBE queries.

In order to overcome the aforementioned problems, we sketched the idea for a web-game in [9] and briefly described our findings from developing a prototype called *BetterRelations* in [10] following the "Games With A Purpose" approach by von Ahn and Dabbish [11].

The rest of this chapter is structured as follows: We first give an overview of existing approaches to rank Linked Data (Section 2) and Games With A Purpose related to BetterRelations (Section 3). Afterwards we provide a detailed description of the game's concept as well as data acquisition and necessary pre-processing steps to present Linked Data triples to players in a comprehensible format (Section 4). Furthermore, we report on a detailed evaluation, consisting of statistics, the results of a user questionnaire and a comparison of the game results with manually generated ranked lists by a test group (Section 5), as well as a discussion of our findings, identifying possible improvements and future work (Section 6).

2   Existing Approaches to Rank Linked Data

The need for mechanisms to rank Linked Data grows with the ongoing adoption of Semantic Web technologies. In recent years, a variety of approaches have been developed. For an easier understanding we want to structure them into approaches which mainly analyze the graph structure of Linked Data itself and approaches which use Linked Data external information sources to rank Linked Data.

2.1   Approaches Using Graph Analyses

As Linked Data can be represented as a graph it is not surprising that many ranking approaches focus on the structural aspects of this graph. Most of these approaches try to apply well known ranking algorithms for the World Wide Web such as PageRank [7] or HITS [8] to the Semantic Web.

ObjectRank [12] was one of the first such approaches applying PageRank on databases modeled as labeled graphs. In order to reduce the Linked Data graph with different link types to a graph with just one link type on which PageRank can operate, ObjectRank requires domain experts to manually assign weights for each link type, which is impractical on large scale, evolving datasets such as Linked Data. As ObjectRank was developed with a single database system in mind, it does not track provenance information and hence is possibly vulnerable to spam.

Swoogle [13] was one of the first search engines for the Semantic Web, using OntoRank and TermRank for ranking. OntoRank ranks RDF documents with PageRank. TermRank ranks classes and properties by their popularity which is composed of their usage counts in other RDF documents and their OntoRank distributed over all classes and properties which are used. One main drawback of Swoogle is its inability to rank instances.

This shortcoming of Swoogle was addressed by the Naming Authority [14] approach. It ranks Linked Data resource and literals by calculating the Page-Rank on the interlinkage of source documents and then propagating the source rank to their resources and literals. The re-use of IDs (URIs) minted by other naming authorities (top level domains or pay level domains) increases their rank and provides spam resistance as it takes the provenance of RDF statements into account. Nevertheless, the same mechanism neglects dataset internal link structures, which are of importance w.r.t. big datasets such as DBpedia.

Hence, DING (Dataset Ranking) [15], which is currently used in Sindice [16] extends [14]. It uses two layers: the dataset graph and the entity graph. As in [14] the dataset graph consisting of links between datasets is used to compute the dataset ranks based on PageRank. The calculated dataset ranks are then combined with semantic-dependent entity rankings (which can be different for different datasets), such as PageRank or a simple in-degree. By this the approach has the ability to better model peculiarities of specific datasets.

In contrast to the aforementioned approaches which are based on PageRank, TripleRank [17] represents the RDF graph as 3D tensor and uses a tensor variant of HITS. By this TripleRank allows the identification of and grouping by similar properties. Despite its promising results, TripleRank is vulnerable to spamming as it does not track provenance information and includes a pruning step which removes properties that could potentially encode very useful information for semantic similarity (e.g., the DBpedia `dbo:wikiPageWikiLink`).

The last approach we want to mention is called SemRank [18] and is an information theoretic approach. Given two resources it ranks possible complex relationships (multi-step paths) between them based on information gain for the user. The user can configure the system to be rather conventional (low information gain) or use it in a discovery mode fashion (high information gain). For this SemRank combines three different components. Aside from providing a semantic keyword matching on the labels of involved properties, SemRank calculates the specificity of properties and refractions of a complex relation. The specificity of a property describes how unique it is w.r.t. the knowledge base and w.r.t. where it could be used due to domain and range restrictions. The refraction count measures how many different vocabularies a complex relation spans. A high specificity or high refraction count increase the rank in discovery mode but decreases the rank in conventional mode.

2.2   Approaches Using Graph External Features

The previously mentioned approaches all limit themselves to information which is available by analyzing Linked Data and especially its graph structure. We now want to focus on approaches which also use external information. Many of the following approaches are not originally devised to rank Linked Data, but instead focus on semantic similarity or semantic relatedness of terms, which are closely related to human association strengths. In order to apply such approaches to Linked Data, usually labels [19] are used to map between Linked Data instances and instances in external data sources.

In order to estimate the semantic relatedness of two concepts, many approaches are based on WordNet [20]. WordNet is a large lexical database of English words. Amongst others, WordNet groups words into synonym sets and provides hierarchical relations between them, such as hypernyms and holonyms. Most WordNet based relatedness measures use features of the hierarchical structure, such as the length of shortest paths between concepts or the overlap of synsets. An evaluation of WordNet-based semantic relatedness measures can be found in [21]. Despite its size and quality the main disadvantage of using Word-Net is that it is far from complete and quickly becomes outdated (trend words such as "iPad" are still missing).

To overcome these issues other approaches are based on Wikipedia and typically focus on structural features of the corresponding articles in Wikipedia, such as the disambiguation pages, hierarchy of categories, listings, and WikiLinks (links between articles). For example, WikiRelate [22] uses the disambiguation pages, letting two concepts disambiguate each other, in combination with text overlap and category tree search for a lowest common category ancestor of Wikipedia articles to calculate the semantic relatedness of the concepts.

Another group of similarity measures focuses on distributional aspects of words and their co-occurrence in large text corpora (e.g., online documents) or social online platforms. Approaches in this group are typically based on the count of scopes in which both terms co-occur, as well as the counts of scopes in which they occur independently and then try to estimate the significance of the co-occurrences. Examples for such similarity measures include the Normalized Google Distance [23] (actually often applied to other search engines as well) and tag relatedness in social bookmarking systems [24]. Further such distributional systems can be found in [25], also including an approach which combines co-occurrence based measures ones based on WordNet-based.

Some of the aforementioned approaches, especially those depending on external datasets such as WordNet and Wikipedia, can actually be performed on Linked Data, as for most of such datasets mappings are existent, nowadays. Still such approaches typically use very specific knowledge about these datasets (and their mappings to Linked Data) in contrast to the methods presented in the previous section.

The last approach we want to mention is DBpediaRanking [26], an approach which makes use of such a mapping which maps Wikipedia to its Linked Data pendant DBpedia. DBpediaRanking finds semantically related terms for a given DBpedia resource. To some extent it can also be seen as a hybrid approach combining graph structural features and external information. DBpediaRanking exploits the graph-based nature for a limited depth-first search restricted to predefined properties (`skos:subject` and `skos:broader`). The discovered nodes are compared to the root node by a scoring mechanism which focuses on nodes that are encountered frequently during the discovery step (important nodes). The scoring includes similarity measures derived from co-occurrences of both `rdfs:labels` in web documents by querying search engines such as Google and Yahoo and online bookmarking services such as Delicious. The scoring mechanism also ranks nodes higher which have bidirectional `dbo:wikiPageWikiLinks` with the root node (an idea which can also be found in [27]), and scores nodes higher which have bidirectional `dbo:abstract` inclusions of their `rdfs:labels` with the root node. The hybrid approach chosen by DBpediaRanking shows promising evaluation results.

The last approach indicates that a combination of procedures using structural features of the graph and techniques using information from external datasources might interesting for future research. As mentioned in the introduction to conduct such research, a collection of Linked Data triples rated by humans would be very helpful, especially considering the fact that in many of the presented approaches evaluations were limited to a small group of people and performed on small fractions of the datasets they should be able to rank.

3   Related Work

In terms of game design, BetterRelations is related to *Matchin* [28]. Matchin is a two player web-game, which confronts pairs of players with two pictures (taken from the WWW), asking them which one they prefer. If the preferences of both players match, the players are rewarded with points and an increasingly higher bonus. In case of a mismatch, they are not rewarded with points and the bonus is reset to 0. In this process, decisions which both players agree on are considered more valuable than mismatches. In the background Matchin records the pairwise user preferences and uses them to compute a global rating of the played images. In contrast, BetterRelations presents two textual facts corresponding to Linked Data triples about one topic to its players. Whereas Matchin creates a globally ranked list of images, BetterRelations computes a ranking for each topic and its related facts. Hence, the rating algorithm, which transforms the pairwise user preferences into the global ratings hence has to deal with significantly smaller lists. As detailed in Section 4.1, BetterRelations includes several additional features in order to make Linked Data issues such as noise or unknown facts tractable.

OntoGame [29] was the first and most prominent game with a purpose focusing on Linked Data. Nevertheless, it collects another type of information than BetterRelations: Players are asked to decide if a Wikipedia topic is a class or an instance, aiming at creating a taxonomy of Wikipedia.

WhoKnows? [30], a *single player* game, judges whether an existing Linked Data triple is known by testing players with (amongst others) a multiple choice test or a hangman game. In contrast to our approach, WhoKnows only uses a limited fraction of the DBpedia dataset and excludes triples not matched by a predefined domain ontology in a preprocessing step. This greatly reduces noise issues, but eliminates the possibility to collect user feedback about triple qualities and problems in the extraction process. Also, WhoKnows intends to rank triples by degree of familiarity. However, the used measurement only relies on the ratio of correctly recognized facts divided by number of times a fact was tested. The quality of this ratio is doubtful as it does not distinguish whether a fact has been tested few or many times.

Other collaborative approaches to create large knowledge bases usable by machines exist, including the Open Mind Common Sense Project (OMCS) [31] or Freebase[2]. Freebase shows some input methods that resemble games, such as: *Typewriter*[3] or *Genderizer*[4]. Answers taken from users in these interfaces are directly converted into statements (e.g., "... is female.") issued by the user and added to the knowledge base, taking them out of the list of items which lack information. In contrast to BetterRelations, such input methods typically do not contain any means of filtering (possibly intentional) disruptive user input and do not provide edge weights.

4   The Game

A straightforward approach to collect association strengths for Linked Data triples is this: First, we select a Linked Data resource of interest (e.g., dbpedia:Facebook or dbpedia:Wiki). We call this a *topic of interest* or simply *topic*. We then show randomly shuffled lists of all related triples to test persons and ask them to order the triples by decreasing importance. In the context of this work, given a topic, we define *related triples* to be the collection of (subject, predicate, object)-triples where the topic is the subject.[5]

The aforementioned approach suffers from the problem that the outcome of each of these experiments, which is a user centric ranking, is not only highly subjective, but sometimes even unstable for one person over time. In order to overcome difficulties for humans when sorting lengthy lists, we could ask for the atomic relative comparisons of two facts about one topic and then use an objective rating algorithm to generate an absolute ranking of the topic's related facts. This leads us to the idea behind BetterRelations.

4.1   BetterRelations

BetterRelations[6] is a symmetric two player output (decision) agreement game in terms of von Ahn and Dabbish's design principles for Games With A Purpose [11]:

A player starting to play the game is randomly matched with some other player for a predefined timespan (e.g., 2 minutes). In every round (see Figure 1) both players are presented with a *topic*, which actually is a Linked Data resource's symbol (e.g., *Facebook*, the symbol for dbpedia:Facebook), and two *items*, which are symbolic forms of facts about the topic (e.g., *key person Chris*

---

[2] http://www.freebase.com/
[3] http://typewriter.freebaseapps.com/
[4] http://genderizer.freebaseapps.com/
[5] Extending the list by triples where the topic is the object (incoming links) typically imports a large number of unimportant facts for the topic (e.g., in Wikipedia and thus in DBpedia one would expect to learn about Facebook by visiting the page about it, not by reading through all the pages linking to its page).
[6] BetterRelations can be played online: http://lodgames.kl.dfki.de

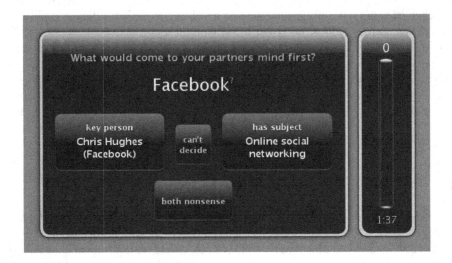

Fig. 1. In a game round, choosing phase

Hughes (Facebook) and *has subject Online social networking*). As in Matchin the facts are presented to the players in randomized order to counter easy cheating attempts.

Both players are asked to select the fact that their partner will have thought of first. In case a player does not know the topic, a quick info can be requested by clicking on the question mark appended to the topic. Doing so will internally mark the player's decision as influenced and the partner's as unvalidated. To decide, each player can either click on the more important fact's button or on two additional buttons in case the player can't decide between the alternatives or thinks that both alternatives are nonsense / noise.

As in Matchin, BetterRelations rewards agreements between both players with points and punishes disagreements without subtracting points, in order to increase game fun. The scoring function bases on the number of successive agreements in the current and preceding rounds: Players are rewarded with $0, 5, 10, 25, 50, 75, 90, 95, 98, 99, 99, 99, 100, \ldots, 100$ additional points for a streak of $0, 1, 2, 3, \ldots$ agreements. In contrast to Matchin (where the streak is reset to 0 on a mismatch), in BetterRelations a mismatch will only decrease the streak by 2 and does not reward the current round with additional points.

BetterRelations includes two more buttons: "can't decide" and "both nonsense" than Matchin. Hence, the scoring function was changed in order to counter easy cheating strategies such as always selecting the "can't decide" button. In terms of the scoring function the both middle buttons are the same button (it counts as an agreement if one player selects "can't decide" and the other "both nonsense") and an agreement on the middle buttons will not be rewarded with additional point, but instead will sustain the accumulated streak. Furthermore, a player who requested a quick info will not be rewarded with points in the current round.

On the server side the game records a large amount of relative decisions between pairs of items, filtered by a partner and uses them to upgrade ratings in case of agreements. A both nonsense agreement will mark both items as nonsense and exclude them from future games. Generating an absolute ranking from such results can be compared to chess rating systems, where based on the outcomes of atomic competitions (player p_1 won against p_2), a global ranking is calculated, just that in this case it is not players competing, but facts [28]. In contrast to Matchin, BetterRelations uses a TrueSkill [32] based algorithm internally to update fact ratings after each agreement, selects next fact pairs for a topic in a way to minimize the overall needed amount of decisions and stops sorting lists with n facts after $n \cdot \log_2(n)$ updates, determined to be a good threshold by simulations.

After rewarding the players with points, the next round starts until the game runs out of time. The next topic is chosen by selecting the topic least often played by both players from a list of topics currently opened for playing, which is based on the topmost accessed Wikipedia articles. In the end, both players see a summary of their performance showing the amount of points gained in this game, the longest streak and their total game score in BetterRelations.

In case no partner can be found or the partner leaves the Game, BetterRelations also provides a single player mode, which will either replay rounds with unvalidated decisions or replay previous two player games if no unvalidated decisions are left. As the latter replays usually waste human decisions, the single player mode can also be configured to initiate two player games with a certain probability and fake the (dis-)agreement by chance, based on the player's historical rate of agreements. The results of such rounds again provide new unvalidated decisions used by other single players.

4.2   Game Data Acquisition and Preprocessing

As BetterRelations tries to rank multiple lists of triples related to one topic each, we first of all have to decide which topics we want to play. Topics should be well known to most players and be interesting, in order to receive valuable feedback and provide an entertaining game. Additionally each of the topics should have associated Linked Data triples. Hence, BetterRelations selects topics (Linked Data URIs) corresponding to the most often accessed Wikipedia pages[7], which include pages such as Wiki, United States, Facebook, Google. Every time the game needs a new game topic and its related triples (e.g., because an existing topic's facts were sorted), it loads the corresponding triples for the next topmost Wikipedia topic from a local DBpedia mirror, which also was pre-loaded with standard vocabularies such as rdf, rdfs, foaf.

As showing URIs to the end-users is of limited use, the users will always see rdfs:labels of such references. Hence, for each URI in the list of related triples of a topic, all English or non language tagged rdfs:labels are acquired. For URIs with multiple labels a best label is selected following a heuristic preferring language tagged literals and such which are similar to the URI's last part if still

---

[7] Stats aggregated from raw access logs, available at http://dom.as/wikistats/

in doubt. Triples having the same labels are merged from a game's point of view and such with missing labels for predicate or object excluded from the game. We call this the *symbolic form* of a triple.

Finally labels and corresponding triples are excluded, which (due to long string length) don't fit into the game's window, end with suspicious file endings (e.g., .jpeg) or which have an object label equal to the topic's label ("Facebook label Facebook").

5   Evaluation

After the previous sections detailed the game's concept, data acquisition and preprocessing, we will now provide a detailed evaluation of the game itself and of the generated output.

5.1   The Game

First, the game's concept and its realization are evaluated by summarizing measurements and derived estimates. Afterwards, the outcomes of a questionnaire are provided which was presented to players of the game.

Measurements and Estimates. In the 18 day period from Jan. 12th until Jan. 30th, 2011, the game was played by 359 Users (re-identified by cookies if possible). In this timespan 1041 games were played, out of which 431 were two-player and 610 were single-player games.

The players played a total amount of $12K$ rounds submitting $14.7K$ decisions, out of which they selected $11.2K$ times an item, $2K$ times "can't decide" and $1.5K$ times "both nonsense". This led to an amount of $3.8K$ mismatches, $4.7K$ matches, including $3.8K$ item matches, and 840 non item matches.

The total amount of time all players together played the game was 42 hours (rounds without any decisions were not counted, they summed up to 5 hours, 46 minutes, e.g., idle tabs). With this, we can calculate the average time a decision takes to be 10.3 seconds. The *throughput*[8] of BetterRelations hence is 350 decisions per human hour of gaming. With the given numbers we can also find out the *average lifetime play*, so the time an average player plays the game, to be about 7 minutes. Multiplication of both numbers gives us an *expected contribution* of 41 decisions per human.

Repeating the above for matches instead of decisions yields a *throughput* of 112 matches per human hour of gaming, and an *expected contribution* of 13 matches per human.

Knowing that the top 1000 Wikipedia topics contain $56K$ game items, and taking into account the observed nonsense ratio of $\frac{1}{10}$, we can estimate that in order to sort the facts known about the top 1000 Wikipedia topic, we would need

---

[8] For a definition of throughput, average lifetime play and expected contribution also see [11].

$313K$ matches. In terms of players, this means that with the current implementation and we would need about $23.9K$ players to sort the top 1000 Wikipedia topics, i.e., 24 players per topic.

Questionnaire. Aside from these measurements and estimates, we wanted to know if the game was fun and wanted to collect feedback for possible future enhancements. For this, an online questionnaire survey was conducted among players of the game. The questionnaire was completed by 35 participants, mainly German (32) computer science students (23) or researchers (8), 31 male and 4 female.

Apart from background questions, the questionnaire consisted of a series of 5-point Likert scale items that are listed in Table 1 and comment fields asking what the participants liked, disliked and what they were missing. The summarized results in Table 1 show that most of the players were between 21 and 33 years old and had played online games before.

The main result from the conducted survey is that the game in its current version is of limited fun and that the majority of people do not plan to play it again. From the collected numerical data we can also see that in average the participants did not know all the topics and knew even less of the game items. At the same time most of the participants agreed that the game contained too much nonsense and too many irrelevant facts.

Apart from these numerical results, a view of the collected comments yields many common aspects. Many users mentioned that they liked the idea of creating a game to collect scientific data and the design of the game. In accordance with the numerical results, most users mentioned that they disliked the high amount of nonsense, consisting for example of unknown or cryptic abbreviations. Many participants also mentioned that they disliked the formatting of dates and often were confronted with facts they did not know anything about. Some of the participants also disliked the waiting period in the beginning of the game and complained about the mixture of German and English facts.

Many of the participants also mentioned that they were missing a button "I don't know any of these" or an initial selection of own interests, so they were not asked things they did not know that often. Many users requested a way to know

Table 1. Results of an online survey answered by 35 game players. Except from *Age* users could select answers from a 5-point Likert scale: 1 (Strongly disagree), 2 (Disagree), 3 (Neutral), 4 (Agree), 5 (Strongly agree).

Statement	μ	σ
The gaming principle was easy	4.43	0.77
I knew all topics	3.11	1.04
I knew all items	2.54	0.91
Too much nonsense	3.68	1.23
Too many irrelevant facts	3.57	1.13
The game was fun	2.66	1.04
I will play it again	2.34	1.29
Played online games before	4.20	1.33
Age	27.68	6.76

Table 2. Example: Gold Standard (left) and Game Output (right) lists for topic *Wiki*. In this case *predicate* and *object* are the symbolic forms of the corresponding triples from DBpedia.

rank	sum	ns	predicate	object
0.0	14.0		has subject	Wikis
1.0	26.0		has subject	Social information processing
2.0	28.0		has subject	Self-organization
3.0	30.0		has subject	Hypertext
4.0	42.5		has subject	Human-computer interaction
5.0	47.5		has subject	Internet history
6.5	74.0	x	Jahr	2007
6.5	74.0	x	tag	10

rating	ns	predicate	object
19.41		has subject	Self-organization
18.33		has subject	Social information processing
15.78		has subject	Human-computer interaction
9.15		has subject	Wikis
5.34		has subject	Hypertext
-1.63		has subject	Internet history
4.24	x	Jahr	2007
4.21	x	tag	10

who they were playing with and even suggested to make it possible to explicitly select a partner to play with. Some of the participants also suggested showing a highscore screen at the end of the game and including user accounts to save their own score and a recap phase after the game listing the questions and selected answers, showing their outcomes and providing more exploratory features.

5.2   Output Quality

Besides evaluating the game itself, the quality of generated results is of special interest in this work. As mentioned in the previous sections, the game calculates rating scores for the facts in each of the topics' related triples lists. The rating score can be used to order each of these lists, generating ordered output rankings. In the testing period, the game completed the generation of 12 such lists ordered by importance ratings.

In order to assess the quality of these lists, a Gold Standard list was generated for each of these 12 topics.

The Gold Standard lists were generated by a test group consisting of 11 people who had played the game before. Each candidate was asked to manually sort each of the 12 randomly shuffled lists of related facts by importance after excluding facts that the candidate identified as nonsense. For each of the topics the manually sorted lists were aggregated by summing up the ranks for each fact and afterwards sorting ascending by rank sum, forming the Gold Standard list. In this process nonsense facts were appended to each list's end and given a rank according to the barycenter of all nonsense items in that list. In the aggregated list a fact is said to be nonsense if the majority of test persons considered it as nonsense. An example of such a manually generated Gold Standard list can be seen in Table 2 (left).

Once a Gold Standard list is generated, the Mean Squared Errors (MSE) can be calculated for each of the individual manually generated ranked lists. The MSE is computed as the average sum of squared rank differences of each fact in the list and can be seen as blue histogram bars in Figure 2.

Calculating the average of these MSEs (so the average error an individual human makes when compared to the Gold Standard) and the deviation thereof (seen as red dashed and dotted lines in Figure 2), we can compare the human results with the game's result (which is shown as green vertical bar).

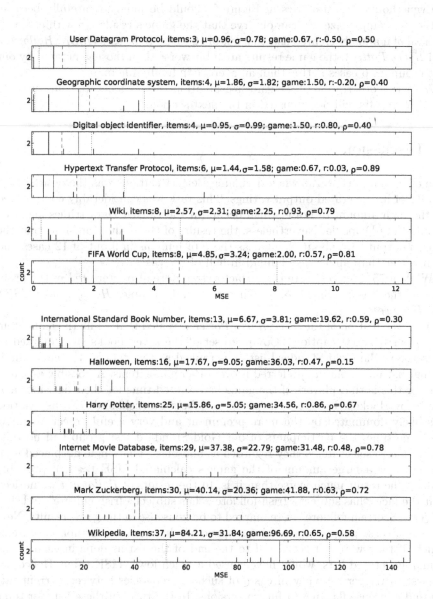

Fig. 2. Comparison of Gold Standard and game output on 12 topics' item lists. Blue histogram bars show the MSEs of each manually generated lists, their mean μ is shown as a red dashed line, their standard deviation σ as red dotted lines. The game's MSE error is shown as a green line. The titles also include the Pearson product-moment correlation coefficient r and Spearman's rank correlation coefficient ρ of the Gold Standard List and the game's output.

Even though the statistics in Figure 2 should be handled carefully because of the low sample size, we can observe that the game's result are within the 1σ interval of manually created lists in 9 out of 12 cases. In 3 cases (*ISBN*, *Halloween* and *Harry Potter*), the game results are a bit worse than those generated by our test group, in 6 cases better than an average individual human.

After this description of the game's evaluation and its generated output rankings, the results will be discussed in the next section.

6   Discussion

One of the main concerns when designing BetterRelations was the desired high quality of its generated output ratings. This task was considerably complicated by the high amount of noise which occurs in the Linked Data triples acquired mainly from DBpedia. Nevertheless, the results of the evaluation show that the game's outputs are about as good as those of humans in 9 out of 12 cases and even better than an average human in half of the cases.

While a 75 % success rate is satisfactory, we were also interested in the problems of the 3 remaining lists, which correspond to topics *Harry Potter*, *ISBN* and *Halloween*.

An investigation of the topic *Harry Potter* revealed that while the game item ((p,o) pair) "image caption · Complete set of the seven books" was marked as nonsense in the Gold Standard list, it is ranked as top item by the game, indicating that many players preferred it over other game items. A possible explanation for this is that players of the game had limited time for their decisions and maybe overlooked the erroneous predicate label in a rush, and their association was likely dominated by the more prominent and very useful object label. At the same time, the participants of our Gold Standard test group had no time restriction to select items they regarded as nonsense. This single misplaced item accounts for a large amount of the game's calculated MSE ($\approx$ 15), probably making the result much worse than it is. In the results of *Halloween* we noticed that the facts "has subject · Irish folklore", "has subject · Irish culture" and "has subject · Scottish folklore" were marked to be nonsense in the game results. Nevertheless, these game items receive suspiciously high ratings for nonsense items which, if they were not reordered to the end of the list as done in each of the human-generated lists, would have caused a much lower MSE value. Hence, we suggest to trigger a review in cases of such discrepancies between current rating and nonsense flagging in future versions. In the third of these lists for topic *ISBN*, we could not identify an obvious reason for the discrepancy.

But even when taking these considerations into account, we are confident that the game—already in its current version—generates good output ratings from pairwise comparisons of items. Nevertheless, it remains part of future work to conduct a survey showing the game outcomes to a test group and asking for immediate feedback about the generated ranking.

Aside from the high quality of the generated ratings, we also evaluated the game itself. The The questionnaire reveals that game principle was easy and straightforward and the majority of topics was known. However, problems related to fun and replay-ability were also mentioned. An investigation of the given comments revealed that the primarily impairing factors were the presence of many cryptic abbreviations, *strange* formatting of numbers and dates, and the mixture of English and German facts. Since improvements of the game's fun factor would further decrease the amount of 24 players needed to sort the facts known about one Wikipedia topic, we performed an analysis on the reported problems. It turned out that many of them originated from errors in the DBpedia 3.5.1 dataset, e.g., German labels which had missing or incorrect language tags, and have been resolved in the more recent DBpedia 3.6. We expect that upcoming releases of the DBpedia dataset will address even more of these problems, as the extraction mappings are improving. Such an enhanced quality of the underlying datasets has the dual effect of reducing the amount of (erroneous) triples to sort and at the same time increasing the fun of the game.

7   Conclusion and Outlook

In this chapter we presented a survey of existing approaches to rank Linked Data and after identifying the need for a collection of Linked Data rated by humans, presented a game called BetterRelations as well as a detailed evaluation of our first implementation.

Our evaluation shows very promising results in terms of the desired quality of the generated collection of importance ratings. We believe that this approach can be used to successfully sort Linked Data triples. While the low average lifetime play indicates a problem with the game's motivation, this appears to be mainly caused by the high amount of noise in the underlying Linked Data triples. As even slight improvements of the average lifetime play could already drastically reduce the number of players needed to sort the facts known about a popular Wikipedia topic, our future work will focus on methods to detect noise and the way how the game deals with it. We also plan to provide the game's output (ranked lists with rating scores) as Linked Data, allowing others to rank result sets of queries by importance for humans, and implement other ways to increase the player's fun, such as user accounts and high scores.

This work was financed in part by the University of Kaiserslautern PhD scholarship program and the BMBF project Perspecting (Grant 01IW08002).

References

1. Berners-Lee, T., Hendler, J., Lassila, O.: The Semantic Web: A new form of Web content that is meaningful to computers will unleash a revolution of new possibilities. Scientific American 284(5), 34–43 (2001)
2. Bizer, C., Heath, T., Berners-Lee, T.: Linked Data - The Story So Far. International Journal on Semantic Web and Information Systems 5(3), 1–22 (2009)
3. Bizer, C., Lehmann, J., Kobilarov, G., Auer, S., Becker, C., Cyganiak, R., Hellmann, S.: DBpedia - A crystallization point for the Web of Data. Web Semantics: Science, Services and Agents on the World Wide Web 7(3), 154–165 (2009)

4. van Elst, L., Abecker, A.: Ontologies for information management: balancing formality, stability, and sharing scope. Expert Systems with Applications 23(4), 357–366 (2002)
5. Crestani, F.: Application of Spreading Activation Techniques in Information Retrieval. Artificial Intelligence Review 11(6), 453–482 (1997)
6. Schumacher, K., Sintek, M., Sauermann, L.: Combining Fact and Document Retrieval with Spreading Activation for Semantic Desktop Search. In: Bechhofer, S., Hauswirth, M., Hoffmann, J., Koubarakis, M. (eds.) ESWC 2008. LNCS, vol. 5021, pp. 569–583. Springer, Heidelberg (2008)
7. Brin, S., Page, L.: The Anatomy of a Large-Scale Hypertextual Web Search Engine. Computer Networks and ISDN Systems 30(1-7), 107–117 (1998)
8. Kleinberg, J.M.: Authoritative sources in a hyperlinked environment. Journal of the ACM 46(5), 604–632 (1999)
9. Hees, J., Roth-Berghofer, T., Dengel, A.: Linked Data Games: Simulating Human Association with Linked Data. In: LWA 2010, Kassel, Germany (2010)
10. Hees, J., Roth-Berghofer, T., Biedert, R., Adrian, B., Dengel, A.: BetterRelations: Using a Game to Rate Linked Data Triples. In: Bach, J., Edelkamp, S. (eds.) KI 2011. LNCS, vol. 7006, pp. 134–138. Springer, Heidelberg (2011)
11. von Ahn, L., Dabbish, L.: Designing games with a purpose. Communications of the ACM 51(8), 58–67 (2008)
12. Balmin, A., Hristidis, V., Papakonstantinou, Y.: ObjectRank: Authority-Based Keyword Search in Databases. In: Proc. of the 13th International Conference on Very Large Data Bases, pp. 564–575. VLDB Endowment (2004)
13. Ding, L., Pan, R., Finin, T., Joshi, A., Peng, Y., Kolari, P.: Finding and Ranking Knowledge on the Semantic Web. In: Gil, Y., Motta, E., Benjamins, V.R., Musen, M.A. (eds.) ISWC 2005. LNCS, vol. 3729, pp. 156–170. Springer, Heidelberg (2005)
14. Harth, A., Kinsella, S., Decker, S.: Using Naming Authority to Rank Data and Ontologies for Web Search. In: Bernstein, A., Karger, D.R., Heath, T., Feigenbaum, L., Maynard, D., Motta, E., Thirunarayan, K. (eds.) ISWC 2009. LNCS, vol. 5823, pp. 277–292. Springer, Heidelberg (2009)
15. Delbru, R., Toupikov, N., Catasta, M., Tummarello, G., Decker, S.: Hierarchical Link Analysis for Ranking Web Data. In: Aroyo, L., Antoniou, G., Hyvönen, E., ten Teije, A., Stuckenschmidt, H., Cabral, L., Tudorache, T. (eds.) ESWC 2010, Part II. LNCS, vol. 6089, pp. 225–239. Springer, Heidelberg (2010)
16. Tummarello, G., Delbru, R., Oren, E.: Sindice.com: Weaving the Open Linked Data. In: Aberer, K., Choi, K.-S., Noy, N., Allemang, D., Lee, K.-I., Nixon, L.J.B., Golbeck, J., Mika, P., Maynard, D., Mizoguchi, R., Schreiber, G., Cudré-Mauroux, P. (eds.) ASWC/ISWC 2007. LNCS, vol. 4825, pp. 552–565. Springer, Heidelberg (2007)
17. Franz, T., Schultz, A., Sizov, S., Staab, S.: TripleRank: Ranking Semantic Web Data by Tensor Decomposition. In: Bernstein, A., Karger, D.R., Heath, T., Feigenbaum, L., Maynard, D., Motta, E., Thirunarayan, K. (eds.) ISWC 2009. LNCS, vol. 5823, pp. 213–228. Springer, Heidelberg (2009)
18. Anyanwu, K., Maduko, A., Sheth, A.P.: SemRank: Ranking Complex Relationship Search Results on the Semantic Web. In: Proc. of the WWW 2005, Chiba, Japan (2005)
19. Ell, B., Vrandečić, D., Simperl, E.: Labels in the Web of Data. In: Aroyo, L., Welty, C., Alani, H., Taylor, J., Bernstein, A., Kagal, L., Noy, N., Blomqvist, E. (eds.) ISWC 2011, Part I. LNCS, vol. 7031, pp. 162–176. Springer, Heidelberg (2011)
20. Fellbaum, C. (ed.): WordNet: An Electronic Lexical Database. MIT Press, Cambridge (1998)

21. Budanitsky, A., Hirst, G.: Evaluating WordNet-based Measures of Lexical Semantic Relatedness. Computational Linguistics 32(1), 13–47 (2006)
22. Strube, M., Ponzetto, S.P.: WikiRelate! Computing Semantic Relatedness Using Wikipedia. In: Proc. of the AAAI 2006, pp. 1419–1424. AAAI Press, Boston (2006)
23. Cilibrasi, R.L., Vitányi, P.M.B.: The Google Similarity Distance. IEEE Trans. Knowledge and Data Engineering 19(3), 370–383 (2007)
24. Cattuto, C., Benz, D., Hotho, A., Stumme, G.: Semantic Grounding of Tag Relatedness in Social Bookmarking Systems. In: Sheth, A.P., Staab, S., Dean, M., Paolucci, M., Maynard, D., Finin, T., Thirunarayan, K. (eds.) ISWC 2008. LNCS, vol. 5318, pp. 615–631. Springer, Heidelberg (2008)
25. Agirre, E., Alfonseca, E., Hall, K., Kravalova, J., Pasça, M., Soroa, A.: A Study on Similarity and Relatedness Using Distributional and WordNet-based Approaches. In: Proc. of the NAACL 2009, pp. 19–27. Association for Computational Linguistics, Boulder (2009)
26. Mirizzi, R., Ragone, A., Di Noia, T., Di Sciascio, E.: Ranking the Linked Data: The Case of DBpedia. In: Benatallah, B., Casati, F., Kappel, G., Rossi, G. (eds.) ICWE 2010. LNCS, vol. 6189, pp. 337–354. Springer, Heidelberg (2010)
27. Waitelonis, J., Sack, H.: Towards Exploratory Video Search Using Linked Data. In: Proc. of the IEEE International Symposium on Multimedia (ISM) 2009, pp. 540–545. IEEE, San Diego (2009)
28. Hacker, S., von Ahn, L.: Matchin: Eliciting User Preferences with an Online Game. In: Proc. of the SIGCHI Conference on Human Factors in Computing Systems, pp. 1207–1216. ACM, Boston (2009)
29. Siorpaes, K., Hepp, M.: OntoGame: Towards Overcoming the Incentive Bottleneck in Ontology Building. In: Meersman, R., Tari, Z. (eds.) OTM-WS 2007, Part II. LNCS, vol. 4806, pp. 1222–1232. Springer, Heidelberg (2007)
30. Kny, E., Kölle, S., Töpper, G., Wittmers, E.: WhoKnows? (October 2010)
31. Singh, P.: The Open Mind Common Sense Project. KurzweilAI.net (January 2002)
32. Herbrich, R., Minka, T., Graepel, T.: TrueSkill(TM): A Bayesian Skill Rating System. In: Schölkopf, B., Platt, J., Hoffmann, T. (eds.) Advances in Neural Information Processing Systems, vol. 19, pp. 569–576. MIT Press, Cambridge (2007)

An Incentive–Compatible Revenue–Sharing Mechanism for the Economic Sustainability of Multi–domain Search Based on Advertising

Marco Brambilla[1], Sofia Ceppi[1,2], Nicola Gatti[1], and Enrico H. Gerding[2]

[1] Dipartimento di Elettronica e Informazione, Politecnico di Milano,
Piazza Leonardo da Vinci 32, I-20133 Milano, Italy
[2] Department of Electronics and Computer Science,
Southampton University, SO17 1BJ, UK
{mbrambil,ceppi,ngatti}@elet.polimi.it, {scllv,eg}@ecs.soton.ac.uk

Abstract. Multi–domain search engines decompose complex queries addressing several issues at a time into sub–queries, and forwards them to one or more domain–specific content providers, typically implemented as Web services. This enables complex searches (e.g., vacation planning, composed of a hotel, flight, and car search), and allows users to receive aggregated and high quality results from a variety of sources. We focus on the design of a revenue sharing mechanism for multi–domain search, considering the general setting in which different actors (content providers, advertising providers, hybrid content+advertising providers, and content integrators) are involved in the search results generation. The design of such a mechanism is paramount for the economic sustainability of multi–domain search. Our revenue sharing mechanism extends the existing sponsored search auctions by supporting heterogeneous participants and allowing the redistribution of monetary values to the different actors.

1 Introduction

General–purpose search engines, which crawl the Web and index Web pages, are the main way for users to access information. However, there is an increasing demand for more sophisticated queries and richer media related to a query, such as images, videos, and pieces of news. While search engines are responding to this need to some extent, they are reaching their limits in terms of effectiveness and utility for the end users. To this end, we argue for a new class of tailor–made systems called *Multi-domain Search Engines (MdSEs)*, which are able to integrate a broad set of data sources and are better able to address the sophisticated user needs. This class of search engines supports the publishing and integration of high–quality data sources for vertical domains (extracted from the deep web or curated data repositories) allowing the user to select sources based on her needs, and route the various pieces of complex queries to such sources, finally reconciling the different result sets in a unified and structured result to be consumed by the user. As of today, general purpose MdSEs do not represent a mainstream class of applications; however, a number of vertical Web

S. Ceri and M. Brambilla (Eds.): Search Computing III, LNCS 7538, pp. 240–254, 2012.
© Springer-Verlag Berlin Heidelberg 2012

applications that apply multi–domain search techniques are well known and widely used. Some very well known examples exist in various fields: the most famous ones are in the travel field, where combined searches of flights, hotels, car rentals, and leisure activities have become the customary way of addressing the travel planning needs both for business and consumers (just think at the cases of Expedia[1] and alike). Other relevant fields where this approach is applied include real estate, where people looking for houses are supported by providing them with advanced search facilities that combine information about houses with contextual information on quality of life, kind of neighborhood, available commercial and utility services, schools, doctors, and so on (e.g., see Zillow[2]).

Importantly, the MdSE must also integrate *advertising service providers*, which are crucial to ensure both the economic sustainability of an MdSE, as well as the quality of the results (existing studies show the positive impact of the relationship between organic and sponsored search [1]). In this chapter, we focus on the latter aspect and introduce a novel mechanism for sharing advertisement revenues between the various providers.

In more detail, with respect to traditional search engines, the aim of the MdSE is to provide: (1) *better results*, through aggregation of domain–specific data (e.g., queries such as "Find the best electronic store in Silicon Valley" can now be solved by aggregating several directories of commercial activities with user reviews); (2) *expanded query complexity*, by responding to questions such as "Which theatre offers an at least–three–stars–rated action movie in London close to a good Italian restaurant?", using multi–domain information integration and enabling the user to select immediately the best options; and finally, (3) *rewards for all the integrated providers* for their contributions to effective search, including content providers, advertising providers, and hybrid ones, according to a suitable revenue model.

Although there is an increasing amount of research that considers how to process complex queries and fuse search results from various sources[3], there is currently no mechanism for adequately compensating the various actors for providing valuable (and often costly) information to the MdSE. That is, it is unclear how the revenue generated by advertisements should be shared among the different actors. A few works have addressed the problem of revenue sharing mechanisms in search applications (e.g., see [2, 3]), but none of them has addressed the general scenario of multi–domain search, where different actors' classes (content providers, advertising providers, hybrid content+advertising providers, and content integrators) are involved in the search results generation.

To address the above problem, in this chapter we propose a novel *ad–hoc revenue sharing mechanism for MdSEs.*[4] Specifically, we introduce a new payment

---

[1] http://www.expedia.com.

[2] http://www.zillow.com.

[3] E.g., see Google Tables (http://www.google.com/fusiontables/), Yahoo! Query Language (YQL) (http://developer.yahoo.com/yql/), and Search Computing (http://www.search-computing.org).

[4] Very preliminary results can be found in [4, 5].

mechanism that: (*i*) ensures all the actors to be truthful (i.e., each agent cannot have a monetary gain from misreporting its private information on the advertisement) and (*ii*) fairly redistributes the yields from advertising to all the actors in the system. Our solution significantly extends the revenue mechanisms for federated search previously presented in the literature [2], which are not able to integrate actors of different classes. Our findings demonstrate that such models are viable through a set of preliminary experimental results based on the *Yahoo! Webscope A3 dataset*, describing a realistic setting.

The chapter is organized as follows: Section 2 describes our MdSE model; Section 3 defines the revenue sharing mechanism; Section 4 reports on our experimental evaluations; Section 5 discusses related work; and Section 6 concludes.

2   Federated Search Engine Model

An MdSE is essentially a sophisticated content integrator that exploits and integrates existing information sources, including both content providers and advertisement providers. The MdSE implements a multi–domain search approach, where users can submit complex queries about different topics or items at a time. The multi–domain query is split in a number of single–domain queries, each one addressed by a domain–specific content service provider; results are then built by combining the various domain–specific items.

The MdSE collects contents and advertisements and publishes them together in every result page generated as a response to a user query. The choice of how many ads and content items to show on the Web page is determined by the MdSE, which also selects the information sources used to generate the results shown. The final outcome consists of an allocation of slots on the page available for ads and for contents. In this section we consider the various actors that provide ads and content, and which need to be compensated for their service. Then we discuss an example scenario which shows how the MdSE works in practice.

2.1   Actors

The MdSE integrates the services of three classes of actors: Content Providers, Advertising Providers, and Integrated Content and Advertising Providers.

Content–Only Providers (CPs). A CP is one of two actors who provide content for the MdSE. The content consists of datasets with a high information value for the users because of their precision, completeness, detail and/or coverage. It represents the core intellectual property for the CP and is costly to produce. Examples of potential CPs include Zillow[5], that provides contents about houses to rent and sell, and Expedia[6], whose contents are related to tourism (e.g., flights and rooms). Other kinds of CPs may not have their own user interface and sell the plain data sets or the access to them through APIs. CPs have a number of

---

[5] http://www.zillow.com/
[6] http://www.expedia.com/

ways to ensure revenue to recoup these costs. Typically, they rely on *third–party* advertisements, user subscriptions, affiliates, transaction fees, or a combination of these. However, if they publish their content through a MdSE, some of these revenue streams will be lost. This loss should be adequately compensated by the MdSE, providing incentives to the CPs for sharing content.

Integrated Content and Advertising Providers (CAPs). This class of actors is distinguished from CPs by serving their own ads together with their own content. Typically, these websites would allow third parties, such as the MdSE, to publish their search engine results by requiring the MdSE to show (some of) their ads too. In that case, revenue sharing agreements are in place that divide the advertisement revenue between the search engine and the publisher. examples of CAPS include the major search engines such as Google, which provides both content and advertisements.

Advertising Providers (APs). These providers do not serve any content, but only advertisement services. They publish ads from a set of advertisers and their goal is to provide targeted ads to users who visit partner web sites. Examples of APs include *ad networks* such as Google's *AdSense*, *ValueClick*, *AdSide*, as well as *ad exchanges* such as Yahoo!'s *RightMedia*, Google's *DoubleClick*, and Microsoft's *AdECN*. In existing revenue sharing models, the revenue from the advertisers is then shared between the advertisement provider and the publishers, where the publisher gets the largest percentage.

In addition to the three classes of providers (CP, AP, CAP), the MdSE involves two classes of stakeholders interested in using the system:

- *end users*, who visit the MdSE web site, submit their queries, read the results and possibly click on the shown advertisements;
- *advertisers*, who provide (and pay) the ads to the APs and CAPs. Advertisers are the only actual source for the revenue in the system. Revenues will then be shared between the three providers' classes mentioned above and the MdSE.

Before we consider how the revenue from the advertisements is shared, we look at an example of how the MdSE works in practice.

2.2   Scenario

The most general paradigm covered by an MdSE is based on the possibility for users to submit complex multi–domain queries, which are decomposed into multiple single–domain queries, which in turn are then forwarded to a domain–specific content provider. The final step is to integrate the responses into a unified list of aggregated items. f

To understand better how an MdSE works, let's consider the scenario depicted in Fig. 1, characterized by the following actors: the user Valentina submitting her query, the MdSE, 2 CPs (depicted with a rectangular shape), 2 APs (depicted with an oval shape), 1 CAP (depicted with a combination of rectangular and oval shapes), and some advertisers submitting their ads to the APs and CAP.

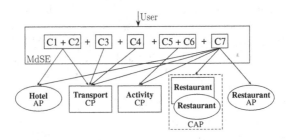

Fig. 1. Reference scenario for an MdSE's instance (for simplicity, advertisers are omitted)

We suppose that Valentina is interested in planning her holiday to Lyon. She wants to book flights from Milan to Lyon and back, and she wants to find a hotel and a few restaurants in Lyon. Moreover, Valentina has decided to see an art exhibition as part of her cultural experience during her stay, and she wants to find the available options. Valentina submits a multi–domain query to the MdSE specifying the following 7 criteria. C_1 date of arrival: April 14th 2012; C_2 date of departure: April 22nd 2012; C_3 the transfer she prefers: airplane; C_4 the departure city: Milan; C_5 the preferred leisure activity: art exhibition; C_6 the date for the leisure activity: April 21st 2012; C_7 the destination: Lyon.

The MdSE decomposes the multi–domain query into single–domain queries and addresses each of them to the pertaining CPs, APs, and CAPs, specifying the respective query parameters[7] as shown in Table 1.

Table 1. Assignment of queries to the providers in our reference scenario, with respective parameters

Provider	Parameter name	Parameter value
Hotel AP	check-in	April 14th 2012
	check-out	April 22th 2012
	city	Lyon
Transportation CP	departure-date	April 14th 2012
	return-date	April 22th 2012
	transportation-type	Plane
	departure	Milan
	destination	Lyon
Activity CP	activity-type	art exhibition
	date	April 21st 2012
	city	Lyon
Restaurant CAP and AP	city	Lyon

---

[7] Notice that we assume here a set of structured data sources and corresponding structured query for illustrative purposes, but the approach is general and is independent of the type of sources or queries.

Each provider communicates its results to the MdSE, which in turn integrates the organic search results (contents) by performing join and union operations over the data sets, merges the ad lists (see [2]), and displays the resulting page.

3   Revenue Sharing Mechanism

We now describe the revenue sharing mechanism. Initially, we informally describe the revenue sources and the sharing and information flows. Subsequently, we present the formal model and the economic mechanism.

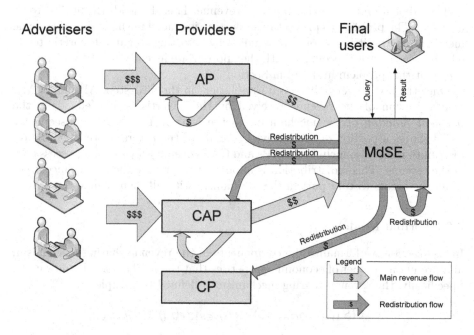

Fig. 2. Revenue flow

3.1   Revenue and Information Flows

We now specify how, using the revenue sharing mechanism detailed below, the revenue flows through the system. The revenue flow is depicted in Fig. 2. The revenue–sharing process starts with the advertisements, which are communicated by the APs and CAPs to the MdSE, which in turn allocates (a subset of) them to the available slots. Once an ad has been clicked, the corresponding advertiser pays the provider (AP or CAP) in which it is registered. For simplicity, we assume that payments are per click and that they are defined according to some auction model (e.g., using GSP [6], although here we do not consider the specifics of the mechanism used by the APs and CSPs, and our revenue sharing mechanism is independent of this choice). However, we remark that our mechanism can be easily extended to the situations in which payments are not purely per click, but also of other formats, e.g., per–per–view and pay–per–conversion. In the following, we define the ad's *value* as the pay–per–click payment associated with a specific ad, and the *expected value* as the payment multiplied by the probability of the ad being clicked. The sum of the expected values of the allocated ads then represents the *total revenue* of the system. The mechanism's aim is to produce an allocation that maximizes this total revenue. In order to achieve that, the mechanism needs to elicit the private information of the providers over the single ads (e.g., values). However, providers could misreport their true information, if they gain more doing that, thereby hindering the mechanism from find the allocation maximizing the total revenue. This also leads the market to be unstable. The problem to prevent misreporting is crucial in the design of revenue mechanisms and it is customarily studied by resorting to game theoretic tools, whereby each actor is provided with the appropriate incentives not to misreport. We treat this problem in detail in Section 3.2.

Once the total revenue has been established, in the next step, APs and CAPs give a portion of the revenue received by the advertisers, as defined by the *payment function* of the mechanism, to the MdSE. The MdSE subsequently redistributes a portion of the received revenue to the actors. Note that this redistribution can also include the APs and CAPs even if they already possess part of the revenue. This redistribution is important to provide the proper incentives to all the actors to take part in the mechanism with all their assets.

3.2 Formal Model

In this section we formalise the components of the revenue sharing mechanism, and present a number of economic properties that the mechanism should satisfy. Specifically, the revenue sharing mechanism is defined by a tuple:

$$\mathcal{M} = \langle S_A, S_C, S_{CA}, A, X, \langle \Theta_s \rangle_{s \in S}, f, \langle p_s \rangle_{s \in S}, \langle r_s \rangle_{s \in S} \rangle$$

where S_A is the set of APs, S_C is the set of CPs, S_{CA} is the set of CAPs, and $S = S_A \cup S_C \cup S_{CA}$. We denote a generic provider in S by s. $A = \{a_1, \ldots, a_{|A|}\}$ is the set of ads and A_s is the set of ads of provider s. For the sake of simplicity, we assume that no ad a appears in multiple A_s (a preliminary study of the situation in which this assumption is relaxed can be found in [7]). X is the set of possible allocations, where an allocation $x \in X$ specifies which ads are displayed on the k available slots and in which order. Θ_s is the set of possible types of provider s; we denote by $\theta_s \in \Theta_s$ the type of provider s. Type θ_s specifies the combination of *value* $v_a \in \mathbb{R}_+$ and *quality* $q_a \in [0, 1]$, one for each ad $a \in A_s$. Value v_a with $a \in A_s$ is the payment s receives once a has been clicked, while quality q_a is a parameter of ad a which affects its click probability (see below for details).

When $s \in S_C$, since only contents are provided, we assume that A_s is composed of a single fictitious ad a with $v_a = 0$ and $q_a = 0$ (and therefore s has a unique type). We denote by Q the set of qualities of all the ads, while

Q_s is the set of the qualities of ads of provider s and $Q_{-s} = Q \setminus Q_s$. Denote by $\theta = (\theta_{s_1}, \ldots, \theta_{s_{|S|}})$ the profile of the types of all the providers and by $\Theta = \times_{s \in S} \Theta_s$ the set of all the type profiles. θ_{-s} is defined as θ except that θ_s is omitted. We use the 'hat' notation to denote types and type profiles (i.e., $\hat{\theta}_s$, $\hat{\theta}$, $\hat{\theta}_{-s}$) reported by the providers. Analogously, we use $\hat{v}_a, \hat{q}_a, \hat{Q}_s, \hat{Q}, \hat{Q}_{-s}$ to denote values, qualities, and set of qualities reported by the providers.

Function $f : \times_{s \in S_A \cup S_{CA}} \Theta_s \to X$ is the social choice function, that, given the communicated type profile $\hat{\theta}$, returns an allocation of ads to slots. We denote by ω an event, defined as the set of clicked ads, therefore $\omega \subseteq A$, and we denote by Ω the set of all the events, defined as the power set of A. Given event ω, the valuation of $s \in S$ over allocation x depends on which ads $a \in A_s$ are displayed in x and in which position, and on the values v_a. Formally, it is defined as $\sum_{a \in \omega \cap A_s} v_a$, i.e., the sum of the values of provider s's clicked ads. (Hence, the valuation of $s \in S_C$ over every allocation x is zero.) The expected (with respect to the user's clicks) valuation of $s \in S$ over allocation $x \in X$ depends also on the click probabilities. We consider only scenarios without ad–dependent externalities [2]. Let $\alpha_a(x, q_a)$ denote the click probability of a as a function of x and q_a. When a does not appear in x we have $\alpha_a(x, q_a) = 0$. The expected valuation of $s \in S_A \cup S_{CA}$ over $x \in X$ is defined as $\sum_{a \in A_s} \alpha_a(x, q_a) \cdot v_a$, while the expected valuation of $s \in S_C$ is obviously zero. The total revenue is the value of the allocation $f(\hat{\theta})$, corresponding to $\sum_{a \in A} \alpha_a(f(\hat{\theta}), \hat{q}_a) \cdot \hat{v}_a$.

Function $p_s : \times_{s \in S} \Theta_s \times \Omega \to \mathbb{R}$ is the payment rule of provider s with $s \in S$. When $s \in S_C$, p_s is either zero or a negative constant (s receiving the payment) defined by a contract, while, when $s \in S_A \cup S_{CA}$, p_s is defined by the mechanism itself in a similar way it happens in the classical federated sponsored search auctions and may depend on the actual events (i.e., user's clicks). Function $r_s : \times_{s \in S} \Theta_s \times \Omega \to \mathbb{R}_+$ is the redistribution to provider s with $s \in S$.

The utility (revenue) u_s of provider s is:

$$u_s((\theta, \hat{\theta})|\omega) = \begin{cases} \sum_{a \in \omega \cap A_s} v_a - p_s(\hat{\theta}|\omega) + r_s(\hat{\theta}|\omega) & s \in S_A \cup S_{CA} \\ -p_s(\hat{\theta}|\omega) + r_s(\hat{\theta}|\omega) & s \in S_C \end{cases}$$

The expected utility (revenue) $\mathbb{E}_\omega[u_s]$ is:

$$\mathbb{E}_\omega[u_s((\theta, \hat{\theta})|\omega)] = \begin{cases} \sum_{a \in A_s} \alpha_a(x, q_a) \cdot v_a & s \in S_A \cup S_{CA} \\ -\mathbb{E}_\omega[p_s(\hat{\theta}|\omega)] + \mathbb{E}_\omega[r_s(\hat{\theta}|\omega)] & \\ -\mathbb{E}_\omega[p_s(\hat{\theta}|\omega)] + \mathbb{E}_\omega[r_s(\hat{\theta}|\omega)] & s \in S_C \end{cases} \quad (1)$$

The revenue R and expected (with respect to the user's clicks) revenue $\mathbb{E}_\omega[R]$ of the MdSE are:

$$R(\hat{\theta}|\omega) = \sum_{s \in S} p_s(\hat{\theta}|\omega) - \sum_{s \in S} r_s(\hat{\theta}|\omega)$$

$$\mathbb{E}_\omega[R(\hat{\theta}|\omega)] = \sum_{s \in S} \mathbb{E}_\omega[p_s(\hat{\theta}|\omega)] - \sum_{s \in S} \mathbb{E}_\omega[r_s(\hat{\theta}|\omega)]$$

Now, in order to produce adequate compensations to the various actors, the mechanism should satisfy some important economic properties. These desirable properties are the following [6].

Allocative efficiency (AE): the allocation chosen by the social choice function maximizes the expected total revenue.

Individual rationality (IR): the utility of each provider $s \in S$ is non–negative. In particular, we consider *ex interim* IR that guarantees the property in expectation w.r.t. the events, i.e., $\mathbb{E}_\omega[u_s((\theta, \hat{\theta})|\omega)] \geq 0, \forall s \in S, \forall \theta, \hat{\theta} \in \Theta$, and *ex post* IR that guarantees the property for each possible event, i.e., $u_s(\hat{\theta}|\omega) \geq 0, \forall s \in S, \forall \theta, \hat{\theta} \in \Theta, \forall \omega \in \Omega$.

Weak budget balance (WBB): the monetary revenue expected by the MdSE is non–negative. In particular, we consider *ex interim* WBB that guarantees the property in expectation w.r.t. the events, i.e., $\mathbb{E}_\omega[R(\hat{\theta}|\omega)] \geq 0, \forall \hat{\theta} \in \Theta$, and *ex post* IR that guarantees the property for each possible event, i.e., $R(\hat{\theta}|\omega) \geq 0, \forall \hat{\theta} \in \Theta, \forall \omega \in \Omega$. When $R(\hat{\theta}|\omega) = 0$ or $\mathbb{E}_\omega[R(\hat{\theta}|\omega)] = 0$ the mechanism is said to be *strongly budget balance* in *ex post* or *ex interim*, respectively.

Incentive compatibility (IC): no provider can gain more by misreporting its true type, and therefore reporting $\hat{\theta} = \theta$ is optimal. In this chapter, we consider one form of IC: *dominant strategy* (DSIC),i.e., when the best action of every provider is to report its true type regardless of the actions undertaken by the other providers). We remark that this property is necessary for determining the allocation with the maximum revenue. In absence of this requirement, the revenue for the providers and of the MdSE would be reduced.

3.3   The Mechanism

In this section, we design the components of mechanism $\mathcal{M}$ (i.e., f, p_s, r_s) such that they satisfy the above desirable properties. First, in order to ensure the WBB property (both in *ex post* and in *ex interim*) we need that $p_s = 0$ for all $s \in S_C$ regardless of the adopted mechanism $\mathcal{M}$. Indeed, for every $p_s < 0$ fixed by a contract, it is possible that the best allocation has a value smaller than $-p_s$ and therefore the MdSE's revenue R is negative (unless violating the IR property). Therefore, if the above property needs to be always satisfied, any revenue received by a provider $s \in S_C$ can only be through redistribution function r_s.

We now detail our mechanism $\mathcal{M}$, which consists of two phases. In the first phase, it determines the optimal allocation $f(\hat{\theta})$ and the payments $p_s(\hat{\theta}|\omega)$ for $s \in S_A \cup S_{CA}$ that are based on a Vickrey–Clarke–Groves (VCG) mechanism (see Section 5). In the second phase, redistributions for all the providers $s \in S$ are computed.

Phase 1. The social choice function is defined as:

$$f(\hat{\theta}) = \arg\max_{\mathbf{x} \in X} \sum_{i=1}^{|\mathbf{x}|} \alpha_{x_i}(\mathbf{x}, \hat{q}_a) \cdot \hat{v}_{x_i}$$

The expected payment $\mathbb{E}_\omega[p_s]$ for $s \in S_A \cup S_{CA}$, defined by the VCG mechanism is:

$$\mathbb{E}_\omega[p_s(\hat{\theta}|\omega)] = \sum_{a \in A \setminus A_s} \alpha_a(f(\hat{\theta}_{-s}), \hat{q}_a) \cdot \hat{v}_a - \sum_{a \in A \setminus A_s} \alpha_a(f(\hat{\theta}), \hat{q}_a) \cdot \hat{v}_a \qquad (2)$$

Let $\mathcal{M}'$ be the mechanism $\mathcal{M}$ when redistribution is zero. Furthermore, let $VCG(\hat{\theta}) = \sum_{s \in S} \mathbb{E}_\omega[p_s(\hat{\theta}|\omega)]$ denote MdSE's expected revenue without redistribution. With expected payments (2), $\mathcal{M}'$ is (by definition of VCG) *ex interim* IR and *ex interim* WBB. In particular, we have $\mathbb{E}_\omega[p_s(\hat{\theta}|\omega)] \geq 0$, and consequently $VCG(\hat{\theta}) \geq 0$.

While with sponsored search auctions it is possible to define contingent payments $p_s(\hat{\theta}|\omega)$ depending on the actual event ω such that they equal in expectation those reported in (2) and IC, WBB and IR are satisfied for each specific event, it is not in the case of our model as shown in [2]. This is essentially because the information about the qualities q_a is private for each agent. Therefore, WBB and IR can be satisfied only in expectation w.r.t. the events and payments are:

$$p_s(\hat{\theta}|\omega) = \mathbb{E}_\omega[p_s(\hat{\theta}|\omega)] \qquad \forall \omega \in \Omega.$$

As a result, we are applying pay–per–impression payments. Therefore, APs and CAPs can pay a positive monetary amount even if their ads are not clicked.

Phase 2. We provide redistributions as defined by Cavallo in [8]:

$$r_s(\hat{\theta}) = \frac{VCG(\hat{\theta}_{-s})}{|S_A| + |S_C| + |S_{CA}|} \qquad \forall s \in S_C, S_A, S_{CA}$$

where $VCG(\hat{\theta}_{-s}) = \sum_s \mathbb{E}_\omega[p_s(\hat{\theta}_{-s}|\omega)]$. In words, $VCG(\hat{\theta}_{-s})$ is the sum of all the expected payments when s is not present in the market. With $|S_i|$ we denote the number of provider of class i. The above redistributions ensure mechanism $\mathcal{M}'$ to be IC (given that the resulting payments are Groves and the mechanism is allocative efficient), IR (given that the payments are smaller than those of $\mathcal{M}$) and WBB (given that the total redistribution is never larger than $VCG(\hat{\theta})$ that is the MdSE's revenue with $\mathcal{M}$).

4 Experimental Evaluation

We empirically evaluate our revenue sharing mechanism in terms of revenue of the actors (MdSE, CPs, APs, CAPs) with and without redistributions.

4.1 Experimental Setting

Our empirical evaluation is based on the *Yahoo! Webscope A3* dataset. This dataset specifies the following over a period of 4 months: for every day, advertiser, keyword, and position it specifies the average bid value, the number of times the ad was displayed and not clicked, and the number of times it has been clicked (from which we derive the click probability). We note that the dataset is not directly applicable to the MdSE scenario, since it specifies average bids submitted by advertisers, but not their payment (and these cannot be derived from the dataset since it does not specify which ads are displayed together). However, we expect a positive correlation between them and so we treat the bids as the payment. Furthermore, to allow a wide range of experimental settings, instead of applying the values directly, we use this dataset to generate probability distributions from which to draw the values and qualities specifically for each of them.

Specifically, we generate a separate pair of distributions for the 100 keywords with the highest numbers of impressions. Each value distribution consists of a truncated Gaussian distribution, where the mean and standard deviation are taken from the dataset, the lower bound corresponds to the minimum bid value in the dataset, and the upper bound to the highest. Furthermore, we use a beta distribution from which to sample the quality. In our experiments, the quality corresponds to the click probability when the ad is displayed in the first position, and thus we use the data from the first position to derive the parameters of the beta distribution. Furthermore, we assume a user model (without ad–dependent externalities) in which the click probability decreases with the position in which the ad is displayed [9]. We model this user behavior by introducing ad–independent discount factors, d_{pos} related to position pos, and then use the dataset to derive these discount factors (in particular, the discount factor for position h is computed as the average click probability of the ads displayed in the first position divided by average click probability of ads displayed in position h). Thus, the click probability, α_a, of each ad $a \in A$ depends on the quality and the position of the ad.

Now, for each ad $a \in A$ we randomly assign one of the 100 value and quality distribution pairs. Then, the qualities and values for the ads of each agent are independently drawn from the corresponding distributions. In our experiments, we consider a wide range of scenarios, which are characterized by the number of APs $\{1, 2, 3\}$, the number of CPs $\{1, 2, 3\}$, the number of CAPs $\{1, 2, 3\}$, the number of advertisers $\{10, 100, 200, 300, 400, 500\}$, and the number of slots $\{3, 6, 9\}$. For each combination, we randomly generate 100 instances, obtaining a total number of instances equal to $48, 600$.

4.2   Experimental Results

Our experimental results are summarized in Fig. 3. We report the MdSE's expected revenue and the average utility (defined as the sum of the value and redistribution minus payment) of a CP, an AP, and a CAP. Note that these results are shown as a proportion of the *total* revenue, which is the system–wide revenue accrued through advertising by all actors. We used the bloxpot diagram: for each box, the central mark is the median, the edges of the box are the 25th and 75th percentiles, the whiskers extend to the most extreme datapoints that are outliers, and the outliers are plotted individually. The first (from the

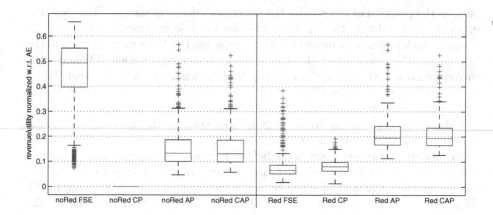

Fig. 3. Revenue/expected utility of the four actors without redistribution and with redistribution

left) four boxplot diagrams are inherent to the situation in which there is no redistribution, while the second four ones are with redistribution. With no redistribution, the MdSE's expected revenue is about 49.3% of the total revenue; the CPs' utility is obviously zero, while APs and CAPs have the same average utility of about 14%. When redistribution is allowed, the MdSE's expected revenue drastically reduces and it is on average about 8%, while the CPs' expected utility is on average about 9% and the APs' and CAPs' utility is on average about 20%. These two situations represent the two extreme cases for the MdSE: maximization and minimization of its revenue, respectively. A new parametric redistribution mechanism that allows one to control the redistribution between the two extreme cases would be useful in practice. Such a mechanism could be used to regulate the redistribution to each actor in order to satisfy specific contracts and, at the same time, maximize the expected revenue of the MdSE.

5   Related Work

Our work is closely related to the auctions for pay–per–click sponsored search and display advertising. In the case of sponsored search, the most common format to allocate ads and to calculate the pay–per–click payments, is the generalized second price (GSP) auction [10, 11]. In this auction, the allocation of an ad is based on a combination of the bid and a quality score, the latter being a function of the click–through–rate (CTR) (the exact function is typically kept secret). The payment is then based not on the bid of the advertiser itself, but on the next–highest bid to encourage truthful bidding. While this auction works well in practice, it has been shown that the mechanism is not incentive compatible [10]. This means that typically there is an incentive for advertisers to misreport their value.

Two issues are crucial for having efficient auctions. The first issue is the estimation of the click probability of an ad [9, 12, 13]. This may depend on parameters such as the position of the ad and the other ads currently shown. There are several models correlating the click probabilities to these parameters. Of these, the *cascade* model, which assumes that the user scans the links from the top to the bottom in a Markovian way [14, 15], is the most commonly used. These models introduce so–called *externalities* in the auction whereby the click probability, and therefore an advertiser's profit depends on which other ads are shown in conjunction. The second crucial issue is the design of auctions that incentivize truthful reporting, and ensure other properties such as the efficiency of the allocation (which maximizes the sum of utilities of all participants, also called the social welfare). This is studied in the field of *mechanism design*, a branch of game theory. The best–known mechanism in this area is the *Vickrey–Clarke–Groves* (VCG) auction, which has been extended to the sponsored search setting by [6]. This auction always computes the efficient allocation, and the payment of the advertiser is calculated by the effect of its presence on the expected utility of other advertisers (the so–called marginal contribution). The allocation is identical to the GSP, but the payment is slightly different to guarantee incentive compatibility.

While there are many papers that study sponsored search, as well as auctions for the more intricate research area of banner ads (which consists of interactions between many classes of actors, including publishers, advertisers, ad networks, and ad exchanges, e.g., see [16–20]), none of these works consider the problem faced by an MdSE who needs to aggregate information from different types of sources, and ensure that they are adequately compensated. An exception is [2] which considers the problem of merging ads from different sources for federated search. However, the paper only considers a single class of actors which provides both content and ads, and does not consider how to compensate actors who only provide ads, or just provide content and no ads. In this paper, we extend this work and study how we can redistribute the MdSE's revenue obtained from advertising to compensate the various actors in the system. In particular, we do this by resorting to the work on redistribution mechanisms by [8]. We choose the mechanism in [8] because it is (asymptotically) optimal, redistributing as much value as it is possible when the number of actors goes to infinity, and it is computationally efficient. (We recall that it is not possible to redistribute all the value in general case, as shown by Green–Laffont [21].) Another possible redistribution mechanism is [22], which allows one to redistribute values in an undominated way according to a given priority over the actors and can be applied to improve the redistribution of [8]. Although this approach seems to be interesting for our scenario, it is computationally intractable and therefore it is not appropriate for web advertising, where allocations have to be computed in the order of milliseconds.

6   Conclusions

In this paper we presented a revenue sharing mechanism for multi–domain search engines (MdSEs). We designed an economic mechanism that complies with the requirements we outlined (*incentive compatibility, individually rationality, weak budget balance*, and *allocative efficiency*), and we have shown it at work on a real–world dataset. The empirical experiments show that the mechanism provides each actor with the adequate compensation.

Future work will extend the model by considering payments from the advertisers that is not only pay–per–click but also, e.g., pay–per–view, which is more realistic for providers like APs, or pay–per–conversion. Furthermore, we plan to integrate our work with models that define how the space on a Web page is allocated to the ads and contents, so as to provide a comprehensive model for both the size of the allocation and the computation of the revenues for MdSEs.

References

1. Danescu-Niculescu-Mizil, C., Broder, A.Z., Gabrilovich, E., Josifovski, V., Pang, B.: Competing for users' attention: on the interplay between organic and sponsored search results. In: WWW, pp. 291–300 (2010)
2. Ceppi, S., Gatti, N., Gerding, E.H.: Mechanism design for federated sponsored search auctions. In: AAAI (2011)
3. Chen, Y., Ghosh, A., McAfee, R.P., Pennock, D.: Sharing Online Advertising Revenue with Consumers. In: Papadimitriou, C., Zhang, S. (eds.) WINE 2008. LNCS, vol. 5385, pp. 556–565. Springer, Heidelberg (2008)
4. Brambilla, M., Ceppi, S., Gatti, N., Gerding, E.H.: A revenue sharing mechanism for federated search and advertising. In: WWW (2012)
5. Ceppi, S., Gatti, N.: An automated mechanism design approach for sponsored search auctions with federated search engine. In: AMEC, pp. 127–140 (2010)
6. Narahari, Y., Garg, D., Narayanam, R., Prakash, H.: Game Theoretic Problems in Network Economics and Mechanism Design Solutions. Springer (February 2009)
7. Ceppi, S., Gerding, E.H., Gatti, N.: Merging multiple information sources in federated sponsored search. In: AAMAS (2012)
8. Cavallo, R.: Optimal decision–making with minimal waste: Strategyproof redistribution of VCG payments. In: AAMAS, pp. 882–889. ACM (2001)
9. Devanur, N.R., Kakade, S.M.: The price of truthfulness for pay–per–click auctions. In: ACM EC, pp. 99–106 (2009)
10. Edelman, B., Ostrovsky, M., Schwarz, M.: Internet advertising and the generalized second-price auction: Selling billions of dollars worth of keywords. American Economic Review 97(1), 242–259 (2007)
11. Varian, H.R.: Position auctions. International Journal of Industrial Organization 25(6), 1163–1178 (2007)
12. Gatti, N., Lazaric, A., Trovo, F.: A truthful learning mechanism for multi–slot sponsored search auctions with externalities. In: AAMAS (2012)
13. Gatti, N., Lazaric, A., Trovo, F.: A truthful learning mechanism for contextual multi–slot sponsored search auctions with externalities. In: ACM EC (2012)
14. Aggarwal, G., Feldman, J., Muthukrishnan, S., Pál, M.: Sponsored Search Auctions with Markovian Users. In: Papadimitriou, C., Zhang, S. (eds.) WINE 2008. LNCS, vol. 5385, pp. 621–628. Springer, Heidelberg (2008)
15. Kempe, D., Mahdian, M.: A Cascade Model for Externalities in Sponsored Search. In: Papadimitriou, C., Zhang, S. (eds.) WINE 2008. LNCS, vol. 5385, pp. 585–596. Springer, Heidelberg (2008)

16. Aggarwal, G., Muthukrishnan, S., Pál, D., Pál, M.: General auction mechanism for search advertising. In: WWW, pp. 241–250 (2009)
17. Ghosh, A., McAfee, P., Papineni, K., Vassilvitskii, S.: Bidding for Representative Allocations for Display Advertising. In: Leonardi, S. (ed.) WINE 2009. LNCS, vol. 5929, pp. 208–219. Springer, Heidelberg (2009)
18. Goel, A., Munagala, K.: Hybrid keyword search auctions. In: WWW, pp. 221–230 (2009)
19. Lang, K., Delgado, J., Jiang, D., Ghosh, B., Das, S., Gajewar, A., Jagadish, S., Seshan, A., Botev, C., Bindeberger-Ortega, M., et al.: Efficient online ad serving in a display advertising exchange. In: ACM WSDM, pp. 307–316. ACM (2011)
20. Muthukrishnan, S.: Ad Exchanges: Research Issues. In: Leonardi, S. (ed.) WINE 2009. LNCS, vol. 5929, pp. 1–12. Springer, Heidelberg (2009)
21. Green, J., Laffont, J.J.: Characterization of satisfactory mechanisms for the revelation of preferences for public goods. Econometrica 45, 427–438 (1977)
22. Guo, M., Conitzer, V.: Undominated VCG redistribution mechanisms. In: AAMAS, pp. 1039–1046 (2008)

Author Index